LIGHTS OF CREATION & TRANSCENDENCE

David Birnbaum / Mesorah Matrix Series

www.MesorahMatrix.com

MESORAH MATRIX
VOLUME 10

David Birnbaum / Mesorah Matrix Series
LIGHTS OF CREATION & TRANSCENDENCE

D'shamru

Editors

David
Birnbaum & Martin S.
Cohen

Associate Editor: **Saul J. Berman**

EXPLORING HIGHER DIMENSIONS

New Paradigm Matrix ®

Published by NEW PARADIGM MATRIX

COPYRIGHT © 2019
NEW PARADIGM MATRIX FOUNDATION

Library of Congress Cataloging-in-Publication Data

Birnbaum, David.

V'shamru / David Birnbaum and Martin S. Cohen.

ISBN   978-0-9843619-8-4

1. V'shamru.   2. Jewish Spirituality.   I. Title.

21st CENTURY PUBLISHING

New Paradigm Matrix
att: David Birnbaum
Tower 49
Twelve E. 49th St.,
18th Floor,
New York, NY 10017

www.MesorahMatrix.com

Direct contact to Editor-in-Chief

David.Birnbaum.NY@gmail.com

Kaunfer

Lockshin

Cook

Dorff

Maayan

Marx

Cohen

Yanklowitz

Ferency

Ornstein

Lerner

Bulka

Levine

Thiede

Frydman-Kohl

Grumet

Kosman

Zion

V'shamru

The Sabbath

David Birnbaum and Martin S. Cohen

Editors

NEW PARADIGM MATRIX

www.NewParadigmMatrix.com

David Birnbaum & Martin S. Cohen

V'shamru

The Sabbath

with essays by

Reuven P. Bulka, Martin S. Cohen, Michael J. Cook,
Elliot N. Dorff, Alon C. Ferency, Baruch Frydman-Kohl,
Zvi Grumet, Elie Kaunfer, Admiel Kosman, Berel Dov Lerner,
Michelle J. Levine, Martin I. Lockshin, David Maayan,
Dalia Marx, Dan Ornstein, Barbara Shulamit Thiede,
Shmuly Yanklowitz, Noam Zion

Saul J. Berman
Associate Editor

New Paradigm Matrix Publishing
New York
2019

21st CENTURY PUBLISHING

ב"ה

From the Editor-in-Chief

May 10, 2019

It is a privilege to be serving as Editor-in-Chief of this unique
10-theme series. I am honored to be working with world-class
editors Benjamin Blech, Martin S. Cohen, Saul J. Berman, and
Shalom Carmy.

It is our hope and prayer that the series be a catalyst for intellectual
and spiritual expansion – as well as a unifying force both for our
people as well as for individuals of good will globally.

Sincerely,

David Birnbaum

דוד אריה בן אברהם יעקב הלוי   5 אייר 5779

בס"ד

Mesorah Matrix series

jewish thought & spirituality

10-theme

10-volume

200+ original essays

150+ global thought leaders

a decade-long unified endeavor

genre: *applied scholarship*

www.MesorahMatrix.com

21st CENTURY PUBLISHING

Mesorah Matrix series

A POTENTIALLY ICONIC LEGACY SERIES
FOR THE 21ST CENTURY

10-VOLUME SERIES......200+ ESSAYS......A GLOBAL EFFORT

150+ ESSAYISTS....SPANNING THE WORLD'S TOP JEWISH THOUGHT LEADERS

A DYNAMIC CONTEMPORARY GLOBE-SPANING ENDEAVOR AND COLLECTION

ESSAYISTS COVER A VERY WIDE SPECTRUM OF JUDAISM:

THE COMPLETE SERIES TO DATE IS AVAILABLE ON-LINE GRATIS
IN FLIP-BOOK FORM......AND DOWNLOAD-ABLE GRATIS
+
AVAILABLE IN SOFTCOVER VIA AMAZON
+
AVAILABLE IN E-BOOK FORM VIA VARIOUS MODALITIES

A UNIQUE STUDY AND REFERENCE TOOL FOR CLERGY, ACADEMICS,
STUDENTS & LAY INTELLIGENSIA

A STELLAR CORE COURSE OF STUDY – WHETHER FOR ONE SEMESTER OR
MULTI-YEAR

AND... AS AN UNINTENDED CONSEQUENCE, THE SERIES HAS
BROKEN DOWN BARRIERS - AND SERVED AS A FORCE-MULTIPLIER –
IN UNIFYING THE JEWISH PEOPLE

IN DEPTH & BREADTH......SCOPE & SPECTRUM
A LANDMARK SERIES
UNIQUE ACROSS THE 3,500+ YEAR SPAN OF JEWISH HISTORY

This New Paradigm Matrix work
is available via multiple modalities:

amazon: www.AmazonX1000.com

eBooks: www.eReader1000.com

online: www.MesorahMatrix.com

contact: NPM1000@yahoo.com

a unique, timeless and potentially multi-semester

Contemporary Jewish Thought

Course Text

a *sui generis* series • all original essays • broad spectrum authorship

a potentially iconic Jewish resource

Am ha-Sefer

Sponsors

Abbe & Debbie Dienstag

Gary Kaufman

David & Lisa Pulver

Aryeh & Rachel Rubin

About the Editors

Martin S. Cohen has been a Senior Editor of the inter-denominational Mesorah Matrix series since 2012.

From 2000-2014, he served as Chairman of the Editorial Board of the quarterly journal *Conservative Judaism*, which was published under the joint auspices of the Jewish Theological Seminary and the Rabbinical Assembly.

Rabbi Cohen also served as the senior editor of *The Observant Life*, a landmark compendium of Jewish law and custom published by the Rabbinical Assembly in 2012.

His weekly blog can be viewed at www.TheRuminativeRabbi.blogspot.com. He has served as rabbi of the Shelter Rock Jewish Center in Roslyn, New York, since 2002.

Rabbi Cohen was educated at the City University of New York and at the Jewish Theological Seminary, where he was ordained a rabbi and received his Ph.D. in Ancient Judaism. He is the recipient of fellowships at the Hebrew University in Jerusalem in 1983 and Harvard University in 1993.

Martin Cohen has taught at Hunter College, the Jewish Theological Seminary, the Institute for Jewish Studies of the University of Heidelberg, as well as at the University of British Columbia and the Vancouver School of Theology.

His published works include *The Boy on the Door on the Ox* (2008) and *Our Haven and Our Strength: A Translation and Commentary on the Book of Psalms* (2004), as well as four novels and four books of essays.

Rabbi Cohen is currently writing a translation and commentary on the Torah and the Five Megillot.

MARTIN S. COHEN MAJOR WORKS

As Senior Editor

Mesorah Matrix series 2012 - present

Conservative Judaism 2000 - 2014

The Observant Life 2012

As Author (Non-Fiction)

Travels on the Private Zodiac: Reflections on Jewish Life, Ritual and Spirituality (1995)

In Pursuit of Wholeness: The Search for Spiritual Integrity in a Delusional World (1996)

Travels on the Road Not Taken: Towards a Bible-Based Theology of Jewish Spirituality (1997)

Sefer Ha-ikarim Li-z'maneinu (2000)

Our Haven and Our Strength: The Book of Psalms (2004)

Siddur Tzur Yisrael (2005)

Zot Nechamati for the House of Mourning (2006)

Riding the River of Peace (2007)

The Boy on the Door on the Ox (2008)

As Author (Fiction)

The Truth About Marvin Kalish (1992)

Light from Dead Stars (1996)

The Sword of Goliath (1998)

Heads You Lose (2002)

About the Editors

David Birnbaum is a philosophical writer, historical chronicler and *conceptual theorist*. His first work *God and Evil* (KTAV, 1988) is considered by many to be a breakthrough *modern day classic* in the field of theodicy. See God-And-Evil.com.

Editor-in-Chief Birnbaum is known globally as "the architect of Potentialism Theory" – a unified philosophy/cosmology/metaphysics. The paradigm-challenging theory (see ParadigmChallenge.com) is delineated in Birnbaum's 3-volume *Summa Metaphysica* series (1988, 2005, 2014). See Philosophy1000.com.

A riposte to *Summa Theologica* of (St.) Thomas Aquinas, the Birnbaum treatise challenges both the mainstream Western philosophy of Aristotelianism and the well propped-up British/atheistic cosmology of Randomness. See Potentialism Theory. com.

The focus of 150+ reviews/articles, Summa Metaphysica has been an assigned Course Text at over 15 institutions of higher learning globally. See SummaCoverage.com.

Summa Metaphysica was the focus of an international academic conference on Science & Religion in April 16-19 2012 (see Conference1000.com). The work has been very widely covered globally. See RewindSumma.com.

David Birnbaum is the Editor-in-Chief of the *Mesorah Matrix* series on Jewish thought and spirituality. The *sui generis* series spans 10-volumes and 10 themes. The entire series is comprised of 200+ specially commissioned original pieces from 150-180 global Jewish thought leader essayists. See Mesorah1000.com.

In the history realm, David Birnbaum is the author/chronicler of the 2-volume *The Crucifixion – of the Jews*, and of the 7-volume *Jews, Church & Civilization*. His Crucifixion series, in particular, traces a direct trajectory from the Canonical Gospels in the First Century to Auschwitz in the Twentieth. See History1000.com.

David Birnbaum has served on the faculty of the New School for Social Research in Manhattan. He is a graduate of Yeshiva University High School (Manhattan), CCNY (City College of New York) and Harvard. His commentary blog is www. ManhattanObserver.com.

See also David1000.com

DAVID BIRNBAUM MAJOR WORKS

As Author

3-volume   *Summa Metaphysica** (www.philosophy1000.com)

2-volume   *The Crucifixion* (www.crucifixion1000.com)

7-volume   *Jews, Church & Civilization* (www.civilization1000.com)

As Editor-in-Chief

10-volume   *Mesorah Matrix* (www.mesorah1000.com)

As Conceptualizer

3-volume   *Summa Spinoffs* (www.Spinoffs1000.com)

8-volume   *Potentialism Theory* via Graphic-Narrative
               (www.TheoryGraphics1000.com)

As Commentator

www.ManhattanObserver.com

YouTube channels

Summa Metaphysica

Mesorah Matrix

*

*Summa I: Religious Man / God and Evil
 Summa II: Spiritual Man / God and Good
 Summa III: Secular Man / The Transcendent Dynamic*

DAVID BIRNBAUM MAJOR WORKS

Summa Metaphysica series

presenting new paradigm
Potentialism Theory
a unified, seamless & fully-integrated
overarching philosophy

www.SummaMetaphysica.com

Summa I:
Religious Man: God and Evil: focus: *theodicy & eternal origins* [1988]**

Summa II:
Spiritual Man: God and Good: focus: *metaphysics & teleology* [2005]

Summa III:
Secular Man: The Transcendent Dynamic: focus: *cosmology & evolution* [2014]

see also secondary site PotentialismTheory.com

see also: RewindSumma.com 140-panel Scroll-Down tour

YouTube Channel: Summa Metaphysica

see also Summa IV: Articles on Summa
(only online - on www.SummaMetaphysica.com)

** see also: www.GodOfPotential.com

** see special YouTube channel: www.UnifyingScienceSpirituality.com

www.Major1000.com

Mesorah Matrix
SENIOR EDITORIAL BOARD

V'Shamru

V'Shamru

TABLE OF CONTENTS

creation on a weekly basis. The significance of Israel's obligation to observe Shabbat is explored by delving into the meaning of *shamor* as it is used in the story of the Garden of Eden, whose utopian environment provides the context for humanity to implement God's will. By observing Shabbat, Israel is thus tasked with recreating this ideal atmosphere, recalling and revitalizing its national spiritual mission to fulfill the purpose for which God created the world.

Shabbat looms large in the religious imagination, literary expression, and halakhic behavior of the Jewish people. Although a stable and sustained sign of a covenantal relationship between God and the people of Israel, its significance and meaning has changed over time. Indeed, the polysemic plasticity of Shabbat is the key to its ongoing vitality and continuing capacity to remain both an indelible sign of the Covenant and also an enduring indicator of a continuing relationship between God and the people of Israel.

This essay survey various scriptural justifications for Shabbat and shows that the biblical attitude labelled here as the societal/humanitarian approach survived into rabbinic times only in the permissive approach to the question of whether beasts of burden may be allowed to graze freely on Shabbat. The essay also surveys those New Testament materials that sought to restore the societal/humanitarian rationale to its central position, and attempts to show how this is an example of how halakhic decisions attributed to Jesus deviated from the rabbinic approach of his day. This restoration of the homilies of Jesus to the rabbinic discussion about the correct way to "keep" Shabbat, and a general consideration of his way of making halakhic decisions, can solve a set of questions that historians have never successfully resolved.

Since Judaism is far more about what one does and how one lives one's life than what one believes, the questions of what exactly one does and why one does it are critical. This essay deals with one aspect of *sh'mirat mitzvot*, the keeping or observing of the commandments, by focusing on the question of what the concept could or should mean for the so-called non-halakhic Jew. The multivalence of traditional concepts of the Eternal as *m'tzavveh* ("Commander"), the Jew as *m'tzuvveh* or *m'tzuvvah* ("commanded"), and the religious deed as *mitzvah* ("commanded action") is explored, considering all three as they appear in Jewish traditional sources and proposing how each might inform the lives of contemporary Jewish people.

The Torah uses the word *mishmeret* to designate the full breadth of commandments and covenantal obligations incumbent upon the faithful Israelite. Underlying that usage is the thought that the covenant needs to be protected or guarded from outside aggression and attack. This idea is explored with regard to the author's life-work: teaching rabbis and lay people how to respond to Christian claims regarding the obsolescence and irrelevance of Judaism in the modern world.

Preface

Martin S. Cohen

The Torah has two basic components: a long, complex narrative that serves as the backstory to the covenant and its literary frame, and the specific commandments that serve as the terms of that covenant. The narrative itself—the long, complex narratives relating to the creation of the world, the great flood, the adventures of the patriarchs and matriarchs of Israel, the descent into slavery in Egypt, the exodus from Egypt, the events at Mount Sinai, and the subsequent journey the edge of the Land of Israel, where the people are camped when the Torah narrative concludes with Moses' death—is relatively well-known even in the secular Western world. And some of the commandments too are well known to the general public in Western lands—some because they were eventually adopted by Christian theologians and made tenets of Christianity, others because they are so overtly characteristic of Jewish life that they have become easily recognizable to anyone who has even casual contact with the Jewish community, and others because they have come to serve as the most basic moral planks in Western ethics even for people who do not self-define as Jews *or* Christians.

But however well known the commandments may be as regards their general content, the Hebrew text of the Torah that preserves the commandments in their literary guise can prove surprisingly difficult. For one thing, Biblical Hebrew is an ancient language in which words do not necessarily mean what they eventually came to mean after millennia of linguistic development. Moreover, classical Hebrew authors regularly presuppose information on the part of their readers and listeners, much of which non-specialist moderns simply do not possess. (For example, Scripture references all sorts of public officials and military officers by their ranks and titles without explaining them because the reader is simply assumed to be familiar with the terminology, somewhat in the same way a contemporary American journalist might refer to someone as a senator from Oklahoma without feeling any need to pause and explain what a senator is. Or what Oklahoma is!) And then there is the question of grammar to consider. For all that modern scholars have analyzed the language of the Bible and attempted to describe its grammatical rules, there are still many passages that feel inconsonant with those rules. These passages likely do not constitute errors of usage on the part of their ancient authors, however, but rather indicate that our understanding of biblical grammar simply does not reflect the nuanced, dynamic way ancient Hebrew was actually spoken in antiquity as a living, vibrant language. And, finally, there is the vexing question of the specific way Hebrew words are related to each other. Classical Hebrew, like all Semitic languages, is built on three-letter combinations of consonants called "roots," and most of the words that constitute the language's vocabulary are built on those roots. Yet some words that appear to be built on the same root seem entirely unrelated in meaning. And still others, mysterious in their own right, do not appear to have triliteral roots at all.

Any study of the commandments that carefully considers such concerns will naturally lead to meaningful insight, and this is precisely the kind of examination that underlies this volume, the tenth and final volume in the Mesorah Matrix series. Like its predecessors in the series, this volume is devoted to the reasoned, thoughtful, and inspiring analysis of specific Jewish ideas, practices, and beliefs. In fact, all of the present essays focus on a single word that lies at the intersection of law, linguistics, spirituality, faith, and modern Jewish practice: *v'shamru*. And although the word will be familiar to most from its liturgical use in the version of the Kiddush prayer recited on Shabbat that cites Exodus 31:16–17, the word appears in other contexts as well and several of the essays in this volume consider those uses.

The key passage that connects that word with Shabbat observance, Exodus 31:16–17, reads as follows, with the English words that correspond to the Hebrew *v'shamru* printed in bold:

> **And so shall** the Israelites **keep** the Sabbath, safeguarding its observance throughout all their generations as evidence of the eternal covenant that binds Me and the Israelites, for the Sabbath is that covenant's eternal sign in that the Eternal made the heavens and the earth in six days and then paused for rest and repose on the seventh day.

It is the specific question of what *v'shamru* means in this context to which our authors who have chosen to write about Shabbat turn their attention.

As noted, the word is not used exclusively with respect to Shabbat observance and it appears elsewhere in the Torah text to designate what Israelites are commanded to "do" with respect to the commandments, or some specific commandment. But it is the Shabbat connection that interests most of our authors, possibly because Moses himself is cited (at Deuteronomy 5:12) as recalling the fourth of the Ten Commandments as beginning with an imperative built on that very root of *shin-mem-resh*, even though the "actual" text presented in Exodus begins with a different word entirely.

Words built on the three-letter root *shin-mem-resh* generally have something to do with guarding, protecting, or keeping safe, but what it is exactly about these specific contexts, and the Shabbat context foremost among them, that *requires* so much guarding or protecting is left unsaid. Is there some specific fragility that inheres in the observance of that specific commandment which makes reasonable the use of some version of a word based on *shim-mem-resh* to qualify its observance? Or is Shabbat simply of such cardinal importance that Scripture uses that specific verb to describe its observance solely to say that that nation must exert itself maximally to guarantee its careful and punctilious observance? Or does this usage hint instead at some specific danger that might be lurking within the details of Shabbat observance, some plausible ideational, doctrinal, dogmatic, or even physical peril against which the people must be commanded scrupulously to guard themselves? To none of these questions does Scripture nod even in passing. Yet the essays in this volume that focus on Shabbat are all attempts, one way or another, to address those specific questions and others that derive from them directly. I hope our readers will find all our authors' efforts both intriguing and uplifting.

The authors who have contributed to this volume are a varied lot drawn from across the spectrum of organized Jewish life—Israelis and diasporan types, rabbis and academics, men and woman, older and younger scholars, seasoned authors and relative newcomers to the world of publishing. Some have contributed to other volumes in our series and one, the indefatigable Reuven Bulka, has contributed essays to all ten; others present their sole contribution to the series in this one volume. All, however, are united by their common belief in the power of the well-written word and the sense that, even in the digital age, the well-structured, convincingly argued essay retains its ability not just to inform but also to influence and to inspire.

Unless otherwise indicated, all translations here are the authors' own work. Biblical citations referenced to the NJPS derive from the complete translation of Scripture published under the title *Tanakh: The Holy Scriptures* by the Jewish Publication Society in Philadelphia in 1985.

As we prepare to publish this, the tenth and final volume in the Mesorah Matrix series, I would like to take this opportunity to acknowledge the other senior editors of the Mesorah Matrix series, David Birnbaum and Benjamin Blech, as well as Saul J. Berman, our associate editor.

And I would also like to add a personal note at this juncture regarding the larger operation. This project has brought together a large number of authors in an almost unprecedented effort to unite people across the spectrum of Jewish affiliation for the sake of *k'lal yisrael*. And despite the way that Jewish people from different parts of the Jewish world are regularly supposed not ever to get along, much less to wish to work together on anything at all of consequence, all of our authors have shown themselves willing to participate in the noble effort that underlies the Mesorah Matrix project: to revitalize the essay form and to make of it a successful vehicle for inspiring Jewish readers to take their Judaism and their Jewishness to an even higher level, to feel ennobled by their membership in the House of Israel, and potentially to feel themselves called upon to embrace a more personal role in the pursuit of Jewish destiny. It has been my privilege and pleasure to work with them all.

As always, I must also express my gratitude to the men and women, and particularly to the lay leadership, of the synagogue I serve as rabbi: the Shelter Rock Jewish Center in Roslyn, New York. Possessed of the unwavering conviction that their rabbi's literary projects are part and parcel of his service to them (and, through them, to the larger community of those interested in learning about Judaism), they are remarkably supportive of my literary efforts as author and editor. I am in their debt and am pleased to acknowledge that debt formally here and whenever I publish my own work or the work of others. I couldn't be me if they weren't them.

Martin S. Cohen
Roslyn, New York
September 9, 2018
Erev Rosh Hashanah 5779

Abbreviations

A.T. – *Arba·ah Turim*

B. – Babylonian Talmud

M. – Mishnah

M.T. – *Mishneh Torah*

S.A. – *Shulhan Arukh*

T. – Tosefta

Y. – Yerushalmi

A Note from the Editors

Every effort has been made to retain a good level of consistency between the essays that appear here in terms of the translation and transliteration of Hebrew. Many of our decisions have, needs be, been arbitrary, but we have done our best to create a book that will be as accessible to newcomers to the study of Judaism as it is inspiring to cognoscenti. All translations are their authors' unless otherwise indicated.

Essays

V'shamru: An Everlasting Preservative

Reuven P. Bulka

The word *v'shamru*—the introductory word in one of the Torah's most oft-cited passages about Shabbat (Exodus 31:16–17) which is, according to many customs, recited as part of the Shabbat morning Kiddush—is one of the more intriguing words in the Torah. Many, many words in the Torah are formed from its triliteral root (*shin-mem-resh*), with varying meanings. What does this word mean when applied specifically to the Shabbat?

Most Hebrew words are built on three-letter roots that are then expanded through the introduction of medial vowels, prefixes, and suffixes to form different words, both nouns and verbs. One of the most popular biblical concordances lists 411 occurrences of words formed from the root *shim-mem-resh* root.[1] All of these instances fall into broad categories of meaning, but each is nuanced in its own way. Most of the time, words built on this root have something to do with "guarding," "protecting," or "preserving," but it is sometimes hard to say why this specific root is being used in a given context. And many passages suggest a meaning for the root closer to "keep," "observe," or "maintain." Though the context will often provide a general sense of what a word with this root may mean, it is still sometimes difficult to pinpoint the precise meaning.

But when the Torah uses the verbal root *shin-mem-resh* to describe what the Israelites are to do with respect to Shabbat, vague translations will not suffice. Shabbat is the cornerstone of Jewish life. What the Torah specifically commands the Israelites to "do" in this regard is thus a matter of great importance.

V'shamru and Shabbat

The general sense of the root is clear enough—"guard" or "protect," or perhaps "keep" or "observe"—but its precise meaning when applied to Shabbat is elusive. What does Moses have in mind, when he frames the Shabbat commandment in the Decalogue with this root: "*Shamor* [the imperative form] the Shabbat day to sanctify it, as the Eternal your God has commanded" (Deuteronomy 5:12)?

When we turn to the *v'shamru* passage in Exodus 31, even the grammar is confusing. The word is formally a third-person plural past tense, prefixed by the "converting *vav*"—and so the time-frame seems to be some sort of future, yet-unfilled action, but the precise sense is still unclear. Is the form *v'shamru* here a command? Is it a prediction? Is it a presumed undertaking? If it is a command, how does it differ from the already enunciated and detailed command to "Remember the Shabbat..." (Exodus 20:8), and the less detailed but potent charge regarding Shabbat just prior to the *v'shamru* statement (Exodus 31:14)?

Let us step back, in order to examine the larger context in which the verb *v'shamru* appears (Exodus 31:12–17):

> God said to Moses: "Speak to the Israelites, saying: However, **you must observe** (*tishmoru*) My Shabbatot, for this is a sign between Me and you for your generations, to know that I am God who sanctifies you. You **shall observe** (*u-sh'martem*) the Shabbat, for it is holy unto you....For six days work shall be done and the seventh day is a day of complete cessation,

sacred unto God....The Israelites **shall observe** (*v'shamru*) the Shabbat, to make the Shabbat an eternal covenant for their generations. Between Me and the Israelites it is a sign forever that for six days God made the heavens and the earth, and on the seventh day God ceased to create and was refreshed."

Interestingly, this Shabbat directive is nestled between the mandate to construct the *mishkan*, the portable Tabernacle, and the unfolding saga of the golden calf. In the space of just a few verses, we move from holy place to holy time to unholy behavior. (More on the connection of Shabbat and idolatry later.)

Of course, this is not the only mention of Shabbat in the Torah: Shabbat is mentioned at the very beginning of the Torah as the culmination of creation (Genesis 2:1–3). Moreover, a lengthy introduction to the observance of Shabbat is found in the instructions regarding the manna, which did not appear on Shabbat (Exodus 16:4–30). And Shabbat is mentioned many more times in the Torah. But no passage is as detailed as the verses from Exodus 31 cited above—or potentially as valuable for nuancing our understanding of how exactly Shabbat is to be observed.

A *V'shamru* Mandate

In the context of a lengthy discussion of the basis for the rule that saving a person's life takes precedence over Shabbat, the Talmud cites Rabbi Shimon ben Menasia's view about our *v'shamru* verse, "The Israelites **shall observe** (*v'shamru*) the Shabbat" (Exodus 31:16). His lesson is truly potent: he teaches that we are hereby told to "violate one Shabbat on a person's account, so that the person may [in the future] observe many Shabbatot."[2]

Undoubtedly, this nuanced meaning of *v'shamru* derives from the latter part of the verse, "...to make the Shabbat an eternal covenant for their generations." In other words, we are urged to do whatever we can to ensure that Shabbat will continue to be observed in the future. This mandate includes setting aside the Shabbat temporarily, if necessary, in order to make the permanent observance of the Shabbat more likely. How meaningful it is that the obligation to observe the Shabbat is, on occasion, fulfilled by not observing it!

The *V'shamru La·asot* Verses

In eleven passages in the Bible, the word *v'shamru* is followed by an infinitive. Of these, three texts are of particular interest for the present inquiry: Genesis 18:19, Exodus 31:16, and Deuteronomy 31:12, where *v'shamru* is followed by the verb *la·asot* ("to do" or "to make," or even "to perform").

Comparison of three different translations of these verses (with the translation of the *v'shamru la·asot* phrase in bold) proves instructive:

	Rabbi Samson Raphael Hirsch (1808–1888)[3]	Original Jewish Publication Society translation[4]	ArtScroll[5]
Genesis 18:19	For I have given him My special Care so that he will command his children and his household after him **that they shall keep** the way of God **to do** benevolence as a duty, and justice, that God may bring upon Abraham that which He hath spoken of him.	For I have known him, to the end that he may command his children and his household after him, **that they may keep** the way of the LORD, **to do** righteousness and justice; to the end that the LORD may bring upon Abraham that which he hath spoken of him.	For I have loved him, because he commands his children and his household after him **that they keep** the way of Hashem, **doing** charity and justice, in order that Hashem might then bring upon Abraham that which He had spoken of him.

Exodus 31:16	**Thus shall** the Children of Israel **keep** the Sabbath, **to observe** the Sabbath throughout their generations as a perpetual covenant.	**Wherefore** the children of Israel **shall keep** the sabbath, **to observe** the sabbath throughout their generations, for a perpetual covenant.	The Children of Israel **shall observe** the Sabbath, **to make** the Sabbath an eternal covenant for their generations.
Deuter-onomy 31:12	Gather all the people together, the men and the women and the children and the stranger that is within thy gates that they may hear and that they may learn and fear *God* your *God*, **and conscientiously fulfill** all the words of this Torah.	Assemble the people, the men and the women and the little ones, and thy stranger that is within thy gates, that they may hear, and that they may learn, and fear the LORD your God, **and observe to do** all the words of this law.	Gather together the people—the men, the women, and the small children, and your stranger who is in your cities—so that they will hear and so that they will learn, and they shall fear Hashem, your God, and **be careful to perform** all the words of this Torah.

The Genesis verse containing *v'shamru la·asot* appears to be a prediction, or perhaps an assurance, of what is destined to be: God expresses love for Abraham, taking special note of the latter's commanding presence, which will be so inspiring that his progeny will surely preserve righteousness and justice. The Exodus verse refers to safeguarding in order to make the Shabbat into an eternal covenant. It is more of a cause-and-effect statement, presented with a tinge of prediction: if the cause (namely, the safeguarding of the Shabbat) is implemented, then the effect (namely, that the Shabbat will be an everlasting covenant) is sure to follow. The *v'shamru la·asot* verse in Deuteronomy is somewhat different. Here, the people are being called to fulfill the entire Torah as a result of its being read aloud to them once every seven years. This *mitzvah* is meant to inspire the Israelites to be careful to observe the Torah in its entirety: *v'shamru la·asot* means that they are not simply meant to obey the law, but that they are to be *careful* to obey, ensuring that they will carry out this great responsibility.

We can therefore say that *v'shamru la·asot* means "to preserve the ability to do"—not merely to do, but to be alert in advance so that one **will** be able to do so. Thus, Abraham's instructions to his progeny will lead to assuring that they will be able to actualize righteousness and justice. Likewise, the Deuteronomy passage is a directive for all Israel, to assure (and ensure) that they will be able to observe the entire Torah.

Meaning of *Shomer Shabbat*

This idea is also at work, even more significantly, when it comes to the verse about Shabbat. In the Exodus passage, *v'shamru la·asot* implies an additional obligation, over and above the mere observance of Shabbat itself. The pious Israelite is to "watch over" Shabbat even before Shabbat, thus assuring that the Shabbat will be observed. In the words of Abraham ibn Ezra to Exodus 31:16, we are to take heed of the days of the week, not to forget which day of the week is Shabbat, and to prepare both materially and spiritually on the sixth day to carefully observe the Shabbat.[6] In this understanding of *v'shamru*, the precise time for fulfilling the commandment *v'shamru* about Shabbat is not on Shabbat itself; instead, it is before Shabbat.

Various regulations concerning Shabbat are permeated by this idea. For example, the Talmud states that one may not set out in a ship within three days of the onset of the Shabbat, if the trip was for a purpose not related to fulfilling a *mitzvah*.[7] Maimonides codifies this law, explaining that since it takes three days to become acclimatized to the realities of life on a ship, one is unsettled prior to that point and therefore unable to properly enjoy Shabbat.[8] This explanation is echoed in the commentaries of Rabbi Yitzhak Alfasi and Rabbi Asher to the Talmud.[9]

Neither the Talmud nor the commentaries mentions the *v'shamru* verse in this context, but it is clear that being a true *shomer(et) Shabbat*, a Shabbat keeper or preserver, is not relegated to one day a week, the Shabbat itself. Watching over the Shabbat demands our ongoing attention.

Rabbi Sofer's Insight

In his *K'tav Sofer*, a most interesting amalgam of observations on the Torah, Rabbi Avraham Shmuel Binyamin Sofer (1815–1871) offers an interesting approach to *v'shamru* as it relates to the Shabbat, by questioning the need for the words "to do the Shabbat" (*la·asot et ha-shabbat*) in Exodus 31:16.[10] Rabbi Sofer points out that many have attempted to explain the logic of Shabbat as based on the human need to take a break from the intense work activity of the week, by resting the body and thereby re-invigorating it. According to this logic, God could actually have chosen any other day of the week to achieve this.

However, says Rabbi Sofer, this explanation does not stand up to scrutiny. After all, the Israelites were commanded about Shabbat at Marah (prior to the Sinai revelation), at which time they were in the wilderness and not involved in labor such as threshing or planting. It must be, Rabbi Sofer concludes, that the Shabbat day is **itself** holy, an eternal sign of creation and the exodus. He thus takes *v'shamru* as a specific directive to the Israelites to immediately commence with Shabbat observance, to effectively make (*la·asot*) Shabbat the eternal covenant between God and Israel. In other words, by starting to observe the Shabbat now (that is, even before Sinai), it will establish Shabbat forever as a covenantal expression—and not as a day set up merely to rest the body.

With the nation Israel beginning its observance of Shabbat in the wilderness, it would become clear to subsequent generations that Shabbat is not merely designed for the good of the body, but rather because of the sanctity of the day itself. The generations to follow, who will live in the Land of Israel and who *will* work every day, are not to observe the Shabbat only with the intent to rest the body. Rather, they are to observe the Shabbat the way it was kept in the wilderness, when there was no need to rest the body. At that time, Shabbat was observed only to sanctify the people themselves, thereby making the Shabbat a covenantal sign between God and the Israelites.

Rabbi Sofer concludes with words he employs quite often after sharing an idea: "So it appears to me." But then he adds a somewhat unusual postscript: "And this observation is correct!"

Shabbat Reinvigoration

The very next verse after the *v'shamru* verse in Exodus reads as follows: "It is a sign forever between Me and the Israelites: that for six days God made the heavens and the earth, and on the seventh day God ceased to create and was refreshed" (31:17). It seems incongruous to ascribe being "refreshed" to God, who creates merely by commanding the reality and "never tires and does not weary" (Isaiah 40:28). Rashi thus concludes that the word "refreshed," as ascribed to God here, is simply intended to make comprehensible to the human ear what it can understand. In other words, the Torah uses an anthropomorphic metaphor—that God might tire and need a Shabbat nap—to say something profound and important.

Thus, seemingly contrary to the insight of Rabbi Sofer to Exodus 30:16, the very next verse appears to introduce the notion of Shabbat as an energizing experience, as an opportunity to be refreshed—even should there be no tiring activity from which one might need to be energized. God does not get tired, yet God is described as in need of refreshment—in order that we might appreciate Shabbat as a refresher, as an energizer. This idea is so important that the Torah uses words that are not self-evident and need Rashi's clarification, lest we misunderstand the essence of God.

It is challenging to embrace Rabbi Sofer's comment on *v'shamru*, rooted as it is in his personal discomfort with the connection of Shabbat with rest from work. Perhaps Rabbi Sofer was attacking the reductionist oversimplification of Shabbat as being only for physical rest and relaxation. Perhaps he does not mean to deny what the Torah suggests almost immediately: namely, the notion that there is an invigorating component to Shabbat. Rather, his comment is intended to reject the suggestion that this is **all** there is to Shabbat.

V'shamru La·asot as a Shabbat Preservative

However we understand Rabbi Sofer, it is evident that he sees *v'shamru la·asot* as a long-range directive, starting in the generation of the wilderness but also looking forward toward the post-wilderness Shabbat of the Jewish people. For Ibn Ezra and others who take a similar approach, the passage is about the thinking and planning every week to assure the observance of the Shabbat.[11] For the Talmud, it has to do with the obligation to sacrifice one Shabbat, or however many may be necessary, to save a life and thus to make possible future Shabbat observance.[12] For Maimonides, the injunction has to do with being extra careful not to embark on activities that may compromise one's ability to truly and meaningfully celebrate the Shabbat.[13]

One might well ask: Why Shabbat? Why does the Shabbat have so many protective rules? Why is the actual preservation of Shabbat, although relegated to a specific day, actually transformed into a full-time endeavor?

For this, we turn to Maimonides, in his climactic conclusion to the Laws of Shabbat.[14] He begins by stating that both Shabbat and idolatry are as weighty as the entirety of all the other precepts of the Torah. The Shabbat, he goes on to say, is a sign between God and the Jews forever. Therefore, one who fails to fulfill any of the other precepts is in the category of a transgressor, but one who desecrates the Shabbat is the equivalent of an idolater. It does not get worse than that! And Maimonides goes on to quote Isaiah's high praise (at Isaiah 56:4–5 and 58:13–14) of those who preserve the Shabbat.

Shabbat, it turns out, is the underpinning of everything, of the entirety of the Torah. It is not just one day of the week. It the very affirmation of creation. It is the quintessential appreciation of the exodus. It is the constant reminder of how we human beings came into existence, and why we Jews came into a life with free choice to serve God—which we do most powerfully and meaningfully on Shabbat. The other side of the serious consequence for failure to keep the Shabbat is the transcending fulfillment achieved by meaningfully embracing the Shabbat. It is no wonder that the Torah draws a ring of *shamor* imperatives around Shabbat, with *v'shamru* standing out as the most expansive of them!

The words *v'shamru la·asot* in the Torah's most famous Shabbat passage celebrate the long-range commitment of the community of Israel to protect, maintain, preserve, and assure that Shabbat continues to be central to our lives: as a manifestation of the covenant, as a reminder of creation and the exodus, and as a symbol of the global and particular affirmations of God's special care for the people of Israel.

Looking at *v'shamru la·asot* from a wide lens, this unique expression—be it a predictor, a directive, or a promise—begins with our first patriarch, Abraham; concludes with a directive from Moses, to embrace the totality of the Torah; and is anchored in the middle with the unique, trans-generational covenantal Shabbat obligation that gives meaningful expression to the Abrahamic promise and the Mosaic directive.

What a wonderful verse to embrace, and to express, on Shabbat!

NOTES

[1] *Konkordantziyah Ḥadashah L'torah N'vi·im U-kh'tuvim*, ed. Avraham Even-Shoshan (Jerusalem: Kiryat Sefer, 1993), pp. 1182–1185.

[2] B. Yoma 85b. This same statement is recorded in Mekhilta, *Ki Tissa,* to that verse in the name of Rabbi Natan.

[3] Rabbi Hirsch's translation was into German. This English translation of his work is by Isaac Levy in *The Pentateuch*, 2nd revised ed. (London, 1930).

[4] The original Jewish Publication Society translation of the Bible was published in Philadelphia in 1917.

[5] *The Chumash*, ed. Nosson Scherman (New York: ArtScroll, 1993); later incorporated in *Tanach: The Stone Edition* (New York: ArtScroll, 1996).

[6] This observation of Ibn Ezra appears in both the short and long versions of his commentary on the Torah. In the short version, he sees *v'shamru* as a warning not to embark on a journey on the sixth day of the week if there is a doubt that the destination will be reached before Shabbat.

[7] B. Shabbat 19a.

[8] M.T. Hilkhot Shabbat 30:13.

[9] Cf. their comments to the talmudic passage reference above in note 7. Rabbi Yitzḥak Alfasi (called the Rif, 1013–1130) was one of the premier talmudists of his day, as was Rabbi Asher ben Yeḥiel (called the Rosh or Rabbeinu Asher, c. 1250–1327) in his.

[10] *Sefer K'tav Sofer al Ḥamishah Ḥumshei Torah* (Tel Aviv: Sinai Publishing, 2009), p. 349.

[11] See, for example, the thirteenth-century commentator Rabbi Ḥizkiyah ben Manoaḥ (popularly called *Ḥizkuni*) in his Torah commentary.

[12] B. Yoma 85b.

[13] M.T. Hilkhot Shabbat 30:13.

[14] M.T. Hilkhot Shabbat 30:15.

"Six Days You Shall Work…"

Berel Dov Lerner

The Sabbath is a day of holiness and pleasure, and it is fundamentally a day of rest, a day without work. Does the prohibition of work on the Sabbath imply that work is antithetical to holiness and human flourishing? In this essay I will argue for the opposite conclusion: that the Sabbath rest must be understood in the framework of the broader Jewish week, which respects the value of both work *and* rest.

The Juxtaposition of Work and Sabbath in the Torah

The Israelites are first introduced to the concept of the Sabbath soon after leaving Egypt. In chapter sixteen of the Book of Exodus, God is described as using a method of experiential learning-through-doing to teach them about this central Jewish institution. The people complain that they are hungry (verse 3) and God tells Moses they will be miraculously supplied with manna to eat during their sojourn through the wilderness (verse 4). God then capitalizes on the situation to get them to discover the idea of a six-day workweek followed by the Sabbath.

In the first stage of this learning process, the Israelites collect their daily portion of manna to eat each morning. Consider how Moses tells the people about their new source of food: "This is what the

Eternal has commanded: Gather as much of it as each of you requires to eat, an *omer* to a person for as many of you as there are; each of you shall fetch for those in his tent" (Exodus 16:16).[1] The people are explicitly commanded by God to collect manna even before they are told about the Sabbath. On the sixth day the Israelite leaders come to Moses to express their surprise that the people managed to collect double portions of manna, whereas previously everyone would end-up, willy-nilly, with just one portion a day.[2] Moses explains that the following day—the seventh day—will be the Sabbath, on which they are not to exert themselves by collecting manna but should rather eat half the food collected and prepared on the previous day. In explaining the Sabbath procedures to the Israelites, Moses once again *commands* the people to collect manna during the working week: "Six days you shall gather it; on the seventh day, the Sabbath, there will be none" (Exodus 16:26).

The story of the manna reveals a basic conceptual truth about the Sabbath: in order for there to be a day of rest, there must be days of work with which it is contrasted. Even in the wilderness in which the Israelites' needs were miraculously supplied by God, they needed to engage in some form of work in order to appreciate the meaning of the Sabbath, and so God required that they go out to collect the manna instead of delivering it miraculously to their tents.

This pairing of Sabbath and workdays is an oft-repeated theme in Judaism. Every extended passage in the Torah dealing with the abstention from work on the Sabbath also includes explicit reference to engagement in work during the preceding six days of the week.[3] Thus, the formulation of the Sabbath law found in the Book of Exodus's version of the Ten Commandments tells us: "Remember the Sabbath day and keep it holy. Six days you shall labor and do all your work, but the seventh day is a Sabbath of the Eternal your God: you shall not do any work…" (Exodus 20:8 10). Although the version of the Ten Commandments found in the Book of Deuteronomy offers a different rationale for the Sabbath than does the Book of Exodus (the former citing the story of creation and the latter the exodus from Egypt), it agrees that the weekdays are devoted to work: "Observe the Sabbath day and keep it holy, as the Eternal your God has commanded you. Six days you shall labor and do all your work, but the seventh day is a Sabbath of the Eternal your God; you shall not do any work…" (Deuteronomy 5:12 14).

The striking thing about these passages is that mention of both working and abstention from work are formulated in the same imperative form: we seem to be *commanded* by the Torah to do each on their appointed days. While the tradition has rarely granted formal recognition to work as an actual commandment of the Torah,[4] the rabbis have forcefully expressed their appreciation of work's great value in celebrated dicta such as the admonition of Pirkei Avot 1:10: "Love work and hate domination." In fact, according to one early source, Rabbi Yehudah Ha-Nasi (Judah the Patriarch), a towering figure of second-century Judaism, drew the obvious and radical conclusion: "'Six days you shall labor'—this is an additional decree, for just as Israel were commanded with the positive commandment of the Sabbath, so too they were commanded to work."[5] But why should the Torah want us to work? Do the workdays merely serve as a drab background against which the splendor of the Sabbath can shine?

Extrinsic Value of Work

Tradition offers both intrinsic and extrinsic reasons to value labor. Intrinsic reasons explain how work is valuable in itself, while extrinsic reasons explain how work is a necessary means for gaining or securing other goals that are valuable in themselves. Let us begin by examining some of the extrinsic ends of work. One obvious goal of working is to make an honest living, and the rabbis were profoundly worried that those who do not work for a living will end up supporting themselves through dishonest means. The great Moses Maimonides (1135–1204) warned that even those who do not work in order to devote all their time to Torah study cannot escape this moral danger: "And any Torah [study] that is not accompanied by work will end up being void and will result in iniquity; this person will end up robbing people."[6]

In this practical vein, money earned and chores accomplished during the week are necessary preconditions for the proper celebration of Shabbat, as is reflected in the popular talmudic maxim: "Those who exert themselves on the Sabbath eve will eat on the Sabbath, but those who do not exert themselves on the Sabbath eve—from where will they eat on the Sabbath?"[7] Avot D'rabbi Natan, a collection of early discussions of the mishnaic tractate Avot, offers a graphic description of a worst possible scenario, in which avoiding work during the week leads to actual defilement of the Sabbath:

> Rabbi Dostai says: How may it happen that if one did no work on the six days, one would work even on the seventh? Suppose that one sits idle all the days of the week and does no work and on the Sabbath eve has nothing to eat. One might then go and fall in with a troop of bandits. Then one would be seized and taken in chains and put to work on the Sabbath! All this because such a person would not work on the six days [of the week]![8]

Fear of destitution leading to crime is not the only extrinsic motivation for work in the Jewish tradition. Classical Jewish texts offer a further extrinsic reason for people to occupy themselves with work: the rabbis feared the psychological effects of idleness and thought that people are better off spending their time in work. Thus, the Mishnah states that inactivity leads to derangement.[9] The classic commentary on the Mishnah by Rabbi Ovadiah of Bertinoro (d. 1515) builds on this idea to explain the dictum "Love work and hate domination" as saying that "even if [without working] one has the means to support oneself, one is required to engage in work because inactivity causes derangement."[10] Rabbi Ovadiah's comment seems also to reflect a passage in Avot D'rabbi Natan:

> Rabbi Yehudah ben Beteira says: If a man has no work to do, what should he do? If he has a run-down yard or run-down field let him go and occupy himself with it, for it is said, "Six days you shall labor and do all your work" (Exodus 20:9). Now, why does the verse say "And do all your work"? To include one who has run-down yards and fields—let him go and occupy himself with them![11]

Even people who don't have an economic reason to work should still keep busy with some constructive activity for their own mental health.

Sabbath, Creation, and the Intrinsic Value of Work

Other classical Jewish sources build upon the Torah's juxtaposition of Sabbath and the workweek to express Judaism's appreciation of the *intrinsic* value of labor. For instance, Avot D'rabbi Natan says the following about the dictum "Love work and hate domination" (Pirkei Avot 1:10): "'Love work'—what does that mean? This teaches that a person should love work and that no person should hate work. For even as the Torah was given as a covenant, so was work given as a covenant, as it is said: 'Six days you shall labor and do all your work, but the seventh day is a Sabbath of the Eternal your God.'"[12]

The comment from Avot D'rabbi Natan requires some unpacking to be properly understood. It seems that the verse it quotes from Exodus is setting up an equivalence between work and the Sabbath. The Sabbath can be understood as standing in for the entire Torah, in accordance with the notion that "the Sabbath is equal to all the commandments of the Torah."[13] As a result, the duty to work should be seen as founded in a covenant with God—just as the obligation to observe the commandments of the Torah derives from Israel's covenant with God. There is, however, a different passage from the Torah, Exodus 31:15–17, that points to an even stronger connection between Sabbath and covenant:

> Six days may work be done, but on the seventh day there shall be a Sabbath of complete rest, holy to the Eternal; whoever does work on the Sabbath day shall be put to death. The Israelite people shall keep [v'shamru] the Sabbath, observing the Sabbath throughout the ages as a covenant for all time: it shall be a sign for all time between Me and the people of Israel. For in six days the Eternal made heaven and earth, and on the seventh day He ceased from work and was refreshed.

This passage explicitly refers to the Sabbath law as a covenant between God and Israel, and it does so in the context of the Jewish Sabbath serving as a commemoration of God's creation of the world. God is portrayed in the Book of Genesis as creating the world in six days and resting on the seventh and, in a kind of imitation of God, the People Israel work six days a week and rest on the seventh. As we shall see, this parallel between divine and human activity points to a deeper understanding of the value of human work in the Jewish tradition.

The first chapter of the Book of Genesis famously describes how God created the world and its inhabitants in the course of six days. We then read, in Genesis 2:1–3:

> The heaven and the earth were finished, and all their array. On the seventh day God finished His work that He had been doing, and He rested on the seventh day from all His work that He had done. And God blessed the seventh day and declared it holy, because on it God ceased from all His work of creation that He had done.

The idea of God needing to rest seems theologically strange; why would an all-powerful deity grow tired? Instead of addressing this obvious question, the Torah seems determined to deepen it. In the quoted passage God is described as resting from the "work" of creation, using the Hebrew word *m'lakhah*, which is consistently used by the Torah to describe work performed by humans during the weekdays. Yet we know from the first chapter of Genesis that God did not expend any effort at all while creating the heavens and the earth; God effortlessly *spoke* things into existence, as in the famous verse, "God said, 'Let there be light'; and there was light" (Genesis 1:3). What is the point of saying that God performed exhausting work, when the act of creation merely consisted of uttering a short series of sentences? And, on the other hand, if God simply spoke the heavenly bodies into being (Genesis 1:14) and told the earth to sprout plants (Genesis 1:11), why couldn't God have just created the entire universe and everything in it at one time and with one utterance?

The rabbis addressed these questions and their answers help us better understand the relationship between divine and human activity in the world. In an early rabbinic midrash on the Book of Exodus, we read:

"And rested on the seventh day." And is God subject to such a thing as weariness? Has it not been said, "Creator of the earth from end to end, He never grows faint or weary" (Isaiah 40:28)? And it says, "He gives strength to the weary" (Isaiah 40:29). And it also says, "By the word of the Eternal the heavens were made" (Psalm 33:6). How then can Scripture say, "And He rested on the seventh day"?

It is simply this: God allowed it to be written about Him that He created His world in six days and rested, as it were, on the seventh. Now by the method of *kal va-ḥomer*[14] you must reason: If God, for whom there is no weariness, allowed it to be written that He created His world in six days and rested on the seventh, how much more should human beings, of whom it is written "But man is born unto trouble" (Job 5:7), rest on the seventh day!

Therefore the Eternal blessed the seventh day and declared it holy.[15]

This midrash tells us that despite God's profound difference from humans, God is deliberately depicted in the creation story as behaving in a way that makes divine actions better available as a model for human behavior. The Creator rests on the seventh day in order to justify the idea of humans resting on the seventh day. Genesis helps us bridge the gulf between the transcendent Creator-God and created-humans, by speaking of God as engaging in work (*m'lakhah*) like a human and needing to rest like a human. Similarly, God takes time with Creation, preceding in stages rather than completing the whole process with one simple command. Pirkei Avot 5:1 explains the message of this drawn-out creation story for human beings:

The world was created through ten utterances. What does this teach? Couldn't the world have been created through a single utterance? Rather, [it was created through ten utterances] in order to hold accountable the wicked who destroy the world, which was created in ten utterances; and to give a good reward to the righteous who sustain the world, which was created through ten utterances.

If we were told that God merely tossed off the act of creation with a single utterance, the world would seem less valuable. Instead, we are told that God went to the trouble of producing ten different utterances in creating the world, thus emphasizing its preciousness and the importance of how we treat it. The ancient midrashic collection Bereishit Rabbah makes a similar statement regarding the Torah's description of God as having performed work in creating the world:

> "[All] His work [that He had done]." Did not Rabbi Berekhiah say in the name of Rabbi Judah, the son of Rabbi Simon: "Neither with labor nor with toil did the blessed Holy One create His world"? But you say, "[He rested on the seventh day] from all His work." This is confusing! But it is [so stated] in order to hold accountable the wicked who destroy the world, all of which was created with labor and exertion; and to give a goodly reward to the righteous who sustain the world, all of which was created with labor and exertion.[16]

These midrashim explain how the creation story of Genesis helps us connect God's acts of creation with human acts of creation—that is to say, with human work. In the first midrash, God is portrayed as resting from the work of creation in order to justify a day of rest for humans. The latter two *midrashim* portray God as demonstrating care for the world by devoting time and work to its creation. For their part, human beings have a choice to make. On the one hand, they can choose to acknowledge the preciousness of God's world by serving as its guardians and by acting as partners in creation by making the world into a suitable home for human beings. Thus, when Genesis tells us about the creation of humans, the role of humanity in the world is also revealed:

> And God said, "Let us make the human in our image, after our likeness. They shall rule the fish of the sea, the birds of the sky, the cattle, the whole earth, and all the creeping things that creep on earth." And God created the human in His image, in the image of God He created him; male and female He created them. God blessed them and God said to them, "Be fertile and increase, fill the earth and master it; and rule the fish of the sea, the birds of the sky, and all the living things that creep on earth." (Genesis 1:26–28)

Human beings are meant to do something with the world, to "fill the earth and master it." God did not complete the work of creation, and God can tell us this because of divine transcendence. God existed before the created world and is not merely part of it. A god who was just part of nature would lack the perspective to tell us that nature stands incomplete. In contrast, the transcendent and eternal Creator of the natural world is in a position to inform us that work was knowingly left to be done. God created humanity to complete the job by humanizing the world, filling the earth and making of it a home. This must be accomplished through human work—work that is the human contribution toward the realization of the goals of creation.

However, as the *midrashim* warn us, human beings can also radically betray their calling by engaging in the destruction of this world. This point must be made clear: the idea that the world is to be made into a home for humanity in no way justifies the descent down a slippery slope toward environmental catastrophe, just as the Torah's concern for society's less privileged members in no way justifies the establishment of communist dystopias. Such destructive behavior is typical of "the wicked who destroy the world all of which was created with labor and exertion," thus demonstrating their contempt for God and God's work, as well as contempt for their fellow human beings who are trying to fashion a viable home in God's creation. As Meir Friedmann, the great nineteenth-century scholar of midrash, wrote:

> The sages taught us that all of these formulations in the creation story did not come to teach us about creation itself, but rather came to teach humanity the great importance of *tikkun olam* [setting the world aright], for it is a cornerstone upon which everything depends; that God created His world, and since He created it, He desires it to persist, and its sustenance and *tikkun* is the goal of humanity, and through this humans become partners in the work of creation, but its corruption and destruction are evil, the very worst kind of human wickedness….[17]

By reenacting God's own rest from creative work each seventh day, we remind ourselves of our partnership with God and we are refreshed, so that we may continue the fulfillment of our own creative responsibilities during the coming week. Returning to the words of Avot D'rabbi Natan: "For even as the Torah was given as a covenant, so was work given as a covenant; as it is said, 'Six days you shall labor and do all your work, but the seventh day is a Sabbath of the Eternal your God (Exodus 20:8 9 and Deuteronomy 5:13 14).'"

NOTES

[1] Biblical quotations are from the NJPS version, with some modifications.

[2] Exegetes disagree as to the exact course events described in Exodus 16. Here I am following Rashi's interpretation, as further expanded by the Maharal (Rabbi Judah Loew ben Bezalel of Prague) in his supercommentary on Rashi, *Gur Aryeh*.

[3] These include: Exodus 20:8–11, 23:12, 31:12–17, 34:21, and 35:1–3; Leviticus 23:1 3; and Deuteronomy 5:12–15.

[4] However, Jewish law does seem to occasionally grant work the status of a formal commandment, such as Shulḥan Arukh Orakh Hayyim 248:4, which cites the opinion that travel for the sake of engaging in commerce is considered a "commanded activity" (*d'var mitzvah*).

[5] Mekhiltah D'rabbi Shimon bar Yoḥai, 20:9.

[6] M.T. Hilkhot Talmud Torah 3:10, based on M. Avot 2:2.

[7] B. Avodah Zarah 3a. Original is in the masculine third-person singular; it has been rendered in the plural in the interest of gender neutrality. The phrase is used metaphorically to refer to the need to do good deeds in this world in order to gain a reward in the world to come.

[8] Avot D'rabbi Natan 11 (Version A); translation (with modifications) is taken from *The Fathers According to Rabbi Natan*, trans. Judah Goldin (New Haven: Yale University Press, 1955) p. 60.

[9] M. Ketubot 5:5.

[10] Commentary to Pirkei Avot 1:10.

[11] See note 8 above.

[12] See note 8 above.

[13] Y. Berakhot 9a, 3c; Y. Nedarim 12b, 38a.

[14] *Kal va-ḥomer* is the rabbinic form of *a fortiori* reasoning: if God, who can't really be fatigued, rested from the divine work of creation, certainly humans should also rest on the seventh day!

[15] Mekhilta D'rabbi Yishmael on Exodus 20:11, copied (with minor alterations) from *Mekhilta de-Rabbi Ishmael*, trans. Jacob Z. Lauterbach (2nd ed.; Philadelphia: Jewish Publication Society, 2006), pp. 330–331.

[16] Bereshit Rabbah 10:9.

[17] Quoted by M. M. Kasher in his monumental *Torah Sh'leimah* (Hebrew; New York: American Biblical Encyclopedia Society, 1954), *Yitro* volume, p. 81, n. 273. Meir Friedman (1831 1908) spent most of his life in Vienna and frequently published under the pen name Ish-Shalom. I am indebted to Kasher's work for its help in locating textual sources for this essay.

The Fragile Sabbath

Martin S. Cohen

The Hebrew verb *shamar* (from the root *shin-mem-resh*) most typically means "to guard" or "to safeguard" in classical Hebrew texts. When God sets cherubim and then some sort of rotating sword in place *lishmor et derekh eitz ha-ḥayyim* (Genesis 3:24), for example, these newly appointed sentinels are meant to "guard" the route to the Tree of Life so that neither Adam nor Eve can sneak back into the garden to eat of its fruit.[1] Similarly, when Cain asks the most famous of all rhetorical questions—*ha-shomeir aḥi anokhi*, "Am I my brother's *shomeir*?" (Genesis 4:9)—the use of a verbal noun derived from *shamar* to denote the role Cain perceives himself specifically *not* to have with respect to his brother clearly suggests that Cain does not see why his fraternal role should include guarding his brother from whatever dangers might befall him.[2] Later on, the *mishmar* (a noun formed from the same *shin-mem-resh* verbal root) in the Joseph story is a jail where prisoners are guarded to prevent them from fleeing.[3]

But there is another *shamar* in Scripture, one that is used to denote allegiance to law and which would thus be better translated into English as "to keep" than "to guard," and there are countless examples of this usage too. The text of the Ten Commandments, for example, describes God as "merciful…to those who love Me and who are *shom'rei mitzvotai*" (Exodus 20:6 and Deuteronomy 5:10), and the word here clearly means to reference people who faithfully "keep" the commandments, not people who "guard" them from some external danger. And there are dozens of other examples I could cite as well in which some form of the verb *shamar* takes as its direct object a word denoting commandments, laws, or statutes, and clearly references obedience to the law.[4] In all these cases, it is clear that what one "does" with respect to a divine law is to observe it, to keep it, to be faithful to its details—but not specifically to guard it from some possible external threat. The verb *shamar* thus bears both meanings, yet the correct meaning in any given verse can almost always derived from context.

Because that second sense of *shamar* generally takes as its direct object a word denoting laws or statutes in general, the Sabbath commandment in the version of the Decalogue that appears in Deuteronomy with Shabbat as its specific direct object (*shamor*[5] *et yom ha-shabbat l'kad'sho*), is puzzling.[6] At first, the puzzle is not that obvious. Jews speak about "keeping" Shabbat so regularly that the injunction to do just that, to keep the Sabbath, seems easy to understand. Indeed, the notion of "keeping" Shabbat is so familiar that the word is almost always inserted into translations of the Exodus version of the Decalogue, where the fourth commandment is regularly rendered as "Remember the Sabbath day to keep it holy," despite the fact that "keep" does not correspond to any word in the Hebrew original at all.[7]

But it is precisely because we so regularly talk about "keeping" the commandments, that it is surprising to learn that Sabbath observance is just one of three *mitzvot* (or rather groups of interrelated *mitzvot*) whose observance is denoted in the Torah specifically with the verb *shamar*. And that usage prompts us to wonder what precisely the verb *shamar* is meant to suggest when used specifically to reference their observance. Does it mean merely that one need be faithful to the Sabbath's many rules and details? Or is the idea that one must guard the Sabbath from external perils that might damage it from without?[8] Both approaches entail difficulties. The former, certainly the simpler solution, founders on the fact that *shamar* is not used in conjunction with other commandments that Scripture also commands the faithful to observe with diligence and assiduity. The latter, the less likely suggestion, founders on the obvious question of precisely what it could be that the commandments which attract the use of *shamar* could possibly need to be guarded *from*.

One group of commandments that attracts the use of the verb *shamar* to denote its observance are those related to the Passover festival. Indeed, one of the stock ways of referencing Passover observance in the twelfth chapter of Exodus is in a series of *u-sh'martem et* ("and you shall keep") clauses: *u-sh'martem et ha-yom ha-zeh* ("you shall keep this day," verse 17), *u-sh'martem et ha-davar ha-zeh* ("you shall keep this thing," verse 24), and *u-sh'martem et ha-avodah ha-zot* ("you shall keep this worship," verse 25). In the first of these clauses, the verb appears twice—once to forbid labor in the course of the holiday and once to command the Israelites to eat *matzah* during the Passover holiday.[9] The second clause uses the expression *u-sh'martem et ha-davar ha-zeh* to command the annual retelling of the story of Israel's liberation from bondage in Egypt.[10] And *shamar* is used in the final clause to remind the Israelites that the *pesaḥ* sacrifice is to be sacrificed annually once they enter the land as an ongoing feature of Israelite worship, and that they are in that specific way to "keep" it as part of their spiritual and ritual heritage.[11] Particularly striking in this regard is the passage at Exodus 23:14–16, where the three pilgrimage festivals are mentioned and the verb *shamar* is specifically used only with reference to Passover. Indeed, this connection between *shamar* and Passover is so intense that the festival is also called a *leil shimmurim* (12:42), which seems to mean that it is the holiday on which so many *shamar* commandments are to be observed, as it were, at once.[12]

A second group of commandments that are described with the verb *shamar* are those that relate to worship in the Tabernacle, regarding which the Torah repeatedly utilizes the word *u-sh'martem* ("and you shall obey") followed by a direct object to denote the complex regimen of rules and regulations that pertain in that sacred place.[13]

And a third specific set of commandments that attract the verb *shamar* has to do with Shabbat. I have already referenced the famous *shamor* that opens the Shabbat commandment as it appears in the Decalogue in Deuteronomy. But the same verb is used to reference Shabbat observance at Exodus 23:13 and at many other junctures in Scripture.[14] As noted above, however, simply taking *shamar* in this context to denote fealty and obedience to this *specific* codicil of the covenant leaves unanswered the question why these specific three commandment groups attract that *specific* verb. And taking the word to denote some sort of special need for protection provokes us to ask what it could possibly be that Shabbat needs to be guarded *from*. I would like to explore the concept with respect to Passover and the Tabernacle at a later time; here I wish to focus specifically on the concept of Shabbat as something in need of special watching-over, of being guarded.

The first thing that comes to mind has to do with complexity: even in their biblical setting, the laws of Shabbat observance are precise and the consequences for even the slightest ritual infraction intense.[15] And, indeed, there are many ancient texts written by non-Jews that derisively mock that aspect of Shabbat observance specifically.[16] These texts have been largely forgotten today, but they were surely known—or at least their authors' attitude was—in antiquity. For example, this perception was surely known to the ancient *darshan* who explained the obscure word *mishbateha* at Lamentations 1:7 (a word that contains within it the letters of the Hebrew word *shabbat*) by explaining that the foe was not intent on mocking in general the pathetic misery of Jerusalem's citizens under siege, but was rather taking aim specifically at the Jews' observance of Shabbat as something ridiculous for a nation to obsess about when its cities were being razed and its population decimated.[17]

Another midrash suggests a different reason that the Sabbath needs to be watched over: because it is fragile and can be "broken" easily by people who are not necessarily innately wicked or hostile to the concept of Shabbat itself, but who are merely careless.[18] In this midrash, Rabbi Shimon bar Lakish imagines a king sending his son off with an empty bottle and some money to a local shopkeeper to purchase something the king wished to acquire.[19] The hapless son breaks the bottle en route and then for good measure loses the money as well, to which series of mishaps his father responds violently at first by twisting his son's ear and yanking at his hair. But then, after calming down a bit, the king decides to give the lad another chance, this time *specifically* instructing the lad not to lose the new coin or break the new bottle. The *darshan* then applies this specific set-up to the double readings of *zakhor* ("Remember!") and *shamor* ("Guard!") that initiate the fourth commandment in Exodus and Deuteronomy respectively. The lesson is daring: the *darshan* suggests that the two different verbs appearing in the versions of the Decalogue in Exodus and Deuteronomy are to be explained sequentially, imagining that God originally thought the Israelites would understand that the original commandment to remember the Sabbath included the (unstated but crucial) injunction *also* to keep its many laws carefully and meticulously—but then, forty years later, realized it was necessary to state unambiguously that the Israelites are to "keep" the Sabbath by obeying its many detailed laws and not merely to "recall" it intellectually by taking note of its weekly return.

The implication of this sermon is clear enough: the Sabbath

actually *can* be broken, thus made useless and meaningless, by people behaving like the careless boy in the parable who failed to understand his father's real intention merely because it wasn't spelled out for him explicitly. The prince in the parable is depicted as neither depraved nor wicked, just irresponsible and careless, and his father, once he calms down, responds rationally to his son's negligent behavior by offering him a second chance to get things right. The take-away is that the child should not be disinherited or disowned because of his recklessness, just made aware how easily glass can break and coins can be lost: these are the specific things that the boy didn't fully understand as he set forth on his errand the first time. And then the boy, having learned his lesson the hard way, earns his second chance and presumably ends up back in his father's good graces. (Are we supposed to understand that Moses actually revised the text on the tablets intentionally? *That* would be a remarkable assertion! But even if the *darshan* would probably not have carried his idea to that extreme, the implication of his parable is still clear enough: the Sabbath can be broken, thus made useless and meaningless, by people behaving like careless children who fail to understand the importance of protecting the treasure that has been entrusted to them.)

A third rationale for the Sabbath being something in need of guarding because of its inherently ethereal nature comes out in a sermon preserved in Midrash Tehillim, the late collection of *midrashim* from the Land of Israel based on the Psalter.[20] Rabbi Judah bar Simon wonders why King Solomon, in his authorial guise as King Kohelet, used the words *hevel* ("vanity" or "nothingness," literally "breath") six times in the opening chapter of the Book of Ecclesiastes. (To get to six, it is necessary to count the two instances that the word appears in the plural as *havalim*.) The simplest understanding is to take the word to denote the king's conviction regarding the ephemeral nature of all existent things, thus to suggest that even the most apparently sturdy things are, when considered honestly and carefully, barely durable at all. But Rabbi Judah has a slightly different twist on Kohelet's use of the word *hevel*: he imagines the king picturing the various things created on each day of creation and labelling the items as *hevel*, as mere breath—adducing biblical verses to prove that all that exists will eventually cease existing. And there is deep meaning to the fact that there is no seventh *hevel* in that opening chapter of Kohelet: that absence corresponds to the seventh day of creation precisely because whatever was created on the seventh day lacked that impermanence that all else that exists shares. "But what," Rabbi Judah asks rhetorically, "*was* created on the seventh day?" The obvious answer—nothing at all, in that Scripture specifically notes (at Genesis 2:2, cf. Exodus 31:17) that God rested on the seventh day from the work of creating the universe—is rejected in favor of the notion that it was "the Sabbath itself" that was created on that day. Rabbi Judah then goes on to imagine that the king actually *was* ready to add a seventh *hevel* to his chapter, one intended to complement the other six and thus to identify the Sabbath as ultimately ephemeral. But he found himself unable to do so, precisely because the Sabbath lacks all physicality: "For [the Sabbath]," the king now notes wisely, "is naught but holiness, light, and repose." And that, presumably, is why it needs to be guarded with special care: because unlike something that can be guarded in a safe or a bank vault, the nature of Shabbat observance requires that it be observed in visible spaces—at home, in the street, in the synagogue, etc.—where any hostile onlooker can easily deride its intricacies and technicalities, thus in effect mocking those who care deeply about its observance. It is from such brazen ridicule that the Sabbath thus needs carefully to be protected.

A fourth rationale for Shabbat being something that should be guarded has to do with its intrinsic value, something it does not share with the other commandments. A different text in Midrash Tehillim speaks to that point directly.[21] Rabbi Isaac wonders about the force of the word "look" in Exodus 16:29, "**Look**, for the Eternal has granted you the Sabbath." More than a mere rhetorical flourish, Rabbi Isaac imagines God actually wishing the Israelites to look at something; he cites a colleague, Rabbi Yosei, who imagines God asking the Israelites to look at Shabbat itself, saying, "This Shabbat that I have given you is a pearl [i.e., something that has value far beyond what the naked eye can easily discern] that doubles all the [otherwise] single things that attend it. The manna, for example, fell in single-day measures every weekday but Friday; in anticipation of the onset of Shabbat, twice as much manna fell on Friday to allow people to collect enough for that day *and* for Shabbat as well." Examples of other doubles then follow: two yearling lambs to be sacrificed (the daily *tamid* offering consisted only of one sole lamb), especially harsh ("double") punishments for Sabbath violators and especially generous (also "double") rewards for those who observe the laws carefully and precisely, a "double" commandment ordaining Sabbath rest given in two different versions (*zakhor* in Exodus and *shamor* in Deuteronomy), and even a double designation in the heading to the psalm for Shabbat (Psalm 92) that begins *mizmor shir l'yom ha-shabbat*, in which phrase *mizmor* ("hymn") and *shir* ("song") more or less mean the same thing, thus "doubling" each other's meaning.

The notion of the Sabbath as a pearl of great value has many different literary echoes, including some outside the corpus of specifically Jewish ancient literature. One example is the Parable of the Pearl in Matthew 13, in which Jesus compares the kingdom of heaven to a pearl. Another is the "Hymn of the Pearl" itself, perhaps the most famous of all Gnostic hymns, in which *gnosis* itself—true knowledge of the purest and most desirable kind—is symbolized by a pearl that a young prince must journey to Egypt to retrieve.[22] But our midrash stands on its own as well because the comparison to a pearl suggests that the Sabbath possesses not only ascribed value but inherent worth as well; unlike the kind of accouterments used to fulfill other commandments that solely have value when pressed into ritual service, Shabbat has true intrinsic value.[23] In that regard, it is indeed like a pearl that is valuable not because of what you can do with it or buy with it, but because of its inmost nature, because of what it is. Such a *mitzvah* therefore needs to be guarded because it might otherwise be stolen—which, in the rabbinic mind, is precisely what did happen as the church took the Sabbath, made a virtue out of ignoring its prohibitions and attendant rituals, and then actually moved it from the seventh day to celebrate it in its new guise as the "Lord's Day" on the first day of the week, on Sunday.[24]

A similar idea is found in the talmudic discussion of Exodus 31:13, where God instructs Moses to command the Israelites to observe the Sabbath, which is to be "a sign between Me and you for all generations, [so that it be known] that I, the Eternal, am the One who sanctifies you." Focusing on the last part of the verse, the third-century sage Rav notes that one has an obligation to inform someone if one has given that individual a gift, presumably so it can then be guarded properly, and he justifies that requirement by citing the verse in Exodus cited above in which God instructs Moses formally to inform the Israelites of the divine munificence that has been visited upon them. And then the Talmud cites an earlier (unnamed) source that imagines God saying to Moses: "I have a gift of great value in My storehouse that I wish to offer to Israel and its name is Shabbat—go and tell the people of the gift [I intend to bestow upon them.]"[25]

For all these reasons, the notion of guarding the Sabbath as one would something precious possessed of inherent value—but also as something easily breakable, easily mocked by ignorant outsiders, and easily lost—seems at least plausibly embedded in Scripture's regular use of the verb *shamar* ("to guard") to denote Sabbath observance.[26]

NOTES

[1] The word *lishmor* is the infinitive of the verb *shamar*.

[2] Similarly, when the poet uses *shomeir* to describe God as "the Guardian" of Israel who neither slumbers nor sleeps (Psalm 121:4), the clear meaning is that God is a watchful sentinel who guards Israel without ever needing even briefly to sleep the way human guards eventually would.

[3] See Genesis 40:3, 4, and 7; 41:10; and 42:17 and 19.

[4] Cf. Rashi's comment to Exodus 19:5, where he notes that the expression *u-sh'martem et b'riti* ("and you shall keep My covenant") denotes allegiance to the "entire Torah" about to be revealed to the Israelites.

[5] An infinitive form of the verb *shamar*.

[6] The commandment is much longer; these are its first five words.

[7] This, with a comma after "day," is both the 1611 King James Version and the 1917 Jewish Publication Society version, as well as many in between. Likewise, NJPS has "Remember the Sabbath day and keep it holy," although there is nothing in the Hebrew that formally corresponds to the "and."

[8] Cf., for example, how the same verb is used in Jacob's prayer to God at Genesis 28:20 to express the patriarch's hope that God will watch over him on his journey by providing him with food to protect him from hunger and clothing to protect him from the elements.

[9] Regarding the notion that the *u-sh'martem et ha-yom ha-zeh* references the prohibition of working on the festival, cf. Rashi *ad locum*, s.v. *u-sh'martem et ha-yom ha-zeh*, and Ramban *ad locum*, s.v. *v'sham*, who says the same thing while narrowing the scope of the reference slightly. Both interpretations are based on a midrash preserved in the Mekhilta D'rabbi Yishmael, *Parashat Bo, parashah* 9, s.v. *u-sh'martem et ha-yom ha-zeh*.

[10] Cf. the way this verse is twice explained in the Mekhilta: in *Parashat Bo, parashah* 4, we read *u-sh'martem et ha-davar ha-zeh—harei pesah l'dorot* ("and you shall keep/guard this thing—this references the actual Passover holiday to be observed throughout the generations"), while in *Parashat Bo, parashah* 11, we read *u-sh'martem et ha-davar ha-zeh—l'havi pesah dorot*, which is just another way to say the same thing.

[11] Cf. Ramban ad locum: *u-sh'martem et ha-avodah ha-zot—zevah pesah*, which means that the phrase *ha-avodah ha-zot* ("this specific manner of worship") literally denotes the paschal sacrifice. The same point, also using the verb *shamar*, is made at Exodus 13:10, where the context makes it clear we are speaking about the Passover festival and not solely the sacrifice.

[12] Cf. the use of *shimmurim* later in that verse unambiguously to denote the commandments of Passover, as opposed to the festival itself, thus leading to the conclusion that Passover is a festival of *shimmurim* because so many

commandments introduced by the verb *shamar* are connected to it. And cf. also Exodus 34:18.

[13] Examples include *u-sh'martem et mishmeret ohel mo·eid* at Numbers 18:4 and *u-sh'martem et mishmeret ha-kodesh* at Numbers 18:5, cf. *u-sh'martem et mishmeret ha-bayit* at 2 Kings 11:6 with respect to the Jerusalem Temple.

[14] E.g. Exodus 31:13,14, and 16, 24:18, or Leviticus 19:3 and 30; and 26:2.

[15] Cf., e.g., the story at Numbers 15:32–36 regarding the man executed for gathering sticks on Shabbat.

[16] See, e.g., J. Hugh Michael's still very useful essay, "The Jewish Sabbath in Latin Classical Writers," *The American Journal of Semitic Languages and Literatures* 40:2 (January 1924), pp. 117–124.

[17] Eichah Rabbati 1:34. Two other suggestions are also made. The phrase in Lamentations *ra·uha tzarim, sahaku al mishbateha* appears in the NJPS version as "when enemies looked on and gloated over her downfall." Much closer to the ancient *darshan*'s reading is the King James Version: "the adversaries saw her and did mock at her sabbaths."

[18] Pesikta Rabbati 23:4. The text was likely compiled in the Land of Israel in the sixth or seventh century.

[19] The notion of an all-powerful monarch sending a child off to the supermarket with some cash and an empty bottle to pick up some beer for supper will seem odd to moderns, but apparently worked for the ancients. For a helpful introduction to the rabbis' "king" parables, see David Stern, *Parables in Midrash: Narrative and Exegesis in Rabbinic Literature* (Cambridge, MA, and London: Harvard University Press, 1991), pp. 19–21. And now, in much more detail, see Alan Appelbaum, *The Rabbis' King-Parables* (Piscataway, NJ: Gorgias Press, 2010).

[20] Midrash Tehillim 92:2, ed. Solomon Buber (ed. Vilna, 1891), p. 401.

[21] Midrash Tehillim 92:1, ed. cit., p. 401.

[22] The Parable of the Pearl appears in the New Testament only at Matthew 13:45-46, and is most easily understood when compared to the Parable of the Great Treasure, which precedes it by one verse in that same chapter. For more regarding the gnostic Hymn of the Pearl, see Johan Ferera, *The Hymn of the Pearl: The Syriac and Greek Texts with Introduction, Translations, and Notes* (Sydney, Australia: St. Paul's Press, 2002).

[23] An example of something used in ritual that has no intrinsic value outside that context would be the myrtle twigs used on Sukkot—something no one would pay money to own other than in the context of preparation for Sukkot—or even a ram's horn, which has no value on the open market other than for use as a *shofar*.

[24] For a general overview, see Samuele Bacchiocchi, *From Sabbath to Sunday: A Historical Investigation of the Rise of Sunday Observance in Early Christianity*

(Rome: Pontifical Gregorian University, 1977), and particularly the seventh chapter, "Anti-Judaism and the Origin of Sunday."

[25] B. Shabbat 10b.

[26] As noted above, there are two other areas of Scriptural law that attract the verb *shamar* as well: laws pertaining to Passover and laws pertaining to the Tabernacle. I hope to return to this topic at a later date to investigate the use of *shamar* in both those contexts and to see if the theory put forward here with respect to Shabbat can be pressed into service in those contexts as well.

V'Shamru: Guarding and Preserving
the Eternal Covenant of Shabbat

Michelle J. Levine

V'Shamru et Ha-shabbat: Israel's Exclusive Commandment

There is a custom to light at least two candles on Shabbat: one recalls the commandment in the Book of Exodus of *zakhor*, to remember this holy day (Exodus 20:8), and one recalls the commandment in the Book of Deuteronomy of *shamor*, to observe this holy day (Deuteronomy 5:12).[1] A midrash cites Rabbi Yudin as saying: "*Zakhor* was given to the nations of the world; *shamor* was given to Israel."[2] According to this explanation, the commandment *zakhor*—remembering Shabbat—has universal relevance, obligating all nations (including Israel) to recognize that God created the world in six days and rested on the seventh day. But the commandment *shamor*—observing the Shabbat—is Israel's exclusive privilege: Israel alone is given specific ordinances that aim to reinforce and solidify its special status as the chosen nation whose spiritual connection to God is unmatched among the nations of the world.[3] Avi Baumol explains: "*Zakhor*, remembering and recognizing Shabbat, is the responsibility of all those creatures for whom God created the world during the six days of creation. His 'resting' should be acknowledged and respected by all of them. *Shamor*, guarding the day from devolving into a mundane, ordinary day, is the additional responsibility of the chosen people. Through the specific laws that support the 'spirit of the day,' we elevate ourselves to great spiritual heights."[4]

Israel's special relationship to Shabbat and Shabbat's spiritual, sanctified purpose is explicated particularly in Exodus 31:16–17, where God commands Israel to observe Shabbat (using the verb *v'shamru*, derived from the same root as *shamor*) "as an eternal covenant (*b'rit olam*) between Me and between the Israelites; it is a sign for all time (*ot hi l'olam*)" that God created the world in six days and ceased work on the seventh day and rested.[5] While the phrase *ot hi l'olam* here is generally understood to refer to Shabbat being an *eternal* sign confirming God as Creator, the medieval Spanish commentator Rabbeinu Baḥya ben Asher (1255–1340) interprets it in a complementary way: that Shabbat is a sign for the creation of *olam* (the world), because by observing Shabbat Israel testifies to the fact that the world is not eternal, but that God brought it into existence through a six-day course of action and then rested on the seventh day.[6] Thus, by fulfilling the commandment of *shamor*, Israel reenacts its covenantal commitment as the nation chosen to sanctify God through its exceptional, lofty spiritual bond to the Divine.[7]

The significance of observing Shabbat (*v'shamru*) as a *b'rit olam*, a covenant for the ages, may be clarified further by examining another occurrence of this unusual biblical phrase, as it appears in Genesis 17, where Abraham is commanded about the rite of circumcision—which is to serve as the distinguishing sign (*ot*) of the eternal covenant between the Divine and Abraham and his descendants (Genesis 17:11). This rite is commanded in conjunction with God's declaration to fulfill an "eternal covenant" to be the God of Abraham and his descendants (Genesis 17:7). This physical sign marks the male Jew as belonging to the nation of Israel; it is the permanent mark of God's servant who has committed to continuous service to the Eternal through observance of the Torah's commandments.[8]

The connection between Shabbat and circumcision, suggested by these parallels in language, illuminates the religious import of Shabbat. Shabbat is, in a sense, the weekly reenactment of the symbolism of the rite of circumcision.[9] On Shabbat, each Jew is to reflect on the act that initially consecrated Abraham as the first Jew, who would beget a nation that would have an exclusive relationship to God (and that nation's accompanying gift of the land of Canaan, where it could thrive and develop spiritually).[10]

An ancient midrash reinforces the connection between Shabbat and Israel's national mission, by noting that the seventh day of creation disrupts the numerical symmetry of the week. While every other day has a corresponding day, organized in pairs—day one is partnered with day two, day three with day four, and so on—Shabbat stands alone. The midrash personifies Shabbat as pleading with God for a matching partner. God responded that Shabbat would have as its partner (*ben zug*) the nation of Israel, which would sanctify the seventh day as a holy day.[11]

The essential purpose of Shabbat observance as signifying Israel's exclusive spiritual relationship with God is also exemplified in the sages' view that Shabbat was the first commandment given to Israel (at Marah, as described at Exodus 15:25), even before they received the Torah at Mount Sinai.[12] As Rabbeinu Baḥya elaborates, Shabbat "is a dogmatic principle of faith (*ikkar ha-emunah*) and it is equal to all of the commandments,"[13] since Israel's observance of Shabbat affirms the essential religious tenet that God created the world. This belief is fundamental: God brought the world into being with deliberate purpose and will, intending to maintain a constant providential interest in and focus on the world and to guide the course of its history and destiny. As Rabbeinu Baḥya explains, belief in a divinely created world serves as the backdrop for the additional, related religious principles of providence (*hashgaḥah*), reward and punishment, prophecy, and thus revelation in the giving of the Torah.[14] Accordingly, the message of Shabbat as codifying the religious principle of a divinely created world serves as the basis for the fundamental principles of faith communicated to Israel at Sinai.

Shamor, the Imperative to Guard and Protect: The Garden of Eden and Shabbat

How can we better understand Israel's specific obligation of *shamor* in relation to Shabbat? How does this obligation serve as an eternal covenant and a sign between God and the people Israel? The answer to these questions may be explored by delving into the meaning and significance of the verb *shamar*, particularly as it first appears in the Torah in the story of the Garden of Eden.

When God created the male Adam, "He placed him in the Garden of Eden to work it and to guard it" (*l'ovdah u-l'shomrah*; Genesis 2:15). While the garden provided Adam with all of his needs, nevertheless, as medieval commentators explain, he was still tasked with the active responsibility to take care of the vegetation: that is, "to work it" by weeding and pruning the trees, hoeing the soil surrounding them and facilitating their irrigation, or even planting additional plants for his pleasure, such as other seed-bearing plants and spices. What, then, is the meaning of *l'shomrah*, "to guard it"? Medieval commentators, from a rationalist and contextual perspective, maintain that this refers to Adam's responsibility to take care of and preserve the garden, as much as he could, by making sure that its domain was not trampled by invasive animals or birds—for only the human being was privileged to eat of the garden's fruits.[15]

I would like to posit a more profound ramification for the task of *u-l'shomrah* in this context, which will elucidate the command of *v'shamru* in connection with Shabbat. Adam, and presumably Eve (who, after she is created, is presented to man as his partner in Genesis 2:22), are tasked to "guard" the garden not only by taking care of its physical environment but also by preserving, protecting, and maintaining their focus on its deep significance for their own lives on earth. The garden was meant to be their home, the place where they were intended to thrive and develop as human beings and fulfill the purpose for which they were created. In this regard, the Provençal commentator David Kimḥi (called Radak, 1160–1235) observes, based on Genesis 2:15, that Adam was not created *inside* the Garden of Eden, but rather somewhere nearby, and only afterward "placed" inside it, "so that this place would be very precious to him (*haviv alav yoteir*) for it was new to him, and that he would acknowledge that God intends to make it good for him."[16] What is the "good" that the humans must acknowledge? The first lessons they are taught are that God created them and that the Almighty intended to have an on-going vested interest in their well-being, manifesting a constant divine providence and presence that would enable them to achieve great spiritual heights by developing an intimate bond and strong relationship with their Creator.[17]

How does this implication elucidate the significance of the command to "guard" (*shamor*) Shabbat? By observing Shabbat, what is the Jewish people "guarding"? The use of this verb in relation to the preservation of the Garden of Eden points to the answer. Just as the first human beings were given the responsibility to protect the garden, as the place where they were to fulfill their purpose in life, Israel is charged with the responsibility to "guard" Shabbat as the separate domain within the weekly cycle in which time is to be taken from their busy daily lives to revitalize their national mission—which is Israel's ultimate collective purpose in life. Just as the Garden of Eden was a gift from God to the first humans, who were charged with preserving and protecting it so that it would help them develop optimally, so too does Shabbat need to be treasured and protected by the Jewish people, because its observance serves to recalibrate the Jews' priorities by refocusing their energies and efforts in fulfilling their role as members of the chosen nation. While the first humans were assigned to take care of their domain, which was meant to assure the fulfillment of their role in life, similarly God expects that, on Shabbat, Jews will recall that they are meant to guard and treasure their chosenness as though it is a precious garden—a priceless divine gift.

The connection between Shabbat and these very tasks imposed on the first human beings in the Garden of Eden is found in an insightful ancient midrash. The verb *va-yanniḥeihu* is used to describe God "placing" Adam in the garden (Genesis 2:15), and the midrash notes its connection to the verb meaning "to rest," as found in the commandment concerning Shabbat: "And He rested (*va-yanaḥ*) on the seventh day" (Exodus 20:8).[18] The verbs regarding humanity's tasks in the garden, "to work" and "to guard" (*avad, shamar*), are the same verbs that appear in the context of the commandment of Shabbat: one should "work" (*avad*) for six days (Exodus 20:8, Deuteronomy 5:13) and then "guard/observe" (*shamor*) the Sabbath to sanctify it (Deuteronomy 5:12). Thus, the midrash concludes that the first humans were given the commandment of Shabbat when they were placed in the Garden of Eden.[19] The implication is that understanding what it means to "guard" the Garden of Eden will elucidate the responsibility given to the future Jewish nation in the commandment to "guard" Shabbat.

God placed the first humans in an environment that was optimal for their physical existence, so that they could focus on developing their greatest spiritual potential by recognizing the Divine as their Creator and serving God to the fullest.[20] According to the midrash, this message was further honed when Adam and Eve were commanded to observe Shabbat, to sanctify this day as a time to acknowledge their creation by God.[21] Thus, later tasking the people Israel to "guard" the Shabbat suggests that Israel's national mission is, in fact, to fulfill the very purpose for which God had originally created humanity at the time when the Creator provided them with a choice place in which to thrive—that is, fulfilling the divine will and sanctifying God's name in the world.[22]

Indeed, the northern French medieval commentator Rashi (1040–1105), based on a midrashic exposition, explains in his first comment to the Book of Genesis that God created the world for the sake of the nation Israel, which would later fulfill the Torah's commandments. The first word of the Torah, *b'reishit*, is explained as a compound word: God created the world "for the sake of" (*b'*) entities described as "beginning" (*reishit*), and the midrash identifies these "beginning" entities as Israel and the Torah. That the world is not eternal, but divinely created at a moment in time, signals that God intended the created beings to acknowledge the Creator's existence and presence in the world.[23]

By observing Shabbat every week, the Jew thus "guards and preserves" (*shamar*) this intent, confirming and bearing witness to the world as a creation whose divine purpose can only be fully realized through commitment to the Torah and its commandments.

Shamar: Torah as a Tree of Life, and Its Relation to Shabbat

The association between Shabbat and the Garden of Eden may be extended by examining a midrash that questions the necessity to work and guard the garden, since God had planted the trees and provided rivers for their constant nourishment (Genesis 2:9–14). The sages therefore interpret the tasks of "working and guarding" the garden from a figurative perspective, applying them to the preoccupation with learning and performing the Torah's commandments: "*L'ovdah*—this is learning (*talmud*); *l'shomrah*—these are the commandments."[24] Based on this midrashic exposition, these two verbs are creatively read by the twelfth-century German tosafist Ephraim ben Isaac as compound words: *l'ovdah*—*la-avod hei* and *l'shomrah*—*lishmor hei*, understanding the final letter, *hei*, of each of these words, which is numerically considered to be equal to five, to hint to the *five* books of the Torah.[25]

Expanding upon this metaphorical meaning, rabbinic sages also note the association of the verb *shamar* with the Tree of Life in Genesis 3:24, "to guard the way to the Tree of Life (*lishmor et derekh eitz ha-hayyim*), seeing the Tree of Life as a metaphor for the Torah. The midrash supports this connection through an associative intertext within the Book of Proverbs, which figuratively describes Wisdom (*hokhmah*) as a tree of life. Presuming that Wisdom is equated with the Torah, the midrash interprets Proverbs 3:18 ("It is a tree of life for those who grasp it…") as a reference to the powers of the Torah for those who observe its precepts.[26] Thus, when Proverbs 11:30 declares "The fruit of the righteous is a tree of life," it is understood to indicate that following the Torah's righteous path will bear the fruit of life-giving sustenance for both body and soul.[27]

In the Book of Proberbs, the verb *shamar* appears in relation to the commandments: if they are observed, they will be a source of life for their adherents. The medieval Provençal philosopher Levi ben Gershon (called Ralbag, 1288–1344) explains:

> "He instructed me and said to me: let your mind hold on to My words, keep (*sh'mor*) My commandments and you will live" (Proverbs 4:4)—Then God instructed me and said to me: "Your heart should hold on to My words and trust in them when it investigates properly the intentions of the Torah's commandments, for then it will reveal the completeness and

wondrous wisdom within the words of the Torah. Guard the words of the commandments in your heart (*sh'mor b'lib'kha divrei mitzvotai*), and through this you will achieve the true life (*ha-ḥayyim ha-amitiyim*), which does not have with it death."[28]

Reciprocally, the poet of Proverbs acknowledges that when one loves the commandments of the Torah, then "it [i.e., Wisdom] will guard you (*tishm'reka*)…it will protect you" (4:6), helping one to avoid choosing the wrong, evil path.[29]

The significance of the verb *shamar*, particularly in conjunction with the Torah as the Tree of Life, is profound. Our understanding may be further sharpened against the backdrop of the nature and constitution of the human being prior to eating from the Tree of Knowledge. As Rabbeinu Baḥya explicates, God placed the human being in the Garden of Eden in order to optimize the inborn synergy that existed between body and soul at the beginning of the human's existence. Humans were brought into this world for the foremost purpose to worship the Divine; this was their single-minded focus and goal. But with eating from the Tree of Knowledge, a competing desire (*ta·avah*, cf. Genesis 3:6) developed within the human psyche, such that bodily and physical needs and lusts competed with spiritual quests and motivations. No longer was there an equilibrium between humanity's two-sided composition of body and soul; these two aspects of humanity now began to act antagonistically. Rabbeinu Baḥya notes that in a future time, after the resurrection of the dead, all individuals will lead a life of synergy between body and soul, with the primary focus on the delight of the soul (*ta·anug ha-nefesh*)—as was the case before the sin of eating from the Tree of Knowledge.[30] We may now understand that God had provided the human beings in the Garden of Eden with the means to optimize their spiritual goal, maintaining their balanced makeup of body and soul by tasking them to "work and to guard"—that is, to learn the Torah and perform its commandments, which is the preservation of the Tree of Life.

Thus, the correlative midrashic association of "to work and to guard" in relation to the command of Shabbat signals that Shabbat is intended to foster and further facilitate a Jew's attentive focus on having been chosen as God's treasured nation (*am s'gullah*, Exodus 19:6), in order to fulfill the Torah and its commandments. On Shabbat, Jews are charged with reinvigorating their focus in order to grasp onto the Tree of Life of the Torah more effectively. Observing Shabbat reminds us of our national mission to perform God's commandments, implementing the Creator's will to the exclusion of the competing egotistical desires and self-driven wants of our own will. Thus, fulfilling *shamor* with regard to Shabbat symbolically recreates the atmosphere of the Garden of Eden within the domain of all Jews—such that their bodies and souls may be sustained throughout the course of the week.

Accordingly, the medieval Spanish exegete Abraham ibn Ezra (1089–1167) explains that when God "*blessed* the seventh day" (Genesis 2:3), "an extra dose of goodness [was added], for on this day bodies are reinvigorated with reproductive power and *souls with the power of understanding and reasoning*."[31] Ibn Ezra thus asserts that it is incumbent upon Jews to study Torah on Shabbat, for this activity strengthens one's commitment to the national spiritual mission to fulfill God's will, and in doing so, one honors God on this holy day.[32]

Fittingly, the German scholar Yaakov Tzvi Mecklenburg (1785–1865), author of *Ha-k'tav V'ha-kabbalah*, interprets the verb *va-yaniḥeihu*—used to describe God's act of placing the human being in the Garden of Eden (Genesis 2:15)—in the sense of *naḥat ruaḥ* ("peace of mind and contentment").[33] In his view, God gave the first human beings the Torah, which is identified midrashically with *m'nuḥah*, rest and contentment—for the Torah was meant to be a source of pleasure and delight.[34] Observing the Torah helps individuals find peace of mind and inner contentment, as it provides them with the tools to overcome the inner lusts of the heart that divert one from realizing one's true potential as a spiritual partner with God. When the wicked chase their desires and impulses, they never find peace and contentment, as Isaiah observes: "But the wicked are like the troubled sea which cannot rest, whose waters toss up mire and mud. There is no safety, said my God, for the wicked" (Isaiah 57:20–21). It is only through adherence to the Torah that the Jew can find a means to overcome the negative forces in life and those temptations that pull one away from the authentic values, proper attributes, noble character traits, and lofty spiritual pursuits that should be one's sole focus.

Based on this reading, one may infer that while Adam and Eve were driven out of the Garden of Eden in a state of misery and anxiety, contentment and pleasure were restored to Israel when God gave them the Torah at Mount Sinai. By associating Shabbat with the tasks to be performed in the Garden of Eden (namely: *l'ovdah u-l'shomrah*), the midrash suggests that this holy day is set apart from the rest of the week in order to reinforce the significance of the Torah in our lives, as a means of recapturing the utopian ideal of contentment and true pleasure that is experienced through spiritual commitment to Judaism and God's laws.

Shabbat and the Creation of the Wisdom of the Torah

Midrashic analysis of the profound relationship between Torah and creation can help deepen our appreciation of the essence of Shabbat's message—namely: to guard and protect Israel's spiritual role of bearing witness to God's creation of the world through observance of the Torah. The relationship between Torah and creation is already embedded in the literary style of the creation story, where the final day of creation is referred to not simply as "sixth day" (*yom shishi*), as is the pattern of the other five days, but rather as "**the** sixth day" (*yom **ha**-shishi*, Genesis 1:31). According to a midrash cited by Rashi, God made a condition with the six days of creation: they would only endure as long as Israel accepted upon themselves the five books of the Torah, which is alluded to by the numerical value of the Hebrew letter *hei* (i.e., the definite article *ha-*, in *ha-shishi*). Moreover, Rashi explains that the world was seemingly in limbo, waiting to see if it would perpetually endure, which was only guaranteed when Israel accepted the Torah on "the sixth day"—that is: the sixth day of Sivan, the presumed date of the Revelation at Mount Sinai.[35]

Within Proverbs 8, Wisdom (*ḥokhmah*)—identified by the midrash as the Torah—speaks about its relationship to the event of creation. This text is unusual within the Bible, for it presents divine *ḥokhmah* as a personified entity that describes both its origins and its subsequent relationship to the other creations of the world in the first person. Wisdom first describes itself as a creation in and of itself, but most notably as an entity that was brought into existence *before* the creation of the entire world including both non-living entities and living beings. Proverbs 8:22 states: "The Eternal created me at the beginning of His course, as the first of His works of old."[36] Through a plethora of temporal adverbs (*kedem, mei-az, mei-olam, mei-rosh, b'terem, li-f'nei, ad*), the Wisdom of Torah recollects that it was brought into being before the creation of heaven and earth and the natural world (8:23–26).

About the creation of the world, Wisdom declares: "I was there" (8:27), apparently as a passive witness and observer to the intricate steps of bringing the world into existence. But, in a most perplexing statement, Wisdom elaborates: "I was with Him as an *amon*, a source of delight every day, rejoicing before Him at all times" (8:30). What is Wisdom—understood by the sages to be the embodiment of the Torah—doing both prior to creation and while God is creating the world? This verse presents the wisdom of Torah figuratively in the guise of a child who is playfully enjoying God's presence, serving as a source of delight to God each day and at all times. The Hebrew word for wisdom, *hokhmah*, is grammatically feminine, and the eighteenth-century Eastern European commentator David Altschuler, in his commentary *M'tzudat David*, explains: "I [Wisdom] was by Him every day as a delight, and at all times, I would play before Him, causing Him to rejoice, as a beloved daughter to her father."[37] In this context, therefore, medieval commentators understand the word *amon* in the verse (based on its Hebrew verbal root, *alef-mem-nun*) to suggest that Wisdom is being described as undergoing a maturation process. Raised up and trained by God so that it is filled with the divine contents and essence of Torah, it thus becomes the gift that is bestowed upon Israel at Sinai as the ultimate delight of humankind. As Proverbs 8:31 relates, after the wisdom of the Torah spends its time by God as a source of delight, it is later "rejoicing in His inhabited world, finding delight with humanity."[38]

Accordingly, when Jews observe Shabbat, it is incumbent upon them to confirm the event of creation with the understanding that the Torah was created *before* all other created entities. We must acknowledge that God intended to reveal the Torah to God's creations as the source of wisdom, to guide the world to bring forth its purposeful intent and meaning optimally. By reaffirming our spiritual commitment to the Torah through the observance of Shabbat, we reinforce our recognition of the priority of the Torah within the context of the creation process.

But one midrashic exposition extends the ramifications of the relationship between Torah and creation even further, and in doing so it provides an extraordinary perspective that deepens the religious message that each Jew guards (taking *shamar* literally) on Shabbat. Reading *amon* as *uman* (both words are composed of the same consonants in Hebrew, differing only in vowels)—an artist or architect—the midrash interprets Proverbs 8:30 as the Torah's declaration of its role as God's blueprint and artistic tool (*k'li umanuto*) for the creation of the world.[39] While God did not need partners for the creation process, this midrash maintains that the Torah served as the foundational pillar upon which the world was built, boldly stating: "God looked into the Torah and created the world (*hayah ha-kadosh barukh hu mabbit ba-torah u-vorei et ha-olam*)." In this rendering, the Torah's wisdom is not merely a passive witness to creation, but it has a very active role in the course of creation.

The underlying ideological message of this reading is that without the Torah's wisdom, the world is not sustainable. As such, the midrash relates that God waited for many generations until Israel accepted the Torah, for it is only in the merit of the Torah that the world was created.[40] The talmudic rabbis go further and audaciously declare that if Israel had not accepted the Torah at Mount Sinai, God would have buried them under the mountain and the world would have returned to its primordial, uninhabitable state—described in Genesis 1:2 as *tohu va-vohu*.[41]

What, then, do Jews guard and preserve—*shamar*—when observing Shabbat? By fulfilling this commandment that is reminiscent of the creation process, Jews reenact the experience of "I served as His *amon*"—in the sense of acknowledging that the world was created with the blueprint and plan of the Torah's wisdom. This acknowledgement bolsters Israel's commitment to accepting the Torah as the guidebook that dictates the divine will, so that every Jew can be that source of delight before God every day, at all times, throughout the entire weekly cycle. On Shabbat, the Jew reaffirms how the fulfillment of the Torah maintains the very pillar upon which the world is built.

This profound religious significance for Shabbat is reiterated in Exodus 31:13, which sees the observance of Shabbat as signifying how God sanctified Israel as the chosen nation: "For this is a sign between Me and you for your generations, to know that I the Eternal have consecrated you." The northern French commentator, Samuel ben Meir (Rashi's grandson, called Rashbam; c. 1085–1174) explains: "[God says to Israel:] When you rest as I did, it is a sign that you are My people."[42] Importantly, the command to "observe" (*shamar*) the Shabbat is clarified by its designation as being "holy for you" (Exodus 31:14), but it is also a day that is qualified as "holy to the Eternal" (Exodus 31:15).[43] Significantly, these juxtapositions indicate that Israel's emulation of God's acts of creation and rest gets to the crux of understanding the relationship between God and Israel. God commands Israel to arrange the cycle of their lives to mirror the divine acts of creation, thus bringing them to understand their role as the chosen nation—and elevating them to become a sanctified nation, as they emulate God's ways.[44] Thus, Shabbat is a holy day for Israel because it is to be treated as a day that is holy for God. Shabbat cannot be merely a day of rest and relaxation, of luxuriating in repose from the chaotic work week. In order for Shabbat to be meaningful, a Jew must use this tranquil time to guard and to protect—*shamar*—its religious symbolic significance through its observance.

The Proper Outlook and Conduct
to Fulfill the Command of V'shamru

Accordingly, only with the proper mindset and conduct will the fulfillment of the command to *shamar*—to guard and protect through observance—be realized. Elaborating on this decorum for Shabbat, Isaiah preaches:

> If you refrain from trampling the Sabbath, from pursuing your affairs on My holy day; if you call the Sabbath "delight," the Eternal's holy day "honored"; and if you honor it and go not your ways nor look to your affairs, nor strike bargains—then you can seek the favor of the Eternal. I will set you astride the heights of the earth….(58:13–14).

Within the context of his rebuke of Israel's oppressive behaviors against the weak, poor, and hungry, Isaiah notes that Shabbat was not being observed with the proper mindset in his time. Isaiah exhorts Israel that they must treasure this day as a day of *oneg*, delight, by setting it apart from all other mundane affairs and treating it as a day in which God is honored.

While Isaiah implores his fellow Israelites to view Shabbat as a means of reinstating the nation's divinely chosen purpose, his spiritual message takes on an added nuance involving relations between one's fellow members of society, particularly the downtrodden. In order to "guard" the message of Shabbat, Isaiah tells Israel that not only must they focus exclusively on God's ways (rather than their own affairs), but they must use this time of the week to recall that as the chosen nation, they are obliged to respect their fellow human beings—which, in turn, is a reflection both of their respect for God's creations and for God.[45]

Paralleling this attitudinal frame of mind, the Moroccan commentator Ḥayyim ibn Attar (1696–1743), author of the *Or Ha-ḥayyim*, explains that perhaps one should understand the command of *v'shamru* in Exodus 31:16 in relation to Genesis 37:11, where this verb also appears. When Jacob hears Joseph's boastful dreams, the narrative relates that "his father kept the matter in mind (*shamar et ha-davar*)," even though outwardly Jacob berated his son. Here, the verb *shamar* indicates that Jacob waited and anticipated when the dreams would be realized; this usage imparts an additional nuance to the idea of guarding the Shabbat through the command of *v'shamru*. Ibn Attar explains that Israel is commanded "that the Shabbat should not be [regarded] as a matter of obligation and bother (*bi-d'var torah*) from the perspective of preventing work of one's affairs and will, but it is necessary to be happy on [Shabbat] with complete will and desire of it, and one should always be waiting and anticipating when it will arrive."[46]

Prayers on the Eve of Shabbat: "Ode to the Woman of Valor" and "Ḥannah's Prayer/Song"

I would like to conclude this essay by applying the ideas presented above to explain the custom of reciting Eshet Ḥayil, the acrostic ode to the Woman of Valor from Proverbs 31, at the Friday evening meal, as well as the lesser-known custom of reciting Hannah's Prayer (taken from 1 Samuel 2) when lighting the Shabbat candles.[47]

On a literal reading, Eshet Ḥayil seems to be recited on the eve of Shabbat as praise for the woman of the household. The midrash, however, provides another viewpoint by seeing the woman of valor symbolically, in the wider context of the Book of Proverbs as a book of wisdom. Since the Hebrew word for wisdom, *hokhmah*, is grammatically feminine, the midrash teaches that the woman of valor symbolically represents the Torah's wisdom, and her "husband" is God and her "children" are the students of Torah.[48] Reciting this ode to usher in Shabbat resonates with the spiritual message that Shabbat is intended to impart to the observant Jew. Shabbat is a time when the Jew must focus on the national purpose to commit to the observance of the Torah and its commandments, realizing the purpose for the world's creation.

Extending the ode's symbolical reading, I would posit that the attributes which characterize the woman of valor may be applied to the Jew's commitment to Torah observance and values. Just as the woman of valor is diligent, industrious, and actively involved in taking care of her family and community, so too devotion to Torah, which is being reinforced on Shabbat, requires *sh'mirah*— that is, active involvement in guarding the Torah, taking care that its commandments are assiduously observed, thus ensuring that one's spiritual relationship with God is treasured and preserved.[49]

The custom of reciting the Song of Hannah at the lighting of the Shabbat candles also resonates with the guarding and protecting— *shamar*—of the religious significance of Shabbat. One of the main motifs of this biblical song is the reversal of one's fortune and circumstances. Having suffered for years as a barren woman, Hannah beseeches God to provide her with a son, whom she would dedicate to God's service in the Tabernacle of Shiloh (1 Samuel 1:10–11). When God grants her wish, Hannah bursts out in poetic song, recounting her good fortune and extolling God as the source of her newfound happiness. But the song does not read as an ode recounting only one individual's change of fate. Instead, Hannah frames her circumstances within a wider theological context, deriving broader religious messages from her particular situation. Her reversal of fortune must be understood, she says, as revelatory of key divine attributes that characterize God's conduct within the world. In particular, Hannah focuses on God's providential involvement in the world, such that the Almighty has the sovereign authority to reverse decrees, change one's destiny and reality, and dole out reward for the righteous and punishment for the wicked. Thus, she declares:

> For the Eternal One is an all-knowing God; by Him actions are measured. The bows of the mighty are broken, and the faltering are girded with strength. Men once sated must hire out for bread; men once hungry hunger no more. While the barren woman bears seven, the mother of many is forlorn. The Eternal deals death and gives life, casts down into Sheol and raises up. (1 Samuel 2:3–6)

Against this backdrop, Hannah asserts, "For the pillars of the earth are the Eternal's; He has set the world upon them" (1 Samuel 2:8). In this statement, she acknowledges that the religious belief in God as Creator underlies the premise of the divine control of the destiny of God's creations, according to the standards of divine justice. "For not by strength shall man prevail" (1 Samuel 2:9). It is God, as the master of the world, who determines the course of history and the future of all individuals, based on their actions.[50] Perhaps this is why Hannah's song is not labeled as a song (*shirah*) in the biblical text, but is rather introduced as a prayer ("And Hannah prayed," 1 Samuel 2:1). Hannah is not asking for anything, as might typically be found in a prayer. Accordingly, why is her poem identified as such? In this context, "prayer" seems to be understood as the special means by which the individual turns to God because here she has gained insight into the ways of God, and this has drawn her closer to her spiritual commitment to serve the Almighty—as evident also through her dedication of her son, Samuel, to divine religious service.[51]

The connection of this prayer to the message of Shabbat is now clear. Reciting Hannah's prayer at the onset of Shabbat at candlelighting, where minimally two candles (which, according to the midrash, represent both *zakhor* and *shamor*) are present, hones the spiritual significance of Shabbat. Hannah teaches that faith in God as Creator serves as the cornerstone from which one may understand further religious principles. On Shabbat, the Jew is urged to guard, treasure, and protect—*shamar*—the essential principles of Judaism, which pivot on the basic understanding that God as Creator is a providential God, who controls the course of human history and destiny. Keeping this message in mind sets the tone for the entire day of Shabbat, and it provides the Jew with renewed energy and vigor to enter the workweek with a deeper understanding that God is at the helm, watching over every Jew and having the power to change the fate of any human being. By observing the laws of Shabbat, we are reminded that all of our accomplishments and successes are due to God and that the Almighty ultimately controls all aspects of the world's progress. As Hannah emphasizes, "He guards (*yishmor*) the steps of His faithful, but the wicked perish in darkness, for not by strength shall man prevail" (1 Samuel 2:9).

Conclusion

In his twentieth-century halakhic compendium, the *Mishnah B'rurah* (a commentary on part of the Shulḥan Arukh), Rabbi Israel Meir Kagan cites the custom of lighting seven candles for Shabbat, each corresponding to one of the seven days of the week, and he cites another custom that one should light ten candles, each corresponding to one of the Ten Commandments.[52] The juxtaposition between these two customs signifies that by observing Shabbat's commandments, Jews guard and protect their eternal spiritual covenant with God through recognizing the essential connection between the fulfillment of the Torah and the realization of the divine will, according to which God created the world in six days and rested on the seventh day, Shabbat.

NOTES

[1] For this custom, see S.A. Oraḥ Ḥayyim 263:1 and the *Kitzur Shulḥan Arukh* of Shlomo Ganzfried (1804–1886) 75:2. And cf. Israel Meir Kagan's *Mishnah B'rurah*, Hilkhot Shabbat §263, note 5, citing the custom that a wax candle was made of two wicks braided together, reminiscent of the rabbinic declaration that God said both *zakhor* and *shamor* in one saying (*zakhor v'shamor b'dibbur eḥad*); for this rabbinic exposition, see B. Shevuot 20b; Mekhilta D'rabbi Yishmael, *Yitro, Baḥodesh, parashah* 7; and Sifrei Devarim §233.

Talmudic and midrashic sources cited in this essay were accessed through *Bar Ilan Responsa, Online Responsa Project*, Bar-Ilan University (www.responsa. co.il), licensed through the Yeshiva University libraries website (www.yu.edu/ libraries), unless noted otherwise.

[2] Pesikta Rabbati, *piska* 23, *aseret ha-dib'rot, parashah t'lita·ah*. This midrash is a compilation of midrashic homilies on the festivals of the year. There is disagreement as to its dating. The first section was composed c. 845 CE according to some, but scholars have noted that it also contains earlier midrashic homilies dating from Palestinian sources of the sixth or seventh centuries. See Daniel Sperber, "Pesikta Rabbati," *Encyclopaedia Judaica*, ed. Michael Berenbaum and Fred Skolnik (2nd ed.; Macmillan Reference USA, 2007), vol. 16, pp. 12–13. See also the commentary of Moses ben Naḥman (called Naḥmanides, 1194–1270) to Exodus 31:13, s.v. *shab'totai*, who notes that the plural form "My Sabbaths" is kabbalistically understood to refer to the double commands of *zakhor* and *shamor*.

Citations from the biblical commentaries of Rashi, Rashbam, Radak, Ibn Ezra, and Naḥmanides derive from *Mikraot Gedolot "Ha-keter"* on the Pentateuch, ed. Menachem Cohen (Ramat Gan: Bar-Ilan University Press, 1997–2013). References to the commentary of Ḥezekiah bar Manoaḥ (called the Ḥizkuni) on the Pentateuch derive from *Ḥizkuni: Peirushei Ha-torah L'rabbeinu Ḥezekiah bar Manoaḥ*, ed. Ḥayyim Dov Chavel (Jerusalem: Mosad Harav Kook, 1981). Citations from R. Baḥya ben Asher's commentary on the Pentateuch derive from *Rabbeinu Baḥya: Bei·ur al Ha-torah*, ed. Ḥayyim Dov Chavel (Jerusalem: Mossad Harav Kook, 1967), vols. 1 and 2 on Genesis and Exodus. Citations from Rabbi Ovadiah Seforno's commentary on the Pentateuch derive from his *Bei·ur al Ha-torah L'rabbi Ovadiah Seforno*, eds. Zeev Gottlieb and Avraham Darom (5th ed.; Jerusalem: Mossad Harav Kook, 1992), henceforth referred to as *Bei·ur Seforno*. Translations of all commentaries are my own.

[3] On the relationship between *shamor*, observing and keeping Shabbat, and the specific laws involved in its observance, see especially Naḥmanides to Exodus 20:8, s.v. *zakhor et yom ha-shabbat l'kad'sho*, who explains (based on B. Eruvin 96a and Shevuot 4a) that *shamor* refers particularly to the negative prohibitions

involved in keeping Shabbat.

[4] Avi Baumol, *The Poetry of Prayer: Tehillim in Tefillah* (Jerusalem and New York: Gefen Publishing House, 2009), p. 199. Baumol observes how the Kiddush text conveys the two perspectives of Shabbat, its universal and national obligations, focusing both on the observance of Shabbat to commemorate God's creation of the world as well as how Shabbat recalls Israel's Exodus from Egypt, zeroing in on the spiritual purpose of Shabbat for every Jew to renew his or her commitment as a member of the chosen nation (pp. 200–201).

[5] Compare Exodus 31:13, which stipulates: "Nevertheless, you must keep (*tishmoru*) My Sabbaths, for this is a sign between Me and you throughout the ages, that you may know that I the Lord have consecrated you" (NJPS translation, cited from www.taggedtanakh.org). All English translations of biblical verses are cited from NJPS online translation, but changing "Lord" to "Eternal" in accordance with the conventions of this series.

[6] Rabbeinu Baḥya to Exodus 31:17, s.v. *beini u-vein b'nei yisrael ot hi l'olam*, in his *Beiur al Ha-torah*, vol. 2, p. 325. Compare Ibn Ezra's commentary (short version) to Exodus 31:17, s.v. *ot hi l'olam*, who cites this reading, although he maintains that *l'olam* in the Bible always means "eternally."

[7] Compare as well the discussion in Baumol, *Poetry of Prayer*, pp. 198 and 201.

[8] On this point, see the supercommentary of Rabbi Judah Loew ben Betzalel (c. 1520–1609, also known as the Maharal of Prague), *Gur Aryeh*, on Rashi's analysis of Exodus 12:6, s.v. *v'hayah lakhem l'mishmeret*, in Yehudah David Hartmann, *Ḥumash Gur Aryeh Ha-shaleim* (Jerusalem: Makhon Yerushalayim, 1991), vol. 3, pp. 190–191, paragraph 12, who explains the significance of the permanent mark of servitude to God through the circumcision in relation to the service to God carried out through the paschal lamb; see also Hartmann's notes 68, 69, and 76, which reference Maharal's other writings on this topic. Compare Samson Raphael Hirsch to Genesis 17:10–11, as translated by Isaac Levy in *The Pentateuch: Translation and Commentary* (2nd ed.; Gateshead, England: Judaica Press, 1989), vol. 1, pp. 299–302, on the importance of the circumcision as a sign of the Jew's eternal covenantal commitment to God's service.

[9] Thus, while circumcision applies only to male Jews, the obligation of female Jews as well in the observance of Shabbat signifies that the overall symbolic message of the rite of circumcision extends to the entire people Israel: *all* Jews are bound permanently to God's service.

[10] Interestingly, Ibn Ezra's long commentary to Exodus 31:17, s.v. *beini*, cites the explanation of the Spanish commentator Saadia Gaon (882–942) that the parallel language of *b'rit olam* and *ot*, which occurs only with the rite of circumcision and Shabbat, signifies these are two primary commandments whose observance particularly single out a Jew's identity.

[11] See Bereishit Rabbah 11:8, as found in *Midrash Bereshit Rabbah: Critical*

Edition with Notes and Commentary, eds. Judah Theodor and Ḥanokh Albeck (1903–1935; rpt. Jerusalem: Shalem Books, 1996), vol. 1, pp. 95–96.

[12] See B. Sanhedrin 56b, based on the stipulation that at this location, "[God] established for it [the nation] a decree and an ordinance (*ḥok u-mishpat*)." Cf. Rashi to Exodus 15:25, s.v. *sham sam lo*.

[13] Rabbeinu Baḥya to Exodus 31:13, s.v. *akh et shab'totai tishmoru* (vol. 2, p. 323), based on B. Ḥullin 5a; and see Rashi on the latter, s.v. *ella lav hakhi ka-amar*. Rabbeinu Baḥya points out that the significance of Shabbat is exemplified particularly in the prophets' rebuke that desecration of the Shabbat was a prime cause for the exile of the Israelites from their land; as he notes, this is a focus of the prophecies at Jeremiah 17:27 and Ezekiel 22:26 (and see also on this point B. Shabbbat 119b). He also cites the sages' explanation that if Israel were to observe even two Shabbatot they would be redeemed (based on the juxtaposition between the exhortation to observe Shabbat and the promise of redemption found in Isaiah 56:4 and 7; see B. Shabbat 118b).

[14] See Rabbeinu Baḥya's introduction to his biblical commentary in his *Beiur al ha-Torah*, vol. 1, pp. 12–13.

[15] For these interpretations, see the commentaries of Abraham Ibn Ezra (1089–1164) and David Kimḥi (Radak, 1160–1235) to Genesis 2:15, s.v. *l'ovdah u-l'shomrah*, noting that the feminine suffix of these verbs refers to the ground (*adamah*), not to the masculine Hebrew noun of garden (*gan*). Cf. Radak to Genesis 2:8, s.v. *va-yasem*, who notes that God appointed Adam as the official "gardener (*gannan*)." On the other hand, cf. Naḥmanides to Genesis 2:8, s.v. *va-yitta YHVH Elohim*, and see as well the commentary of the twelfth-century Joseph Bekhor Shor to Genesis 2:15, s.v. *l'ovdah u-l'shomrah*, who read the two verbs as a hendiadys—that is, two words connected by "and" that are meant to convey the same overall meaning of improving the garden (in Bekhor Shor's words, *tikkun ha-gan*), by planting additional plants and beds of spices, harvesting them so he may eat as he desired. Naḥmanides maintains that the trees of the garden that God had planted (as noted in Genesis 2:8–9) were meant to be eternally fruit-bearing and did not need any cultivation or pruning, such that when humanity was expelled from the garden, they continued to thrive.

[16] See Radak to Genesis 2:15, s.v. *va-yikkaḥ…va-yanniḥeihu*. Compare Ḥizkuni to Genesis 2:8, s.v. *va-yasem sham et ha-adam*. It should be noted, however, that the woman specifically is created inside the garden, based on the sequence of events in Genesis 2.

[17] See the commentary of Seforno (1470–1550) to Genesis 3:8, s.v. *mit·haleikh ba-gan*, who interprets this phrase to signify that God's "movements" throughout the garden reflected the divinely motivated, purposeful will—that God was personally and constantly present among them in the garden. Thus, Seforno

interprets *ru·ah* figuratively as God's will (*ratzon*), used to conduct the divine activities each day in the garden (ibid., s.v. *l'ru·ah ha-yom*).

[18] Both verbs come from the same root, *nun- vav-het*.

[19] See Bereishit Rabbah 16:5 (Theodor-Albeck, vol. 1, p. 149). The midrash also associates the two verbs describing the humans' tasks in the garden—*avad* and *shamar*—with verbs that appear in relation to the sacrifices (see Exodus 3:12 and Numbers 28:2).

[20] Compare Seforno to Genesis 2:15, s.v. *l'ovdah*, who maintains that the feminine suffix to the verbs *l'ovdah* and *l'shomrah* does not refer to the soil of the garden (*adamah*), but rather to the "soul of life" (*nishmat hayyim*) referenced in Genesis 2:7. In his view, the garden was the optimal environment to nurture the human's well-being so that the focus could be on developing the *tzelem elohim*, which, for Seforno, refers to the intellect. As noted by Seforno in his comment to Genesis 1: 27, s.v. *b'tzelem elohim*, the human's intellect is only bestowed as a potential capacity, but it must be developed and actualized to truly attain the realization of one's divinely bestowed gift of *tzelem elohim*. For a discussion of Seforno's philosophy of humanity in this context, see (with references to other scholarship on this facet of his commentary) my "Havdalah— Emulating God in Mind and Deed: Israel's Divine Mission and the Quest for Salvation" in *Havdalah*, eds. David Birnbaum and Martin S. Cohen (New York: New Matrix Publishing, 2017), pp. 223–226.

[21] Note, however, that there is midrashic debate regarding whether Adam and Eve were expelled from the Garden of Eden before the onset of the Sabbath or at its conclusion. See, for example, the discussion in Bereishit Rabbah 11:2 and 12:6 (Theodor-Albeck, vol. 1, pp. 88–89 and 103, respectively), as well as in Pirkei D'rabbi Eliezer, chap. 20.

[22] Regarding Israel's divine mission as the chosen nation, see also my discussion in "Havdalah—Emulating God in Mind and Deed," pp. 226–228.

[23] See Rashi to Genesis 1:1, s.v. *b'reishit bara Elohim*, based on midrashic sources; see Bereishit Rabbah 1:6 (Theodor-Albeck, vol. 1, p. 2) and Tanhuma Buber, Bereishit §3. The entities identified as *reishit* are Israel (based on Jeremiah 2:3) and the wisdom of the Torah (based on Proverbs 8:22).

[24] See Sifrei Deuteronomy, *Eikev, piska* 41; and cf. Pirkei D'rabbi Eliezer, chap. 12.

[25] See Ephraim ben Isaac's reading cited in *Sefer Tosafot Ha-shaleim, Otzar Peirushei Ba·alei Ha-tosafot*, ed. Jacob Gellis (Jerusalem: Mifal Tosafot Ha-shaleim Publishing, 1982), vol. 1, p. 104, comment 6, to Genesis 2:15. And cf. the Aramaic translations of Targum Yonatan ben Uzziel and Targum Yerushalmi to Genesis 2:15, who likewise interpret these verbs as referring to observing the Torah and its commandments.

[26] See Pirkei D'rabbi Eliezer, chap. 12, which associates Genesis 3:24 with the

Torah metaphorically being described as the Tree of Life, in relation to Proverbs 3:18. For parallel midrashic identifications of the Tree of Life in Genesis 3:24 and Proverbs 3:18 with the Torah, see Bereishit Rabbah 12:6 (Vilna edition) and Vayikra Rabbah 35:6. Cf. Burton L. Visotzky, *Midrash Mishle: A Critical Edition* (New York and Jerusalem: Jewish Theological Seminary of America, 2002), pp. 12–13; and cf. also p. 84, where the midrash declares "There is no wisdom but the Torah," citing Psalm 19:8. See as well, for example, Rashi to Proverbs 1:20, s.v. *ḥokhmot ba-ḥutz taronah*; 2:2, s.v. *l'hakshiv la-ḥokhmah*; and 8:1, s.v. *halo ḥokhmah tikra*—who, like the midrash, identifies Wisdom in the Book of Proverbs as the wisdom of the Torah.

[27] For a discussion of the metaphor of the Tree of Life in the Book of Proverbs, see Karolien Vermeulen, "The Tree of Metaphors: Etz Chayyim in the Book of Proverbs," in *Conceptual Metaphors in Poetic Texts: Proceedings of the Metaphor Research Group of the European Association of Biblical Studies in Lincoln 2009*, ed. Antje Labahn (Piscataway, NJ: Gorgias Press, 2013), pp. 91–112. Compare the commentaries of Rashi and Malbim to Proverbs 11:30, s.v. *p'ri tzaddik*. In relation to this angle of analysis, Ḥayyim ibn Attar (1696–1743), author of *Or Ha-ḥayyim,* notes in his commentary to Genesis 2:15, s.v. *va-yikkaḥ…l'ovdah u-l'shomrah*, how the Torah is often described metaphorically in the Bible with agricultural imagery, such as in Deuteronomy 32:2 and Hosea 10:12. Extending this metaphor, he elaborates that study and commitment to religious faith and observance requires work, *avodah,* as well as guarding and preserving its importance, so that its fruits and produce are reaped properly.

[28] Ralbag to Proverbs 4:4, s.v. *va-yoreini*. Compare Proverbs 4:21 and Ralbag *ad locum* as well.

[29] See Ralbag to Proverbs 4:6, s.v. *al ta·azveha*.

[30] See Rabbeinu Baḥya to Genesis 2:15, s.v. *l'ovdah u-l'shomrah* (vol. 1, p. 69). Compare Naḥmanides to Genesis 2:9, s.v. *v'eitz ha-da·at tov va-ra*, in relation to his commentary to Deuteronomy 30:6, s.v. *u-mal YHVH elohekha et l'vav'kha*.

[31] Abraham ibn Ezra to Genesis 2:3, s.v. *va-y'varekh Elohim*. Compare Seforno to Genesis 2:3, s.v. *va-y'varekh Elohim et yom ha-sh'vi·i* and to Exodus 31:17, s.v. *u-va-yom ha-sh'vi·i shavat*, who explains that God provides an "additional soul (*nefesh y'teirah*)" on Shabbat to enable one to better actualize one's spiritual potential. On the concept of the extra soul on Shabbat, see Martin S. Cohen, "The Extra Soul and the Common Heart," in *Havdalah*, eds. David Birnbaum and Martin S. Cohen (New York: New Paradigm Matrix, 2017), pp. 91–105.

[32] Abraham ibn Ezra to Exodus 20:8–11, long commentary, s.v. *beirakh YHVH*. Compare on Ibn Ezra's insights regarding the intellectual component of Shabbat and its ramifications in Rabbi Mordechai Torczyner, "The Shabbat Influence," *To-Go Shavuot 2012/5772* (Yeshiva University To-Go series, Sivan 5772), eds. Joshua Flugund Michael Dubitsky, pp. 40–41. See as well Naḥmanides to

Exodus 20:8, s.v. *l'kad'sho*.

[33] See Yaakov Tzvi Mecklenburg, *Ha-k'tav V'ha-kabbalah: Bei·ur al Ḥamishah Ḥumshei Torah* (New York: Om Publishing Co., 1946), to Genesis 2:15, s.v. *va-yaniḥeihu b'gan eiden*, referencing Pirkei Avot 3:10 and Proverbs 29:17, as well as the idea of *rei·aḥ niḥo·aḥ* in relation to the sacrifices.

[34] See Mecklenburg, *Ha-K'tav V'ha-kabbalah*, ibid., citing the midrashic association of *m'nuḥah* with the Torah; see Tanḥuma to *parashat Va-y'ḥi*, §11.

[35] See Rashi to Genesis 1:31, s.v. *yom ha-shishi*, based on Tanḥuma to *parashat Bereishit*, chap. 1, §1.

[36] While the verb for "created" in this context is *kanah*, which could have the connotation of "acquisition," medieval commentators, and the NJPS translation cited, opt for the meaning of "creation" based especially on the ensuing verses that speak of Wisdom being brought into being before the various components of the earth. Note as well that in Genesis 14:19 and Deuteronomy 32:6, the verb *kanah* has the sense of creation. This is reiterated by explaining *reishit darko* to mean before the creation of the world (see Rashi to Proverbs 8:22, s.v. *reishit darko*, as well as the NJPS translation). See also how other verbs indicate the idea of creation in relation to the entity of wisdom: *nisakhti* in Proverbs 8:23 (from the root *nun-samekh-kaf*, meaning "to be poured out" [as in Job 10:10] or "to be fashioned" [as in the parallel usage of this verb in Psalm 139:13]), and *ḥolalti* in Proverbs 8:25, which is used to reference the birth process, as in Deuteronomy 32:18. Note that the eighteenth-century Eastern European commentator David Altschuler, author of *M'tzudat David*, sees both meanings of the verb *kanah* at play here, explaining that God created Wisdom so that it would be the divine possession (see his comment to Proverbs 8:22, s.v. *YHVH kanani*).

[37] *M'tzudat David* to Proverbs 8:30, s.v. *va-ehyeh*. The term *sha·ashu·im* is used in the context of a child's delight in Jeremiah 31:19, and see the commentary of Radak *ad locum*. Compare Zechariah 8:5, where the verb *l'saheik* appears in the context of children joyfully playing in the streets.

[38] Compare Rashi to Proverbs 8:30, s.v. *amon*, who cites Lamentations 4:5, "who are raised up (*ha-emunim*) in purple splendor." See as well Altschuler's *M'tzudat Tziyon* to Proverbs 8:30, s.v. *va-ehyeh*, who cites the parallel in Isaiah 49:23, which has the plural noun, *omnayikh*, understood as those who raise and nurture. Similarly, Bereishit Rabbah 1:1 (Theodor and Albeck, vol. 1, p. 1) cites Numbers 11:12, which has the noun *omein*, understood as a nurse for an infant, but interestingly rendered by the midrash with the Greek term *pedagoga*, a teacher. See as well Esther 2:7, with the noun *omein*, and 2:20, with the related verb *v'om'nah*, indicating how Mordecai raised up Esther as an adoptive parent. Compare also Ralbag to Proverbs 8:30, s.v. *va-ehyeh*, who specifies that Wisdom is trained and taught by God, raised up in the matters of knowledge, and in that way, she was a source of delight to the Divine. The meaning of *amon* in Proverbs

8:30 has been the source of extensive discussion as well among modern scholars. See, for example, Avi Hurvitz, "*L'diyyuko Shel Ha-munah Amon B'sefer Mishlei 8:30*," in *Ha-mikra Bi-r'i m'far'shav: Sefer Zikkaron L'Sarah Kamin*, ed. Sarah Yefet (Jerusalem: Magnes Press, Hebrew University, 1994), pp. 647–650; Michael V. Fox, "Amon Again," *Journal of Biblical Literature* 115:4 (1996), pp. 699–702; Cleon L. Rogers III, "The Meaning and Significance of the Hebrew Word *Amon* in Proverbs 8,30," *Zeitschrift für die alttestamentliche Wissenschaft* 109:2 (1997), pp. 208–221; and Victor Avigdor Hurowitz, "Nursling, Advisor, Architect? *Amon* and the Role of Wisdom in Proverbs 8, 22–31," *Biblica* 80:3 (1999), pp. 391–400. Note, in particular, the latter's description of Wisdom, based on his preference to render *amon* as "nursling" (ibid., p. 398): "Wisdom relates that she received her education or early training in the house of the creator of the universe who was her father and nurse, and one may imply thereby that she learned all she could about the cosmic order by watching her parent at work. As God's daughter she has inherited His wisdom. She has observed creation (*sham ani*) and has been raised by the creator Himself (*va-ehyeh etzlo amon*) so she knows everything there is to know about the world."

[39] See Bereishit Rabbah 1:1 (Theodor-Albeck, vol. 1, p. 2). Compare Tanḥuma, *parashat Bereishit*, chap. 1, § 1. One may also note that the noun *aman* is used at Song of Songs 7:2 to denote an artisan.

[40] See Bereishit Rabbah 1:4 (Theodor-Albeck, vol. 1, p. 7).

[41] See B. Shabbat 88a.

[42] Rashbam to Exodus 31:13, s.v. *ki ot hi*. Compare Rashi to Exodus 31:13, s.v. *ki ot hi beini u-veineikhem*, and s.v. *la-da·at*, that this sign is also meant for the nations of the world to recognize that God sanctifies Israel as the chosen nation. On this latter point, see as well Ḥizkuni to Exodus 31:13, s.v. *ki ot hi beini u-veineikhem*, who notes the text's emphasis that when Israel rests like God did after the six days of creation, it is a sign between God and Israel to the exclusion of the world's nations—for when Israel observes the Shabbat, the nations will know that only Israel is God's chosen nation. Seforno to Exodus 31:13, s.v. *ki ot hi beini u-veineikhem*, draws this point out further, noting the correlation in this context between the command of Shabbat and the building of the Tabernacle. He infers that if Israel does not observe Shabbat, then the whole purpose for the construction of the Tabernacle—which aims to reveal God's manifest presence among them—is null and void.

[43] See Rashi to Exodus 31:14, s.v. *kodesh l'YHVH*.

[44] See Seforno's introduction to his biblical commentary in *Bei·ur Seforno*, p. 4, who focuses on humanity's mission, with which Israel was ultimately charged: to imitate God's ways and, in doing so, to become more godly in their personae and essential character.

[45] On Isaiah 58 in relation to one's decorum on Shabbat, see also Naḥmanides

to Exodus 20:8, s.v. *l'kad'sho*.

[46] See Ḥayyim Ibn Attar, *Or Ha-ḥayyim* to Exodus 31:16, s.v. *v'shamru v'nei yisrael*.

[47] For the custom to recite Hannah's prayer at candle lighting, see Ganzfried, *Kitzur Shulḥan Arukh*, siman 75, paragraph 2. Note the caveat given that a woman who is barren or having trouble raising her children should particularly say this prayer as a *s'gullah* (i.e., as a prayerful undertaking) to reverse her circumstances. I would like to thank Hindishe Lee, librarian at the Hedi Steinberg Library, Stern College for Women, for assistance in finding this source, which appears to be the only halakhic source that I was able to locate for this custom.

[48] See *Midrash Mishle* to Proverbs, chap. 31 (ed. Visotzky, p. 190, and see also p. 192). See as well the end of Rashi's commentary to Proverbs 31, where he provides a symbolic reading of the poem and, after explaining the text literally, identifies the woman of valor symbolically as the Torah. In this regard, Rashi to Proverbs 31:28, symbolically identifies the "sons" as the students of Torah, and the "husband" as God (s.v. *kamu vaneha* and *ba·alah*). Similarly, *Midrash Mishle*, chapter 5 (ed. Visotzky, p. 38) figuratively identifies "the wife of your youth" as the Torah. In contrast, Rashi to Proverbs 2:16, s.v. *mei-ishah zarah*, symbolically identifies the strange, foreign woman as heresy (*k'neisiyah shel apikorsut v'hi ha-minut*). See as well Rashi to Proverbs 6:24, s.v. *lishmorkha mei-eishet ra*, who identifies the evil woman symbolically as idolatry.

[49] *Sh'mirah* is the nominal form ("guarding") related to the verbal forms *shamor* and *v'shamru*.

[50] For an analysis of the religious dogmatic principles of faith explicated in Ḥannah's song, see Avraham Ahuviyah, "*Va-titpalleil Ḥannah*," *Beit Mikra* 26:4 (1981), pp. 319–324. Compare Eliyahu Yedid, *Sheva Ha-n'vi·ot: Sarah, Ḥannah, D'vorah, Miriam, Avigayil, Ḥuldah, Esther* (Jerusalem: Hoza·at Ari, 2002), pp. 172 and 175–177.

[51] Regarding the identification of this song as belonging to the genre of prayer, see Ahuviyah, "*Va-titpalleil Ḥannah*," pp. 319–320.

[52] *Mishnah Berurah*, Hilkhot Shabbat 263, n. 6. For this custom, see as well the *Kitzur Shulḥan Arukh* 75, paragraph 2, but without Kagan's explanation for the custom. Kagan, however, concludes that there is "no need to have all of these candles on the Shabbat table."

Shabbat as Sign: Creation, Covenant, Communion, and Universal Community

Baruch Frydman-Kohl

Covenantal Sign and Liturgical Affirmation

The Sabbath is one of the central theological and behavioral aspects of Jewish life, one with roots in Genesis that continue to flourish in contemporary life. Although it is a stable and sustained sign of a covenantal relationship between God and the people of Israel, its significance and meaning has changed over time. Indeed it is precisely the polysemic plasticity of Shabbat that is the key to its ongoing vitality and continuing capacity to remain meaningful to successive generations.

In one of the first Torah statements about the significance of the seventh day, after detailing the structure of the Wilderness Sanctuary, Moses is directed to proclaim that the Sabbath is to be observed as a "sign between" the people of Israel and God.

> You must preserve my Sabbaths. This will be a sign (*ot*) between me and you (*beini u-veineikhem*) for all generations, so you may know that I am the Eternal, who makes you holy. (Exodus 31:12)

The significance of the sign is to "know that I am the Eternal, who makes you holy." This passage continues as follows:

The Children of Israel shall preserve [*v'shamru*] the Sabbath, establishing it for generations as an enduring[1] covenant [*b'rit olam*]. It will be an enduring sign (*ot olam*) between me and the Israelites, for in six days the Eternal made the heavens and the earth, and on the seventh day [God] rested and was refreshed. (Exodus 31:16-17)

The observance of Shabbat is identified as an abiding expression of the covenant and as a "a sign between" God and the people. The divine cessation of activity in Genesis becomes a call in Exodus for the Hebrew nation to "preserve" the Sabbath. Taking all these verses together, we see that by "making" or establishing Shabbat, Israelites acknowledge the Divine who has sanctified them and recognize Shabbat as a sign of the covenant and as a reminder of the culmination and cessation of creation.[2]

As with the Hebrew word *et*, a pointer word used to designate the definite direct object of a transitive verb, the word *ot* (spelled almost identically in Hebrew) denotes a sign that directs attention to something. A sign is a "mark, symbol or portent, serving to convey a particular idea or meaning."[3] Throughout the Bible, there are many references to signs. Some examples are the mark on Cain (Genesis 4:15), the rainbow (Genesis 9:12-17), the burning bush (Exodus 3:12), the incense censors on the altar (Numbers 17:3), the staff of Aaron (Numbers 17:25), a heap of stones in the Jordan (Joshua 4:6), and an iron plate at the wall of Jerusalem (Ezekiel 4:3).

In addition to Shabbat, two other *mitzvot* serve as signs. Circumcision (Genesis 17:11) is an indicator of the covenant and *t'fillin* (Exodus 13:9, 16, Deuteronomy 6:8, and 11:18) are reminders of the Exodus from Egypt. Along with Shabbat, these three *mitzvot* pre-date Sinai with its expanded covenantal system of commandments. While *t'fillin* and circumcision are actual physical signifiers, all three are intended to convey an idea or message to others, indicating that what occurred in the past is expressive of divine engagement in history and an affirmation of comparable concern in the present.

The prophet Ezekiel also uses the term *ot* in relation to Shabbat. Responding to a consultation by some elders, Ezekiel reviews the sacred relationship between God and the people, reminds them of the covenantal Land of Promise, and demands loyalty to God by prohibiting images. Ezekiel then declares:

> I gave them my decrees and made known to them my laws; the person who obeys them will live. I also gave them my Sabbaths as a sign between us, so they would know that I the Eternal made them holy. (Ezekiel 20:11-12)

Ezekiel, of priestly lineage, reflects the language of Leviticus by identifying *mitzvot* as life-giving.[4] He then uses the terminology of Exodus, designating Shabbat as a "sign between" the Israelite people and God to "know" that God had "made them holy."

This reference to Shabbat as a sign was placed in the central part of the Amidah recited on Shabbat morning as a formal statement of the significance of the Sabbath.[5] Following the liturgical preface that alludes to a tradition that the Sinai revelation occurred on Shabbat and after quoting the two verses from Exodus 31:16-17, the passage continues:

> You did not grant [the Sabbath] to the [other] nations of the earth,
> nor was it a heritage … to those who worship images;
> those who are uncircumcised will not dwell with its rest.
> For You have given [the Sabbath] to Your people Israel,
> the descendants of Jacob whom you have chosen.
> …a remembrance of the work of Creation.[6]

This paragraph mirrors the biblical idea that Shabbat is a reminder of Creation and the rabbinic conception of Shabbat as a time of exclusivity and intimacy "between" God and the community of Israel.[7]

Shabbat is also designated as a "sign" through one of the poems sung during Shabbat meals. The Sabbath table song "Ki Eshm'ra Shabbat" was composed by the poet and Bible commentator, Rabbi Abraham ibn Ezra (1089–1164). Well-known among Jewish communities from India to North America, the refrain of the *piyyut* affirms

> When I preserve Shabbat
> God preserves me.
> It is an enduring sign
> Between [God] and me.[8]

Ibn Ezra introduces a word-play where the root *shin-mem-resh* (which usually generates words related to guarding or preserving) refers both to the observance of Shabbat and to divine protection. Sabbath signifies a covenantal relationship that links the individual Jew to the Holy One who, in turn, extends divine concern and love to that person.

What is meant when Exodus states that Shabbat is a sign of creation and holiness? What is the significance of connecting Shabbat to the liberation of the Hebrew slaves from Egypt? What is intended when Ezekiel repeats that that Shabbat is a "sign between" God and Israel? How does Ibn Ezra transform Shabbat into a sign of divine protection?

In rabbinic literature—both midrashic and liturgical—Shabbat observance will be understood as a sign of particular significance to Jews. Medieval halakhic authorities and philosophical commentators will identify the Sabbath as a sign that affirms significant theological beliefs. Jewish mystics will see the seventh day as a sign of the constant connection of the divine to the material world. And modern Jewish thinkers will identify Shabbat as a sign of universal aspirations with value for all humans. Shabbat will remain as a stable behavioral sign "for generations;" what it signifies will demonstrate change over time.[9A]

An Exclusive Sign

Shabbat was a significant element of the religion of ancient Israel[9] and post-biblical literature also indicates a deep concern for Shabbat observance. The Book of Jubilees, for example, describes the day as "a great sign" which the descendants of Jacob will preserve as a "sign" of sanctification and covenantal relationship with God.[10] Accounts of the Maccabean conflict indicate that Shabbat was a defining characteristic of Jewish identity.[11] Similarly, the Qumran community was deeply committed to the observance of Shabbat.[12] Reports from Philo, Josephus, as well as from non-Jewish authors writing in Greek and Latin, indicate ancient awareness of Jewish Sabbath practices and indicate that attitudes about them "varied from respect and accommodation to misunderstanding and even abuse."[13] Shabbat observance appears to have been normative and widespread within Jewish communities of the Diaspora and the Land of Israel.

The two other commandments identified as signs are the *mitzvot* of the daily binding of *t'fillin* and of circumcising male infants on the eighth day. However, the commandment to bind *t'fillin* is superseded by the Sabbath which serves as an alternative sign of the covenant.[14] Circumcision, also identified as a "sign of the covenant between Me and you" (Genesis 17: 9-13), was attacked in the ancient world and by the Church Fathers.[15] However, because *brit milah* is specifically ordained for the eighth day of the child's life, it is considered a time-specific commandment that takes precedence even over Shabbat.[16]

While much of the Gentile world may have seen Jewish Sabbath practice as an oddity, rabbinic literature emphasizes Shabbat as a sign of Jewish identity.

> The Sabbath confers holiness upon Israel. "Why is that person's shop closed?" "Because that one is a Sabbath observer." "Why is that individual not working?" "Because that one is a Sabbath observer." Such a person testifies about the One who spoke and brought the world into being that [God] created this world in six days and rested on the seventh. So is it written (Isaiah 43:12) "And you are My witnesses, says the Eternal, that I am the Almighty."[17]

Sabbath observance was seen as a practice particular to Jews and as an emblem of an exclusive relationship with God. Two second-century teachers, Rabbi Natan and Rabbi Yehudah Hanasi, commenting on the words, "It is a sign between Me and you" (Exodus 31:13), emphasize: "And not between Me and the nations of the world."[18] This may reflect a reaction to a growing interest in Sabbath practices by followers of Hellenistic and Roman religions, as well as by Gentile Christians.[19]

Michael Wyschogrod observed that the Sabbath has "two faces," one of delight and dignity and another, if violated, of danger and death.[20] This duality is also true for non-Jews. Although non-Jewish workers are supposed to rest on Shabbat and Jews are prohibited from asking them to perform labor on their behalf, non-Jews are forbidden to observe the Sabbath.[21] Resh Lakish, a third-century sage of Eretz Yisrael, taught, "A gentile who observed Shabbat is liable to receive the death penalty, as it is stated: 'And day and night [that person] shall not cease [from work]'" (B. Sanhedrin 58b, citing Genesis 8:22). Another teacher of the same period, Rabbi Yossi bar Ḥanina, taught, "A [male] gentile who observes Shabbat, but who has not been circumcised, is liable for death."[22] Complete cessation from labor would, theoretically, lead to a death penalty.[23]

Rabbi Ḥiyya bar Abba, a fourth–century scholar, brought a tradition in the name of Rabbi Yoḥanan, a colleague of Resh Lakish, that focuses on the Sabbath as a time of intimacy between God and the people of Israel:

> Is it not generally known that when a sovereign and his noblewoman are sitting and speaking intimately, one who sticks his head between them is liable to death? Shabbat is a sign [of intimacy] between the Holy One and Israel, as [Scripture] states: "between Me and the people of Israel." Therefore a pagan who insinuates himself between them before undertaking circumcision is liable [to the penalty of] death.[24]

The insertion of the Other into what is an exclusive relationship warrants severe punishment. Other rabbis imagine Moses anxious about non-Jewish observance of Shabbat: "Sovereign of the universe, since pagans were not commanded regarding the Sabbath, were they to observe Shabbat, would you show them favor [over us]?" God then reaffirms the status of Israel and reassures Moses: "By your life! Even if they would observe all the *mitzvot* of the Torah, they would not replace you."[25]

This exclusivity parallels a sense expressed by Rabbi Yehudah bar Shalom that the Oral Torah must not be translated. It was to be a *mystyryn*, a secret reserved for the people of Israel.[26] Shabbat is described as a special gift for the people of Israel and was to be protected from cultural expropriation.

> Rabbi Yoḥanan said in the name of Rabbi Shimon ben Yoḥai: The blessed Holy One gave all the *mitzvot* to the Jewish people in public except for Shabbat, which was given to them in private (*b'tzina*). As it is stated: "It is an enduring sign between Me and the children of Israel."[27]

As a "sign between" God and the people of Israel, Shabbat is understood to be a private gift between the covenanted partners. But since the Sinai revelation was public, the sign of intimacy will be a particular aspect of the Sabbath: the additional Shabbat-soul.

What is this "additional Shabbat-soul," known in Hebrew as *nefesh y'teiriah*? Offering a word-play on the root-stem *nun-pay-shin* that yields *nefesh* ("soul"), suggesting that in ceasing from the act of creation God was "refreshed" (*va-yinafash*, based on the same root-stem), Rabbi Shimon ben Lakish (cited earlier about the intimacy between the people of Israel and God) states:

> The blessed Holy One gives each person an additional soul (*nefesh y'teiriah*) on Shabbat eve and takes it back at the conclusion of Shabbat, as it is stated: "He ceased from work and was refreshed [*va-yinafash*]" (Exodus 31:17). When Shabbat cessation [concluded, the additional soul is removed and *va-yinafash* is split into two words:] woe [*vay*, for the additional] soul [*nefesh* that is] lost.[28]

By refraining from work activity on Shabbat, one is given an enhanced or doubled soul, an enrichment of spiritual capacity on the seventh day. According to this talmudic discussion, non-Jews are unaware of and unable to experience this extra ensoulment, which remains a "sign between" God and the Jewish people. The individual nature of this ensoulment may be the basis of Ibn Ezra's personalization of the "enduring sign between God and me."

A Theological Sign

The rabbinic portrayal and practice of Shabbat had great "structural longevity," shaping Jewish life and endowing it with the capacity to absorb "new movements and modes of interpretation without undergoing a fundamental shift in praxis or behavioral paradigms."[29] Medieval rabbis with an halakhic or philosophical orientation built on the biblical, midrashic, and talmudic sources regarding the Shabbat to identify the seventh day, for Jews or for those around them, as a theological indicator, as a reminder of Creation and the Exodus, as a witness to the Covenant, and as an affirmation of belief in God. Shabbat, a day for study, for physical rest, and for the pleasures of personal and social life, was part of this world.

One of the earliest commentators to the Torah, Rabbi Saadia ben Yosef (c. 882–842), is cited by Abraham ibn Ezra regarding the use of the terms "covenant" and "sign" for both circumcision and Shabbat. Saadia noted that just as a male Jew's circumcision would, if exposed, indicate his identity, so a Jew would be known to belong to God "by avoiding work on Shabbat or by not engaging in commerce."[30] Typically, after quoting another opinion, ibn Ezra offers his own: "[Shabbat is a] sign that the world was made in six days. One who labors on Shabbat denies that act of creation.[31] While both Saadia and ibn Ezra base their comments on the Mekhilta's idea that Shabbat is a visible sign, each emphasizes a different element of the midrash. Saadia stresses how the Jew will be perceived, with the words "you are my witnesses" referring to the society around the Jew. For Ibn Ezra, Shabbat is a sign directing internal theological awareness for Jews themselves, writing explicitly that "such a person [i.e., the Sabbath observer] testifies about the One who spoke and brought the world into being...."[32]

In *"Yom Shabbaton"* ("Day of Rest"), one of the most famous poems of Yehudah Halevi (c. 1075–1141), the poet offers a soulful song which indicates that on the Sabbath Noah's dove, a symbol of the people of Israel, finds rest and respite.[33] Halevi returns to the spiritual healing power of Shabbat in his great philosophical work, *The Kuzari*, where he writes as follows:

> The body repairs on the Sabbath the waste suffered during the six days, and prepares itself for the work to come, whilst the soul remembers its own loss through the body's companionship. He cures himself, so to speak, from a past illness, and provides himself with a remedy to ward off any future sickness.[34]

In addition to this functional role, Shabbat serves

> "as a remembrance of the exodus from Egypt," and as a "remembrance of the work of creation"….The observance of the Sabbath is itself an acknowledgment of His omnipotence, and at the same time an acknowledgment of creation by the Divine word.[35]

Elsewhere, Halevi adds that in addition to being a sign of Creation and of the Exodus, Shabbat also is a reminder of the revelation of Torah.[36] The seventh day is a time for spiritual memory, theological affirmation, and soul renewal, as well as a sign that the Jewish people maintain a relationship with God and national dignity despite the degradation of Exile.

One of the most prolific and influential scholars of the Middle Ages, Rabbi Moses ben Maimon (1135–1204), dedicates much attention to the details of Shabbat observance in his Commentary to Mishnah and his legal code, the *Mishneh Torah*. The concluding chapter of Maimonides' codification of the Laws of Shabbat begins by explaining four key terms related to Shabbat: "From the Torah, [the terms in play are] 'remember' and 'preserve', and from the prophets, [they are] 'honor' and 'delight'."[37] After reviewing what these concepts entail, he culminates his detailed codification with a summary statement about the significance of the Sabbath:

> [Observance of] Shabbat and [not] worshiping false deities are each comparable to [following] all the *mitzvot* of the Torah. Shabbat is the enduring sign between the blessed Holy One and us. One who violates the Sabbath is considered as an idolater....[38]

Maimonides probably based the equivalence of Shabbat to all the other *mitzvot* on a discussion in the Talmud Yerushalmi which specifically mentions Shabbat along with a general statement about the commandments.[39]

In his *Guide for the Perplexed*, Maimonides comments as follows:

> God commanded us to abstain from work on the Sabbath and to rest for two purposes: one, to confirm the true belief in Creation, which immediately and clearly leads to the belief in the existence of God; and, two, to remember God's kindness in freeing us from the burden of the Egyptians. The Sabbath is therefore a double blessing: it gives us correct beliefs and promotes the well-being of our bodies.[40]

Later, he returns to the subject of the Sabbath and observes

> The object of Sabbath is obvious, and requires no explanation. It is known to afford people rest; one-seventh of the life of every person, whether small or great, may pass in comfort and rest from trouble and exertion. This is in addition to the

perpetuation and confirmation of the grand doctrine of the Creation.[41]

As with Halevi, Maimonides seems to regard Shabbat observance not as an end in itself, but as a means to other purposes: physical repose (utilitarian), faith in Creation (theological), and recognition of divine care (theological). Maimonides' legal code stresses the details of observance, while his philosophical opus accentuates the elements of Shabbat which have universal significance.[42]

Among Ashkenazic commentators, Rashi (1040–1105) returns to the Mekhilta (fusing the perspectives of Saadia and ibn Ezra) to suggest that Shabbat observance is a sign for Jews of a relationship with God and, for other people, an indicator that God has made the Jewish people significant and sacred. Shabbat "is a great sign between us, [confirming] that I chose you, as I have bestowed upon you the day of my rest for [your] rest. [Through it,] the nations will know that I make you holy."[43] However, his grandson, Rabbi Shmuel ben Meir (popularly called Rashbam, 1085–1158), sees Shabbat as a sign of love directed exclusively to the Jewish people: "Your resting is comparable to mine, for you are my people."[44]

Rabbi Yaakov ben Asher (1269–1343) was an Ashkenazic halakhic authority who migrated to Spain and served as a bridge to the Sephardic interpretive tradition. In his legal work, the *Arba·ah Turim*, which set the organizational framework for all subsequent Jewish codes of law, he identifies the central blessing of the three Shabbat Amidah prayers with three Sabbaths venerated by Jewish tradition.

"You sanctified Shabbat" [on Friday night] relates to the Shabbat of Creation, as seen from its content. "Moses rejoiced" [on Shabbat morning] refers to the Shabbat of the Giving of Torah, for all accept that the Torah was given on

Shabbat. "You are one" [on Shabbat afternoon] relates to the Shabbat of the future [Messiah].[45]

His conceptualization links the liturgy of Shabbat to creation, revelation and redemption, indicating the arc of theological history.[46]

Sign of Communion

The rabbis who followed a mystical tradition amplified aggadic imagery, emphasizing the sacral nature of Shabbat to give Shabbat cosmic significance as something capable of affecting God and enabling Jews to share in the life of the Divine.[47] The teachings of Provençal Kabbalah changed the understanding of the "sign" of Shabbat from a day that reminds Jews and others of important theological beliefs into a day which enables Jews to spiritualize the material world and participate in the divine life. The constellation of ideas that bring together midrashic ideas in this novel way is first found in *Sefer Habahir*, one of the most influential works of early Kabbalah, which was composed in Provence around the end of the twelfth century.[48] Through the use of a highly symbolic language, *s'firot*, first mentioned in *Sefer Yetzirah*,[49] came to be understood as ten aspects of a divine unity that, through a process of emanation, bring the world into being.[50]

Each of the *s'firot* has a specific role in the creation process and refer to different days of creation. In the *Bahir*, the seventh *s'firah*, Yesod, is linked with the Sabbath because of the idea that Yesod

> served as the Sabbath of the sefirotic world: standing at the center of the seven "active" *s'firot*, Yesod nourished the surrounding rungs much like the Sabbath vitalized the six surrounding weekdays.... just as the weekdays are the temporal symbols of the six *s'firot* surrounding Yesod, the

Sabbath day is the manifestation of the divine Shabbat, the temporal vessel for Yesod's manifold blessings.[51]

Building on the midrash in which Shabbat was given to the Community of Israel (*k'nesset yisrael*) as a partner,[52] *Sefer Habahir* interpreted "You shall preserve my Sabbaths" (Leviticus 19:30) and other plural references to Shabbat as alluding to the union (or reunion) of those aspects of Shabbat which carried male and female associations.

> That is why it is said [in the two statements of the Decalogue]: "Remember [the Sabbath]" [Exodus 20:8] and "Preserve [the Sabbath]" [Deuteronomy 5:12]. "Remember" [Hebrew: *zakhor*] refers to the Male [*zakhar*] and "Preserve" refers to the Female.[53]

The sacred union also will be linked to the concept of an additional Shabbat-soul. Shabbat is truly "between" God and the Jewish people, giving human beings an active role in the inner life of the Divine and, in turn, enabling God to ensoul the Jew with an enhanced spiritual life.

One of the great medieval commentators on Torah and Talmud, Rabbi Moshe ben Naḥman (called Naḥmanides, 1194–1270), often differed from Maimonides in matters of Jewish law and theology. He also distinguished himself from the methodologies of Rashi and ibn Ezra by integrating emerging insights from the Kabbalah of Provence and Catalonia with his literary, linguistic, and aggadic interpretations.[54] "Between the lines of his rich commentary on the Torah, Ramban scatters kabbalistic allusions designated with the title "*derekh ha-emet*," presenting an approach to two different audiences.[55] As public discursive commentary (that is, the level commonly referenced as "the *p'shat*"), Ramban notes that remembering Shabbat through celebration and joy on the seventh day leads to an affirmation of the "the foundations of faith in creation, providence, and prophecy.[56] He also observes that while the Christian community gives each day an individual name, the Jewish pattern is to identify the weekdays by their relationship to Shabbat (Sunday, for example, is the "first day toward the Sabbath"). This verbal signification also ensures that Shabbat will be part of the consciousness of a Jew.[57]

Ramban then adds a kabbalistic conception of Shabbat as the mystical linkage between the divine *s'firot* and the world, citing the *Bahir* regarding the two verbs associated with the observance of the Sabbath:

> In the Midrash of Rabbi Neḥunia ben Hakaneh (*Sefer Bahir* §182), [there is] another great esoteric [teaching regarding] *zakhor* [remember] and *shamor* [preserve].... This relates to the statement of the Sages (in B. Bava Kamma 32b) that on the eve of Shabbat we recite "Come in, O Bride; come in, O Bride. Let us go out to meet the Shabbat Queen and Bride." They called the blessing [over wine] during the day the Great Kiddush, which [alludes to God who is called] the great Holy [One]. Understand this.[58]

Ramban refers to the concept that the female aspect of divinity, the Bride/Queen, is associated with the Community of Israel at the beginning of Shabbat, while the masculine aspect of divinity, the Holy One, corresponds to Sabbath day. Shabbat not only points toward a theological idea. Shabbat ritual unites the *s'firot*, unifies the Godhead, and creates a flow of divine energy into the world.

In his comment on "It is a sign between Me and you," Ramban returns to this theme:

> By way of truth... the reason for [the plural form], "My Sabbaths" and twice declaring that Shabbat is a "sign

between Me and you"… is that the seventh day is a Sabbath
of Sabbaths, Holy to the Eternal, because it is the foundation
(*y'sod*) of [the existence of] the world.[59]

He takes the use of the plural form, *shabbtotai* (literally, "my Sabbaths")
to refer to *shamor* and *zakhor*, which represent the male and female
aspects of divinity. When the Sabbath is celebrated during the evening
and the day, the rituals indicate intimacy and peace in the "divine
household," bringing about divine restoration and reunification. A
Great Shabbat, also called a Shabbat Shabbaton, occurs when these
two aspects of Shabbat provide a conduit for divine energy to flow
into the material world. Focusing attention on the biblical phrases
"an enduring covenant" (Exodus 31:15) and "a sign between Me and
the Children of Israel" (Exodus 31:17)," Naḥmanides adds: "The sign
of the [supernal] Shabbat is on the seventh day, because the [seventh]
day is a sign and [the supernal] Shabbat is an enduring sign…. The
one who is wise will understand."[60] The temporal Sabbath day is a
sign of the eternal and supernal Shabbat. In turn, the additional soul
[*n'shamah y'teiriah*] "which comes from Yesod, the Foundation of the
World 'though whom the soul of all lives' (Job 12:10)" provides a
partial experience of eternal life, the ultimate Sabbath, during the
temporal Shabbat.

Rabbi Baḥya ben Asher ibn Ḥalawa (also known as Rabbeinu Baḥya,
1255-1340) followed the model of Ramban, establishing contextual
meaning, adding rabbinic aggadah and elements of philosophy, and
then bringing the recently diffused teachings of Kabbalah. Initially,
Rabbenu Baḥya follows the commentators who link Shabbat to
the belief in creation *ex nihilo*,[61] through which "we can also derive
the beliefs in providence, prophecy, and reward and punishment."[62]
He goes on to direct attention to the kabbalistic conception of
Shabbat. "Shabbat is the last *s'firah*, just as the day completes the

entire creation and is named Community of Israel. Our Sages have hinted at this by stating that the Sabbath is the partner of the Jewish people…."[63] Going beyond the Talmudic delineation of thirty-nine categories of labor involved in the Sanctuary construction which are prohibited on Shabbat, Bahya identifies Shabbat with Sanctuary, thus understanding it to serve the Israelite seeking communion with God in time in an analogous way to how the Sanctuary served the same individual in space.[64]

As a temporal day that falls each week and that marks the seventh day of creation, Shabbat becomes a sign designating a transcendent union among the divine array of *s'firot*.[65] Just as when the people of Israel experienced the "great hand" of God at the Reed Sea, there are moments when the expression of a covenantal relationship through an "enduring sign" allows for a special spiritual insight. For the people of Israel who observe the Shabbat, "this is called "Pleasure" [Hebrew: *oneg*] because it is a pleasure for the souls above and below. *Oneg* is [thus] an expression of the heavenly and human harmony identified with the *neshamah y'teiriah*, the supernal or additional Shabbat-soul.[66] Even though non-Jews may know of the Sabbath, and even though this cosmic harmony is believed to affect all of existence, kabbalistic teaching reserved and restricted this aspect of Shabbat to the covenant community in comunion with the Divne.

While Bahya can be seen as someone who is deeply linked to the emergence of the Kabbalah in Spain, a later colleague, Rabbi Yitzhak Arama (c. 1420–1494) was one of the first to occasionally use kabbalistic terminology without being deeply involved with kabbalistic ideas, somewhat in the way modern authors with limited personal engagement in mystical endeavors might use terms derived from Kabbalah. His commentary arose from Shabbat sermons and is both homiletical and analytical, seeking to reaffirm the significance of *mitzvah* observance as an expression of faith and a means of attaining *d'veikut* (which, for Arama, is spiritual communion, rather than mystical ecstasy) and ultimate flourishing with God.[67] Arama, who felt that sacred times were the embodiment of theological verities, restates an idea we have already seen: cessation from work on Shabbat not only enables the Jew to study Torah, it confirms belief in creation and revelation, and constitutes a sign of eternal felicity.[68] Arama goes beyond the symbolic and ideational significance of the Sabbath to introduce a kabbalistic explanation: Shabbat is the seventh of divine *s'firot* involved in the construction of the cosmos, so that the Jew, by observing the seventh day, partakes of all the commandments and draws the Divine into relationship with the material world.[69] Through Rabbi Arama, we are able to see how kabbalistic ideas about Shabbat moved from a small circle of scholars to commentaries intended for learned Jews into the homilies which were shared with the public that attended synagogue.[70]

The distinctive features of the kabbalistic Shabbat as identified by Elliot Ginsberg are:

1. Shabbat signifies an intra-divine harmony which is a source of cosmic blessing. Serving literally as the life-blood of the cosmos, Shabbat is far more than mere devotional practice, theological idea, or sacramental moment for the individual or nation;

2. Shabbat rituals affect the mystical drama and mythic system of the *s'firot*, stressing the marriage of two aspects of divinity to provide a sacred union that restores and sustains the individual Jew, the people of Israel, divinity, and the material world.

3. Shabbat is not just a recollection of the past: the immediate spiritual moment is significant for the covenant and for the celebrant, transforming the self through the additional Shabbat-soul, and enabling the individual partially to partake of perfected time;

4. Shabbat is more than a gift *from* God; it is a gift *of* God
   establishing adivine-human communion.[71]

Eventually, many of these ideas found their way into Jewish liturgy.
The most well-known example, universally included in Kabbalat
Shabbat, is Lekha Dodi, the hymn that welcomes Shabbat.[72]

A Universal Sign

Although Jewish mysticism, particularly in its Zohar and Lurianic
expressions, maintained a significant role among traditional Jewish
authorities, its influence and authority waned within nineteenth–
century European rabbinic circles and Kabbalah "ceased to enjoy
an authoritative and sanctified status among most of the circles
which in one way or another adopted the values of the European
Enlightenment."[73] Heinrich Graetz (1817-1891), whose narrative
of Jewish history was extremely influential into the middle of the
twentieth century, saw a continuing struggle within Judaism between
the rabbinic tradition (characterized as rational) and the "corrosive
effects of mysticism."[74] Modern Jewish historians and thinkers
turned away from a mystical understanding of Shabbat as a sign of
divine presence in the world but gravitated toward the more universal
aspects of the philosophical conceptions of Shabbat. In keeping
with the kabbalistic emphasis on redemption, modern thinkers also
stressed the proto-messianic elements of Shabbat.

Generally speaking, Orthodox Jewish thinkers from Samson
Raphael Hirsch (1808–1888) to Joseph B. Soloveitchik (1903–1993)
understood the Sabbath as a sign and "a witness to the authority
[of Jewish law] and freedom of God's will."[75] Hirsch explained
the commandment to construct the Wilderness Sanctuary as a
"sanctification of human labor and creativity" and the cessation

from that project on Shabbat as "an acknowledgment of human allegiance to God."[76] Although concerned with religious inwardness, Soloveitchik explicitly excludes a mystical path to holy life. It is through adherence to Jewish law that the Jew indicates devotion to Divine will, sanctifies God, and honors the Sabbath.[77] Refraining from creative activity, according to Rabbis Emanuel Rackman and Norman Lamm, also has a personal influence on the practitioner. By observing the Sabbath, the Jew "might, in a kind of imitation of God, catch a glimpse of that freedom which is the essence of God's nature," and, in a reimagining of the traditional concept, create "a new and better identity," which is what is intended by an additional soul.[78]

More liberal Jewish thinkers accentuated the universal quality of Shabbat, seeing it as a sign of monotheistic belief and messianic hope. Hermann Cohen (1842–1918) celebrates Shabbat as a sign of the love of God and the mission of Israel: "The Sabbath is given first to Israel," but the world has accepted it, enabling Judaism to fulfil its "mission of spreading monotheism over the earth ...in the Sabbath the God of love showed himself as the unique God of love for mankind." Shabbat is "the quintessence of the monotheistic moral teaching."[79] Rabbi Leo Baeck (1873–1956), while acknowledging the distinctiveness of the Sabbath for Jews, was attentive to its universal messianic quality: "From this people, the Sabbath made its way through many lands and times. As this people [Israel] was blessed by it and is to remain blessed, so did it bless the people to whom it came." The sign of Shabbat "points and reaches toward a world of harmony, toward a great peace."[80]

For Martin Buber (1878–1965), Shabbat is not unique for Israel. "Rooted in the very beginnings of the world itself… the Sabbath is the common property of all, and all ought to enjoy it without restriction." Shabbat is a sign of the hoped-for quality of relationships every day, "the regular articulation of the year… valid at all times."[81] While recognizing the universal qualities of Shabbat, Buber shifts the emphasis from the abstract to the personal, stressing the implications of Shabbat for individual ethics. That turn to the personal and existential is also seen in Buber's colleague, Franz Rosenzweig (1886–1929). While stressing the uniqueness of Judaism and the liturgical pattern of the synagogue, Rosenzweig also believed that Judaism had an essential role to play for Western civilization. "In the Sabbath, the year is created… it is a holiday that commemorates creation." At the same time, Shabbat infuses the week with a holiness that anticipates redemption: "In celebrating it, we go in the midst of creation, beyond creation and revelation…the congregation feels as if it were already redeemed." Shabbat exemplifies an eternal anhistorical religious life as a future aspiration for all humanity.[82]

Rabbi Abraham Joshua Heschel's writing about the Sabbath was part of his lifelong attention to religious experience. Heschel pushed back against the Maimonidean understanding of God and joined Arama and others in emphasizing the significance of *mitzvah* as a "leap of action" that defines Judaism. Heschel refers to Shabbat as a reminder of creation and as a time to recall both the Exodus and the experience of Sinai, but it seems to be most significant as a signal pointing toward redemption. As with Rosenzweig, Shabbat is a temporal step into eternity: "Israel is engaged to eternity… their soul is claimed by the seventh day." Thus the Shabbat is a sign of "our Messianic hope… of the end of days."[83]

Although focused on Judaism as "a *religion of time* aiming at *the sanctification of time*," Heschel reflects on its universal implications. "There is no moment which I possess exclusively. This very moment belongs to all living men as it belongs to me." Thus Shabbat, as "a palace in time with a kingdom for all" is a sign of possibility for all human relationships: "The seventh day is the armistice in man's cruel struggle for existence, a truce in all conflicts, personal and social, peace between man and man, man and nature, peace within man....[84] *The Sabbath* is subtitled *Its Meaning for Modern Man* and Heschel does not quote any rabbinic text that identifies Shabbat as a sign limited to the Jewish people. "More than any other thinker since Emancipation, Heschel launched Judaism on the venture of pursuing its most obvious particularity in the point of universality."[85]

The idea of Shabbat as a sign pointing toward concepts and actions of universal and redemptive significance is an important contemporary theological development.[85A] Jonathan Sacks describes Shabbat as conveying a message about environmental ethics: "a weekly reminder of the integrity of nature and the boundaries of human striving."[86] Yosef Yitzhak Lifshitz contends that the secret of the Sabbath includes "the promise of healing the rift between man and the world, and between the created and the Creator."[87] Irving Greenberg characterizes Shabbat as a "foretaste of messianic redemption," a way to keep Jews faithful to the dream of "peace, with abundant resources and an untrammeled right to live... [with the world] structured to sustain the infinite value of the human being."[88]

Others have directed attention to the pace of modern life and the need to consciously slow down to enhance personal reflection and relationships. Francine Klagsbrun writes that the Fourth Commandment "offers a balance to the bonds of boundless labor, an opportunity one day a week to shut down the phone and faxes and reconnect instead with family and friends—and with oneself."[89] Judith Shulevitz discusses "time sickness," the "social morality of time", and how "a structured period of non-productivity could be very useful for an overscheduled society."[90]

As part of an exhibit in the Contemporary Jewish Museum of San Francisco, Rani Jaeger points to Shabbat as a vision for a transformed society. "Sabbath is a revolutionary tool for comprehensive social change—pertaining to all echelons of society... It reflects on the entire week; indeed, on the entire cycle of life." It should turn humanity "back to the inner value of people in particular and the world in general.[91]

Shabbat is personalized by the Sabbath Manifesto, "a creative project designed to slow down lives in an increasingly hectic world," in which we read as follows:

> We created ten core principles completely open for your unique interpretation. We welcome you to join us as we carve a weekly timeout into our lives…These ten principles are: Avoid technology. Connect with loved ones. Nurture your health. Get outside. Avoid commerce. Light candles. Drink wine. Eat bread. Find silence. Give back.[92]

Not only is Shabbat personalized, it is removed from any particular Jewish historic or theological context.

The Sign of an Enduring Covenant

In contradistinction to this reading of Shabbat, another approach suggests a way in which Shabbat might, as Heschel suggested, retain a covenantal significance for Jews with a message of significance for a universal audience. Rabbi Shimon Gershon Rosenberg (widely called Rav Shagar, 1949–2007) eschewed grand conceptual understandings of Judaism, allowing for doubt, uncertainty, and personal decision while still maintaining traditional Jewish observance. For him, Shabbat is a sign of holiness, attained by a personal choice arising from

> the struggle against slavery and bondage, and the [desire to] return to a natural unity and harmony. The two dimensions

are interlinked, as the demand for freedom from bondage is part of the very nature of man, who was created in God's image and is thus worthy of freedom.[93]

Shabbat is both a sign of the universal desire for freedom and harmony with nature as well as an indicator of the covenantal relationship between the Jewish people and God. This covenant is not a fact about the past to be affirmed or denied, but a very real option to be chosen in the present.

Steven Kepnes, a leading figure in the Society for Scriptural Reasoning, draws on the image of the additional Shabbat-soul to suggest that "Shabbat represents a process through which humans, God, and creation itself are re-ensouled," becoming "an everlasting sign of this ensoulment process that necessarily occurs once a week to ensoul the world."[94] Pointing to Shabbat both as a *b'rit olam*, an "everlasting covenant" and an *ot olam*, an "everlasting sign" between God and Israel, he suggests that Jews are obligated "to perform the liturgies of Shabbat" and the Holy One is obligated "to continue to re-ensoul Israel in the world," so that Israel becomes "a sign of creation". The covenant carries "the connotation of a mutual project. God and Israel working together to ensoul the world. Israel sharing the responsibility to bring God's power of ensoulment into the world."[95]

In the Bible, Shabbat begins as a sign of Creation and a reminder of the Covenant. In rabbinic sources and liturgical settings, Shabbat becomes a sign of the exclusive relationship between God and Israel, with the additional Shabbat-soul reserved for those who observe the Seventh Day. Medieval scholars identified Shabbat as a sign of belief in Creation and Revelation, with social implications for the community and individual. For followers of Kabbalah, Shabbat became a temporal sign of the transcendent structure of the universe and the interdependence and communion of heaven and human. Modern thinkers conceptualized the Sabbath as being a sign of universal monotheistic and messianic meaning, while more contemporary writers stressed the significance of Shabbat for our understanding of time, the need to moderate our pace of activity and a universal reminder of the importance of restricting human dominance of the earth.

Governed by the grammar of Jewish law and intended to be part of the covenantal system which brings God and Israel into relationship with one another, Shabbat looms large in the religious imagination, literary expression, and halakhic behavior of the Jewish people. Shabbat is polysemic, with a plasticity allowing for multiple meanings in different contexts, and having both variation and contiguity of meaning as a constituent element of the ethical-spiritual language of Judaism.[96] Shabbat can be sign of Creation and Liberation, a reminder of divine cessation from activity and an expression of a personal relationship with God, a day of exclusive delight for Jews and one that infuses the cosmos with divinity, an opportunity for an additional Shabbat-soul and a time that points toward the fulfilment of the promise of freedom for all people and harmony with the world. Always, it will be a call to holiness, an enduring sign of the Covenant, and an indicator of a continuing relationship "between God and the people of Israel."

NOTES

[1] In Biblical Hebrew, *olam* probably meant "enduring" or "everlasting," rather than "eternal."

[2] In Deuteronomy, Shabbat evokes a different memory: "Remember that you were a slave in the land of Egypt and the Eternal your God freed you from there… therefore the Eternal your God has commanded you to observe the Sabbath day" (Deuteronomy 5:15). Cf. the comment of Francine Klagsburn in her *The Fourth Commandment: Remember the Sabbath Day* (New York: Harmony, 2002), p. 23, where she notes that Shabbat with the promise of human respite is a way of "remembering the Israelites' slavery and showing gratitude to God for redeeming them and their descendants from it."

[3] W. Stewart McCoullough, "Sign in the OT", *The Interpreter's Dictionary of the Bible*, ed. George Arthur Buttrick (Nashville: Abingdon, 1962), vol. 4, p. 345. See also Albert Atkin, "Peirce's Theory of Signs", *The Stanford Encyclopedia of Philosophy* (Summer 2013 Edition), ed. Edward N. Zalta, who identifies a sign as having three parts: an object that means something to a particular interpreter. (Atkin's essay is available online at https://plato.stanford.edu/archives/sum2013/entries/peirce-semiotics.

[4] Leviticus 18:5. "You shall keep my statutes and my ordinances; the person who does them shall live; I am the Eternal."

[5] In distinction from weekday and festival services, each of the Shabbat Amidah prayers has a unique liturgical poem, consisting of a preface, a Torah quotation, an interpretation of the Biblical citation, and a prayer that God accept with favor the repose of the people of Israel on the Sabbath. See *Siddur Rav Saadia Gaon*, 2nd edition, eds. Israel Davidson, Simha Assaf, and B. Issachar Joel (Jerusalem: Mekitzei Nirdamim/Reuben Mass, 1963), p. 111: "I have found that the custom regarding the middle blessing of the four prayer services on Shabbat is that each differs from the other." Shlomit Elitzur, "The Ancient Prelude for the Blessing of the Day on Sabbath" (Hebrew) *Nitu·im* 2, pp. 1–18, available online at http://herzogpress.perzog.ac.il, reviews the numerous versions of this prayer and contends that originally there was a single prayer-poem repeated at each of the Sabbath services.

[6] For the idea that the Sinai revelation took place on Shabbat, see B. Shabbat 86b.

[7] *Siddur Sim Shalom: A Prayerbook for Shabbat, Festivals and Weekdays*, ed. Jules Harlow (New York: The Rabbinical Assembly, 1989), p.356, with translation slightly modified by me. The Mekhilta D'rabbi Yishmael 31:17 discusses exclusivity, B. Shabbat 10a describes Sabbath as a gift of love, and Devarim Rabbah 1:21 delineates Shabbat as a time of intimacy between God and Israel. At some point the Exodus verses came to be recited as a public proclamation

of Shabbat just prior to the Friday evening Amidah, thus framing the Amidah between the words from Exodus and a citation from Genesis 2:1–4, both affirming Shabbat as a reminder of Creation.

[8] *Piyyut* is a liturgical poem. "An Invitation to Piyut," a web-site that catalogs, explains and records liturgical poems and music, lists twenty-two renditions of the song at http://old.piyut.org.il/tradition/english/1904.html?section=more Performances (14Jan2019).

[9] See, for example, Isaiah 58: 13–14 and Nehemiah 13:15–2.

[9A] On the genre of providing rationales for the commandments, see Isaac Heinemann, *The Reasons for the Commandments in Jewish Thought: From the Bible to the Renaissance*, trans. Leonard Levin (Brighton, MA: Academic Studies Press, 2008).

[10] The Book of Jubilees, composed 160-150 BCE, presents a sacred history of the world in fifty-year jubilee cycles. See Jubilees 2:21.

[11] 2 Maccabees 6: 6–11, 15:1–4. 1 Maccabees 2: 34–41 reports a refusal to enter into battle on the Sabbath and a reluctant decision that bearing arms in defense would be permissible.

[12] Eli Lizorkin-Eyzenberg, "Sabbath Keeping In Qumran," Israel Institute of Biblical Studies, available online at https://blog.israelbiblicalstudies.com/jewish-studies/sabbath-keeping-in-qumran/.

[13] Willy Clarysse, Sofie Remijsen and Mark Depauw, "Observing the Sabbath in the Roman Empire: a Case Study," *Scripta Classica Israelica* 29 (2010), p. 52. See also Bezalel Bar-Kokhva, *The Image of the Jews in Greek Literature: The Hellenistic Period* (Berkeley, CA: University of California Press, 2010), pp. 296–303 and passim.

[14] See Mekhilta D'rabbi Yishmael 13:10 and B. Eiruvin 96a. At https://thetorah.com/the-origins-of-t'fillin/, Yehudah Benjamin Cohn suggests that "The blanket exclusion of Shabbat *t'fillin* practice can be explained in [relation to amulets and protection]…. Upon leaving the house… wearing them would have led to an immediate conflict with the Shabbat rules that prohibited "carrying" in public spaces–as clearly shown by Mishnah Shabbat 6:2. In a later stage of halakhic development, the rabbis ultimately elected to ban *t'fillin* wearing on Shabbat altogether." See his *Tangled Up in Text: Tefillin and the Ancient World* (Providence, RI: Brown Judaic Studies, 2008), pp. 135–136.

[15] The perspective of classical Greco-Roman writers is found in F.M. Hodges, "The Ideal Prepuce in Ancient Greece and Rome: Male Genital Aesthetics and Their Relation to Lipodermos, Circumcision, Foreskin Restoration, and the Kynodesme, "*The Bulletin of the History of Medicine* 75:3 (2001), pp. 375–405. Daniel Boyarin discusses the attack on "carnal Israel" by the Church Fathers in *Carnal Israel: Reading Sex in Talmudic Culture* (Berkeley: University of California Press, 1993), pp. 31–60. Opposition to circumcision continued into

secular society. Robin Judd details opposition in pre-Nazi Germany and before in *Contested Rituals: Circumcision, Kosher Butchering, and Jewish Political Life in Germany, 1843–1933* (Ithaca: Cornell University Press, 2007), pp. 86-121, 244. Jehoshua A. Gilboa reviews the unofficial campaign conducted by the USSR in *A Language Silenced: The Suppression of Hebrew Literature and Culture in the Soviet Union* (London: Associated University Press, 1982), pp. 34–35. Dan Bollinger presents an extensive listing of contemporary anti-circumcision efforts in "Circumcision (And Its Opposition) As Causes", *The New Encyclopedia Of Unbelief*, ed. Tom Flynn (New York: Prometheus, 2007) pp. 193–195.

[16] "On the eighth day the flesh of his foreskin shall be circumcised" (Leviticus 12:3), M. Shabbat 19:2 and B. Shabbat 132b take this to be an obligation which overrides Sabbath restrictions.

[17] Mekhilta D'rabbi Yishmael: *Shabbata* 1, commenting on Exodus 31:14.

[18] Mekhilta D'rabbi Yishmael: *Shabbata* 1, commenting on Exodus 31:17.

[19] R.J. Bauckham, "Sabbath and Sunday in the Post-Apostolic Church" in Don A. Carson, *From Sabbath to Lord's Day* (Grand Rapids, MI: Zondervan, 1982), pp. 252–98. And cf. also Hugh Michael," The Jewish Sabbath in the Latin Classical Writers," *The American Journal of Semitic Languages and Literatures*, 40:2 (1924), pp. 117–124.

[20] Michael Wyschogrod, "On the Christian Critique of the Jewish Sabbath" in *Sabbath: Idea, History*, ed. Gerald Blidstein (Beersheva: Ben-Gurion University Press, 2004), pp. 48–49.

[21] Regarding the question of whether it is licit to ask a non-Jews to perform forbidden labors for a Jewish person on Shabbat, see Yehoshua Neuwirth, *Sh'mirat Shabbat* (New York: Feldheim, 1989), section 30:1–7; and cf. also Jacob Katz, *The "Shabbes Goy": A Study in Halakhic Flexibility*, trans. Yoel Lerner (Philadelphia: Jewish Publication Society, 1989).

[22] Devarim Rabbah 1:21

[23] This remains a valid halakhic ruling, leading to discussions by contemporary Orthodox rabbis regarding the correct way for prospective convert to Judaism to be instructed to keep the Sabbath in advance of his or her conversion. See David Bleich, "Observance of Shabbat by a Prospective Proselyte and by a Ger She-mal V'lo Taval," in *Contemporary Halakhic Problems, Volume 4* (New York: KTAV, 1995), pp. 145–170. Elchanan Adler, explores some of the nuanced differences between talmudic, midrashic and Maimonidean perspectives in his "The Sabbath Observing Gentile: Halakhic, Hashkafic and Liturgical Perspectives." *Tradition: A Journal of Orthodox Jewish Thought* 36:3 (2002), pp. 14–45.

[24] Deuteronomy Rabbah 1:21.

[25] Ibid., referencing Jeremiah 1:17 as a prooftext and as a kind of wordplay on Deuteronomy 2:31, the verse that starts this homily.

[26] See Pesikta Rabbati 5:1, ed. M. Ish-Shalom 14b (also Midrash Tanḥuma:

Ki Tissa 34:2): "The blessed Holy One knew that the Nations would translate the Written Torah and read it in Greek. And they would say: 'The Jews are not Israel!' Said the blessed Holy One to Moses: 'Moses! The Nations will say, We are Israel… the children of the One who is always Present!' And Israel will say, 'We are the children of the One who is always Present! And the scales are in balance!' Said the blessed Holy One to the Nations: 'You claim to be my children, but I recognize only the one who holds my mystery in his hands! Only that one is my son!' They said to God: 'What is this mystery?' [God] said: 'It is the Mishnah!'" Martin Jaffee, in his "Oral Transmission of Knowledge as Rabbinic Sacrament: An Overlooked Aspect of Discipleship in Oral Torah," in *Study and Knowledge in Jewish Thought*, ed. H. Kreisel (Beersheva: Ben Gurion University Press, 2006), pp. 65–79, sees the Aramaic term *mystyryn* as an indication that the Oral Torah had a sacramental quality (comparable to the Christian eucharist) which was to be carefully guarded and preserved by the Jewish community.

27 B. Beitzah 16a.

28 Ibid.

29 Elliot K. Ginsburg, *The Sabbath in the Classical Kabbalah* (Albany: State University of New York Press, 1989), p. 66.

30 Ibn Ezra (short commentary) on Exodus 31:13

31 Ibid.

32 Mekhilta D'rabbi Yishma'el: *Shabbata* 1 based on Exodus 31:14. In *The Book of Beliefs and Opinions* 3:2, Saadia offers functional and anthropological reasons for cessation from activity on Shabbat: physical rest, time to study, opportunity for prayer, social relationships, and public announcements of religious matters. See Nehama Leibowitz, *Studies in Shemot* 2, trans. Aryeh Newman (Jerusalem: World Zionist Organization, 1976), p. 544.

33 See Yaakov Jaffe, "No Rest for the Weary? Ambiguity in Yehudah Halevi's 'Yom Shabbaton', *Lehrhaus* April 30, 2018, available online at https://www. thelehrhaus.com/scholarship/no-rest-for-the-weary-ambiguity-in-yehudah-halevis-yom-shabbaton/ and cf. also Rahel Eretz, "Yom Shabbaton," *Mi-ma·amakim* 12 (November 2007), available online at http://www.daat.ac.il/daat/ktav_et/maamar.asp?ktavet=1&id=411.

34 *Kuzari* 3:5, in *The Kuzari: An Argument for the Faith of Israel*, trans. Hartwig Hirschfeld (New York, E. P. Dutton, 1905), republished with introduction by H. Slonimsky (New York: Schocken, 1964) p.140.

35 Ibid, 2:50, p. 114. The words that appear in quotes are from the Torah.

36 Ibid., 3:10, p. 142.

37 MT Hilkhot Shabbat 30:1.

38 MT Hilkhot Shabbat 30:15. Maimonides intense opposition to false worship is well known. See Moshe Halbertal, *Maimonides: Life and Thought* (Princeton:

Princeton University Press, 2015).

[39] Y. Nedarim 3:14, 38a, citing Ezekiel 20:12–22 and Nehemiah 9:13–14. "You made known to them your holy Sabbath and gave them *mitzvot*, decrees and laws through your servant Moses."

[40] *Guide for the Perplexed* II 31, trans. M. Friedlander (London: Routledge & Kegan Paul, 1904), p. 219.

[41] Ibid., III 43, p. 352.

[42] David Novak, in "The Mind of Maimonides," *First Things* 90 (1999), pp. 27–33, sees Maimonides as moving from the rabbinic exclusivity of Shabbat to a more universal message: "…although the strict observance of the Sabbath is considered by the Talmud to be for Jews alone, Maimonides saw great human value in the way the Sabbath teaches human beings to appreciate divine creation of the universe and the way it creates true rest for human beings, enabling them to interact regularly with each other in a way based more on spiritual equality and less on physical inequality." Another rabbinic commentator and philosopher, Levi ben Gerson (called Gersonides, 1288–1344), articulates a similar universal understanding of Shabbat as a reminder of creation, along with it serving as a sign of distinctive holiness and a recollection of slavery and liberation. See his commentary to the Torah on Exodus 31:13 and 31:1, available on-line at on the www.sefaria.org website.

[43] Rashi on Exodus 31.13, s.v. *v'atah dabbeir el b'nei yisrael.*

[44] Rashbam on Exodus 31:13 is available on line: https://www.sefaria.org/Exodus.31.13?lang=en&aliyot=0&p2=Rashbam_on_Exodus.31.13.2&lang2=en.

[45] A.T. Hilkhot Shabbat 292.

[46] In the twentieth century, Franz Rosenzweig would also draw attention to the relationship of Shabbat to this liturgical triad. See his *The Star of Redemption*, trans. Barbara E. Galli (Madison: University of Wisconsin Press, 2005), pp. 330–332.

[47] Isaiah Tishby, *Wisdom of Zohar*, trans. David Goldstein (Liverpool: Littman Library Of Jewish Civilization, 1989), vol. 3, p. 1220.

[48] Although traditionally identified as Midrash of Rabbi Nehunya Hakaneh and ascribed to this first-century scholar, it was written and circulated in medieval Provence. See Aryeh Kaplan, *The Bahir* (York Beach, Maine: Samuel Weiser, 1979), p. xi.

[49] One of the most influential sources of Jewish mystical speculation about creation, *Sefer Yezirah* (Book of Formation) was probably composed during the Mishnah period.

[50] See Arthur Green, *A Guide to the Zohar* (Berkeley: Stanford University Press, 2003), pp. xxxviii-li, and Aryeh Kaplan, ibid., pp. xxi and 176–178.

[51] Elliot K. Ginsburg, *The Sabbath in the Classical Kabbalah* (SUNY Press, Albany, NY, 1989), p. 70.

[52] Bereshit Rabbah 11:8,

[53] *The Bahir*, ed. Kaplan, §180.

[54] In his commentary on the Torah, Ramban is one of the first to quote the *Bahir* under the title *Midrash R. Nehunya ben Ha-kanah*. His imprimatur was significant for the legitimization of Kabbalah in Spain and elsewhere and for its diffusion beyond a small circle of adepts. See Elliot R. Wolfson, "By Way of Truth: Aspects of Nahmanides' Kabbalistic Hermeneutic," *AJS Review* 14:2 (Autumn, 1989), pp. 103–178. Also see Martin I. Lockshin, "Bible Studies," in *The Cambridge History of Judaism, Volume Six: The Middle Ages, The Christian World*, ed. Robert Chazan (Cambridge: Cambridge University Press, 2018), pp. 555–581.

[55] Moshe Halbertal, *By Way of Truth: Ramban and the Formation of Tradition*. (Jerusalem: Keter 2006), p. 11

[56] Ramban to Exodus 20:8.

[57] Ibid., citing Mekhilta D'rabbi Shimon Bar Yohai on Exodus 20:8.

[58] Ibid.

[59] Ibid. to Exodus 30:13. The Hebrew word for foundation, *y'sod*, is identical to the name of the *s'firah* Yesod.

[60] Ibid.

[61] See Harry A. Wolfson, "The Meaning of *ex nihilo* in the Church Fathers, Arabic and Hebrew Philosophy, and St. Thomas" in *Mediaeval Studies in Honor of Jeremiah Denis Matthias Ford*, eds. Urban T. Holmes, Jr. and Alex J. Denomy (Cambridge: Harvard University Press, 1948), pp. 355–370.

[62] Rabbenu Bahya to Exodus 20:8.

[63] Ibid.

[64] Abraham Joshua Heschel may have based the concept of Shabbat as a "palace in time" on this kabbalistic concept. See his *The Sabbath: Its Meaning for Modern Man* (NY: Farrar Straus Giroux, 1951), p. 15. See also Arthur Green, "Sabbath as Temple: Some Thoughts on Space and Time in Judaism," in *Go and Study; Essays and Studies in Honor of Alfred Jospe*, eds. Raphael Jospe and Samuel Z. Fishman (Washington, DC: B'nai B'rith Hillel Foundations, 1980), pp. 287–305, who contends that by equating Shabbat and Sanctuary, kabbalists compensated for the sanctity of the lost Temple through the speech-act rituals of Shabbat.

[65] Rabbenu Bahya to Exodus 31:13.

[66] Ibid., linking Isaiah 58:13 to Exodus 31:17.

[67] For more on Arama, see my doctoral dissertation, *Hazut Qashah: Faith, Felicity and Fidelity in the Thought of Yitzhaq Arama*, submitted at the Jewish Theological Seminary in New York City in 2004.

[68] *Akeidat Yitzhak* 4:1 (ed. Lvov, 1868, pp. 109-110), and 55:13 (ed. Lvov, 1868, pp. 609- 610). Cf. Bereshit Rabbah 11:8, where the text reads "Why did God

bless Shabbat? Rabbi Berechia says: 'Because it has no partner...' Rabbi Shimon bar Yoḥai taught: God said: 'The community of Israel will be your partner.' And when they stood before Sinai, God said to the Israelites: '*Remember* what I said to Shabbat, that the community of Israel is your partner: [therefore the text of Scripture says] "*Remember* Shabbat and keep it holy"' (Exodus 20:8)."

[69] Ibid. 55:13, p. 615.

[70] See Marc Saperstein, *Jewish Preaching, 1200–1800: An Anthology* (New Haven: Yale University Press, 1989), pp. 263–266 and 392–393.

[71] Elliot K. Ginsburg, *Sabbath in Classical Kabbalah*, pp. 68–69 and 78–136.

[72] For a scholarly analysis, see Reuven Kimelman, *The Mystical Meaning of Lekha Dodi and Kabbalat Shabbat* (Jerusalem: Magnes Press, 2003). A breadth of information is synthesized by Noam Zion in his "L'cha Dodi and the Kabbalist Background to Kabbalat Shabbat," available on the website of the Shalom Hartman Institute in Jerusalem.

[73] Boaz Huss, "Admiration and Disgust: The Ambivalent Re-Canonization of the Zohar in the Modern Period," *Study and Knowledge in Jewish Thought*, ed. Howard Kreisel (Beersheva: Ben-Gurion University of the Negev Press, 2006), p. 204.

[74] Jonathan M. Elukin, "A New Essenism: Heinrich Graetz and Mysticism," *Journal of the History of Ideas* 59:1 (1998), p. 135.

[75] Roy Branson, "The Sabbath in Modern Jewish Theology," in *The Sabbath in Scripture and History*, ed. Kenneth Strand (Washington: Herald Publishing Association, 1982), pp. 266–277.

[76] Samson Raphael Hirsch, *The Pentateuch* (New York: Judaica Press, 1973), vol. 2, p. 661, commenting on Exodus 35:2.

[77] Joseph B. Soloveitchik, *Halakhic Man* (Philadelphia: Jewish Publication Society, 1983), p. 46. However, in his "A Tribute to the Rebbetzin of Talne," (published in *Tradition* 17: 2 [Spring 1978]), pp. 76–78, he also wrote that "Judaism expresses itself not only in formal compliance with the law but also in private, poignant, living experience."

[78] Branson, "The Sabbath in Modern Jewish Theology," pp 268–269, citing Emanuel Rackman, "Sabbath and Festivals in the Modern Age" in *Studies in Torah Judaism*, ed. Leon D Stiskin (New York: Yeshiva University, 1969), p. 55; Norman Lamm, *Faith and Doubt: Studies in Traditional Jewish Thought* (New York: KTAV, 1971), p. 204.

[79] Branson, "The Sabbath," p. 269, citing *Reason and Hope: Selections From the Jewish Writings of Hermann Cohen*, trans. Eva Jospe (New York, Norton, 1971), pp. 117 and 157.

[80] Ibid., p. 270, citing Leo Baeck, *This People Israel: The Meaning of Jewish Existence* (Philadelphia: Jewish Publication Society, 1964), p. 137; and cf. also his "Mystery and Commandment," in *Contemporary Jewish Thought*, ed. Simon

Noveck (Washington: Bnai Brith, 1985), p. 202.

[81] Ibid., 270, citing Martin Buber, *Moses: The Revelation and the Covenant* (Oxford: East West Library, 1947), pp. 85–86.

[82] Ibid., p. 271, citing Franz Rosenzweig, *Star of Redemption*, trans. William Hallo (Notre Dame: University of Notre Dame Press, 1985), pp. 310–312. See also Steven Kepnes, *Jewish Liturgical Reasoning* (Oxford: Oxford University Press, 2007), p. 106, who notes that for Rosenzweig, "the spiritual year finds its foundation, regulation and sense of wholeness" from the Sabbath which moves Jews away from history to preserve the eternality of the Jewish people.

[83] Abraham Joshua Heschel, *The Sabbath: Its Meaning for Modern Man* (New York: Farrar Straus and Giroux, 1951), pp. 8 and 48.

[84] Ibid., pp. 8, 21, 29 and 99.

[85] Branson, "The Sabbath," p. 276.

[85A] David Hartman, *From Defender to Critic: The Search for a New Jewish Self* (Woodstock, VT: Jewish Lights Publishing, 2012), p. 261, where the author also argues that "it is through the intimate covenantal relationship that we are able to access the universal aspects of our consciousness."

[86] Jonathan Sacks, *The Dignity of Difference* (New York: Continuum, 2003), p. 167.

[87] Yosef Yitzhak Lifshitz, "The Secret of the Sabbath," *Azure* 10 (Winter 5761/2001), pp. 35-66, available online at the Azure website at http://azure.org.il.

[88] Irving Greenberg, *The Jewish Way: Living the Holidays* (New York: Touchstone, 1993), p. 127.

[89] Francine Klagsbrun, *The Fourth Commandment*, p. xiv. Also see Tilden Edwards, *Sabbath Time: Understanding and Practice for Contemporary Christians* (Nashville, TN: Upper Room, 1992), where the author calls for a recovery of a "rhythm of Sabbath awareness" to "both balance and ground our working time…. as a major contribution of the church to the whole society, one that offers an alternative to the growing societal rhythm between driven achievement and narrow escape."

[90] Judith Shulevitz, *The Sabbath World: Glimpses of a Different Order of Time*, (New York: Random House, 2010), p. xviii.

[91] Rani Jaeger "Give Me Your Tired: On the Toil and Hope of Shabbat," in conjunction with the exhibition "Sabbath: The 2017 Dorothy Saxe Invitational," https://www.thecjm.org/learn_resources/346.

[92] The full text is available at http://www.sabbathmanifesto.org/.

[93] Rav Shagar (Shimon Gershon Rosenberg), *Faith Shattered and Restored: Judaism in the Postmodern Age*, ed. Zohar Maor (Jerusalem: Maggid Books, 2017), p. 72. For more on Rav Shagar, see the material gathered at http://shagar.co.il.

94 Steven Kepnes, *The Future of Jewish Theology* (West Sussex: John Wiley & Sons, 2013), pp. 71–72. For Society for Scriptural Reasoning, see http://jsr. shanti.virginia.edu/statement-of-purpose/.

95 Ibid.

96 Sanford Drob, "Judaism As a Form Of Life," *Tradition* (23/4, 1988), pp. 78–89, explores Ludwig Wittgenstein's use of language "games" or "activities" as a means of understanding Judaism. The notion of Shabbat as having multiple, yet related, meanings subject to context may be similar to the idea of "value concepts" that Max Kadushin developed to give some coherence to the diversity of rabbinic thought. See his *The Rabbinic Mind* (New York: Bloch, 1972). Future exploration of the relationship between Kadushin on value concepts and Wittgenstein about language games might be fruitful.

"The Israelite People Shall Keep the Sabbath": The Homiletical Rationale for Shabbat Observance, from Second Temple Times to the Talmudic Era

Admiel Kosman

Translated from the Hebrew by Martin S. Cohen

Introduction

The concept of weekly rest from the toil and travail of the workplace is not found solely in the Bible but also in the works of several other ancient cultures. And it is just as much a feature of the modern world, where every country that maintains even minimal societal standards sees employers as obligated to give workers weekly days of rest.[1] It is thus reasonable to ask: How does the concept of Sabbath rest ordained by the Torah differ (if it does) from the concept as it has evolved elsewhere? When the Torah decrees that the Israelites must "keep" the Sabbath, using the famous *v'shamru* terminology that inspired the title of the present volume, what exactly does the text mean to say?

In responding to this question, I will first consider the specific rationales offered in the Bible for the concept of Shabbat.[2] Three in particular are important in this regard:[3] the societal/humanitarian rationale, which proposes a weekly day for rest for master, slave, and beasts of burden; the theological rationale, which proposes a weekly day away from secular pursuits to create an opportunity for the pursuit of spiritual ones; and the historical/national rationale, which sees the Sabbath as an ongoing weekly memorial to the exodus from Egypt.[4] I will consider each of these theoretical reasons, attempting to address the ultimate meaning of each in the context of real life. I will, however, spend much more time on the first two rationales than on the third, since those two (apparently far more than the third[5]) have far-reaching implications for real-life Sabbath observance. The third rationale, the historical/national one, can be seen as a secondary reason, easily joined to the other two.[6]

The Societal/Humanitarian Rationale

This approach explains the whole concept of Shabbat rest as essentially related to the need for physical respite from the labors that occupy us during the rest of the week. Consider, for example, the following formulation of the Sabbath commandment: "Six days you shall do your work, but on the seventh day you shall cease from labor, in order that your ox and your ass may rest, and that your bondman and the stranger may be refreshed" (Exodus 23:12). In this verse, the concept of Sabbath holiness is not mentioned, only the need for weekly rest—and it is possibly for that reason that the familiar reference to "Sabbath of the Eternal your God" is also absent here.[7]

There is no hint here that there is anything inherently base or wrong with the concept of labor on the Sabbath, only that there exists a human need to occasionally desist both from physically strenuous labor as well as from all sorts of business-related undertakings. Practically speaking, then, the prohibition of work on Shabbat may be interpreted as an effort to regulate the economic pressure that the workplace creates by its very existence.[8] We can separate this societal/humanitarian rationale into two complementary aspects, as follows.

The first is rooted in a concern for the wellbeing of the worker (represented in the verse cited above by the slave, the stranger, and the beast of burden), and a strong interest in laborers not being exploited by their employers. This interest leads directly to such workers being granted at least one day per week for restorative rest. Indeed, this is the specific concern of passages like the Ten Commandments as it appears in the Book of Deuteronomy:

> For six days shall you work and attend to all your labors, but the seventh day shall be a Sabbath unto the Eternal your God on which you shall do no work—you and your son and your daughter, your male and female slaves, your ox and your ass and all your livestock, and the stranger in your gates—in order to allow your male and female slaves to rest just as you do. Thus you shall recall that you yourself were a slave in the land of Egypt, and that the Eternal your God brought you out from there with a mighty hand and an outstretched arm—and for that reason the Eternal your God has commanded you to observe the Sabbath day. (Deuteronomy 5:12–14)

The second aspect is not as explicit in these verses, but will be noticed upon a more intensive reading. Note that the rationale for Sabbath observance here is directed not solely at employees but also at employers, who are also instructed to observe a weekly Shabbat, so their every effort will not be directed to pursuing commercial success. Indeed, it seems that the whole point of invoking the exodus from Egypt in this context is to remind employers that they themselves must not become enslaved to the pursuit of wealth and ever-increasing profit.[9] Employers too are thus depicted as needing weekly liberation from this kind of inner slavery.[10] And the gift of a weekly Sabbath is thus extended not solely to workers and slaves, but also to those workers' employers and those slaves' masters.[11]

The Theological Rationale

In the version of the Ten Commandments found in the Book of Exodus, the rationalization of a weekly Sabbath day is rooted in the concept of the Creator resting from the work of creation on the seventh day: "For in six days did the Eternal make the heavens and the earth, and the sea and all it contains, and rested on the seventh day—for which reason the Eternal blessed the Sabbath day and sanctified it" (Exodus 20:10). According to this text, those who keep the Sabbath are engaging in an act of *imitatio Dei*; the Sabbath serves as a sign of their dedication to God, and they are therefore sanctified by the very fact of keeping the Shabbat of God.[12] The same idea can be found in the creation story itself: "Thus were completed the heavens and the earth, and their hosts. God completed on the seventh day the work He had [earlier] undertaken and rested on the seventh day from all the labors [earlier] taken on. God blessed the seventh day and made it holy [*va-y'kaddeish oto*], for on it He rested from all the work of creation that God had [earlier on] done" (Genesis 2:1–3).[13]

This approach (which I am calling the "theological" rationalization[14]) sees the act of resting on the Sabbath as intended to turn an individual's attention from the secular pursuits that characterize weekday activity to the pursuit of holiness (*k'dushah*), the quality that Scripture defines as a state of separateness from the secular world and devotion to the Divine.[15] As we shall see presently, however, many of those who rationalize their Shabbat observance by emphasizing this line of thinking also tend to assimilate the societal/humanistic rationale into it—sometimes to the extent that the latter rationale simply disappears entirely from the halakhic consciousness of specific groups. This way of thinking will be explained below in length; at this point, let me just say that one can imagine an argument that if God ordained a total cessation from all labor on the Sabbath for whatever reason, it would surely also imply that slaves and beasts of burden likewise are to be granted their weekly rest—which blurs the distinction between the two schools of rationalization.[16]

It should also be noted that the theological rationalization (as presented, e.g., at Exodus 31:14–15) is not necessarily tied to the theological/cosmological argument in the Genesis 2 passage. One could say, in fact, that Shabbat is a day of self-sanctification before God, a kind of personal "day of the Eternal"—and that this need not be tied specifically to the mythological motif of God "resting" from the labors of creation on the seventh day, as found in some scriptural texts. I shall return to this topic later on in this essay.

The Relationship Between the Societal/Humanitarian and the Theological Rationales for Shabbat Observance

Among critical biblical scholars, it is widely accepted that the theological rationalization for Shabbat observance was eventually attached to older scriptural texts that offered the societal/humanistic rationalization. This argument, first put forward by Julius Wellhausen in the nineteenth century, posits that the earliest biblical texts about the Sabbath (such as Exodus 23:12, cited above) describe it as a day of simple rest, obligating both native and foreign workers, and even beasts of burden, to rest on it.[17] According to Wellhausen, it was only later—when the so-called priestly documents were being composed (around the sixth and fifth centuries BCE)—that the societal/humanistic concept of Sabbath rest was transformed into what I have called the theological rationalization, seeing the goal of the Sabbath's total cessation of labor as the sanctification of the individual before God. In fact, Wellhausen saw the description of the Sabbath in these later documents as "a statute that presents itself with all the rigour of a law of nature, having its reason with itself, and being observed even by the Creator."[18] According to Wellhausen, it is to this new stage in the conceptualization of Shabbat as a day sacred unto God that we can date the verses that explain why no manna fell on Shabbat (namely, because it would have been forbidden to collect it; Exodus 16:25–27); the story of the stick collector who was executed for profaning the Sabbath (Numbers 15:32–36); and the laws explicitly prohibiting the kindling of flames on Shabbat (Exodus 35:3). Only in this late stage of literary development, in the so-called P document, do we find for the first time explicit language forcefully condemning anyone who would profane the Sabbath, together with terrible punishments decreed against such people (e.g., Exodus 31:14–15 and 35:2, and Numbers 15:32–36).[19]

These theories of Wellhausen regarding the development of the Sabbath laws remain widely accepted today—although with more recent refinements that have identified an additional source, unknown in Wellhausen's time, now known in scholarly circles as H, the "Holiness Source."[20] At first, many scholars believed that the "school" that produced this document was merely a part of the priestly school that produced the P document, and that H was possibly the older of the two sources. Today, however a different theory holds sway.[21] The biblical scholar Simeon Chavel, for example, has recently summarized things nicely, noting that in the texts of the Holiness School collected at Leviticus 17–26 we find

a series of additions that are clearly different from earlier texts in terms of their literary goals, their style, and their terminology. This section of Scripture, because of its palpable closeness to the Book of the Covenant attributed to the E source,[22] has for many years been considered an early priestly work, the so-called "Book of Holiness," and as such has been considered to constitute part of the larger priestly corpus.

However, many of its characteristics also appear elsewhere in Scripture…in many places in the Book of Numbers, for example, and, as a result, many today believe that the reverse process is closer to the truth and that the texts attributed to the Holiness School constitute the later literary layer. That being the case, it follows that either its authors were the individuals who created the P document, and included in it the very old priestly material found in Leviticus [and on that old level they have added their own later level, i.e., H] (according to Israel Knohl), or the P document was already a completed literary work at the time that H, constituted of new material oriented in a new direction, was added to it (according to Baruch Schwartz). At any rate, both theories concede that early priestly literature was primarily focused on the Tabernacle and everything connected to it [i.e., the temple and the priestly word], whereas the secondary material was focused instead on the people in the camp [i.e., out of the temple and the priestly world].[23]

As this discussion demonstrates, there was a wide gap separating the literary orientations of the Holiness School and the Priestly School.[24] We can see—and this is the most important point for this essay—that the literary layer responsible for creating the theological rationalization of Shabbat is undeniably the layer that was only eventually added to the work of the Priestly School. Thus Israel Knohl writes as follows:

> In ritual context, the Sabbath is represented only by an additional sacrifice. There is no hint in the PT (=Priestly Torah) laws of the prohibition of labor on the Sabbath.[25]

This should be understood in specific opposition to the work of the Holiness School; Knohl writes that "with the Festival law in HS (=Holiness School), the picture changes completely.…Here the

Sabbath, the foundation of the extra-Temple holiness, is put on a parallel with the Temple. The prohibition of labor is discussed at length and serious punishments are specified for transgressors."[26]

Now a new question arises: What could possibly have inspired the authors of the Holiness School to forbid work on Shabbat, and thus to transform the Sabbath from a day relaxation and rest into a day of strict prohibitions relating to specific kinds of activity? Knohl answers as follows:

> That PS (=the Priestly School) refrains from any prohibitions of labor and withholds from the Sabbath the title of *mikra kodesh* is worthy of attention. Leaving full treatment of this question for another time: I would say briefly that PT's (=Priestly Torah's) attitude resulted from the conflict between two sacral spheres: Temple and Sabbath. Despite the similarities between these two institutions…at certain points they unavoidably clash. On the one side is the Sabbath, an all-Israelite sacred entity, grounded on the cessation of all labor on the seventh day. On the other side is the Temple, the exclusive sacral precinct of the priests, to which entry by ordinary Israelites is forbidden. Its central feature is the daily sacrificial service, which it is inconceivable to interrupt even for a single day. PT (=Priestly Torah), which attempts to strengthen the sanctuary of the priesthood, here prefers the Temple and the Temple service over the Sabbath, while HS (=Holiness School), which sees the attainment of a holy life as the goal of the entire people, views the Sabbath as an expression of the sanctity of all Israel, and therefore places the command to observe the Sabbath before that of respect for the Sanctuary (Exodus 31:13; Leviticus 19:30, 26:2).[27]

Assuming that the Holiness School was active in a period after the Priestly School, we may next attempt to identify the specific period of time in which the former flourished. There is general disagreement about this point, however. For example, Knohl and Milgrom believe that it was active at the end of the eighth century BCE in the days of Kings Aḥaz and Hezekiah.[28] Other scholars, however, assign the Holiness School to a later date, sometimes around the return from the Babylonian Exile and the beginning of the Second Temple period.[29]

Nonetheless, one point is quite certain: the late date of the theological/cosmological rationalization for Shabbat observance. Strong support for this view can be found Yair Hoffman's research on the opening chapters of Scripture, where we find the first creation story. Hoffman convincingly demonstrates "that the minuscule number of biblical texts that reference the first creation story teaches us clearly that that story was not deemed authoritative by the majority of biblical authors."[30] Hoffman demonstrates that "the position of great prominence eventually awarded this story in the post-biblical period does not correspond to its place in the internal structure of biblical texts."[31] He concludes:

> The [first] creation story was not known to the majority of biblical authors because it is a late text. And how late exactly is it? It is hard to imagine that the author of the Ten Commandments text in Deuteronomy would not have cited it had it been known, just as it is hard to imagine that Second Isaiah would have failed to cite it had he known it. And the same could be said about the so-called "Sabbath prophecy" preserved in Jeremiah 17:19–27 or about the authors of other texts regarding the Sabbath who fail to make any mention of the creation story....It seems to me that all the evidence suggests the conclusion that the [first creation] story was written in the time of Ezra as a kind of etiology intended to justify the Sabbath laws. Dating the story to such a late date nicely explains the absence of references to the creation story in biblical literature before the time of Ezra, plus the

etiological argument corresponds nicely to the work of Ezra and Nehemiah, both of whom stressed the cosmic importance of the Sabbath.[32]

Based on Hoffman's work, it seems reasonable to conclude that even toward the end of the biblical period—when the authors of the Holiness School understood the Sabbath to require a complete cessation from all labor, and so added to its biblical description specific prohibitions and a set of dire consequences for their contravention—the theological/cosmological rationalization for Shabbat observance was still not in place. That line of rationalization, so Hoffman, was added in the very latest period of biblical creativity.[33]

Scriptural Exegesis at the End of the Second Temple Period

Consideration of a wide range of texts dating to the end of the Second Temple period suggests that although the Bible, once canonized, was surely taken as a unique and interiorly consistent work, it is nonetheless likely that the gap between these two approaches to Shabbat troubled at least some in the Jewish community in those days.[34] Indeed, it would be hard to imagine that the existence of two such varying approaches to Shabbat within the same literary work—the humanitarian, on the one hand, and the theological, on the other—would somehow have escaped their notice.[35] Moreover, it seems to me that this tension was solved in antiquity in different ways. I believe the various proposed solutions fall into three distinct categories: one particularly stringent, one particularly liberal, and one that sought to find a path between those extremes. And it seems reasonable to suppose that there also existed other approaches that were some sort of variations on these main three ways. Allow me to explain.

Perusing the earliest exegetical texts about Shabbat that have survived from this period allows us to identify, at least in general terms, a distinct tension between the two efforts at rationalizing Shabbat observance presented above. Yitzḥak Dov Gilat addresses this reality as follows:

> It seems logical…that in earliest times there were extant in Israel two basic approaches to the Sabbath. One saw in the Sabbath a day that was wholly holy to God, a day to be used to repent of one's sins and to pursue the perfection of one's soul; to engage in Torah study and in deep, meditative prayer; to ponder religious questions and to seek to feel God's influence [in one's life]. This approach suggested limiting pleasures, including eating; as well as ascetic practices and even fasting.[36] The second approach understood the uniqueness of the Sabbath as a day to rest in the pleasure it occasioned, in joy and rest…[seeing it as] a day given to Israel "to eat and to drink and to rest and to observe a Sabbath from all work of that day and to bless the LORD your God, who gave to you the day of festival and the holy day" (Jubilees 50:9).[37]

These approaches laid out by Gilat differ from each other substantially and, as I see it, they correspond to the inner-biblical efforts at rationalization described above: the societal/humanistic approach encouraging Shabbat rest, relaxation, and the pursuit of physical pleasure; and the theological one (found in the latest section of Scripture, deriving from the Holiness School) painting a much more dour picture of the Sabbath, depicting it as a day of self-sanctification and ascetic withdrawal from daily life.[38] In the biblical texts about Shabbat rooted in this latter approach, we find depictions of the Sabbath that include some degree of fear and worry about the severity of punishment for even the least infraction of its laws—just as entering an ancient temple would have instilled a spirit of nervous awe and worry in any who would enter the holy precincts.[39] After all, the Holiness School sought to underscore the parallel between the Sabbath and the Temple; consider, for example, the verse that appears twice in Leviticus: "Keep My Sabbaths and hold My sanctuary in awe; I am the Eternal" (Leviticus 19:30 and 26:2).[40] Moreover, it is not surprising that in late Second-Temple period texts, we have at least some depictions of Shabbat in grim, severe terms characterizing it as a day to be given over to ascetic discipline.

There were also efforts to chart a middle course that effectively mitigated the severity of the latter approach with verses that underscored the physical pleasures said to inhere in Shabbat observance in line with the societal/humanistic approach to Sabbath observance, which saw the Sabbath as having more to do with the human observer than with God. Although never stated explicitly in ancient texts, we can find echoes of this idea in passages that speak openly about the "pleasure" (*oneg*) inherent in Shabbat observance— for example, the prophet's declaration that on Shabbat "you shall take pleasure before God" (Isaiah 58:14). The prophet's words do not actually suggest that the sole goal of Shabbat is the physical pleasure that may be derived from its observance,[41] but they do seem in line with a general tendency (evident in Isaiah) to see the Shabbat in light of what we have been calling the societal/humanistic rationale.[42] I suggest, however, that the approach to Shabbat in late Second Temple times that was the most lenient in terms of law itself was a direct outgrowth of the societal/humanitarian approach to Sabbath observance. Indeed, texts that feature this approach to Shabbat can be read as counterweights to those scriptural passages that promote the other view.

Let me elaborate on this idea. The strictest approaches to Shabbat observance known from ancient times were those practiced by *ḥasidim* ("pietists"),[43] by the Qumran sect,[44] and by some other ancient sects as well.[45] For example, Flavius Josephus writes: "They [the Essenes] are…stricter than all Jews in abstaining from work on the seventh day; for not only do they prepare their food on the day before to avoid kindling a fire on that one, but they do not venture to remove any vessel [from their homes] or even to go to stool [i.e., to the toilet]."[46] This approach seems to me aligned with the stringent legal approach that characterized the theological approach to Sabbath observance in biblical times. It merely takes it somewhat further, in order to create an atmosphere on Shabbat that features complete disassociation with secular life and that is more extreme than any other approach.

We can find different approaches to the level of the strictness in keeping Shabbat among those groups who followed the theological reasoning. Some extremists saw Shabbat as a day of extreme ascetic disconnection from the world, for the sake of total engagement with the Divine. We have already mentioned those who observed Shabbat as a day of fasting. Many groups in Second Temple times deemed it wrong to ignore any Sabbath stricture—even for the sake of saving a life,[47] if that effort involved any desecration of Shabbat.[48] In this spirit of sanctification before God, many also assumed that marital relations are forbidden on Shabbat—probably because sexual relations induce a state of impurity[49] potent enough to prevent anyone so contaminated from entering the Temple.[50]

Perhaps we can formulate the concept of the Sabbath on the extreme side of the scale as follows: this view sees the Sabbath as a day on which one is required solely to serve God, as it may be understood from the biblical phrase *shabbat l'YHVH elohekha* ("a Sabbath for the Eternal, your God").[51] The idea is thus to deny the validity of any activity intended solely to benefit or to provide pleasure to the Sabbath observer—and instead to promote rituals designed solely as acts of divine worship, just as things were "before

God" in the Temple.[52]

As noted above, there were also middle-of-the-road approaches to Shabbat, permitting the pursuit of physical pleasure on the Sabbath to some degree. In addition to the severe approach that forbids any effort to seek physical comfort or pleasure on Shabbat, there is also the approach featured in the texts from Qumran. Yosef Elimelekh Baumgarten writes that "Despite the tendency toward stringency with respect to Sabbath prohibitions"[53] in the Qumran texts, there is also an eager willingness to respond to the prophetic injunction to "proclaim the Sabbath [to be] a delight" (Isaiah 58:13). Alongside the lists of things one is forbidden from discussing on Shabbat, permission is specifically granted to discuss details of eating and drinking needs.[54] Even Jubilees (at 50:12–13) describes taking pleasure in Shabbat as a divine commandment, specifically encouraging Sabbath worshipers "to eat and to drink and to be satisfied on this day of festival (=Shabbat)."[55]

In contrast to these strict approaches, we also find a more lenient position which, in my opinion, underlies the pronouncements about the Sabbath attributed in the Gospels to Jesus[56]—although I admit that this is not the usual way of reading those New Testament passages. Support for my approach may be found in the oppositional attitude attributed to the Pharisees in the New Testament[57]—as, for example, in a narrative about plucking ears of wheat from the stalk on Shabbat that appears several times in the Gospels.[58] In this tale, Jesus' disciples were ravenous on Shabbat and plucked some ears of wheat from their stalks[59] in the presence of their master, who was later attacked by outsiders who considered such activity to be forbidden on the Sabbath. In defense of his disciples' actions, Jesus argued that they in fact behaved licitly because such behavior *is* permitted under such circumstances. In that context, Jesus formulated the principle that "the Sabbath was made for man's sake, man was not made for the sake of the Sabbath, so that the son of man is the lord also of the Sabbath" (Mark 2:27–28).[60] This pronouncement will serve as a cornerstone for our discussion (below) of Jesus' halakhic attitude toward the Sabbath.

Already in that remark can we see how Jesus' argument moves the societal/humanistic argument to the center of the discussion. Indeed, this notion that the Sabbath was intended to provide rest for the exhausted body and the weary soul, and not to afflict Sabbath observers with onerous rules, corresponds exactly to the sources we have identified that take the societal/humanitarian approach to Shabbat. In other sources, we find that Jesus himself cured the sick on Shabbat, albeit without preparing drugs as the physicians of his day would have done but instead using the power of speech alone to heal.[61] The narratives in the Gospels suggest that this method of speaking to the ill was often deemed to effect healing (for example, in the case of the man with the withered hand, or to expel the demon that had lodged itself in the sick individual in question and who was causing the latter's misery).[62]

A full review of the many books and essays that consider Jesus' attitude toward the *halakhah* of his day is beyond the scope of this essay, and so I will simply outline the most widely accepted approaches.[63] Nonetheless, I should note at the outset that one specific point has yet to be made with respect to Jesus' attitude specifically to Shabbat—and it is one that can potentially explain the basis of his thinking. The key to understanding Jesus' approach to Sabbath laws rests precisely in the fact that, when asked about the details of Shabbat observance, his answers are always rooted overtly in the scriptural texts that feature the societal/humanistic approach.[64] This approach is almost entirely absent from the halakhic texts of rabbinic literature that discuss the rationale for Shabbat observance[65]—as well as from the even more strict approach to Shabbat evident in the surviving works of the Essenes and their fellow travelers.

The central issue raised by scholars about Jesus' attitude to the Shabbat laws of his day is as follows. According to the Mishnah and the Talmud, the sole justification for anyone ever intentionally to break the laws governing Sabbath rest is when such activity is necessary to safeguard or to save a human life. However, none of the instances in which Jesus argues with the Pharisees about the Sabbath laws has to do with setting aside the law in order to save a life. This has puzzled scholars attempting to find the legal basis in Jesus' reasoning for his apparently lax approach to Sabbath observance. How, they wonder, *did* he justify his approach?

The various solutions suggested to the question fall into distinct categories. Some claim that none of the various incidents mentioned above constitutes a real deviation from standard tannaitic *halakhah*. The best known proponent of this approach was David Flusser (1917–2000), who argued unremittingly that the synoptic Gospels do *not* depict a Jesus opposed to halakhic observance, as is so often depicted.[66] According to Flusser, the sole incident that seems to constitute an exception to this generalization is the one mentioned above, regarding the disciples and the ears of wheat on Shabbat.[67] Even in that case, however, Flusser maintains that the Gospels present a version of a well-known halakhic dispute that fits into the legitimate parameters of rabbinic halakhic discourse in Jesus' day. Flusser believes that the evangelists, who were distant from the world of Jewish observance, misunderstood their own sources: they presumed the issue had to do with plucking ears of wheat from their stalks on Shabbat—which seems to Flusser highly unlikely, since the *halakhah* was entirely clear in Jesus' day that such a thing was completely forbidden. Rather, Flusser maintains that the original version of the incident must have featured the ravenous disciples gathering up ears of wheat that had fallen to the earth, and they then crushed the kernels with their own hands in order to make them edible.[68] Flusser claims that although there were surely those in Jesus' day who considered that kind of kernel-crushing illicit on the Sabbath, Jesus himself was simply following the custom of the Galileans of his day, who were lenient in this particular matter. To prove this point, Flusser cites the example of Rabbi Judah bar Ilai (first half of the second century), who permitted one to crush kernels with one's own fingers on Shabbat.[69] Since Rabbi Judah was a Galilean, Flusser imagines the Galileans in general—including Jesus—following his decision and being lenient in the matter.

A different position that has been suggested is that Jesus simply did not feel at all bound by the *halakhah*. One of the best-known proponents of this view is Harvie Branscomb (1894–1998). In bold contradistinction to many earlier scholars—who claimed that Jesus repudiated the legal force of the oral traditions (the so-called *torah she-be'al peh*, as, e.g., at Mark 7:5 where he appears to repudiate the rabbinic obligation ritually to wash one's hands before a meal[70]) but retained a sense of fidelity to the commandments of the written Torah—Branscomb believed that Jesus essentially saw himself as a prophet, empowered by his office to ignore the laws of the Torah of Moses, however important they might have been,[71] when they did not correspond to an oracle that he personally had received. Moreover, to Branscomb it was also clear that Jesus was not a scholar able to preach along the lines of the Pharisaic scholars of his day. Branscomb argues:

> Jesus was untrained in the schools. He did not have the weapons with which to meet his critics on their own ground and answer with authority. But the law and prophets he did know. In the controversies which arose, therefore, he would turn naturally to this authority to answer tradition with citations of Scripture.[72]

It seems to me, however, that in this matter Branscomb was in error.[73] He is mistakenly learning from the confusion that prevails in some of the Gospel accounts resulting from the unfamiliarity of the evangelists with the style of Jesus' discourse that *was* indeed similar to the rabbinic style. The canonical Gospel texts, written many years after Jesus' death, presented his argumentation in a particularly confused way because their authors were unfamiliar with that style of preaching.[74] Jesus himself did not preach in a way that was particularly different from how *darshanim* in the tannaitic period typically preached. And it seems that many of Jesus' homilies were certainly lost and, moreover, much of the material that did survive is confused (and, in some cases, incoherent).

The careful reconstructive effort undertaken by Menaḥem Kister,[75] a professor of Talmud at the Hebrew University of Jerusalem, represents an entirely different approach from Branscomb's.[76] Kister reconstructs Jesus' sermons so as to present, on the one hand, Jesus as an independent preacher; but, on the other, as someone well trained in the homiletic arts[77] and fully conversant with every detail concerning the Torah.[78] Kister stresses that Jesus rebuked the Pharisees specifically because their sermons were, in his eyes, perverse and imprecise (exactly the rebuke expected from someone adept at preaching with precision!), and because the Pharisees were constantly defending the status of late traditions that were not written in the Torah. Jesus thus rebuked them for preaching in a way that distorted the simple meaning of Scripture for the sake of justifying current practice—which was, in many cases, distant from the specific divine laws contained in Scripture.[79]

I wish now to highlight a fascinating detail, whose importance to this discussion cannot be overstated. None of the ancient *midrashim* preserved in the Mekhilta (the oldest rabbinic work on the Book of Exodus) that seek[80] to permit forbidden labor on Shabbat when human life is in play references any of the verses that are rooted in the societal/humanistic tradition.[81] By comparison, it seems that Jesus *did* choose to emphasize verses from the societal/humanistic tradition in the Torah.[82]

A further example supports my argument. Kister convincingly reconstructs a sermon of Jesus given in a synagogue on Shabbat, which was intended to justify his efforts to enable a hunchbacked woman to stand up straight.[83] And this (theoretical) sermon supports the notion that Jesus' preaching used verses rooted in the societal/humanistic argument to set a context for understanding the correct way to observe Shabbat. In the Gospel of Luke, we read that Jesus saw a woman in synagogue one Shabbat who was severely "bent over, with none to support her or to help her stand up straight" (13:11), and so he placed his hand on her as a curative gesture. As a result, "she stood to her full height and spoke [words of] glory to God" (13:13). The head of the synagogue[84] responded angrily by asking "Is it so that Jesus healed on the Sabbath?" The people responded in the affirmative, whereupon the leader cited Scripture (slightly misquoting Exodus 35:2 or Leviticus 23:3) to bolster his argument: "'For six days shall you do all your work'—on those six day of the week shall you come to be healed, but not on the Sabbath day" (Luke 13:14).

It is reasonable to suppose that, as Kister wrote, in this incident the *archisynagogos* also had in mind the verse (Exodus 23:12) about working for six days and then allowing one's slaves and beasts of burden too to rest. It was to that thought that Jesus responded: "Every single one of you would release his ox or his ass from the pen and lead the animal to drink on the Sabbath, so does it not follow that this daughter of Abraham, who has been bound up by Satan for eighteen years, does it no follow that she too should be set free on the Sabbath day?" (Luke 13:16). Kister takes this confused text and reconstructs the ideas of the original homily as Jesus may have uttered it (understanding that we cannot be sure about the specific words he may have used to express these ideas), as follows:

> "For six days shall you attend to your tasks but on the seventh day shall you rest, so that too may rest your ox and your ass, and be refreshed the son of your maidservant and the stranger in your midst" (Exodus 23:12): If you are prepared, as you surely are, to release your ox and your ass from their pens to grant them some rest, will you do for this daughter of Abraham no less?[85]

This example has special importance for our effort to analyze the different places in Jewish literature occupied by the theological rationale for Shabbat on the one hand, and the societal/humanitarian, on the other. Because we can easily now compare the various *midrashim* to Jesus' homily it is possible to see how Jesus in this homily resurrected *de novo* the societal/humanitarian rationale.[86] In my estimation, the sages took it upon themselves to continue the earlier traditions of the Pharisees.[87] The Mekhilta teaches, with respect to the verse, Exodus 23:12, about allowing beasts of burden to rest on Shabbat, as follows:[88]

> "That Thine Ox and Thine Ass May Have Rest." This passage gives an additional rest to the animal, intimating that it should be allowed to pluck food from the ground and eat it. You say it comes for this. Perhaps however it only means that one should lock it up in the house? You must admit however that this would be no rest but suffering. And when Scripture says: "That thine ox and thine ass may have rest," it must mean to give an additional rest to the animal, that it be allowed to pluck food from the ground and eat.[89]

The issue raised by this verse was a legal one, for the rabbis: the Torah commands us (in several different places) not to perform specific labors on Shabbat, and plucking grass from the ground is one of these; are we to then assume that animal-owners must pen up their animals on Shabbat, so as to prevent them from plucking grass on Shabbat? The answer, as found in the Mekhilta, is: in addition to the theological framework for the Sabbath, Scripture also speaks explicitly of Shabbat as a day of rest and relaxation—and the societal/humanitarian framework includes the rest of animals. Hence, if we forbid animals from grazing the fields, we will be accomplishing precisely the opposite—by denying them the very rest promised them by Scripture![90]

This appears to be precisely the homily preached by Jesus (according to Kister's reconstruction), as he considered his options regarding the hunchbacked woman on Shabbat. He likely argued along the following lines: all who claim that healing is forbidden on Shabbat and that the woman should be left her in her misery are ignoring the Torah's commandment, where the societal/humanitarian framework for Shabbat observance would obligate us to do precisely the opposite. Jesus' *a fortiori* argument would unfold as follows: if it is permitted to allow an animal to graze on a field on Shabbat, because it would otherwise suffer from hunger—even though it will surely pluck grass from the ground and eat it, thus transgressing a Sabbath law—how much the more so a similar kind of transgression must be permitted in order to relieve the suffering of a daughter of Israel, since the societal/humanitarian rationale was formulated to apply to human beings, in the first place!

I could even suggest that the evangelist in Luke 13—who wrote in a later period and was likely not familiar with the Jesus' original sermons—confused the cases, and this sermon of Jesus was originally said about his hungry disciples who were ravenous and plucked ears of wheat on Shabbat. After all, such an act (plucking) is precisely parallel to the situation of the animal on Shabbat, who is set free to graze—even though such activity will inevitably involve plucking grass from the ground.[91]

In any case: if this was indeed the approach to Shabbat-observance put forth by Jesus, we can only conclude that he was interpreting the Torah in a way that had not been accepted by the Pharisees of his day or by their rabbinic successors—and even less so by the extremely strict Essenes.[92] Indeed, this assumed homiletical framework of Jesus manages to negotiate the chasm between the theological and societal/humanitarian arguments more successfully than any other halakhic text known to us from ancient times.

We may even posit that Jesus understood the obligation to desist from labor on Shabbat as akin to the rabbinic understanding of the parallel set of prohibitions of working on the festivals. That is to say: on Shabbat it should be licit to prepare meals that could not be prepared in advance in order to prevent suffering from hunger on the day of rest—just as it is on the festivals.[93] And Jesus might even have argued that *any* act that leads to a diminution of suffering should be permitted on Shabbat, on order to fulfill the societal/humanitarian mandate.[94] It should be also be noted in this regard (as Gilat has shown) that the thirty-nine labors forbidden on Shabbat, detailed in the Mishnah at Shabbat 7:2, is a relatively late tannaitic composition that may have been unknown in Jesus' day. (The list was apparently unknown to both Philo of Alexandria and Josephus.[95] Nor is there any reference to it at Qumran or in the part of the Damascus Covenant dealing with Sabbath laws. Similarly, it was unknown to the Jews of Ethiopia.[96]) In fact, there is no evidence for the existence of the list until its formulation at the end of the mishnaic period, about 150 years after Jesus' day.[97]

I would like to focus now on the statement attributed to Jesus to the effect that "the Sabbath was made [in the first place] for man's sake (that is, to grant a respite from the labors of the six-day week and to lessen misery, as suggested by the societal/humanitarian argumentation), man was not made for the sake of the Sabbath (that is, as suggested by those texts rooted in the theological argument for Shabbat observance), so that the son of man[98] (that is, man, and *not* God, who is according to the theological rationalization of Shabbat the one that requires Sabbath observers to give themselves over entirely to the worship of God—against it, says Jesus, that he, the human being) is the lord also of the Sabbath" (Mark 2:27–28).

A comparison of the way Jesus thought about Shabbat to the way the rabbinic midrash from the Mekhilta cited above thought about Shabbat makes it clear that Jesus was motivated in his interpretation of the biblical verse by an *a fortiori* reasoning that used the societal/humanitarian argument to learn from the case of how animals are to be treated on Shabbat how people too should be treated on Shabbat, and this did not take root in rabbinic thought. The reason for this seems clear enough: the rabbinic midrash did not discuss the societal/humanitarian argument for the scriptural Sabbath law[99] with regard to its practical application to Jews. Indeed, their midrashic reasoning applies differently to Jews and non-Jews with respect to Shabbat observance, as now becomes clear: when the person likely to benefit from forbidden labor is a Jew (in the story in Luke, a "daughter of Abraham"), we find only the theological argumentation; when the possible beneficiary is not a member of the Jewish community— regardless of whether we are speaking about non-Jewish people[100] or about animals—then the societal/humanitarian line of thinking comes into play in determining the *halakhah*. Therefore, there was in their minds no logical reason to apply the law concerning animals grazing in a field to Jewish people.[101]

We may conclude that—in contradistinction to my earlier argument that the third biblical reasoning for Shabbat (the historical/national rationale, which sees the Sabbath as an ongoing weekly memorial to the exodus from Egypt) apparently had no influence at all on the practical side of things[102]—the sages did indeed employ that line of reasoning as a central tenet of their halakhic theorizing. They did, however, make a clear distinction between the concept of a universal Shabbat experience, intended for all humanity (as is found in the creation story), and the concept of an Israel-specific Shabbat, intended to provide national sanctification on a weekly basis and to serve as a testimony to the covenant between Israel and its God (to which non-Jews are not summoned, since the covenant is by definition unique to the relationship between Israel and its God).[103] In light of the latter line of thinking, the authorities of the talmudic era exaggeratedly decreed that a capital offense for any gentile[104] to rest on the Sabbath.[105]

It would be reasonable, then, to ask: What held the sages back from going even further, and folding the societal/humanitarian argument into the *halakhah* as it pertains to Jews—just as Jesus did in his day?[106] A full exploration of this topic is beyond the scope of this essay, but I can note here that the reason they did not do so was apparently rooted in the fact that the sages (and before them, the Pharisees) felt far more restricted than did the various sectarians of their day when it came to altering the traditional understanding of Shabbat that prevailed among the Jews of their day. The sources we have make it clear that healing on Shabbat was widely understood to be forbidden, just as it was widely understood that plucking ears of wheat on Shabbat was forbidden; and the sages simply affirmed these widely-held opinions without altering them at all. Indeed, when they did consider these issues, it was specifically in order to provide scriptural justification for these practices according to their rich talents at drawing hidden meaning from the biblical text.[107]

In extra-rabbinic circles, however, there was more exegetical freedom, which enabled them to search the Torah for its underlying principles—what scholars today would call the meta-*halakhah*[108] (i.e., the "foundational principle," called *k'lal gadol* in Hebrew[109])— and to use them to develop a kind of halakhic hierarchy based on those principles.[110] The meta-halakhic principle that undergirded Jesus' teaching, and according to which he made halakhic decisions, becomes clear from the New Testament sources when read in that way. For Jesus, all Torah legislation was correctly to be subjugated to one single principle rooted in two scriptural texts: Deuteronomy 6:5 ("you shall love the Eternal your God with all your heart, with all your soul, and with all your might") and Leviticus 19:18 ("You shall love your neighbor as yourself").[111]

It is easy to find similar statements in rabbinic literature, which see in these two verses (or in the idea they encapsulate, the love of God and the love of humankind) the foundational principles of the Torah. One well-known example is found in Pirkei Avot 6:1: "All who study Torah for its own sake merit many different rewards... [such a one] is called [a true] friend [of God], [even God's] beloved, [and should be acclaimed as one who truly] loves God and who loves humankind, as one who makes God rejoice and who makes rejoice humankind [as well]."[112] Flusser long ago pointed out the similarity between the sources that cite this text in Jesus' name and those passages in rabbinic literature that also do.[113] But Flusser omitted to mention one specific detail, which is of paramount importance: not one of the rabbinic texts he cites allows this remark to influence halakhic discourse with respect to practical matters of law, while Jesus presents the idea that animates the text from Avot as the practical basis for his halakhic pronouncements![114] It even seems plausible to posit that Jesus' leniency in halakhic matters pertaining to Shabbat may well have been overtly tied to the concept of the love of humankind enjoined by Scripture, thus transforming it from a mere idea into a pivotal meta-halakhic principle that influenced practical decisions about Jewish practice.[115]

At any rate, as far as rabbinic literature is concerned, we can certainly say that the societal/humanitarian argument did not play any meaningful role in the development of the *halakhah* as it concerned the daily behavior of Jews. Indeed, the basic rabbinic text that enumerates the specific labors forbidden on Shabbat (M. Shabbat 7:2) shows no interest at all in the societal/humanitarian argument.[116] The development of the *halakhah* relating to Shabbat in the tannaitic and amoraic periods was focused, albeit only from a certain period, on the precise delineation of the thirty-nine forbidden labors that appear in the *mishnah* mentioned above.[117] The biblical passages that depict the master and all his servants, slaves, and workers resting on a weekly Sabbath seems to have lost any relevance at all (apart from the case of the beast), in the effort to say what exactly constituted an infringement of the biblical injunction not to labor on the Sabbath.

A detailed discussion of this point, citing the talmudic passages that support my argument, is beyond the scope of this essay.[118] However, I will seek to support my contention by citing some medieval authorities who understood the talmudic and halakhic texts as I myself do, and who clearly expressed the view I am putting forth here.[119]

Rabbi Yehudah Halevi (c. 1075–1141), for example, expressed the relationship between the *halakhah* and the societal/humanitarian rationale for Shabbat observance in his *Kuzari*. In the following passage, he undertakes a passionate diatribe against the Karaites, a sect that embraced Scripture but rejected the oral traditions that the rabbis saw as an indispensable dimension of the Written Torah.

Halevi argues that without the traditions passed down from our ancestors, we cannot hope to fathom the meaning of the Written Torah. To prove his point, he raises the issue of how we are to define "work," as it applies to the prohibition of labor on the Sabbath:

> I should, further, like to know where the prohibition of work on the Sabbath commences? Why pens and writing material are not admissible in the correction of a scroll of the Law (on this day), but lifting a heavy book, or a table, or eatables, entertaining guests and all cares of hospitality should be permitted, although the guests would be resting, and the host be kept employed? This applies even more to women and servants, as it is written: "That thy manservant and thy maidservant rest as well as thou" (Deuteronomy 5:14).[120]

Against the Karaite view, Halevi argues that without the traditions of the Oral Torah, there is no way to understand the common practice of requiring servants to work on Shabbat (especially to serve the meals for their masters and their masters' guests), as this goes against the explicit injunction of the Written Torah with its endorsement of the societal/humanitarian argument in requiring Israelites to grant even slaves a weekly day of rest and refreshment! This, Yehudah Halevi argues, proves that it is impossible to rely solely on what is found in the Written Torah; we must accept that the Oral Torah alone can provide us with the correct interpretation of the written law.[121] At any rate, it should be sufficient to say, in this stage of our discussion, that rabbinic *halakhah* turned away (almost) entirely from the societal/humanitarian argument with respect to the Sabbath—without dwelling on this point at any greater length.[122]

As far back as the twelfth century, Ramban (1194–1270, also called Naḥmanides) did attempt to restore *de novo* principles to the *halakhah* that derived directly from the principle that rest and restoration should be key features of Shabbat observance, but his words were taken as a wellspring of extra-halakhic sermonizing that had no bearing on the "actual" *halakhah*, which remained solely rooted in the theological argument.[123] Much later, in the eighteenth century, the Ḥatam Sofer (Rabbi Moses Schreiber, 1762–1839) attempted to revive interest in Ramban's opinion in order to determine the practical *halakhah*, as part of his own relentless struggle against the earliest proponents of what was to become Reform Judaism—but even he did not propose that that the Bible's societal/humanitarian argument be revived as a basis for Shabbat observance. Indeed, the sole use of Ramban's work that the Ḥatam Sofer could bring to actual *halakhah* was in literarily buttressing the threats he was making against those would perform any forbidden labors on Shabbat.[124] He did not attempt to use the straightforward meaning of the scriptural texts featuring the societal/humanitarian argument to encourage a Shabbat observance that would provide a respite from labor and real rest to employer and employee alike.[125]

An aspect of psychological reality must be stressed as well. By increasing the restrictive nature of behavior on Shabbat, and by infusing such activity with a sense of terror, by making those who intentionally transgress even the most picayune prohibitions liable for capital punishment or excision at the hands of heaven (*kareit*)[126]— prohibitions such as selecting nuts that one does not want to eat on Shabbat and putting them to the side of a pile of mixed dried fruits that one wants to eat now, or pouring boiling water directly from a pot onto loose tea at the bottom of a cup[127]—Shabbat observance moves further and further away from the scriptural model of Shabbat as a day of relaxation and restoration[128] suffused with the simple sense of the biblical mandate that we have labelled the societal/humanitarian.[129]

Summary

In this essay, I began by enumerating the three scriptural justifications for Shabbat: the societal/humanitarian rationale, the theological rationale, and the nationalistic rationale. I then tried to bring modern biblical scholarship to bear to explain the historical relationship between the earlier societal/humanitarian rationale and the later theological approach. Finally, in the last part of the essay, I discussed the relationship between Pharisaic sermons regarding the Sabbath and their rabbinic descendants, which I attempted to demonstrate left only scant space available to elaborate or develop the societal/humanitarian approach in their homiletic statements on the matter.

I have tried to show that the only meaningful way that the societal/humanitarian approach survived in rabbinic times was in the permissive ruling that allowed beasts of burden to graze freely on Shabbat. Against that, I presented some material attributed in the Gospel literature to Jesus of Nazareth, taking him seriously as an independent Galilean preacher and Torah expositor, and attempted to show how he restored the societal/humanitarian argument to its once central position in Jewish thought. That, I believe, constitutes the most logical way of explaining the series of halakhic decisions attributed to Jesus that deviated from the standard halakhic approach of his day—fostered by those whose opinions would later be preserved in the pages of the Mishnah and the Talmud.

NOTES

[1] For some examples from the ancient world, see Roland De Vaux, *Ancient Israel: Its Life and Institutions*, trans. John McHugh (London: Darton, Longman & Todd, 1961), pp. 479–480, and cf. the discussion of the parallels to the concept of a weekly Sabbath in the ancient world in Yaakov Hayyim (Jeffrey) Tigay, *Mikra L'yisrael: Peirush Mada·i L'mikra – D'varim* (Jerusalem: Magnes Press, 2016), vol. 1, pp. 254–256.

[2] Yair Hoffman, in his "The First Creation Story (Genesis 1:1–2:3): Canonical and Diachronic Views" (Hebrew), in *Meḥkarim B'shomronit, B'ivrit, U–v'aramit Mugashim L'avraham Tal*, eds. Moshe Bar-Asher and Moshe Florentin (Jerusalem: Mossad Bialik, 5765 [2005], pp. 142–143 (the entire article: pp. 135–157), writes that Shabbat is mentioned forty-five times in the Torah, of which thirty-one appear in just five chapters: Exodus 16 and 31, and Leviticus 23, 25, and 26. In the books of the prophets, Shabbat is mentioned thirty-three times; in the Hagiographa, twenty-two times. And cf. also the material referenced below in note 30.

[3] Regarding these three, cf. my doctoral thesis, *L'toldot Ha-kateigoriyah shel Issurei "Ovadin D'ḥol" B'shabbat V'yom-tov V'yiḥusah La-kateigoriyah shel Issurei Ha-"sh'vut"* (Ramat Gan, Israel: Bar Ilan University, 1993), pp. 11–12, and cf. also Naftali Tocker's essay, "Biblical Texts Regarding Shabbat: Their Linguistic Features, Their Ideas, and Their Mutual Relationships" (Hebrew), *Meḥk'rei Ḥag* 2 (5750 [1999/2000]), pp. 69–85.

[4] Regarding how this line of rationalization was integrated into the two earlier ones presented in the Bible, see my *Ovadin D'ḥol*, p. 12, n. 59.

[5] I stress the word "apparently," and I frame the issue in this way for textual-pedagogic reasons only. We shall see below that the sages of classical times attributed great importance to this line of thinking when they considered the matter practically. See below in the text before note 102.

[6] If we consider this line of thinking alongside the societal/humanitarian one, its basic nature will be understood as I have explained below in the text before note 9. Different explanations are possible. One is that this understanding is brought in the Torah in order to establish God's authority to command the observance of the Sabbath—namely, that Israel are indeed slaves of God and if Israel had not been freed by God then they would still be slaves in Egypt. Or, we might say that this reason was brought in order to strengthen the argument that human are in need of regular rest, a point made clear by the misery of the Israelite slaves, who were not permitted any respite from their labors. Another possibility, however, is that this line of reasoning is an appeal to the masters to free their slaves from their labors on Shabbat, just as God once liberated the Israelites from their labors for their Egyptian masters. In this latter regard, e.g., cf. Tigay,

Encyclopedia Mikra·it, vol. 7, pp. 504–508. If we fold this line of reasoning into the one I have labelled the "theological" approach, then we can say that the Sabbath serves as a sign between God and Israel (as is explicitly set forth in Scripture at Exodus 31:17), and this is why Shabbat observance serves as a sign of Israel's divine sanctification (see Yaakov Shalom Licht, *Mo·adei Yisrael: Z'manim U-mo·adim Bi-t'kufat Ha-mikra U-vi-yemei Bayit Sheini* [Jerusalem: Mossad Bialik, 1988], p. 87).

[7] The Sabbath is referenced as "Sabbath of the Eternal" at Exodus 16:23 and 25; cf. Leviticus 23:3 and Deuteronomy 5:13, as well as in other verses.

[8] This explanation focuses on the communal level but this line of thinking can also be understood to operate on the personal level in line with the prophet's call to make the Sabbath into a day of physical delight: "If you restrain your feet because of Shabbat [and keep] from going about your [weekday] business on My holy day, then you shall have proclaimed the Sabbath [to be] a delight, a dignified [celebration] day for the Holy One of Israel. And you can grant it such dignity by [refraining] from going about your [weekday] ways and by neither seeking [to accomplish] your [normal] tasks nor speaking [profane] words, for then shall you take [true] pleasure before God, and I shall set you up to ride upon the high places of the earth" (Isaiah 58:13–14). The prophet suggests that when people refrain from pursuing the affairs of commerce and other workplace matters that occupy them during the week, the result will be a source not solely of satisfaction to God but of personal physical delight. (Interestingly, Moshe Weinfeld has shown, relying on parallel expressions in Akkadian, that the Hebrew expressions *asot heifetz* ["doing your wishes"] and *asot derekh* ["turn back your foot from"], translated above as "going about your [weekday] business" and "going about your [weekday] ways," are both references to commerce; see his "The Advice of the Elders to Rehoboam" [Hebrew], *Leshoneinu* 36 (5732 [1971/1972]), p. 9, n. 43.) Another possibility, perhaps even more logical, would be to imagine the prophet referencing not the kind of pleasure that moderns derive from a weekday off from work, but rather spiritual pleasure, as suggested in the Hebrew *titannag al YHVH* (translated above as "take pleasure in the Eternal"). (Regarding the theoretical mutual exclusivity of these two possibilities, see the comment of Moshe Alshekh cited below in note 42). In this approach, the prophet may be seen as referencing not the societal/ humanitarian rationale for Shabbat observance (or not solely that rationale), but rather a Shabbat devoted to the kind of spiritual pursuits that can bring those who pursue them closer to God. I shall return to this concept in detail below in my discussion of the second scriptural rationale for Shabbat observance, the one that focuses on Shabbat as a day designed for self-sanctification.

[9] This reasoning then extends beyond the notion of Shabbat as a weekly reminder of the Creator's efforts during the week of creation, or the societal/

humanitarian rationale, and is linked then to the third line of reasoning.

[10] This point is made by John I. Durham in his commentary on Exodus in the *Word Bible Commentary* series (Waco, TX: Word Books, 1987), p. 414: "If even God stopped to catch his breath after six days of customary labor, so also should Israel. And in stopping, as Israel came to know God, Israel would come also to know themselves." Among modern thinkers, this point was stressed especially by Karl Marx, who failed, however, to reference any Jewish sources in its presentation. Marx's point was that enslavement to the need to produce profit can bring an individual to self-alienation: "The externalization of the worker in his product implies not only that his labour becomes an object, an exterior existence, but also that it exists outside him, independent and alien, and becomes a self-sufficient power opposite him, that the life that he has lent to the object affronts him, hostile and alien" (Marx, *Selected Writings*, ed. David McLellan [Oxford: Oxford University Press, 2000], p. 86). This line of thinking was developed as well by Erich Fromm, who emphasized in his own work the spiritual implications of Marx's writings, particularly the importance of seeking liberation from enslavement to the kind of physical needs that can entirely erase the inner self of an individual. In this regard, cf. his *Marx's Concept of Man* (New York: Ungar, 1969) and *To Have or To Be?* (1976; rpt. London: Bloomsbury Academic, 2015). It is interesting to note that Marx can be read as an effort to interpret (presumably unintentionally) the specific feature that makes the Jewish Sabbath unique in this regard. Cf. his argument that the inner selves of people would be altered entirely if they could somehow stop all creative endeavor for the space of several years (see his *Selected Writings*, p. 191), and also Meshullam Groll, *K'tavim (vol. 2): Marx, Nietzsche, Heidegger* (Tel Aviv: Sifriyat Po·alim, 1969), pp. 24–25. One could even argue that this is yet another argument in favor of Shabbat observance; cf. the material presented below in note 125.

[11] Licht (in *Mo·adei Yisrael*, p. 87) sees it differently: he thinks that Scripture assumes that masters and employers can always find time to rest, and so the commandment is directed to them so that they allow their workers and beasts of burden some time to rest as well.

[12] Ibid.

[13] This understanding that the heavens, the earth, and all that is in them were created in six days and that the Creator then stopped creating on the seventh day—and that the holiness of Shabbat inheres in that detail—does not appear in the second creation story (i.e., the one that begins with Genesis 2:4). Cf. in this regard Alexander Rofé's introduction to his *Mavo L'sifrut Ha-mikra* (Jerusalem: Carmel, 2006), p. 37.

[14] Cf. Exodus 20:7–10 and 31:12–17. The theory that the Sabbath is meant as a kind of "tithe" in time and is a holiday for that specific reason accords well with this position. Cf. Licht, *Mo·adei Yisrael*, p. 88; and Kosman, *Ovadin D'ḥol*, p. 11,

n. 55.

[15] There is another meaning to the Hebrew word *k'dushah* as it appears in Scripture, one related to cleanliness and purity; see Yaakov Barukh Schwartz, *Torat Ha-k'dushah: Iyyunim B'hukkah Ha-kohanit She-ba-torah* (Jerusalem: Magnes, 5759 [1999]), pp. 251–255. However, that meaning does not suit this context particularly well. Nevertheless, see note 36 below.

[16] See the explanatory material cited below in this regard in note 100, and see the explicit comments of Rabbi Yehudah Halevi in his *Kuzari* (as discussed below the in the material referenced in note 120) strongly opposing this theory.

[17] Wellhausen actually defined this concept of "rest" as a day of "satisfaction for the labouring classes" and as a day of "refreshment for the people and the cattle, and is accordingly employed for social ends in the same way as the sacrificial meal is" (Julius Wellhausen, *Prolegomena to The History of Israel*, trans. John Sutherland Black and Allan Menzies [Edinburgh: Adam & Charles Black, 1885], p. 114). Bible critics attribute the passage in Exodus 23 to the early Elohistic school, dating to the eighth century BCE; cf. Shuvi Hoffman, *Yihudo shel J Ba-hok U-va-sippur* (Hebrew University of Jerusalem: M.A. Thesis, 2007), p. 82.

[18] Wellhausen, *Prolegomena*, p. 115.

[19] Ibid. To sense the sharp differences between how Shabbat was understood in the early biblical period and in later times, cf. 2 Kings 4:22–23, where we read that after her son felt pain in his head and then died, the Shunamit called to her husband and said, "Send me one of the [servant] lads and one of the she-asses and I will race to the man of God [that is, to Elisha, so that he might revive the boy] and then return." To this, her husband, who has not been told of the tragedy that has struck his family, responds in amazement, "Why would you go to him today? It is neither a New Moon nor a Sabbath! Are you going just to greet him?" From this passage, it seems clear that Israelites of ancient times undertook lengthy journeys in order to spend a Shabbat or a Rosh Hodesh in the company of a "man of God." This passage, however, directly contradicts Moses' admonition to the people in the in Exodus 16:29, concerning the manna: "Behold, the Eternal has granted you a Sabbath and for that reason is also granting you a double share of the 'bread' on Fridays. Stay close to home! None shall go out from his place on the seventh day." (Indeed, even if we were to argue that the original prohibition in Exodus was not about going out on a major journey but specifically about going out to collect manna [as did Moshe Weinfeld; cf. Licht, *Mo·adei Yisrael*, pp. 85–86], it still seems amazing that the Shunamit was prepared to ride on a donkey, which the text in 2 Kings suggests was common practice and fully permitted—and this obviously is diametrically opposed to the societal/humanitarian argument). Cf. in this regard Kosman, *Ovadin D'hol*, p. 9, n. 42 and the material presented below in note 101.

[20] Israel Knohl, "The Priestly Torah versus the Holiness School: Sabbath and the Festivals," *Hebrew Union College Annual* 58 (1987), p. 66 (the entire article: pp. 65–117).

[21] This follows Knohl's theory, now widely accepted by many scholars because it convincingly answers many questions that earlier theories (which assumed that the Holiness School operated before the Priestly School) could not explain logically. See Knohl, "Participation of the People in the Temple Worship: Second Temple Sectarian Conflict and the Biblical Tradition" (Hebrew), *Tarbiz* 60:2 (5751 [1991]), p. 146, n. 22.

[22] The Book of the Covenant (Exodus 20:22–23:33, also called the Covenant Code) is generally understood to be a collection of laws created by the Elohistic school that operated in the eighth century BCE; cf. Shuvi Hoffman, *Yiḥudo*, p. 82.

[23] Simḥa (Simeon) Chavel, "Biblical Law" (Hebrew) in *Sifrut Ha-mikra: M'vo·ot U-meḥkarim*, ed. Tziporah Talshir (Jerusalem: Yad Ben Zvi, 2011), vol. 1, p. 250.

[24] Knohl, "The Priestly Torah versus the Holiness School," p. 66.

[25] Ibid., p. 103. It is hardly necessary to note that, according to Knohl, the various prohibitions of labor on Shabbat are left entirely unmentioned in the texts that derive from the earliest biblical schools: J (ninth century BCE), E (eighth century BCE), and D (seventh century BCE). Knohl explains the prohibition of gathering manna on Shabbat (Exodus 16) and the story of the man gathering sticks on Shabbat (Numbers 15:32–36) as a much later reworking of earlier material by the Holiness School (ibid., pp. 75–76). Not all scholars dealing with this text prior to Knohl saw this; cf., e.g., Hoffman, *Yiḥudo*, pp. 82–93. Nonetheless, Knohl's opinions are widely accepted by scholars today.
I myself would respond to those who find in the manna story a clear indication of forbidden labor on Shabbat by noting that there is no specific prohibition of baking or cooking in this whole pericope (as we find in Exodus 16:23, "bake what you wish to bake and cook that which you wish to cook, and the rest leave over as guarded foodstuffs for the morning"). The Israelites were instructed to divide the double portion of manna collected on Friday, one half to be baked and cooked for consumption on that same day, "and the rest shall you leave over as guarded foodstuffs for the morning"—which clearly implies that they may bake and cook it on Shabbat. On the gap between the Priestly School and the Holiness School, see also Jeffrey Stackert, "How the Priestly Sabbaths Work: Innovation in Pentateuchal Priestly Ritual," in *Ritual Innovation in the Hebrew Bible and Ancient Judaism*, ed. Nathan MacDonald (Berlin: Walter de Gruyter, 2016), pp. 79–111.

[26] Knohl, "The Priestly Torah versus the Holiness School," p. 104.

[27] Ibid., p. 103, n. 118.

[28] Israel Knohl, *The Sanctuary of Silence* (Minneapolis: Fortress Press, 1995), pp.

204–212, and Jacob Milgrom, "Does H Advocate the Centralization of the Worship?" *Journal for the Study of the Old Testament* 88 (2000), pp. 59–75.

[29] See Erhard Blum, *Studien zur Komposition des Pentateuch* (Berlin: De Gruyter, 1990), pp. 218–332; Yairah Amit, "Creation and the Calendar of Holiness" (Hebrew) in *Tehillah le-Moshe: Biblical and Judaic Studies in Honor of Moshe Greenberg*, eds. Mordechai Cogan, Barry L. Eichler, and Jeffrey H. Tigay (Winona Lake, IN: Eisenbrauns, 1997), Hebrew section, pp. 25–29 (entire article: pp. 13–30); and, recently, Gali Dinur, *Mizbaḥ Sh'nayim Va-ḥeitzi Ha-sh'vatim* (Tel Aviv: Resling, 2017), p. 148, n. 343.

[30] See above, note 2. To make this point, Hoffman ("First Creation Story", pp. 143–144) bases himself on his own extensive research, in the course of which he found in the entire Torah only forty-five references to Shabbat (and, as mentioned above, among them the thirty-one references concentrated in just five specific pericopes: Exodus 16 and 31, as well as Leviticus 23, 25, and 26). In all of those verses, it would be reasonable to expect to find some reference to the connection between Shabbat and the creation story, but in fact only one passage references such a connection. (Hoffman refers to Exodus 31:17, "For in the course of six days the Eternal made the heavens and the earth, and then spent the seventh day in rest and repose." But he maintains that "more than constituting a reference to the story of creation, we should see [this verse] as a quotation from the 'Sabbath' commandment in the Ten Commandments at Exodus 20:11" [ibid., p. 143].) This phenomenon is known from prophetic literature as well, where the Sabbath is referenced thirty-three times (principally in the books of Jeremiah and Ezekiel), and never is it tied to the story of creation. With respect to the Hagiographa, Hoffman notes that Shabbat is mentioned a total of twenty-two times (mostly in the Book of Nehemiah), and the sole effort to tie Shabbat observance to the story of creation appears in the Levites' prayer at Nehemiah 9:6. And the same is true in observing the situation from the opposite direction: Hoffman noted this phenomenon not only with verses concerning Shabbat, but also with verses referring in any way to the creation of the world—none includes a reference to Shabbat. In light of these findings, Hoffman concludes that "the more than one hundred scriptural passages that have to do with the creation of the world create an obvious opportunity to cite the [first creation story that begins the Book of Genesis…yet] only a very few actually do so" (ibid, p. 153).

[31] Ibid., p. 154.

[32] Ibid., p. 155.

[33] According to Hoffman, as noted above, it was in the days of Ezra that the books of the Torah were organized in a specific order, with the creation composed at that time as a kind of prologue to the Torah. See Hoffman, "First Creation Story," p. 155.

[34] Israel Knohl's argument that the Pharisees constituted a direct continuation of work of the Holiness School (whose tendency is to give the laymen the option to take part in the rituals), whereas the Priestly Torah was continued by both the Sadducees (in a manner characterized both by severity and leniency) and the sectarians of the Judean desert (in a particularly extreme and severe manner) is unconvincing to me. In my opinion, it is tendentious to describe such late schools of thought as the "continuation" of much earlier ones. One example (among many that could be brought to oppose Knohl's theory) has to do specifically with the laws of Shabbat: the Priestly Torah is particularly lenient about this, but there is no evidence that the Sadducees were any more lenient than the Pharisees, nor could this possibly be said with reference to the Judean Desert sectarians. For Knohl's argument, see his "Participation of the People in the Temple Worship," p. 146, and in particular n. 25.

[35] It seems to me that the tension between the societal/humanitarian argument and the theological one never really disappeared, and is still evident today. In the Middle Ages, Naḥmanides was troubled by the fact that Rabbinic Judaism had almost totally abandoned the societal/humanitarian rationale for Shabbat observance and, in his own way, he attempted to revive it (see below, the material presented before and after note 122). It is even possible to find traces of this tension in the Christian world, despite the fact that Christianity formally abandoned Shabbat observance in the Jewish sense millennia ago; even in Christian circles, there are some who continue to ask why Christianity really abandoned Shabbat observance. In this regard, see Roy Gane, "The Sabbath and the New Covenant," *Journal of the Adventist Theological Society* 10:1–2 (1999), pp. 311–332; cf. also the account of a contemporary Christian believer who sought to return to traditional Sabbath observance (on Sunday!), as related by Keri Wyatt Kent in her *Rest: Living in Sabbath Simplicity* (Grand Rapids, MI: Zondervan, 2009). Regarding why Christianity treats the theological imperative for Shabbat observance so casually, despite it being so explicit in Scripture (and even in the Ten Commandments!), see Samuele Bacchiocchi in his *From Sabbath to Sunday: A Historical Investigation of the Rise of Sunday Observance in Early Christianity* (Rome: Pontifical Gregorian University Press, 1991), who documents in detail the shift from Sabbath to Sunday worship, as well as the specific way that Shabbat observance was formally devalued in Christian circles. Cf. also the work of Willy Alwin Rordorf, who has collected many sources connected with the issue through the end of the patristic period in his *Sunday: The History of the Day of Rest and Worship in the Earliest Centuries of the Christian Church* (London: SCM Press, 1968). Also of interest in this regard is *From Sabbath to Lord's Day: A Biblical, Historical, and Theological Investigation*, ed. Donald Arthur Carson (Eugene, OR: Wipf and Stock, 1999). Regarding the so-called "pagan" influence on latter-day converts to Christianity

with respect to Shabbat observance, see Franz Cumont, *Astrology and Religion Among the Greeks and Romans* (New York: Putnam, 1912), pp. 162–163, and Rivka Nir, *Ha-natzrut Ha-k'dumah: Sh'losh Ha-mei·ot Ha-rishonot* (Raanana, Israel: Ha-universitah Ha-p'tuḥah, 2009), pp. 274–275. Regarding the place Shabbat observance played in the early church's efforts to distinguish its faith from Judaism, see Michael Wyschogrod, "On the Christian Critique of the Jewish Sabbath," in *Sabbath: Idea, History, Reality*, ed. Gerald J. Blidstein (Beersheva: Ben Gurion University Press, 2004), pp. 54–55 (English section). Another important factor, which all historians who write on the topic see as the beginning of the popular embrace of Sunday worship, is the emperor Constantine's proclamation (in the first half of the fourth century CE) that the *dies Solis* (i.e., Sunday) was henceforth to become the weekly day of rest and respite from work. This imperial decree was, of course, part of Constantine's larger effort to Christianize the empire; cf. Klaus Martin Girardet, "Vom Sonnen-Tag zum Sonntag: der *dies solis* in Gesetzgebung und Politik Konstantin des Großen," *Zeitschrift für antikes Christentum* 11 (2007), pp. 279–310; and Gerard Rouwhorst, "The Reception of the Jewish Sabbath in Early Christianity," in *Christian Feast and Festival: The Dynamics of Western Liturgy and Culture*, eds. P. Post, P. G. Rouwhorst, A. Scheer, and L. van Tongeren (Leuven: Peeters, 2001), pp. 223–266. Of course, there are contemporary Christian groups, such as Seventh-Day Adventists, who seek to re-establish the sanctity of Shabbat within the context of Christian worship. For example, William Warren Prescott (1855–1944), one of the leaders of that denomination, wrote: "There is at present a widespread agitation over the Sabbath question. For nearly half a century the attention of the public has been called to this subject anew; but a growing tendency to religious legislation in recent years, and the misguided efforts to enforce 'Sabbath-keeping' by pains and penalties, have done more than anything else to make this topic a living issue of the day" (in his "Christ and the Sabbath," at http://www.path2prayeRabbicom/article/1109/revival-holy-spirit/books-sermons/new-resources/bible-study-resources/w-w-prescott-christ-and-the-sabbath).

[36] It is worthwhile to consider a source that Gilat does not mention: an anonymous Greek text cited (in English translation) in *Mark: Ancient Christian Commentary on Scripture*, eds. Thomas C. Oden and Christopher A. Hall (Downers Grove, IL: InterVarsity Press, 1998), p. 36. In this text, the author explains that Shabbat was meant to be a day of repentance and atonement for the sins of the six days of the workweek. The author was formally a Christian, but his content suggests a Jewish-Hellenistic worldview regarding the Sabbath, one that held sway long before Christendom decided to "move" the Sabbath to Sunday. This source should be linked, however, to the sources recorded from early Christian world in regard to the Sabbath by Gedalyahu Alon, *Meḥkarim*

B'toldot Yisrael Biymei Bayit Sheini, vol. 1 (Tel-Aviv: Ha-kibbutz Ha-me·uḥad, 1957), p. 306, n. 26. And cf. above, note 15.

[37] Yitzḥak Dov Gilat, *P'rakim B'hishtalsh'lut Ha-halakhah* (Ramat Gan, Israel: Bar Ilan University Press, 5754 [1994]), p. 117. The translation of the verse into English is taken from: *The Old Testament Pseudepigrapha*, ed. James H. Charlesworth (Garden City, NY: Doubleday, 1985), vol. 2, p. 142 (henceforth, OTP). For a detailed discussion of these two positions, both of which left behind traces in the rabbinic corpus, see Anat Sharbat, *T'fisat Ha-miniyut B'olamam shel Ḥakhamim: B'ḥinat Ha-hityaḥasut Ha-erkit shel Ḥazal La-miniyut Ba-ma·arakh Ha-teologi al Reka Maḥlokot T'kufatam* (Ramat Gan: Bar Ilan University doctoral dissertation, 2011), pp. 67ff.

[38] This approach, which supposes that attaining a state of holiness must inevitably entail ascetic withdrawal from daily life and the needs of one's own body—and therefore leads to the conclusion that Shabbat observance must necessarily be painted in dark and dour colors—is hardly the only way to interpret the data. Indeed, it is possible that the theological/cosmological argument for Shabbat observance was influential here. For example, Gutmann argues that the opening of Genesis presents an image of a world in which "nature has substantial life of its own, but is conceived as inanimate and subordinate to the purposes of God, which, as such, are foreign to it. Man himself…is not conceived solely as part of nature, but as standing over and against nature, as the image of God. This anthropocentric conception grants man the right to conquer the earth, and relegates astral 'divinities' to the role of mere luminaries for the earth; it redirects all religious feeling from nature towards the transmundane God. Henceforth man sees himself as a being superior to the forces of nature, which in natural religion would be considered as divine"(Guttman, *The Philosophy of Judaism: The History of Jewish Philosophy from Biblical Times to Franz Rosenzweig*, trans. David W. Silverman [New York: Holt, Reinhart, and Winston, 1964], pp. 10–11). Indeed, if we merely substitute the word "body" for the word "nature" in this quotation, it becomes clear why the concept of holiness would be interpreted in light of Genesis 1 as involving a kind of ascetic separation from one's own body. (Some of the historical sources I will mention below do indeed suggest that Shabbat was taken that way by proponents of that approach to Scripture.) Nevertheless, to demonstrate the viability of an alternate approach, I recommend here the comments of Martin Buber, who discusses the biblical view of Shabbat in his *The Prophetic Faith*, trans. Carlyle Witton-Davies (New York: Harper Torchbooks, 1960), pp. 52–54. Buber supposes that even proponents of the theological rationale for Shabbat observance did not see it as a day of ascetic withdrawal at all, but rather as a day on which the nation sought to sanctify itself to God without any ceremonial or ritual component but instead through meditative contemplation on God and the meaning of the religious life for the individual and the community.

[39] Regarding the notion of the Temple precinct as a place of danger, see Hannah K. Harrington, *Holiness: Rabbinic Judaism in the Graeco-Roman World* (London: Routledge, 2001), pp. 57–58 and 80–81, and cf. Deuteronomy 5:22 ("What manner of flesh has ever heard the voice of the living God speak from within the fire as have we and survived?"). In a similar vein, cf. Leviticus 16:1, where God speaks to Moses "after they [i.e., Nadav and Abihu] came nigh unto the Eternal and died." Cf. also the remarks of Avigdor Shinan in his "The Sins of Nadab and Abihu in Rabbinic Literature" (Hebrew), *Tarbiz* 48 (1979), p. 206 (entire article: pp. 201–214), and the ensuing discussion between Shinan and Elimelech A. Halevi in *Tarbiz* 51 (5742 [1982]), pp. 310–312. Regarding the awe due the Temple as it was set into law in later generations, see Maimonides, M.T. Hilkhot Beit Ha-b'ḥirah 7:1–23. Regarding the sense of danger that proximity to the divine occasions in all religious people, see Rudolph Otto, *The Idea of the Holy*, trans. John W. Harvey (New York: Oxford University Press, 1923), pp. 12–19 and 74–84. For Otto, the danger dimension is related to the nominal experience. Otto coined the term "numinous" (from the Latin *numen*, meaning "divine power" or "divine will") to note the peculiarities of the religious experience. He claimed there was no parallel, in any other human experience, of the combination of two mental poles that he called *tremendum-fascinans*. The first term expresses great fear and a terrifying sense of danger from God; at the same time, the other expresses a sense of pleasantness, love, and joy arising from contact with the Divine. (In Jewish thought, these two would be labelled *yirah* and *ahavah*, awe and love.) This concept of the numinous is also identified, in other sources, with the experience of drawing near to the holy. Regarding the terrifying face of the Divine when confronted with human proximity (an image featuring demonic elements as well), see Buber, *The Prophetic Faith*, pp. 51–52, referencing Exodus 4:24: "And it came to pass as they were underway, in an inn, that the Eternal encountered him and sought to kill him." For a description of this terrifying side of God that is a feature of the entranceway to temples across the globe, see Joseph Campbell, *The Hero with a Thousand Faces* (1949; rpt. Princeton, NJ: Princeton University Press, 2004), pp. 84–88, who convincingly explains why the entrances to so many temples feature terrifying creatures of various sorts: these are the doorkeepers, whose task it is to warn those who might enter the temple that within its precincts a kind of supernal silence prevails. These doorkeepers are, according to Campbell, the earliest embodiment of this dangerous side of divine presence in a sacred space. The terrifying aspect of these monsters is thus meant to remind those about to enter the temple that penetrating its inner precincts is going to bring them into contact with the divine holiness that inheres in that sacred space, which experience is going to require of them a deep, personality-altering transformation.

[40] In this regard, see Knohl, "The Priestly Torah versus the Holiness School," p.

74: "Why did HS (= the Holiness School) juxtapose the Sabbath injunctions to the commandments regarding the construction of the Tabernacle? There is certainly a great deal of truth in the view of the sages and medieval commentators who underscore that this emphasizes that the work of the Sanctuary does not stop on Shabbat. However, there also seems to be an expression here of the tendency of HS to magnify the Sabbath and to place its sanctuary on the same level as that of the Sanctuary. This tendency is expressed in the twice-mentioned formula 'You shall keep My Sabbaths and venerate My Sanctuary' (Leviticus 19:30, 26:2), in which HS lists the Sabbath before the sanctuary. It seems that the desire to elevate the importance of its observance was what led the HS editors to add the Sabbath passage to the PT (=Priestly School) list of festivals, thus teaching that the Sabbath is no less important than any of the other annual holidays and is also a day of 'proclaimed holiness' (Leviticus 23:3). The highest expression of this view is the designation of the Sabbath as a design of the holiness with which the Lord sanctified Israel (Exodus 31:13)." For more about biblical texts that juxtapose Sabbath and sanctuary, see the sources martialed by Gary Anderson in his "The Garden of Eden and Sexuality in Early Judaism," in *People of the Body*, ed. Howard Eilberg-Schwartz (Albany, NY: State University of New York Press, 1992), pp. 55-56; Arthur Green, "Sabbath as Temple: Some Thoughts on Space and Time in Judaism," in *Go and Study: Essays and Studies in Honor of Alfred Jospe*, eds. Raphael Jospe and Samuel Z. Fishman (Washington, DC: B'nei B'rith Hillel Foundations, 1980), pp. 287–305, and also my own *Gender and Dialogue in the Rabbinic Prism*, pp. 185–191, as well as my *Ovadin D'ḥol*, p. 158, n. 230.

[41] In this regard, see above, note 8.

[42] This claim may be bolstered by noting that the verse from Isaiah can serve as a kind of mantra for those interested in revivifying the societal/humanitarian argument, especially in order to counter the halakhic extremism and obfuscatory asceticism that the theological argument seems to inspire. Regarding the larger problematic (noted by the rabbis) of using prophetic sources as the basis for halakhic rulings, see Cana Werman and Aharon Shemesh, *L'gallot Nistarot: Parshanut Va-halakhah Bi-m'gillot Qumran* (Jerusalem: Mossad Bialik, 2011), p. 102. On the other hand, some commentators have no doubt declined to interpret the halakhic principle of seeking "joy in the Sabbath" (namely, in rest, food, or sex) in the most obvious way precisely because of the sense of danger presumed to inhere in the endlessly demanding Shabbat strictures associated with the theological argument, and so they have generally sought to diminish both areas of potential indulgence to the greatest extent possible. For example, Moshe Alshekh (1508–1593) wrote that the preparing meals for Shabbat should not be undertaken as responses to mere physical joy; rather, those preparing Shabbat meals should feel as though "the Shekhinah were present in their personal ambit

and were actually cleaving unto them and emptying the reified stuff of Divinity (*shefa*, a kabbalistic term) from beneath the wings of the Shekhinah into those specific individuals, [and should thus feel as though] such people are granting pleasure to the blessed God in seeking to find pleasure in Shabbat" (in his *Torat Moshe* commentary to Exodus 35:3; ed. Jerusalem, 5750 [1989/1990], p. 386). Alshekh thus rejects the possibility of seeing Shabbat as a day of rest and physical pleasure that an individual exhausted by a week of work might enjoy—in distinction to those who would argue that "the point of the Sabbath is to grant comfort to workers and respite from the pain induced by their workaday labors, and so God commanded [Shabbat observance] to create a day on which the exhausted could finally find some rest—rest and leisure time for those who spend their lives working. But that is not the kind of rest and leisure intended here, which applies to flesh and muscles and bones—which is naught but vanity, and which is addressed to flesh that will eventually be buried deep in the earth in the realm of worms and maggots. Rather, [it is] the kind [of rest] intended to serve the weary as their portion in God, [which should be] the ultimate striving as human beings utilize the Sabbath as an opportunity to approach the God who ordained its observance and invested in those who keep it an additional [Sabbath] soul" (ibid., p. 387). Thus, as a practical result of his own theorizing, Alshekh finds himself in opposition to those who would dare to read secular literature on Shabbat because they find pleasure in doing so: "We must take note of the enormous sinfulness of those who find pleasure on Shabbat in reading books featuring the tales of kings and their wartime escapades, and who insist that that is their *oneg shabbat*. Woe is them, for they have allowed the holiness [of Shabbat observance] to be swallowed up by their secular pursuits, thus scorning the [true] holiness of Israel" (ibid.). In this regard, cf. the remarks of Brevard Childs cited below in note 64.

[43] Cf. Baruch Sharvit, "The Sabbath of the Judean Desert Sect" (Hebrew), *Beit Mikra* 21 (5736 [1975]), p. 509: "The Jews of this period did not go out to war on Shabbat even when they were under siege, thus placing their own lives in danger. Later on, Mattathias [i.e., the father of Judah Maccabeus] declared it permitted to fight on Shabbat in a defensive war so as not to perish, as had perished so many in earlier times. We see further evidence of the severity that prevailed in contemporary Sabbath observance in the teaching of the *ḥasidim* ("the pious") teaching noted in the Talmud (at B. Shabbat 121b) that 'any who kill snakes or scorpions on Shabbat earn the displeasure of the pious.'" For more on this notion, see below, note 48; and also Menaḥem Ben Shalom, *Ḥasidut Va-ḥasidim Bi-t'kufat Bayit Sheini U-vi-t'kufat Ha-mishnah* (Tel-Aviv: Ha-kibbutz Ha-me·uḥad, 2008), pp. 229–230. It has been noted that those early pietists (i.e., the *ḥasidim rishonim* of rabbinic literature) took severe restrictions upon themselves, forbidding themselves even a whisper of something profane

on Shabbat. (See Shlomo Naeh, "*Shabbat, Shivta, Shivt'na,*" in *Meḥkarim B'lashon* 7 (5756 [1995/1996]), p. 99, n. 8. This was already discussed by Philo, as demonstrated by Yitzḥak Dov Gilat in his *P'rakim*, p. 256, n. 31.) Regarding the term *ḥasidim* as it was used in the Hellenistic period, see Yitzḥak Baer, "The Ancient Ḥasidim in Philo's Writings and in Hebrew Tradition" (Hebrew), *Zion* 18 (5713 [1953]), pp. 107–108 (entire article: pp. 91–108). Baer identifies these early *ḥasidim* with the Essenes, whose existence was reported by both Philo and Josephus. See also Adolph Büchler, *Types of Jewish-Palestinian Piety From 70 B.C.E.to 70 C.E.: The Ancient Pious Men* (London: Jews College Publications, 1922); Louis Jacobs, "The Concept of Hasid in the Biblical and Rabbinic Literatures," *Journal of Jewish Studies* 8 (1957), pp. 143–154; and see Ben Shalom, *Ḥasidut*, pp. 111–114.

⁴⁴ Regardless of whether the Qumran community is identified as part of the Essenes (as most researchers think) or not. For an up-to-date summary of the scholarly debate on this subject, see Eyal Regev, "How Many Sects Were at Qumran? Distinguishing Between the *Yaḥad*, the Damascus Covenant, the Essenes, and *Khurvat Qumran*" (Hebrew), *Cathedra* 148 (5713 [2012/2013]), pp. 7–40, and cf. particularly his comment at p. 19, n. 49, regarding those who oppose the idea that there were Essenes at Qumran. (Regev himself partially espouses this position at the conclusion of his article, pp. 38–40.)

⁴⁵ For a brief summary of how the laws of Shabbat are presented in the writings of the Judean Desert sect and in the Damascus Covenant, see Yosef Elimelech Baumgarten,"Common Legal Exegesis in the Scrolls and Tannaitic Source" (Hebrew), in *M'gillot Qumran: M'vo·ot U-meḥkarim*, ed. Menaḥem Kister (Jerusalem: Yad Ben Zvi, 2009), vol. 2, pp. 653–656.

⁴⁶ *Jewish War* II:147, in Josephus Flavius, *The Jewish War: Books I–III*, trans. Henry St. John Thackery (Cambridge, MA: Harvard University Press, 1956), p. 379. Cf. also the editor's note in Steve Mason's translation of the *Jewish War* (Leiden: Brill, 2008), pp. 117–118.

⁴⁷ This approach appears to accord with straightforward reasoning: if the punishment for profaning the Sabbath is death, does that not suggest that the value of Shabbat is greater than the parallel value of life? In this sense, it is possible to see the various homilies of the sages cited in the Mekhilta (see below, note 81), attempting to justify the preference for saving lives over strict adherence to the Shabbat laws, as distant from the simple meaning of Scripture if a decision were to be made solely to follow the theological rationale for Shabbat observance. For sources supporting this interpretation, see Aharon Shemesh, *Onashim V'ḥatta·im: Min Ha-mikra L'sifrut Ḥazal* (Jerusalem: Magnes Press, 2003), particularly pp. 498–501 (and cf. also note 82 below.)

⁴⁸ The touch of death is one of the signs of Shabbat's severity at the most extreme end of the scale. This touch has two faces. One assumes that the laws of Shabbat

are *not* suspended when human life is in play. According to the tradition preserved in 1 Maccabees 2:32–41 (ed. Uriel Rappaport [Jerusalem: Yad Ben Zvi, 2004], pp. 129–131, and in English, *I Maccabees: A New Translation*, ed. Jonathan A Goldstein [Anchor Bible vol. 41; Garden City, NY: Doubleday, 1976], p. 234), Mattathias and his followers permitted acts of self-defense on Shabbat even if they contravened the Sabbath laws; this tradition is also preserved in Jubilees 50:12–13 (*OTP*, p. 142). Thus we can see that not all Jewish sects in ancient times adopted such an extreme approach to the Sabbath laws, and it seems that Mattathias was specifically addressing extremist groups when he issued his permission to fight on Shabbat. Cf. Rappaport's comments to 1 Maccabees 2:32–41 (pp. 131–132), focusing on verse 41. See also: Moshe David Herr, "The Problem of War on the Sabbath in the Second Temple and Talmudic Periods" (Hebrew), *Tarbiz* 30:3 (5721 [1961]), pp. 242–256 and 341–356; Ben Shalom, *Ḥasidut*, pp. 103–106; and David Nakman, *Ha-halakhah B'kitvei Yosef ben Matityahu* (Ramat Gan, Israel: Bar-Ilan University doctoral dissertation, 2004), pp. 281–293. Regarding how such a liberalization of the law became accepted by Mattathias' followers in such conservative circles, see Aharon Shemesh, "The History of the Halakhic Concept *Piku·aḥ Nefesh Doḥeh Shabbat*" (Hebrew), *Tarbiz* 80:4 (5772 [2012]), pp. 502–504 (entire article: pp. 481–505).

The other approach, the more severe one, takes seriously the theological rationale for Shabbat observance as found in Scripture. It is possible to suppose that the passages that impose the death penalty for desecrating the Sabbath (e.g., at Numbers 15:32–36, regarding the man caught collecting sticks on Shabbat) simply see performing forbidden labors on Shabbat as something to be pursued through the justice system in earnest—even though the sources suggest that the death penalty for profaning Shabbat was enacted very rarely. Such a case is found in the Talmud (B. Yevamot 90b and Sanhedrin 46a), where it is noted that such things only occurred "in the days of the Greeks." (Note, however, that the parallel at Y. Ḥagigah 2:3, 78a, does not mention when this incident occurred.) Nevertheless, even if the death penalty was imposed rarely, the very fact of its existence must surely have wafted constantly over the heads of the Sabbath profaners, thus lending to the Sabbath day itself a monitory ambience rooted in nervousness and fear. See below, note 125.

[49] Regarding the question of why sexual activity was considered capable of imparting ritual impurity, see Anat Sharbat, *T'fisat Ha-miniyut*, pp. 131–135, as well as the material in the following note.

[50] See Leviticus 15:16–18: "And any man from whom comes forth seminal ejaculate shall wash his flesh in water and then be impure until evening. And any garment or pelt upon which any of that ejaculate lands shall also be washed in water and considered impure until evening. As for a woman with whom

a man shall lie [thus bringing her into contact] with [his] seminal ejaculate, they shall both be impure until evening." Although it is possible that the man referenced in verse 16 as being contaminated with impurity could be a *ba·al keri* (that is, one who experienced an instance of involuntary ejaculation) as opposed to one who engaged in sexual relations with his wife, this is unlikely, given the following verse. Nevertheless, that is precisely how the verse was understood both by the rabbis and by other sects. In the wake of that observation, we can understand how the expression *ba·al keri* in rabbinic literature, which originally referred solely to a man who experiences an involuntary seminal emission, came to denote any man who experiences any seminal ejaculation, even in the context of marital relations. For the original concept, cf. Deuteronomy 23:11: "Should there be among you a man contaminated with impurity by virtue of a *mikreh lailah* [literally "a nocturnal event," the word for "event" being related to the word *keri* in the rabbinic phrase]—such a one must go out from the camp." Regarding the expression *mikreh lailah* in the Bible, see Elisha Qimron, "Biblical Philology and the Dead Sea Scrolls" (Hebrew), *Tarbiz* 58:3/4 (5749 [1989]), pp. 297–315, and Menaḥem Kister, "Some Observations on Vocabulary and Style in the Dead Sea Scrolls," in *Diggers at the Well: Proceedings of a Third International Symposium on the Hebrew of the Dead Sea Scrolls and Ben Sira*, eds. T. Muraoka and John F. Elwolde (Leiden: Brill, 2000), pp. 149–150. This expansion of the term's original meaning appears in the Talmud as well, such as at B. Berakhot 22a. (Another example appears in the text of edict attributed to Ezra, as given at B. Bava Kama 82a: "Ezra instituted…[the custom] of bathing [in a *mikveh*] for *ba·alei k'riyan*," where the context makes clear that the edict also applied to men who had marital relations. Moreover, there are examples in the rabbinic corpus of the expression *ba·alat keri* (i.e., the feminine form of the same expression) to denote a woman who has had sexual relations with her husband; regarding this usage, see the *Entziklopeidiah Talmudit* (Jerusalem: Yad Ha-rav Herzog, 2001), vol. 4, col. 130, s.v. *ba·al keri*.

At any rate: we see that if a couple engages in marital relations, both parties become contaminated with impurity that derives from the man's semen, and both can be purified—according to the simple meaning of the Bible, with the arrival of evening of the day on which they sought purification by washing their flesh. (Rabbinic tradition understood this to reference specifically the act of bathing in a *mikveh*.) It is thus clear that both men and women who engage in sexual relations are by Torah law forbidden to enter into the Temple in their state of impurity. Even if that is not explicit in the passage cited above (Leviticus 15:16–18), it seems obvious that both men and woman in that state would be included in the general prohibition of anyone contaminated with *tumah* (ritual impurity) passing through the gates of the Temple until being purified of that impurity. In the Temple Scroll, this is not only made explicit with respect to the

Temple, but is also made even more stringent in two different ways: the waiting period is a full three days (and not merely until the fall of evening), and the prohibition is extended from the Temple precincts proper to the entire city of Jerusalem. The text of the Temple Scroll 48:7–12 states: "And if o[ne] has an emission of a semen in the night, then he may not enter the whole sanctuary until he has [comp]leted three days. He shall wash his clothes and bathe on the first day, and on the third day he shall wash his clothes [and bathe], and after the sun has set, he may come to the sanctuary. But in their sexual impurity they may not come into my sanctuary to make [it] unclean. If a man lies with his wife with emission of semen he may not enter any (part) of the city of the sanctuary, in which I cause my name to dwell, for three days." (See *M'gillot Midbar Y'hudah: Ha-ḥibburim Ha-ivriyim*, ed. Elisha Qimron [Jerusalem: Yad Ben Zvi, 2010], vol. 1, p. 184; the English translation is taken from *The Temple Scroll*, ed. Johann Maier [Sheffield: Journal for the Study of the Old Testament, 1985], pp. 40–41, and cf. also Warman and Shemesh, *L'gallot Nistarot*, pp. 116–117).

Given this material, we can understand finally just how daring the rabbinic act of permitting a married couple to engage in sexual relations on Shabbat truly was—since such permission flew directly in the face of other groups in Jewish antiquity who did not permit marital intimacy on Shabbat. We find, for example, the following statement in the Talmud: "The pious of olden times (*ḥasidim rishonim*) only engaged in marital intercourse on Wednesdays, lest their wives end up profaning the Sabbath" (B. Niddah 38a–b). For a summary of the discussion concerning this law, see Sharbat, *T'fisat Ha-miniyut*, pp. 94–102. The *halakhah* that obtained among the Judean Desert community seems to have been the same (cf. Magen Broshi, "Anti-Qumranic Polemic Texts in the Talmud" [Hebrew], in *Or L'ya·akov: Meḥkarim B'mikra U-vi-m'gillot Midbar Y'hudah L'zikhro shel Ya·akov Shalom Licht*, eds. Yair Hoffman and Frank Polak [Jerusalem: Bialik Institute, 1997], pp. 216–217), as was apparently also the *halakhah* that prevailed among the Samaritans (and until modern times, at that; cf. Sharbat, *T'fisat Ha-miniyut*, pp. 120–124), and possibly among the Sadducees and the Karaites as well. (We have no explicit textual evidence regarding the Sadducees, but cf. Sharbat's comment in *T'fisat Ha-miniyut*, pp. 116–117, as well as her comments regarding the Karaites on p. 124.) Even among the Jews of Ethiopia (called in earlier works Falashas), who maintained very old traditions, we find that although feasting and drinking were promoted on Shabbat, marital intimacy was forbidden—as it was forbidden to break any of the Sabbath laws, even to save a human life. (In this regard, see Aharon Zev Eshkoly, *Sefer Ha-falashim: Y'hudei Ḥabash, Tarbutam U-m'soroteihem* [Jerusalem: Reuven Mass, 5733 (1972/1973)], pp. 36–37.) In Jubilees 50:8 (*OTP*, p. 142), engaging in sexual relations on Shabbat is a capital offense. Some scholars, however, maintain that this passage was a later addition to the book by a scribe from the Qumran community; cf. Sharbat, *T'fisat Ha-miniyut*, pp. 104–105. In any case, Lutz Doering argues that the origin of the death penalty as punishment for engaging in marital relations on Shabbat may be found at Exodus 19:15 where, in instructing the Israelites how to prepare for the theophany about to occur at Sinai, the men are instructed not to "draw near a woman" (see his *Schabbat: Sabbathalacha und -praxis im antiken Judentum und Urchristentum* [Göttingen: Mohr Siebeck, 1999], p. 191). But it isn't really necessary to pin the concept on a specific verse, because our earliest biblical exegetes—at least, those whose works were left behind at Qumran—found the Torah to inflict the death penalty on any who would enter into the sanctuary in a state of impurity. (In this regard, see Aharon Shemesh, *Onashim V'ḥatta·im*, pp. 117–119.) And from that, we can easily argue that the same would apply to the "sanctuary" of the Shabbat.

When seen in this light, the ancient rabbis did not merely rule that sexual relations on Shabbat were permissible for a couple; in fact, they effected a powerful ideational revolution by interpreting sexual activity itself as belonging to the realm of holy behaviors—even going so far as to recommend that a *talmid ḥakham* (literally, "a student of the wise") specifically engage in intimate relations with his wife on Shabbat. (This, of course, was in diametric opposition to the simple meaning of Scripture, as is obvious from even a cursory survey of the sources listed above with respect to the question of permitting self-contamination with impurity on Shabbat; cf. the comments of Anat Sharbat in her *T'fisat Ha-miniyut*, pp. 20–28, providing an even more detailed picture.) Although more detail about the dialogic implications of this innovation for the larger theology of our ancient sages is beyond the scope of this essay, interested readers may consult Sharbat, *T'fisat Haminiyut*, p. 113, as well as my own two books. *Massekhet Nashim: Ḥokhmah, Ahavah, Ne·emanut, T'shukah, Yofi, Min, K'dushah* (Jerusalem: Keter, 2007), pp. 127–166, and *Gender and Dialogue in the Rabbinic Prism*, trans. Edward Levin (Berlin: De Gruyter, 2012), pp. 154–213. For a rabbinic text in this vein, see, e.g., B. Ketubot 62b: "When is the correct time for rabbinic scholars to engage in marital relations? Rav Yehudah said in the name of Samuel, 'Only on Shabbat eve.'" And the Talmud then goes on to discuss a verse from Psalms: "[Such a one shall be as a tree planted alongside flowing waters] that gives fruit in the appointed time [and whose leaves do not wither, and that knows only success in all endeavors]" (Psalm 1:3)—Rav Yehudah, or some say it was Rav Huna and still others say Rav Naḥman, said: 'This [verse] references one who engages in marital relationships only on the eve of Shabbat." In regard to this text, see Sharbat, *T'fissat Ha-miniyut*, p. 95, n. 60. Regarding the question of the earliest rabbinic (or even Pharisaic) date to which we can assign the formal permission to engage in sexual relations on Shabbat (or at least the earliest text recommending such activity), Yair Lorberbaum maintains that this notion was already current in the tannaitic period and was not solely a feature of the amoraic; see his *Tzelem Elohim: Halakhah Va-aggadah* (Jerusalem: Schocken, 2004, p. 441, n. 19). Moreover, it seems likely that at least some Jews followed the recommended practice as early as the late second and early first centuries BCE. In this regard, see Efraim Elimelekh Urbach, *The Halakhah: Its Sources and Development*, trans. Raphael Posner (Ramat-Gan, Israel: Massadah, 1986), p. 363, n. 38, who points readers to the text of Meleager of Gadara (cited in Menahem Stern, *Greek and Latin Authors on Jews and Judaism: Volume One: From Herodotus to Plutarch* [Jerusalem: Israel Academy of Sciences and Humanities, 1976], p. 140), who writes derisively regarding the Jews of his day that "if thy lover is some Sabbath-keeper, no great wonder! Love burns hot even on cold Sabbaths"—which is to say that even Jews who suffer from the cold on Shabbat because they will not kindle the flames necessary to heat their homes, even such Jews find warmth in the sexual relations in which they engage on Shabbat. Regarding this text, cf. Gedalyahu Alon, *Meḥkarim B'toldot Yisrael Biymei Bayit Sheini*, vol. 1, p. 306, n. 26, and Sharbat, *T'fisat Ha-miniyut*, pp. 92–23, n. 148. For his part, Raphael Pattai sums up the rabbinic attitude in a few short words: "Intercourse with one's wife on Friday night was a sacred duty" (*The Hebrew Goddess* [Detroit: Wayne State University Press, 1991], p. 256). And cf. also Daniel Boyarin, *Carnal Israel: Reading Sex in Talmudic Culture* (Berkeley: University of California Press, 1993), pp. 149–150, and the comprehensive summary of Sharbat in *T'fisat Ha-miniyut*, pp. 67–128.

It should be noted that there are later sources that indicate that engaging in sexual relations on Shabbat should be understood as part of the larger mandate to make Shabbat a delight (*oneg shabbat*) within the bosom of the Jewish family. See, e.g., the words of Moshe Matt, one of the great rabbis of sixteenth-century Poland, who wrote in his *Matteh Moshe* (p. 58b, sect. 441) that the phrase "those who taste of it merit life," known to worshipers from the Shabbat Musaf service, references the consummation of sexual relations on Shabbat (with the word "taste" referencing "the taste of intercourse on the eve of Shabbat"). In this regard, see also Elliott Horowitz, "Sabbath Delights: Toward a Social History," in *Sabbath: Idea, History, Reality*, ed. Gerald J. Blidstein (Beersheva: Ben-Gurion University of the Negev, 2004), pp. 131–159.

To return to the subject raised in the beginning of this very long note: it seems to me that the sages in the Sifra limited the contaminative nature of semen specifically to the semen itself and claimed that coitus by itself, but without seminal ejaculation, did not render one impure. See Sifra, *M'tzora, Perek Zavim*, chap. 6 (ed. Isaac Hirsch Weiss [Vienna, 5626 (1865/1866)], p. 77d: "Seminal ejaculate: as opposed to penetration"—which is to say that, in the opinion of the Sifra, *tumah*-contamination does not occur as a result of penetration, but only after semen itself comes into play. For more on this topic, see the comments of

Menaḥem Mendel Kasher in his *Torah Sh'leimah* (Jerusalem: Mekhon Torah Sh'leimah, 5752 [1991/1992]), vol. 29, p. 274. This approach accords well with the opinions of those who theorize that, from the biblical perspective, sexual relations occasion *tumah*-contamination not because sexuality itself is somehow contaminative, but rather because of a direct nexus in the biblical view between impurity and death (and thus totally divorced from the divine realm, the source of life), such that the so-called "fluids of life" that were brought out into the world without leading to conception were understood to represent instead the realm of death. Regarding this notion, see Sharbat, *T'fisat Ha-miniyut*, pp. 131–135.

[51] Exodus 20:9 and Deuteronomy 5:13. The Talmud (at B. Pesaḥim 68b) presents a neat distinction between the theological basis for Shabbat observance and the approach we have labelled the societal/humanitarian one: "For the Eternal" (Exodus 20:9 and Deuteronomy 5:13), as opposed to "for you [i.e., for your own enjoyment]." The talmudic discussion concerns both Shabbat and the festivals, and the "for you" is a citation of Numbers 29:35, where the phrase "an assembly shall it be *for you*" appears. See Sharbat, *T'fisat Ha-miniyut*, pp. 61–63.

[52] This is the formulation of Elisha Qimron, taken from a popular interview he gave which is now available online at https://www.makorrishon.co.il/magazine/dyukan/30827/. There is no doubt that this extreme view was influenced by Exodus 16:29 ("See how the Eternal has given the Shabbat to you, and so [God] also gives you two days' worth of food on Fridays. Let each of you [therefore] stay home [on Shabbat]; let none go out from one's place on the seventh day"), which was interpreted among the extremist sects as a severe and unyielding prohibition; and cf. above, note 19.

[53] Baumgarten notes in his "Common Legal Exegesis," p. 653: "There is no distinction made in the Damascus Covenant between the kinds of labor forbidden by the Torah and rabbinic edicts [*d'oraita* and *d'rabbanan* laws], and neither is there any reference to the thirty-nine kinds of labor forbidden by rabbinic law to be undertaken on Shabbat. Even the principle of setting aside the Sabbath laws in order to save a human life was not accepted by the members of that sect." The fact that the sect had no distinction between *d'oraita* and *d'rabbanan* laws leads to a much more severe approach to the *halakhah* in general and to the laws of Shabbat observance in particular, since everything which is not allowed is forbidden on a biblical level. Cf. Yitzḥak Dov Gilat, *P'rakim*, pp. 88–92.

[54] 4Q264a, part 1, lines 7–8.

[55] Baumgarten, "Common Legal Exegesis," pp. 655–656 (the verse is cited here, in the English translation, from *OTP*, p. 142 [in this edition the verse appears in the Book of Jubilees 50:10]) observes that Jubilees too imposes the death penalty on anyone who fasts on Shabbat (see Jubilees 50:12–13; *OTP*, p. 142).

He thus rejects Gilat's theory that in antiquity there were, among those who promulgated the notion of an ascetic Shabbat, also those who fasted on that day. However, I believe that that Gilat is right: the very fact that the author of Jubilees feels such a strong need to forbid fasting on the Sabbath suggests that there were those who did not see things the author's way and who, in fact, did promote the notion of fasting on Shabbat.

[56] My use of the language of "leniency" and "severity" with respect to Shabbat laws is merely a function of how we speak today about halakhic matters. It is perhaps reasonable to suppose that Jesus saw himself not as seeking to make the law more lenient, but rather as stressing strict allegiance to the law as a virtue (i.e., as treating even the least infraction as an offense of great seriousness) when it came to laws governing interpersonal behavior and the respect due to others. See below, note 114.

[57] Even though the historicity of the account matters little in this specific context, it should be noted that there are scholars who take these oppositional encounters with the Pharisees as fictitious, arguing that the Gospel sought to depict the Pharisees of the past as earlier versions of the Rabbinic Jews of their own day. In this regard, see Morton Smith, "Palestinian Judaism in the First Century," in *Israel: Its Role in Civilization*, ed. Moshe Davis (New York: Jewish Theological Seminary of America, 1956), pp. 67–81; David S. Williams's response to Smith in his "Morton Smith on the Pharisees in Josephus," *Jewish Quarterly Review* 84:1 (1993), pp. 29–41; Jacob Neusner, *The Rabbinic Traditions about the Pharisees before 70* (Leiden: Brill, 1971); idem, *Early Rabbinic Judaism: Historical Studies in Religion: Literature and Art* (Leiden: Brill, 1975); and Rivka Nir, *Ha-natzrut Ha-k'dumah*, pp. 91–92. And cf. also below, notes 73, 76, and esp. 87. David Flusser argues that those opposed Jesus and were described by the authors of the Gospels as scribes and Pharisees were actually "anonymous, self-appointed spokesmen of local [Galilee's villages] bigotry, [who only] later are described [by the evangelists] unhesitatingly as scribes and Pharisees" (in his *Jesus*, trans. R. Steven Notely [Jerusalem: Magnes Press, 1998], p. 66).

[58] Mark 2:23–28, Luke 6:1–5, and Matthew 12:1–8.

[59] Regarding the translation of the Greek word στάχυας (*stakhuas*) as "ear of wheat," see below, note 68.

[60] The English translation follows *Mark 1–8:26*, ed. Robert A. Guelich (*Word Biblical Commentary*, vol. 34A; Dallas, Texas: World Books, 1989), p. 119. The amount of research devoted to the interpretation of this passage is enormous and complex, and it is beyond the scope of this essay to treat it all. Nonetheless, see below for some attempts at elucidation.

[61] Regarding the question of whether there was any sort of rabbinic prohibition of healing with words, see Menaḥem Kister, "Plucking of Grain on the Sabbath and the Jewish-Christian Debate" (Hebrew), *Meḥk'rei Y'rushalayim B'maḥshevet*

Yisrael 3 (1984), p. 355, n. 19b.

[62] Regarding the distinction between these two types of healing in which Jesus engaged on Shabbat, see Lutz Doering, "Much Ado about Nothing?: Jesus' Sabbath Healings and Their Halakhic Implications Revisited," in *Judaistik und neutestamentliche Wissenschaft*, eds. Lutz Doering, Hans-Günther Waubke, and Florian Wilk (Göttingen, Vandenhoeck & Ruprecht, 2008), pp. 226–227 (entire article, pp. 217–241).

[63] Interested readers should see the references to the variety of approaches in notes 72–73 and 75–76 below. I am glossing over the question of the methodology developed in this immense field of scholarly endeavor because this essay is not about research into the question of historical Jesus and his life. I will note, however, that the personality of the historical Jesus is a very tough nut to crack. Most scholars who write about the life of the historical Jesus attempt to ferret out clues from Christian and non-Christian sources in order to construct a broad portrait of the man and his faith. All we know with certainty regarding the historical Jesus are a few scattered details. According to Anthony Earnest Harvey (writing in his *Jesus and the Constraints of History* [London: Duckworth, 1982], pp. 5ff.), we can only know with certainty that Jesus was known in his own day in the Galilee and in Jerusalem, that he was a teacher who taught the Torah, that he healed sick individuals (primarily by exorcising the demons he perceived to have possessed them), that he was embroiled in controversies with various contemporary Jews about certain specific halakhic matters, and that he was eventually crucified by Pontius Pilate. On the various tendencies that were developed in the research, as well as the current state of affairs of the historical Jesus, see the summary of Rivka Nir, *Ha-natzrut Ha-k'dumah*, pp. 141–142.

[64] From this suggestion arises the question of how Jesus himself would have explained his reason for preferencing the societal/humanitarian rationale for Shabbat observance over the theological. My sense is that the commandments related to love (such as the commandment to love God [Deuteronomy 6:5 and 11:1], to love one's neighbor [Leviticus 19:18], and to love the stranger in one's midst [Leviticus 19:33]) represented the overarching values that subsumed the rest of the Torah in Jesus' eyes. If that is so, the obligation to care for one's suffering neighbor could easily have become the decisive mandate—and as such, the one that inspired the halakhic discourses attributed to him. This seems particularly likely when the incident under discussion required preferencing one rationale over the other. Roy Gane argues (in his "Sabbath and the New Covenant," p. 311–317) that Jesus understood the theological/cosmological rationale not as an answer to the question of why one is obligated to mimic God's rest on the seventh day (and thus to make every seventh day sacred unto God by behaving on it in a way that overrides the natural inclination to act on behalf of other people and for their benefit), but rather as a reflection of

the belief that God rested for the sake of humankind—i.e., as an act of divine benevolence—thus teaching those who work during the week to learn from God's example and to cease from labor one day a week, and to rest and relax on that day. This explanation seems reasonable to a large degree. However, even if it does succeed in setting one of the most important scriptural texts concerning the theological rationale on its head and making it argue instead on behalf of the societal/humanitarian rationale, it still fails to accord with the other texts regarding Shabbat that feature the theological rationale with its severe overtones regarding Shabbat (and that severely delimit the activities that may be undertaken on it). If we are talking about the possibility of those who hold the social/humanitarian rationale to explain at least some of the verses that deal with theological rational according to their method, one can also show that the opposite possibility can be suggested: the verses that present the social rationale can be explained not in this manner (i.e., as having a social purpose) but rather as having a religious (theological) goal—namely, that the slaves can be sanctified to God on this day. In this vein, see Brevard S. Childs, *The Book of Exodus: A Critical, Theological Commentary* (Louisville, KY: Westminster Press, 2004), p. 417. With respect to domesticated animals, it is thus possible to say that the obligation to allow them to rest is mentioned only in order to make it impossible for a human being to work them on Shabbat; cf. the comment of Moshe Alshekh cited above in note 42.

[65] This is not true for aggadic texts, however. See my *Ovadin D'hol*, pp. 162–163.

[66] Regarding the question of healing the sick on Shabbat, see David Flusser, *Jesus*, pp. 61–69. With regard to the question of ritual handwashing, see below, note 70. And with regard to the *halakhah* cited by Jesus that it is possible to bring up from a pit an animal who has fallen into it, see the conclusions of Aharon Shemesh in his "The History of the Halakhic Concept *Piku'ah Nefesh Doheh Shabbat*," and cf. also the material below in note 86.

[67] Flusser bases himself principally on the version of the story preserved at Luke 6:1–5 because he believed it to be the earlier one (see below note 74). The text there reads: "It happened on a Sabbath that he was going through grainfields and his disciples were plucking and eating the heads of grain, rubbing them in their hands. Some of the Pharisees said, 'Why do you do what is not lawful on the Sabbath?' Jesus answered them, 'Have you not even read what David did when he was hungry, and those who were with him, how he went into the house of God and took and ate the Presentation loaves which it is not lawful to eat, except for the priest alone, and gave them to those who were with him'? Then he said to them, 'The son of Man is Lord of the Sabbath'" (*Word Biblical Commentary*, vol. 35A; *Luke 1:1–9:20*, ed. John Nolland [Dallas, TX: World Books, 1989], p. 252). And cf. the discussion in Menahem Kister, "Plucking of Grain on the Sabbath," pp. 358ff.

[68] The explanation is that a στάχυας (*stakhuas*), translated here as "ear of wheat," has almost reached its full state of readiness for human consumption and the grains can be separated from it easily. Manually separating the kernels from the husk is a kind of crushing, which results in the separation of the edible from the inedible part of the plant. For more about the Hebrew terminology behind the Greek text, *m'lilot*, see Eliezer Ben Yehudah's *Milon Ha-lashon Ha-ivrit Ha-y'shanah V'ha-ḥadashah* (Jerusalem: Makor, 5740 [1979/1980]), vol. 6, p. 3040. It is clearly possible to undertake this kind of separation while the ear is still attached to the stalk planted in the ground, and, of course, it is also possible to remove the kernels from an ear that has fallen on its own to the ground and is therefore no longer growing in the earth. According to Flusser (*Jesus*, p. 58, n. 2), there are clear indications that the original story did not discuss plucking ears from the stalk, but rather removing kernels from the ears by hand after the latter had fallen on their own to earth. If Flusser is correct, it would be interesting to compare the halakhic statements of Jesus about shucking kernels from ears of wheat on Shabbat to contemporary rabbinic legal statements about the same matter. For a discussion of the various labors forbidden under the rubric of "threshing," see Efraim Zalman Margoliot's *Yad Efraim*, printed as a commentary on the Shulḥan Arukh, O.H. 252:19. See also Rabbi Israel Meir Hakohen of Radin's *Mishnah B'rurah* to SA. O.H., *Hilkhot Shabbat* 319, n. 6. Admittedly, there is a complicated halakhic problem here, which Flusser does not address at all. The entire discussion about the permissibility of crushing kernels of fallen grain on Shabbat in order to eat them relates only to those grains that had fallen down *before* Shabbat; those that fall down *during* Shabbat are certainly forbidden according to all opinions. See *Mishnah B'rurah*, ibid., §335, n. 3. However, if we would like to defend Flusser's position in this case (in light of this additional halakhic complication), we can say that the laws of preparation for Shabbat (which use the term *mukhan* to denote previously prepared materials) were not seen by Jesus as severe issues—although many sects did consider this prohibition in Shabbat as a severe one (in line with Exodus 16:5, "and it shall come to pass, that on the sixth day they shall prepare that which they bring in"—which many sects understood to mean that one should not use on Shabbat anything that was not prepared, i.e., made *mukhan*, before Shabbat). See Vered Noam, "Beit Shammai and the Sectarian *Halakhah*" (Hebrew), *Mada'ei Ha-yahadut* 41 (5762 [1982]), pp. 60–62 (entire article: pp. 45–67). However, the Talmud mentions the opinion of Rabbi Shimon bar Yoḥai, another Galilean rabbi) who is very lenient and allows almost all cases of *muktzeh* on Shabbat. (In this context, the term *muktzeh* denotes everything that is not *mukhan*, thus forbidden for use on Shabbat.) His opinion is that the term *muktzeh* does not apply to food, as it is all considered to be prepared. See E. Itzhaki, "Muktzeh," *Sidra* 16 (2000), pp. 81–104; and Yoel Kretzmer-Raziel,

"The Category Muqṣe [Muktzeh] and its Development in Amoraic Literature (Ben-Gurion University: Ph.D. dissertation, 2015), esp. pp. 193–210. Another possibility is simply to suggest that Jesus assumed that the grains in this field had fallen down to the earth before Shabbat.

[69] Cf. B. Shabbat 128a. This Babylonian tradition is based on a tannaitic source; see T. Shabbat 14 (15):11 (in *The Tosefta: Order of Mo·eid,* ed. Saul Lieberman, [New York: Jewish Theological Seminary, 1962], p. 67). See also Lieberman's comments in his *Tosefta Ki-f'shuta* (Part 3, *Seder Mo·eid* [New York: Jewish Theological Seminary of America, 1962], p. 237), regarding the difficulty in identifying the precise version of the citation of Rabbi Judah; the same is also true for the version of the sages who disagree with him. Another important point not mentioned by Flusser: even for the sages who disagree with Rabbi Judah, this was not actually forbidden. Rather, they only demanded that the action of crushing the grain would be done in *shinu·i*—namely, not in the regular way it is done on weekdays—while Rabbi Judah did not demand any change.

[70] Regarding this story, Flusser writes (in his *Jesus,* p. 59) that it hardly constitutes a real halakhic statement, because unlike the commandments of the Written or Oral Torah, the ritual washing of hands before eating was not a halakhic requirement for all Jews, but "only incumbent upon those particular groups of Jews who had accepted them as an obligation for life." And cf. his extended discussion of the matter in ibid., pp. 59–61.

[71] No one suggests that Jesus intended to render the legal authority of the Torah void, in the way that Paul would do. But cf. Harvie Branscomb (in his essay "Jesus' Attitude to the Law of Moses," *Journal of Biblical Literature* 47:1/2 [1928], pp. 37–38 [entire article: pp. 32–40]; as well as in his book *Jesus and the Law of Moses* [New York: Abingdon-Cokesbury Press, 1931]), as well as the critique of Louis Finkelstein ("The Earliest Christian Attitude toward the Torah," *Jewish Quarterly Review* 21:4 [1931], pp. 469–470), who attempted to create some sort of logical, although highly dubious, progression between Jesus and Paul. The latter's life's work began after Jesus died, and he sought vigorously and categorically to declare the authority of the *halakhah* to be void—at least for non-Jews; Branscomb promulgated the extreme position that Jesus had seen himself as a prophet who was by definition not bound to obey the *halakhah* when he was in a position to receive instructions directly from God that contradicted the accepted *halakhah* of his day. (Interestingly, rabbinic *halakhah* also accepts as valid the premise that a prophet may have the right to alter the accepted *halakhah* of his day, by introducing behavior that contradicts the norm, under the rubric of *hora·at sha·ah,* a "temporary decree." In this regard, see Eliezer Berkovits, *Ha-halakhah, Koḥah V'tafkidah* [Jerusalem: Mossad Harav Kook, 1981], pp. 78–83.) It is unimaginable that Jesus intended to initiate a complete

break with the accepted *halakhah* of his day, because many preserved traditions feature Jesus relating to the laws of the Torah with great respect, as laws that must be obeyed. See, e.g., the words attributed to Jesus that he had come not to void even a single letter in the Torah (Matthew 5:18), and see below, notes 75 and 76. A clear proof for the strict observance of the law of Shabbat by Jesus and his disciples is brought by Michael Wyschogrod, "On the Christian Critique of the Jewish Sabbath," pp. 54–55. For discussions on another tradition of Jesus that ostensibly contravenes Jewish dietary laws (*kashrut*), see the summary of those discussions in Menahem Kister, "Law, Morality, and Rhetoric in Some Sayings of Jesus," in *Studies in Ancient Midrash*, ed. James L. Kugel (Cambridge, MA: Harvard University Center for Jewish Studies, 2001), pp. 145–154.

[72] Harvie Branscombe, "Jesus' Attitude to the Law of Moses," p. 35. For Menaḥem Kister's argument against the similar position of David Daube, see the former's "Plucking of Grain on the Sabbath," p. 354, n. 18.

[73] Peter J. Tomson (in his "Jesus and his Judaism," in *The Cambridge Companion to Jesus* [Cambridge: Cambridge University Press, 2001], p. 32) admits that there are widespread misunderstandings among researchers about Jesus' statements concerning Torah law. Even in academic circles, these discussions are often highly charged with the tension that inheres in the relationship between Judaism and Christianity. Tomson stresses that it is important for some Christian scholars to present Jesus as someone who came to void the obligatory nature of the *halakhah*, in order to tie Jesus to later Pauline tradition that indeed preached freedom from the law (see above, note 71). But he stresses that it is difficult to accept this line of thinking, given passages (such as Matthew 5:17–20) where the *ipsissima verba* of Jesus to the contrary are preserved, apparently going against the church's later teaching that there was no spiritual value to be had in following the Torah's commandments. (The passage he refers to reads as follows: "Do you think that I have come to destroy the law or the prophets: I did not come to destroy them but to bring them to their intended goal. Truly I say to you: as long as heaven and earth last, not the slightest aspect of the law will fail until everything has been accomplished. Whoever, therefore, breaks one of the least of these commandments and teaches others so shall be called the least in the kingdom of heaven. But whoever shall do and teach them, this person shall be called great in the kingdom of heaven. For I tell you that unless your righteousness surpasses that of the scribes and pharisees, you will no way enter the kingdom of heaven." [*Word Biblical Commentary*, vol. 33A; *Matthew 1-13*, ed. Donald A. Hagner (Dallas, TX: World Books, 1993), p. 103].) Another recent example for that can be found in the difficulty of a Christian researcher such as Donald Hagner to accept the conclusion of John Meier's research. Meier unequivocally states: "All questers for the historical Jesus should repeat the following mantra even in their sleep: the historical Jesus is the halakhic

Jesus. This is the positive gain of this chapter that we must never forget" (in his "A Marginal Jew: Rethinking the Historical Jesus," in *Law and Love* [Anchor Yale Bible Reference Library, vol. 4; New Haven: Yale University Press, 2009], p. 297). Donald Hagner, however, forcefully rejects Meier's conclusion, and protects the conception of many Christian researchers in the past, declaring: "The fact remains that the historical method, strictly practiced à la Meier, is ill-equipped to deal with the uniqueness represented by the story of Jesus" ("Jesus and the Synoptic Sabbath Controversies," *Bulletin for Biblical Research* 19:2 [2000], p. 248 [entire article: pp. 215–248]).

In light of the above discussion, it seems that Tomson is justified in agreeing with scholars like David Flusser, that texts like Mark 3:6 and 7:19; Matthew 12:14, and John 5:18 (all of which feature Jesus in halakhic dispute with his opponents, the Pharisees, and then depict the latter as scheming to murder him) cannot be taken at face value (see above, note 57), and were introduced into the Christian narrative by those seeking to stir up anti-Jewish feelings. Nevertheless, Tomson also notes that it is correct to say that there exists a certain tension between the halakhic decisors and adherents to Jewish custom, on the one hand, and the pietists who sought to follow a different path, on the other (p. 33). He offers as proof of that assertion the story of the tension that existed between one such pietist, known to tradition as Ḥoni the Circle-Drawer, and Shimon ben Shetaḥ, who was so frustrated with the former that he is reported to have said, "If you weren't Ḥoni, I would put you under a ban" (M. Taanit 3:8). But the truth is, according to Tomson, that this tension cannot really explain the intense antagonism that is reflected in the New Testament toward the Pharisees; it seems much more likely that these are later additions inserted in the Gospels.

[74] Most scholars today agree that the Gospels were written between the years 70 and 100 CE. The Gospel of Mark is apparently the oldest, probably having been composed around the year 70 CE, and the next oldest is presumed to be Matthew, and then Luke. John was clearly the last to be written. See the summary of Rivka Nir, *Ha-natzrut Ha-k'dumah*, pp. 19–21. David Flusser, however, supported the view that Luke is the earliest Gospel (see ibid., pp. 20–21).

[75] I am thinking specifically of Menaḥem Kister's classic essay, "Between Jesus' Remarks and Midrash" (Hebrew; published in *Meḥk'rei Y'rushalayim B'maḥashevet Yisra·el* 2 [5742 (1982)], pp. 7–17), where Kister takes his place among those scholars who understand Jesus as a Jew of his own day and not as an outsider (as scholars like Branscomb see him). Others in Kister's group, each with his own twist on the basic concept, would be David Flusser, Philip Sigal, Hyam Maccoby, Geza Vermes, and Ed Parish Sanders. For a detailed bibliography of all their relevant works on the topic, see Lutz Doering, "Much

Ado about Nothing?," p. 218, n. 3. Regarding the huge gap between scholars
considering the specific issue of Jesus's attitude towards the *halakhah*, see below,
note 76.

[76] Branscomb stands in here for an entire generation of scholars who thought
about the matter as he did. More recently, the most prominent scholar of the
historical Jesus whose approach is quite similar to Branscomb's, Ernst Käsemann,
has influenced many scholars, especially in his essay on the historical Jesus ("The
Problem of the Historical Jesus," in *Essays on New Testament* [London: SCM
Press, 1964], pp. 15–47). He expresses an opinion almost identical to Branscomb's
with respect to Jesus' relationship to the laws of the Torah: "Jesus felt himself in
a position to override, with an unparalleled and sovereign freedom, the words
of the Torah and the authority of Moses. This sovereign freedom not merely
shakes the very foundations of Judaism and causes its death, but, further, it cuts
the ground from under the feet of the ancient worldview with its antithesis of
sacred and profane" (ibid., p. 40). Regarding this whole school of scholarship,
John S. Kloppenborg writes: "An earlier generation of scholars influenced by
neo-orthodoxy happily pronounced Jesus to have transcended and superseded
'Judaism,' to have 'broken free' of it (as if Jews generally believed themselves to
be enslaved). Such a view, besides being unduly misled by the Pauline polemic
in Galatians, generally assumed an exceedingly narrow, not to say inaccurate,
definition of what constituted 'Judaism.' Ironically, the more recent wave of
Jesus scholarship, which variously concedes important diversities in practice
and belief in Judaism, often holds the historical Jesus to a higher standard of
conformity with a 'common Judaism' than that allowed for other Second Temple
groups and persons" (in his "As One Unknown, Without a Name? Co-opting
the Historical Jesus," in *Apocalypticism, Anti-Semitism, and the Historical Jesus:
Subtexts in Criticism*, eds. John S. Kloppenborg and John W. Marshall [London:
T&T Clark International, 2005], p. 3). Cf. also Kister, "Plucking of Grain on the
Sabbath," p. 360, concerning the Pauline polemic. For a comprehensive survey of
the various approaches that have been suggested regarding Jesus' approach to the
halakhah and his struggle with the Pharisees regarding the laws of Shabbat, see
Doering, "Much Ado About Nothing?," pp. 217–241; and Holger M. Zellentin,
"Jesus and the Tradition of the Elders: Originalism and Traditionalism in Early
Judean Legal Theory," in *Beyond the Gnostic Gospels: Studies Building on the
Work of Elaine H. Pagels*, eds. Eduard Iricinschi, Lance Jenott, Nicola Denzey
Lewis, and Philippa Townsend (Tübingen: Mohr Siebeck, 2013), pp. 379–403.
Also useful in this respect is the survey of Herold Weiss, *A Day of Gladness: The
Sabbath among Jews and Christians in Antiquity* (Columbia, SC: University of
South Carolina Press, 2003), pp. 86–110. Cf. also Ed Parish Sanders's important
introduction to his *Jesus and Judaism* (London: SCM Press, 1985), pp. 1–58.
Also of interest is the unusual and exceptional approach of Morton Smith, who

stressed the texts featuring Jesus as someone involved in magic and sorcery; cf. the summary and evaluation of his work in Sanders, *Jesus and Judaism*, pp. 5–6.
[77] Cf. also Serge Ruzer, *Mapping the New Testament: Early Christian Writings as a Witness for Jewish Biblical Exegesis* (Leiden: Brill, 2007) and Tzvi (Herbert) Beser, "An Echo of an Early Midrash in the New Testament" (Hebrew), in *Divrei Ha-kongress Ha-aḥad-asar L'mada·ei Ha-yahadut* (Jerusalem: World Union of Jewish Studies, 5753 [1993]), part 3, vol. 1, pp. 124–128.
[78] Menaḥem Kister, "Between Jesus' Remarks and Midrash," p. 14, n. 31, and see above, note 74.
[79] For this rebuke see Mark 7: 9–13, and also Menaḥem Kister, "Between Jesus's Remarks and Midrash," p. 14, n. 30. Indeed, we know that a large portion of the sermons that came down to us from the sages (who are, to a large extent, the followers of the Pharisees) are simply justifying existing customs. (These are called *midrash m'kayyeim*; see Vered Noam, "Creative Interpretation and Integrative Interpretation in Qumran," in *The Dead Sea Scrolls and Contemporary Culture: Proceedings of the International Conference Held at the Israel Museum, Jerusalem, July 6–8, 2008*, eds. Adolfo D. Roitman, Lawrence H. Schiffman, and Shani Tzoref [Leiden: Brill, 2011], pp. 363–376; and see in this regard the important point brought below in notes 107 and 110.
Regarding the question of where and from whom Jesus learned his Torah, Tomson writes: "From the teachings attributed to him we know he must have studied with Pharisaic teachers; where and when, we cannot say. We do however, know one of his other teachers: the one whose message of repentance, forgiveness, and baptism he accepted and made his own (Mark 1:4): John the Baptist, whose prophetic reputation is confirmed by Josephus." (See his "Jesus and His Judaism," pp. 27–28.)
[80] This was clearly meant to oppose the stricter sects; see the comments of Shemesh cited below in the following notes.
[81] I will cite here the oldest surviving text, as an example of the other *midrashim* of its kind. The following passage appears in the edition of the Mekhilta D'rabbi Ishmael, *Massekhta D'shabbata, parashah* 1, eds. Ḥayyim Shaul Horovitz and Yisrael Avraham Rabin (1930; rpt. Jerusalem: Wahrman, 1970), pp. 340–341, based on Ms. Oxford 151. The translation is taken from the edition of Jacob Lauterbach published by the Jewish Publication Society in 1933–1935, pp. 493–494:

> Once Rabbi Ishmael, Rabbi Eleazar ben Azariah, and Rabbi Akiva were walking along the road followed by Levi the netmaker and Ishmael the son of Rabbi Eleazar ben Azariah. And the following question was discussed by them: Whence do we know that the duty of saving life supersedes the Sabbath laws? Rabbi Ishmael, answering the question, said: Behold it says: 'If a thief be found breaking in,' etc. (Exodus 22:1). Now of what case does

the law speak? Of a case when there is a doubt whether the burglar came merely to steal or even to kill. Now, by using the method of *kal va-ḥomer*, it is to be reasoned: Even shedding of blood, which defiles the land and causes the Shekhinah to remove, is to supersede the laws of the Sabbath if it is to be done in protection of one's [own] life. How much more should the duty of saving [another's] life supersede the Sabbath laws! Rabbi Eleazar ben Azariah, answering the question, said: If in performing the ceremony of circumcision, which affects only one member of the body, one is to disregard the Sabbath laws, how much more should one do so for the whole body when it is in danger! The sages however said to him: From the instance cited by you it would also follow that just as there the Sabbath is to be disregarded only in a case of certainty, so also here the Sabbath is to be disregarded only in a case of certainty. Rabbi Akiva says: If punishment for murder sets aside even the Temple service, which in turn supersedes the Sabbath, how much more should the duty of saving life supersede the Sabbath laws! Rabbi Yosei the Galilean says: When it says: 'But My sabbath ye shall keep,' the word 'but' (*akh*) implies a distinction. There are Sabbaths on which you must rest and there are Sabbaths on which you should not rest. Rabbi Simon ben Menasiah says: Behold it says: 'And ye shall keep the Sabbath for it is holy unto you' (Exodus 31:14). This means: The Sabbath is given to you— but you are not surrendered to the Sabbath. Rabbi Nathan says: Behold it says: 'Wherefore the children of Israel shall keep the Sabbath to observe the Sabbath throughout their generations' (v. 16). This implies that we should disregard one Sabbath for the sake of saving the life of a person so that that person may be able to observe many Sabbaths.

Regarding the various questions that arise from reading this sermon, see above, note 47. Note that Jesus' reason for his lenient approach to Shabbat law (i.e., that the Sabbath was given to humankind and not vice versa) is identical to the rationale offered in the above passage by Rabbi Shimon ben Menasia (who lived in the second half of the second century CE) to justify his opinion that saving a human life could supersede the laws that of Sabbatlh rest: "'And ye shall keep the Sabbath for it is holy unto you' (Exodus 31:14)—This means: The Sabbath is given to you but you are not surrendered [given] to the Sabbath (*lakhem shabbat m'surah v'i atem m'surin la-shabbat*, trans. Lauterbach, p. 494). This is a very interesting parallel, already noted by many others (e.g., Michael Wyschograd, "On the Christian Critique of the Jewish Sabbath," p. 46, or Aharon Shemesh, "The History of the Halakhic Concept *Pikuaḥ Nefesh Doḥeh Shabbat*," p. 497; note, however, that the tradition preserved at B. Yoma 85a attributes a different sermon to Simon ben Menasiah). However, the difference between the sages' approach to *halakhah* and the approach attributed to Jesus should be noted. For the sages, this only impacts on the theological rationale, and thus the argument only matters for an observant Jewish soul when human life is in danger—but not simply to eliminate suffering. (That seems to be the meaning of Rabbi Shimon ben Menasia's comment in the Mekhilta passage, and that is also how this *d'rashah* was understood in the Talmud at B. Yoma 85a.) Thus, we may conclude that Jesus simply believed that the Sabbath laws could be set aside to relieve human pain or suffering. Below, I shall attempt to explain Jesus' position as merely one rooted in the societal/humanitarian rationale for Shabbat observance, as opposed to the purely theological one.

[82] Shemesh (in his "The History of the Halakhic Concept *Piku·aḥ Nefesh Doḥeh Shabbat*," p. 501) describes how the Pharisees (and, later, the rabbinic sages) abandoned the earlier, more uncompromising *halakhah* that forbade engaging in acts of warfare on Shabbat, as part of a general trend toward a new halakhic approach to Shabbat observance and as "a development that symbolized the development of the *halakhah* in a humanitarian direction." This assessment makes it is possible to understand how the same humanitarian impetus that brought the ancient rabbis to permit deviation from the strict letter of the law when human life was in danger on Shabbat also allowed Jesus to develop the law in the same direction, taking the underlying concept even further in an effort to make the *halakhah* conform to humanitarian principles—a direction he found supported in the exegesis of Scripture in the societal/humanitarian mode.

[83] Menaḥem Kister, "Between Jesus' Remarks and Midrash."

[84] The title "head of the synagogue" was *archisynagogus* in Greek. Regarding this position in the old synagogue, see Tessa Rajak and David Noy, "Archisynagogoi: Office, Title and Social Status in the Greco-Jewish Synagogue," *Journal of Religion* 83 (1993), pp. 75–93. (Regarding the *archisynagogus* in the story discussed here from the Gospel of Luke, see their comments on p. 79.) From the comments of Yeshayahu (Isaiah) Gafni, *Y'hudei Bavel Bi-t'kufat Ha-talmud: Ḥayyei Ha-ḥevrah V'ha-ru·aḥ* (Jerusalem: Merkaz Zalman Shazar, 1990), pp. 112–113, we can see that the role of the *archisynagogus* in the Jewish communities of the Land of Israel and in the diasporan communities of the Hellenistic-Roman world were largely identical to the position of the *rosh ha-k'hillah* ("the head of the community") among the Jews of Sassanian Persia. In this regard, cf. also the comments of Shmuel Safrai, *B'shilhei Ha-bayit Ha-sheini U-vi-t'kufat Ha-talmud: P'rakim B'toldot Ha-ḥevrah V'ha-tarbut* (Jerusalem: Merkaz Zalman Shazar, 5743 [1982/1983]), p. 157.

[85] Kister (in his "Between Jesus' Remarks and Midrash," p. 9, n. 9) reasonably emphasizes that "there is perhaps a specific reason for the text to stress that the woman in the story is a 'daughter of Abraham'"—to wit, that she was neither a beast of burden nor a Gentile woman, but a daughter of Israel. For us this point is crucial, as it shows clearly the difference between the approach of Jesus and the rabbinic midrash. The latter relied solely on the theological rationale

for Shabbat observance. Thus for the rabbis, in complete opposition to Jesus, the prohibition applied first and foremost to a Jewish woman (i.e., to Jews in general), while they excluded from the prohibition the non-Jew and the beast of burden. Cf. below, the material referenced in notes 100–101 and 105.

[86] The problem that has elicited so much discussion (see above, note 66; and see also Menaḥem Kister, "Plucking of Grain on the Sabbath," pp. 355–356, n. 20; Christopher M. Tuckett, *Reading the New Testament: Methods of Interpretation* [Philadelphia: Fortress, 1987], pp. 90–93 and pp. 112–114)—namely, how can it have been licit, according to Jesus, to bring a beast out of a pit into which it has fallen on Shabbat (see Mark 2:25–28)—can now tentatively be considered solved in light of Jesus' reconstructed sermon, in which he clearly understood an obligation to relieve the misery of any suffering animal on Shabbat as an outgrowth of his acceptance of the societal/humanitarian argument for Sabbath observance. Regarding the question of how the Pharisees can apparently have agreed with such a ruling (cf. Matthew 12:10–14), the sole reasonable answer, in my opinion, is that the author of Matthew was simply jumping to conclusions and assuming that the Pharisees agreed with Jesus when, in reality, it was Jesus alone who held the opinion attributed to him above. In light of this, there is no need for the complicated sort of explanation offered by Aharon Shemesh in his "The History of the Halakhic Concept *Piku·aḥ Nefesh Doḥeh Shabbat*," pp. 499–501.

[87] I can only respond here briefly to this question, which has elicited so much debate in scholarly circles. Some historians see direct continuity between the Pharisees and the *tanna·im*, and there are those who separate the Pharisees from the *tanna·im* and do not see simple continuity between them. See the sources summarized in Sharbat, *T'fisat Ha-miniyut*, p. 98, n. 170; and also those brought by Vered Noam in her "Did the Rabbis Know Josephus' Works?" (Hebrew), *Tarbiz* 81 (5773 [2012]), p 394, n. 117; Galit Hasan-Rokem, "Were the Sages Aware of the Concept of Folklore?," in *Higayon L'yonah: Hebbeitim Ḥadashim B'ḥeiker Sifrut Ha-midrash, Ha-aggadah, V'ha-piyyut*, eds. Joshua Levinson, Jacob Elbaum, and Galit Hasan-Rokem (Jerusalem: Magnes Press, 5767 [2006]), pp. 212–213 (and particularly the position of Hyam Maccoby cited there, which identifies the close relationship between Jesus and the Pharisees); and Annette Yoshiko Reed, "When Did Rabbis become Pharisees? Reflections on Christian Evidence for Post-70 Judaism" in *Envisioning Judaism: Essays in Honor of Peter Schäfer on the Occasion of His Seventieth Birthday*, eds. R. S. Boustan, K. Herrmann, R. Leicht, A. Y. Reed, and G. Veltri (Tübingen: Mohr Siebeck, 2013), vol. 2, pp. 859–896. See also above, note 57.

[88] Mekhilta D'rabbi Ishmael to *Parashat Mishpatim* (*Massekhta D'khaspa*), commenting on Exodus 23:12 (ed. Horovitz-Rabin, p. 331).

[89] Mekhilta, ed. Lauterbach, p. 479.

[90] It is not surprising, then, that Karaite sages did, in fact, understand there to be a biblical injunction obliging owners to prevent their animals from plucking grass in the field on Shabbat. See, for example, Yehudah Hadassi, *Eshkol Ha-kofer* (Güzliev, Crimea: Tirishken Print, 1836), §149, pp. 56a–56b; Baruch Ehrlich, *Laws of Sabbath in Yehudah Hadassi's Eshkol Ha-Kofer* (New York: Yeshiva University dissertation, 1974), p. 250, and also pp. 55–56.

[91] Furthermore, I would suggest considering a different sort of midrash, which might have been addressing the issue of healing on Shabbat: namely, the one Jesus himself might preached to cast his own acts of healing on Shabbat in a less harsh light by stressing that he used no medicaments and so could qualify all his healing as spiritual in nature, and intended solely to relieve the misery of people suffering from various diseases or conditions (because although the illnesses and conditions were obviously physical in nature, they actually originated within the psyches of the sufferers). If we understand the *nun-vav-het* root that appears in parallel passages in Isaiah 14:3 (*b'yom hani·ah YHVH l'kha mei-otzb'kha u-mei-rog'zekha*) and 28:12 (*zot ha-m'nuhah hanihu la-ya·eif*) as essentially denoting healing and the abatement of (psychic) suffering, then it should be possible to imagine something like the midrash that Jesus could have had in mind as he connected the concept of Sabbath rest (cf. Exodus 23:12, *l'ma·an yanu·ah*, "so that rest...") with the concept of relieving the suffering of their misery. Cf. above, note 61. And cf. also Horst D. Preuss, "נו״ח," in *The Theological Dictionary of the Old Testament*, eds. G. Johannes Botterweck, Helmer Ringgren, and Heinz-Josef Fabry, trans. David Green (Grand Rapids, MI: Eerdman Publishing, 1998), pp. 278, who writes that in Scripture there are seven instances in which the root *nun-vav-het* generates words with this meaning. Cf. also Roy Gane, "Sabbath and the New Covenant," p. 312, n. 1.

[92] And cf. the hesitation regarding Kister's remarks in his "Plucking of Grain on the Sabbath," p. 359, n. 27. My argument here strengthens the already decisive argument of Dan M. Cohn-Sherbok in his "An Analysis of Jesus' Arguments Concerning the Plucking of Grain on the Sabbath," *Journal for the Study of the New Testament* 2 (1979), pp. 31–41. Also, Wyschogrod's explanation of Jesus' opinion regarding Shabbat (in his "On the Christian Critique of the Jewish Sabbath") provides support to the direction in which I am trying to explain Jesus' midrash of the Torah in this essay. (In general, Wyschogrod's points in his essay strengthen many different points that I am making in the current essay.)

[93] It is possible that a fragment, or perhaps just a hint, has survived of an ancient source that sees the prohibition of work on Shabbat as identical to the parallel prohibition that applies on festival days, but the idea appears somehow to have been transferred to the *geir toshav*, the resident alien. That is what we find in the Mekhilta D'rabbi Ishmael to Exodus 23:12 (ed. Horovitz-Rabin, p. 330), where the biblical verse ("and the son of thy handmaid and the stranger may

be refreshed") is interpreted to mean that the alien in question is defined as a *geir toshav*, for whom Shabbat rules are the same as those that pertain to Jews on festivals. (Regarding this text, cf. B. Keritot 9a.) For a detailed exposition of the halakhic situation of the *geir toshav*, see B. Avodah Zarah 64b, where Rabbi Meir rules that a gentile who wishes to live in the Land of Israel (only the *geir toshav* is allowed to live in the Land of Israel) must not perform idolatry and, moreover, must take upon himself all of the seven Noahide commandments. Another opinion offered there submits that the gentile must accept all the commandments of the Torah, apart from eating *n'veilah* (meat of an animal that was not slaughtered according to the *halakhah*).

This possible similarity of Shabbat and festival laws recalls the suggestion of the biblical scholar Graf Reventlow (cited by Brevard S. Childs in his Westminster Press volume on Exodus [see above, note 64], pp. 414–415), who stressed the remarkable similarity between the phrasing of the laws that pertain on Shabbat as found in Exodus 20:7–10 and those that pertain specifically to those festivals that have a period of separation between their opening and closing days (i.e., which contain a *ḥol ha-mo·eid.*) According to Reventlow, the Sabbath entered the biblical world because of the error of a scribal transmission that somehow created a weekly "festival." This suggestion seems extremely implausible and difficult to take seriously, as Childs himself noted. (Childs himself, on p. 415 of his Exodus volume, writes that the Sabbath had an ancient forgotten precedent, in light of which he explains the multitude of so many different attempts to "explain" the institution of the Sabbath in Scripture.) However, Childs does agree that Reventlow's jumping-off point—that the parallels between how the Sabbath law is formulated and how certain festivals laws are formulated—is indeed surprising. And so, even if we reject Reventlow's thesis with respect to the history of the biblical text, we can still admit that it is conceivable to consider, in light of the issue of parallel terminology he raises, the possibility of having been some sort of early exegetical effort, now long lost, that did indeed tie the laws of the festivals to the laws that of Sabbath rest, attempting to make them each other's equal.

[94] As far as I know, there is no evidence in rabbinic literature of any sentiment akin to the simple understanding of the matter that may well have been Jesus'. I have, however, located a single commentator who acknowledged how the societal/humanitarian rationale for Sabbath observance derives directly from Exodus 23:12, and who claims that the Torah demands that the Sabbath bring pleasure to animals and not be a cause of any pain or suffering to them—even if he did not extrapolate the same lesson to human beings. See Moshe Lieb Shaḥor, *Avnei Shoham La-torah: Bei·urim U-feirushim, Hei·arot V'ḥiddushim* (Jerusalem: Defus Akiva Yosef, 5728 [1967/1968]), p. 148, who comments on the Mekhilta passage: "We can learn from here that within the verse 'so that

your ox and ass too shall rest' (Exodus 23:12) is also included the obligation not to cause animals any inconvenience at all [on Shabbat, as it is a day of rest and pleasure for them]; it is for that reason permitted to allow an ox or an ass to graze in a grassy field and not to pen them up in barns, which confinement would bring them not pleasure, but pain."

Nevertheless, we normally find, in rabbinic commentaries to that verse (and to the midrash cited from the Mekhilta), discussions rooted in the theological argument, of which I shall cite one single example. Yeḥiel Mikhel Stern (b. 1949), *Ḥamishah Ḥumshei Torah Im Midrash Halakhah: Midr'shei Ḥazal B'inyanei Halakhah* (ed. Jerusalem, 5760 [1999/2000]), vol. 2 (Exodus), p. 429, ties himself up in knots trying to answer the question of how our sages cited in the Mekhilta could possibly have permitted an ass to pluck grass from the ground on Shabbat. If we try to avoid the question by noting that the owner has simply allowed his ass to wander about in a field, and it is the animal itself who plucks the grass from the soil, then we must acknowledge that the *halakhah* does not even allow actions that, although permitted in and of themselves, will inexorably lead to the commission of forbidden acts on Shabbat. (In halakhic literature, this kind of action is known as a *p'sik reisha*, literally "cut off his head," which is shorthand for "if you cut off its head, will the chicken not die?" The idea is that you can't cut off a chicken's head, then claim that it died on its own because *all* you did was remove its head.) However, it is possible to skip the byzantine reasoning in his response to the Mekhilta, because the question itself proves my point: rabbinic exegesis entirely abandoned the simple meaning of the verse from which the entire societal/humanitarian argument about Shabbat derives.

[95] Cf. Philo, On the Special Laws II §60–69, in *Philo with an English Translation*, vol. 7, trans. Francis Henry Colson (London: Loeb Classical Library, 1937), pp. 345–351. See also Jutta Leonhardt, *Jewish Worship in Philo of Alexandria* (Tübingen: Mohr Siebeck, 2001), pp. 64–74.

[96] See David Nakman, *Ha-halakhah B'kitvei Yosef ben Matityahu*, pp. 256–257. Ed Parish Sanders, writing in his *Judaism: Practice and Belief: 63 BCE–66 CE* (London: SCM Press, 1992), pp. 197–200 and 210–211, concludes that keeping the Sabbath laws and gathering in synagogue on Shabbat were two of the practices shared by all Jewish groups at the end of the Second Temple period (and later on, as well). But even he stresses that there was no general agreement in ancient times about what specific kinds of labor were forbidden on Shabbat. Indeed, the only kind of labor that was universally understood to be interdicted was overt strenuous labor, like harvesting or plowing or creative labor of any sort—the kinds of things that derive from the straightforward exegesis of scriptural verses. Moreover, in none of the ancient sources cited above is there any distinction between the terms *avodah* and *m'lakhah*, both of which are

ancient Hebrew terms for work, but the distinction between the two eventually became crucial to the *halakhah* with respect to Shabbat, as in later rabbinic literature where *m'lakhah* is taken specifically to denote labors forbidden by the Torah as opposed to the concepts of "business" or "work" taken in a far broader sense. Regarding the later attempt to justify this distinction linguistically, see my *Ovadin D'hol*, p. 165, and also Ulrike Kleinecke, *The Meaning of the Term "Melakha" in the Biblical and Talmudic Literature and Its Implications to the Shaping of the Halakha* (Potsdam University: M.A.Thesis, 2010).

[97] According to Yitzḥak Dov Gilat, *P'rakim*, pp. 32–62, the crystallization of the thirty-nine forbidden labors on Shabbat was the result of several stages of development. First, in Second Temple times, the Shabbat laws became strict to the point that the authorities forbade any work that could possibly fall under the general scriptural rubric of "you shall do no manner of work" (Exodus 20:9), but without formally distinguishing between various categories of forbidden labor. In the wake of the dispute between Rabbi Akiva and Rabbi Eliezer (as recorded at M. Keritot 3:10), the concept of certain specific activities being grouped together as subcategories of the same "labor" began to develop. (The text in Keritot reads as follows: "Rabbi Akiva said, 'I once asked Rabbi Eliezer about the law concerning an individual who does many labors on Shabbat, all of which are considered derivative of the same larger rubric of forbidden activity. Is such an individual obligated to offer up one sin offering to atone for all of those actions, or does such a person have to bring a separate offering for each?'") But the final determination of the law is found elsewhere in the Mishnah, in a view attributed to Rabbi Akiva in M. Shabbat 7:1, where we read that "the individual who does many forbidden labors on Shabbat that are all considered derivative of the same larger rubric of forbidden work is obligated only to bring one sin offering." A third stage of development ensued when teachings were developed that formally categorized all plausible activities into specific groups, such as the one mentioned at T. Shabbat 9 (10):17–18: "One who digs, plows, and prepares a furrow—these are all subsets of the same larger rubric of forbidden work. Similarly, one who tramples grain, crushes, or beats [flax or some other substance]—these too are all subsets of the same larger rubric of forbidden work. And [similarly so] are considered the acts of plucking, picking grapes from the vine, harvesting, plucking olives from the tree, picking dates from the tree, picking figs from the tree—these too are all considered subsets of the same larger forbidden labor." Here, then, we find examples of groups of labors that are subsumed under the same larger rubric, as part of the larger effort to define the concept of labor groups with respect to the obligation of inadvertent sinners to offer up a single sin offering for any number of related (but also distinct) offenses. At a subsequent stage of development, specific labors were selected from these groups, to serve as their representative labors—thus as

a kind of archetype for each group—which came to be called the *avot m'lakhah*, as listed at M. Shabbat 7:2. The list of labors there is organized according to earlier attempts that were themselves widely known in that period and which had been developed through the simple act of considering the daily work of regular people: baking bread, preparing garments to wear, cooking food, etc. At this stage, there was no specific list of labors that was accepted by all; indeed, many sages probably created their own lists, so that it was only later on that the term *toladah* came into use to denote the derivative labors that were understood to constitute the subset of labors subsumed under the larger rubric of each *av m'lakhah*. In earlier texts, there is no distinction between *avot* and *tol'dot*. See my *Ovadin D'hol*, pp. 107–108.

[98] There is no need for the later christological explanation favored by those exegetes who attempted to find deep messianic meaning in the epithet "son of man." (See, e.g., Timothy J. Geddert, ed., *Mark*, in the Believers Church Bible commentary [Scottsdale, PA: Herald Press, 2001], p. 71.) Both David Flusser (in his *Jesus*, pp. 61–62, nn. 11 and 126) and Menaḥem Kister (in his "Plucking of Grain on the Sabbath," pp. 354–355) believe that there is no specific messianic meaning here and that the text is simply translating into Greek the Aramaic expression *bar enash*, which is regularly used simply to mean "human being." (Kister notes, however, that the parallel passages in Matthew and Luke have already misused the term by investing it with messianic meaning.) Cf. also Shemesh, "The History of the Halakhic Concept *Piku·aḥ Nefesh Doḥeh Shabbat*," p. 497, n. 62.

[99] This is not true with respect to aggadic passages (but those have no practical halakhic implications at all); cf. above, note 65.

[100] Although this is a basic principle, it is also true that the *halakhah* concerning slaves became very complex as it was developed during the talmudic and medieval periods, and it eventually became distinct from the law concerning animals. This was primarily because the *halakhah* eventually came to understand the gentile slave to be someone who has abandoned gentile ways but who has not yet become fully Jewish. In other words, the gentile slave was not considered in the same halakhic category as other non-Jews and was deemed responsible for observing at least some of the commandments as though he or she were Jewish. The conversion procedure for such a gentile slave was distinct as well: there was the need for "partial conversion" for one who was liable only to perform "part of the commandments" (see Rambam in his M.T. Hilkhot Issurei Bi·ah 13:1, and cf. Hilkhot Avadim 5:5). In this regard, see also the explanation of Menaḥem Finkelstein in his *Ha-giyyur: Halakhah U-ma·aseh* (Ramat Gan: Bar Ilan University, 2003), pp. 69–90, esp. pp. 69–70. As a result, the situation became very complicated and the case of the gentile slave can no longer be explained merely as connected only to the societal/humanitarian rational, like

the beast. It thus becomes clear why the *halakhah* eventually determined that "the male and female slave, being endowed with intelligence [as opposed to beasts of burden], have placed upon them the same Shabbat prohibitions [that apply to Jewish people], and thus their masters are commanded to oversee their activities to guarantee that no [forbidden] labors are performed [by them on Shabbat]" (Yeḥiel Mikhel Epstein, *Arukh Ha-shulḥan, Oraḥ Ḥayyim, Part 2*, Hilkhot Shabbat 346:17).

It is also important to note the dramatic changes in how Shabbat laws are worded. In early biblical texts rooted in the societal/humanitarian tradition, the law requires that owners of slaves grant their male and female slaves the weekly opportunity to rest and be refreshed. This command is phrased very differently in those later halakhic texts rooted in the theological rationale for Shabbat observance, which require the masters to ensure that their slaves do not perform any of the thirty-nine forbidden labors (or any of their derivatives). Furthermore, the text by Yeḥiel Mikhel Epstein cited above does not even include the word "rest," in order to clarify that this is something the master must provide. An interesting halakhic question related to the issue we are considering concerns the master who overburdens his slaves with a surfeit of commands that, while requiring no specific violation of any Shabbat laws, is nonetheless keeping them busy with work throughout Shabbat. This would be something the *halakhah* could reasonably countenance, and it is discussed by Judah Halevi in his *Kuzari*, whose discussion reveals that this was something that happened to slaves in his time. See below, the material referenced in note 120, and see more broadly my own *Ovadin D'ḥol*, pp. 137–139, n. 127.

It is reasonable to imagine that just as Jesus understood the laws of Shabbat that applied to the rest due to beasts of burden, he also understood the legal principles that applied to slaves on Shabbat—namely: those rooted in the societal/humanitarian rationale for Shabbat observance. We can thus surmise, in the absence of compelling arguments to the contrary, that Jesus would have taught that masters must allow their slaves to rest on Shabbat—and this applies even to gentile slaves, who must be allowed to relax however they wish (just as they may spend their time as they wish whenever they are off-duty); the master is not responsible to ensure that his slaves do not violate any of the laws that govern Sabbath rest (or at least on his own property—although it is likely that in Jewish public spaces gentile slaves would not be completely free to behave as they wished). This accords with what we find in Philo: "He [Moses] not only requires free men to abstain from work on the Sabbath, but gives the same permission to menservants and handmaids, and sends them a message of security and almost of freedom after every six days, to teach both masters and men an admirable lesson. The masters must be accustomed to work themselves without waiting for the offices and attentions of their menials, and so…they may not through unfamiliarity with personal service lose heart at the outset and despair of accomplishing the tasks set before them, but use the different parts of their body with more nimbleness and shew a robust and easy activity; while on the other hand the servants are not to refuse to entertain still higher hopes, but should find in the relaxation allowed after six days an ember or spark of freedom, and look forward to their complete liberation if they continue to serve well and loyally" (*Philo with an English Translation*, vol. 7, trans. F. H. Colson The Special Laws, II, §§66–67, pp. 349–351).

Note also that the halakhic decisors of the Middle Ages went even further in this regard. In the eleventh century, for example, Rashi (unlike Maimonides) explained that the talmudic passage found at B. Sanhedrin 58b (s.v. *amar ravina*) claims that not only is it forbidden for a gentile to observe all the Shabbat laws restricting labor, but also that it is forbidden for a gentile to fix a specific day of the week as a day of rest. Such an individual is thus obliged to work all seven days of the week with no respite at all! Cf. in this regard the comments of Yaakov Blidstein in his "On the Legitimacy of Gentile Worship in Maimonides and the Meiri" (Hebrew), *Daat* 61 (2007), pp. 41–47. Regarding the correct interpretation of this talmudic passage, see the comments of Reuven Margaliyot to B. Sanhedrin 58b, in his *Margoliot Ha-yam* to Tractate Sanhedrin (Jerusalem: Mossad Harav Kook, 1977), vol. 2, §28. Note too that in the Roman Empire, at least, it was customary to give slaves days off, whether they were urban slaves or rural slaves; see Keith. R. Bradley and Paul Cartledge, *The Cambridge World History of Slavery*, Volume 1, The Ancient Mediterranean World (Cambridge: Cambridge University Press, 2011), p. 340 and n. 12. It should be further noted that regarding a slave who is not a Torah-observant Jew (that is to say, a gentile slave who has undergone neither circumcision nor immersion in a *mikveh*), some would permit even the most blatant acts of public labor on Shabbat to whatever extent the slave wishes (and without restraint or boundary), while others would permit such an individual solely the specific kinds of labor that would be permitted to a Jewish person on the intermediate days of *ḥol ha-mo·eid*. And there are also those who would rule, even more narrowly, that such an individual is permitted only labor necessary to prepare one's meals, just as is permitted to a Jewish person on the festival days themselves (i.e., *yom tov*). See the discussion on this question in B. Keritot 9a.

[101] Given that the societal/humanitarian rationale for Sabbath observance seems entirely absent from classical rabbinic discourse about Shabbat (as the sages focused their exegetical prowess almost exclusively on developing the theological rationale), the question of riding animals on Shabbat eventually took on an absurd air. According to the societal/humanitarian rationale, the *halakhah* should clearly forbid such activity using in strict language—whereas actual rabbinic *halakhah* is entirely confused about this matter. For example,

the sages whose opinions are recorded in the Babylonian Talmud (although not in the Yerushalmi) do not think that riding an animal on Shabbat is forbidden in the Bible—and so they conclude that such riding is actually permitted by Torah law, and it was only the sages themselves who forbade it based on the fear that such riding will lead to the performance of forbidden *m'lakhah* on Shabbat. Their specific worry was that someone riding a horse might be pluck a branch from a tree to use to swat the horse's flanks and make it move along more quickly. See above, note 19, and, in more detail, my *Ovadin D'ḥol*, p. 124–125, n. 42. Cf. also R. Yeruḥam Fischel Perla's commentary to Saadia Gaon's *Sefer Ha-mitzvot* (Jerusalem: Keset, 5733 [1972/1973]), vol. 1, pp. 392 ff.), where he presents a complicated discussion about how rabbinic tradition understands the relationship between the prohibition of "using the work" of an animal on Shabbat and the commandment ordaining rest for one's animals on the Sabbath day.

[102] See above, the material referenced in note 5.

[103] See B. Beitzah 16a, as well as Ulrike Kleinecke's discussion of that source in her *The Meaning of the Term "Melakha."* A similar view was held by various sectarians in ancient times; cf. Cana Werman and Aharon Shemesh, *L'gallot Nistarot*, pp. 39–40.

[104] For a definition of the term "gentile" in this context and in talmudic literature generally, see Reuven Margaliyot's *Margaliyot Ha-yam* commentary to B. Sanhedrin 58b, §§26 and 27, pp. 27–28.

[105] B. Sanhedrin 58b. I must admit that the situation is not as simple as all that. We would wish at this point to cite some rabbinic sources that counter this notion with the argument that the societal/humanitarian rationale for Shabbat observance was meant to apply to all humanity and, for that reason, anyone who owns slaves and beasts of burden is obliged by Torah law to grant them all a weekly day of rest and restoration—whereas those focused solely on the theological rationale would restrict the obligation to allow slaves and animals to rest to Jewish people. Along this line of thinking, one must admit that the idea of capital punishment for any gentile who keeps the Shabbat is quite unexpected. However, I have been unable to find any tannaitic sources that support the idea that keeping Shabbat should be a capital offense for gentiles; even the Yerushalmi does not echo that extremist point of view. All I can find in tannaitic sources in this regard is an emphasis on the intimacy between Israel and God, for which Shabbat provides a weekly forum. See, e.g., the sermon delivered by Rabbi Shimon bar Yoḥai preserved in Bereshit Rabbah 11:8 (ed. cit., pp. 95–96), which speaks intimately about Israel and Shabbat as husband and wife. (A different sermon, suspected to be a later one although attributed as well to Rabbi Shimon bar Yoḥai, is presented at B. Beitzah 16a, where Shabbat is depicted as a gift offered privately to Israel, specifically so that the gentile world will know

nothing of this secret gift that links Israel and God.) Taken all together, then, the tradition that a gentile who observes Shabbat deserves execution appears to be a late Babylonian tradition that has merely been presented in the name of Rabbi Yoḥanan, the Palestinian *amora*. (It certainly feels suspicious that such a remarkable statement specifically does not appear in the Yerushalmi!) Indeed, the sole parallel I could find, which itself appears to have been influenced by the text in the Babylonian Talmud, is the text preserved in Devarim Rabbah 1:21, where the lesson is attributed to Rabbi Yosei ben Ḥanina. (On the late date of Devarim Rabbah, see Reuven Kiperwasser's "Midrash Ha-gadol, the Exempla of the Rabbis (Sefer *Ma·asiyot*), and Midrashic Works on Ecclesiastes: A Comparative Approach" (Hebrew), *Tarbiz* 75 (5766 [2006]), p. 421, n. 50, and the sources mentioned there.) At any rate, it seems to me that this tradition is the result of a late, extremist tendency to guard the Sabbath as something solely Jewish in which gentiles may have no part even if they were to wish to have one. Cf. this conclusion to the one Kleinecke puts forward in her M.A. thesis referenced above in note 96.

[106] Please note the specific way I have framed this question. In my opinion, the question is not how Jesus could have dared to widen the scope of the *halakhah* (as Menaḥem Kister argues in his "Plucking of Grain on the Sabbath," p. 352), because he was merely preaching the *halakhah* from his own vantage point (that is, to use Kister's terminology: as an independent preacher). The better question therefore would be to ask why the Pharisees, and the sages of classical times after them, *did not* develop the relevant texts in Scripture in that midrashic direction.

[107] See the material above referenced in note 79. Regarding this freedom to argue against accepted popular customs characteristic of sectarians, see Cana Werman and Aharon Shemesh, *L'gallot Nistarot*, p. 126, regarding the Qumran sectarians: "Their dedication and faithfulness to biblical law were destined to bring the sectarians to the point not solely of developing *halakhah* consonant with their understanding of the biblical text, but also to deny in the most stringent terms all the traditions that had developed among the people that were not anchored in biblical legal texts. It was in this light that the author of the Damascus Covenant [at 16:1–2] asks of any who would join his community to take an oath 'to return to the Torah of Moses in which all [correct] behavior is spelled out.'"

[108] Regarding the expression "meta-*halakhah*" and how it is understood today by philosophers of *halakhah*, see Avinoam Rosenak's "Meta-*Halakhah*, the Philosophy of *Halakah*, and Yosef Schwab" (Hebrew), in *Halakhah, Meta-halakhah, V'filosofiyah: Iyyun Rav-t'ḥumi*, ed. Avinoam Rosenak (Jerusalem: Magnes, 2011), pp. 17–34. The term itself was originally coined by Eliezer Goldman, as noted by Rosenak, "Meta-*Halakhah*," p. 20.

[109] Cf. Serge Ruzer, "The Double Love Precept in the New Testament and the Rule of the Congregation" (Hebrew), *Tarbiz* 71 (5762 [2002]), pp. 353–354.

[110] Regarding the dramatic distinction between the relative freedom that the sectarians allowed themselves in the exegesis of the Torah according to their own overarching principles and the restrictedness that the sages of classical times felt with respect to their own Torah exegesis, see Werman and Shemesh, *L'gallot Nistarot*, p. 11, regarding the sectarians of the Judean desert. But the same applies in my opinion to the ways of the midrash of Jesus: " I intend [writes co-author Werman] to claim that the difference between priestly *halakhah* and the *halakhah* of the sages flows…from the different way both groups related to the biblical text. *The decisive factor in the priestly enterprise flows directly from their interiorization of the foundational values that the law in Leviticus set before them.* At the basis, then, was the concept that slaughter was fundamentally akin to murder and that the blood of the [slaughtered] ox, sheep, or [other] animal, therefore, has the capacity to render the earth impure just as does the blood of human beings. This basic belief is not dependent on geographic location or on historical era, but does need to be taken into account as the Israelites prepare to transfer from [a nomadic life in] the desert to the land [of Israel], even if this transition does create a new reality that cannot fully accommodate the ideal. *On the other hand, the sages did not seek [to ground their work] in the worldview of biblical law and so made no attempt to formulate the laws [they promulgated] in conjunction [with the text of Scripture]…*" (emphasis added). See also ibid., p. 123, where Werman writes that in contrast to the midrash of the Judean Desert sect, the tannaitic midrash (the one that she compared to the Qumran text) is in truth "not loyal to the Bible itself."

I can note further that even many years after the close of the Second Temple period, we remain unsurprised by the degree to which Orthodox rabbis remain unaffected by such considerations, and that even contemporary talk about the concept of meta-*halakhah* is capable of arousing truly vehemently negative responses from those authorities. Regarding this, cf. Rosenak, "Meta-*halakhah*," pp. 17–34.

[111] Cf. Mark 12:28–31, Luke 10:25–28, and Matthew 22:34–40. See also Flusser, *Yahadut Bayit Sheini: Hakhameha V'sifrutah* (Jerusalem: Magnes, 2002), pp. 161–182, who discusses the similarities between some rabbinic statements (alongside even earlier sources) and Jesus' remarks in this regard.

[112] Albeit in an odd way, our rabbinic sources emphasize solely the idea of the love of humankind, as in the well-known principle that appears as early as the Sifra (*K'doshim, parashah* 2, ed. Weiss [Vienna, 5622 [1861/1862], p. 89a), where we read regarding Leviticus 19:18: "Rabbi Akiva says this is a foundational principle [*k'lal gadol*] of the Torah." David Flusser (in his *Yahadut Bayit Sheini*, p. 170) believes it is mere happenstance that fragments of *midrashim* taking

two different approaches to the meaning of the verse from Leviticus 19 haven't come down to us. Indeed, the only source in which this is stated unequivocally in Jewish sources that have survived to our day is a medieval midrash entitled *"Pitron Torah."* Cf. *Sefer Pitron Torah: Yalkut Midrashim U-feirushim*, ed. Efraim Elimelekh Urbach (Jerusalem: Magnes, 1978), pp. 79–80 and cf. also Flusser on this passage in his *Yahadut Bayit Sheini*, p. 178.

The citation from Avot is from the sixth chapter, which is not part of the original tractate but rather a collection of *b'raitot* that were added to Avot after its original editing. See *Massekhet Avot L'doroteha: Mahadorah Mada·it*, ed. Shimon Sharvit (Jerusalem: Mossad Bialik, 2004), pp. 214–236 and pp. 276–277.

[113] Flusser, in his *Yahadut Bayit Sheini*, pp. 161–182, presents the similarities between rabbinic dicta (and also even earlier sources in the Apocrypha and Pseudepigrapha) and the relevant dicta of Jesus in great detail; cf. also Ruzer, "The Double Love Precept," particularly the sources he analyzes on p. 253, n. 2.

[114] To be more precise, Flusser (in his *Yahadut Bayit Sheini*, p. 172) notes that Jesus demanded that his disciples be even stricter than the Pharisees in matters relating to the *halakhah*, but the specific issues in play are all related to ethical behavior. Flusser sees this an example of Jesus' own supererogatory piety, whereas it seems to me not a matter of piety at all but rather a question of a general approach to *halakhah*, whose demands led him to conclude that these specific commandments of the Torah are requirements for all—the kind of obligations that would be labelled *d'oraita* (i.e., rooted in the text of the written Torah) in rabbinic circles.

[115] We can suppose De Vaux (in his *Ancient Israel*, vol. 2, p. 282–283), was speaking to this point when he wrote about Jesus as one who did not condemn the Sabbath itself, but did reject narrow-minded interpretations of the laws about it. De Vaux says that Jesus preached that the Sabbath obligation yielded before the precept of love of one's neighbor. In truth, how De Vaux frames his remarks places him closer to Branscomb than to the stance I am trying to articulate here. I am claiming that Jesus did not reject the larger framework of *halakhah* in favor of the meta-halakhic concept of love for one's neighbor, but instead developed an approach to *halakhah* that led him to his own conclusions and showed how his presentation of the law grew into an articulated approach to the law derived from his own scriptural exegesis—however different that work turned out to be from the halakhic framework developed by the Pharisees as they attempted to develop laws for daily life from Scripture as well.

[116] To demonstrate this approach clearly, see the collection of various *midrashim* presented in Menaḥem Mendel Kasher's *Torah Sh'leimah*, vol. 19, pp. 191–194, to Exodus 23:12. Not a single one of the *midrashim* cited there from ancient and medieval rabbinic sources goes anywhere near the societal/humanitarian argument that derives directly from the simple meaning of Scripture!

Regarding the rights of workers in *halakhah* in general, it is important to stress that I am not saying the there are no rabbinic laws at all that are rooted in the human basic rights of laborers, just that the rabbis of ancient times did not allow this halakhic mandate to serve as a basis for the laws they developed as the framework of the *halakhah* of Shabbat. Regarding the rights of workers in *halakhah* in general, see Hayyim Reines, *Ha-po·eil Ba-mikra U-va-talmud* (New York: Moinester, 1935). Regarding rabbinic and lay responses in the Orthodox world to the socialist and communist approaches to workers' rights, see Henry Berkowitz, *Judaism on the Social Question* (New York: J. B. Alden, 1888); Yitzhak Blau, "Rabbinic Responses to Communism," *Tradition* 40 (2007), pp. 7–27; and Binyamin Brown, "Professional Unionism, the Right to Strike, and the Renewal of Halakhic Laws Pertaining to Work: Ideology in the Halakhic Decision of Kook, Uziel, and Feinstein" (Hebrew), *in Ha-halakhah: Heksheirim Ra·ayoni·yim V'idiologi·yim G'luyi·im U-s'muyi·im*, ed. Avinoam Rosenak (Jerusalem: Van Leer Institute, 5772 [2011/2012]), pp. 187–217. Regarding the positive approach to communism of Rabbi Yehudah Ashlag, one of the greatest kabbalists of the last century, see Boaz Huss, "'Altruistic Communism': The Modernist Kabbalah of Rabbi Yehuda Ashlag" (Hebrew), in *Iyyunim Bi-t'kumat Yisrael* 16 (5766 [2006]), pp. 109–130.

Even a modern thinker like Rabbi Samson Raphael Hirsch (1808–1888), one of the most important German rabbis of the nineteenth century, who did emphasize the societal side of Judaism, omitted the societal/humanitarian argument for Shabbat observance almost entirely from his explanation of the Jewish Sabbath. Cf. in this regard Isaac Heinemann, *Ta·amei Ha-mitzvot B'sifrut Yisrael* (1942; rpt. Jerusalem: Horeb, 1993), pp. 120–121 and 150–154. Heinemann's argument is that Hirsch minimized the importance of the societal/humanitarian argument because he feared that stressing it would make him sound too close to Hermann Cohen (1842–1918), the well-known Jewish philosopher who understood the commandments as solely ethical precepts and who thus distanced himself entirely from the Orthodox rabbinic concept of the *halakhah*.

[117] Regarding this development, see above, note 97.

[118] I will, however, say briefly that a perusal of the Mishnah's list of *avot m'lakhah* does not suggest that inclusion on list has to do with the degree of strenuous effort required to perform the labor in question; indeed, many of the labors listed do not require particularly strenuous effort. (Consider, for example, the forbidden labor of *potzei·a/botzei·a*, which involves separating the warp from the woof to prepare the loom for new weaving efforts; or *makkeh b'fattish*, which involves aligning the walls of the loom in the final stage of preparation by means of simple hammer blows.) From this, we learn that the definition of "labor" (*m'lakhah*) by the rabbis of classical times has to do with the concept of creation, not exertion, and thus features acts that lead to the creation of something that

did not previously exist (that is, an act that involves its doer in the natural world through the creation of a new "thing.") This emphasizes the passage of the created thing from its pre-existent setting in nature to its entry into the world of cultural endeavor. For example, a cook who takes something from the world of nature and makes it into the kind of edible food that belongs to the domain of human culture is, in the eyes of the sages, engaging in an act of *m'lakhah*— even if the actions themselves do not involve any serious exertion. Cf. Samson Raphael Hirsch, *Ḥorev*, ed. Moshe Zalman Aronson (Bnei-Brak: Ha-makhon L'hafatzat Sifrut Datit B'yisrael, 5744 [1983/1984), p. 70, and also my *Ovadin D'ḥol*, pp. 162–188.

[119] For a list of additional commentators who summarized the rabbis' opinion in this regard, see my *Ovadin D'ḥol*, pp. 164–165.

[120] Kuzari III 35, cited from *The Kuzari (Kitab al Khazari): An Argument for the Faith of Israel*, trans. Hartwig Hirschfeld (London: George Routledge, 1905), pp. 167–168.

[121] In truth, Halevi's logic here isn't all that clear. The classical commentators on the Kuzari all claimed that Yehudah Halevi relied in his argument here on the fact that the Karaites whom he personally knew apparently admitted that there is no prohibition of work for servants, but that writing itself was nonetheless forbidden on Shabbat. For a general description of Halevi's understanding of Shabbat, see Shlomo Weissblueth, "The Meaning of Shabbat in the Writings of Rabbi Judah Halevi" (Hebrew), *Meḥk'rei Ḥag* 2 (5750 [1989/1990]), pp. 86–92.

[122] Readers interested in a more detailed discussion of this point may consult my *Ovadin D'ḥol*, pp. 162–188.

[123] Cf. my *Ovadin D'ḥol*, pp. 169–188, for a more detailed discussion.

[124] For more details on this point, see my *Ovadin D'ḥol*, pp. 195–219, and also my "The Central Role of the Category of Prohibitions of *Ovadin D'ḥol* in the Halakhic Argumentation of the Ḥatam Sofer against Reform Leniency in the Employment of Devices Utilizing Newly Developing Technology on the Sabbath and Religious Holidays" (Hebrew), in *Mishpat V'historiyah*, eds. D. Gutwein and M. Mautner (Jerusalem: Zalman Shazar Center for Jewish History, 1999), pp. 75–101.

[125] As I noted a bit ironically in note 10 above, this biblical humanitarian approach that requires both master and servant to abandon the hierarchal strictures that explain their relationship and together to rest from their labors has surfaced in modern terms without any relationship to Shabbat at all, and has become enormously influential in the world though the writings of a different Jew, Karl Marx—who not only appears not to have been influenced at all by classical Jewish texts, but who unabashedly considered himself a confirmed atheist. In the ranks of the philosophers of modern Zionism, there were many who longed to alter the halakhic feel of traditional Shabbat observance by re-introducing a

revivified version of this ancient biblical approach. An outstanding example of this is the socialist author Naḥman Sirkin who, despite the fact that he adopted an uncompromisingly negative attitude toward halakhic Judaism in general for most of his life, nonetheless believed strongly that there is a place for Shabbat in today's world, as an institution of social worth. Cf. the summary of Sirkin's thoughts on the matter by Tzvi Tzameret in his "'We Must Turns Our Sabbaths into Cultural Institutions': Non-Orthodox Zionist Positions Regarding the Sabbath" (Hebrew), in *Sabbath: Idea, History, Reality*, ed. Gerald J. Blidstein (Beersheva: Ben Gurion University Press, 2004), p. 104 (Hebrew section): "The Sabbath…is first and foremost the result of the bitter historical experience of Israel in Egypt. We were redeemed from Egypt, and from that experience we learned the obligation of [transmitting] freedom to subsequent generations. The Sabbath was thus [in Sirkin's opinion] the socialist, egalitarian response to the suppression of the poor by the rich, and it was this that Israel was commanded to bequeath to the nations. Sirkin called [upon the nation] to keep the Sabbath above all as a social achievement. But he also preferred that this be a forum for individual freedom of behavior, thus a totally secular version of Shabbat." Even today, we occasionally hear this topic coming up in dialogue concerning the Jewish character of the State of Israel between halakhically committed Jews and others less committed to traditional observance, in which the "secular" side proposes that Shabbat be recast in the societal/humanitarian mold that calls for a weekly day of rest from labor and restoration, at least in public. Thus, for example, Shabbat was depicted in the Gavison-Medan Agreement in 2000. (See *Amanat Gavison-Medan: Ikkarim V'ekronot*, ed. Yoav Artzieli [Jerusalem: Ha-makhon Ha-yisraeili L'demokratiah, 2003], chap. 3, which deals exclusively with Shabbat. The Gavison-Medan Agreement, written by law professor Ruth Gavison and Rabbi Yaakov Medan, was an attempt to assist religious and secular elements in Israeli society come to a reasonable relationship with each other. For more details, see the material gathered at https://gavisonmedan.wordpress.com/english/.) And cf. further Nadav Eliash, Aviad Hominer, Eyal Berger, and Ariel Finkelstein, *Shabbat Yisraelit: Hatza·ah L'hasdarat Ma·amad Ha-shabbat B'yisrael B'ru·aḥ Amanat Gavison-Medan* (Jerusalem: Hamakhon L'istrateigiah Tziyyonit, 2014) and Ariel Pikar, "Shabbat and Life" (Hebrew), *Kikkar Ha-ir: Bimah L'yahadut Yisraelit* 2 (2017), pp. 55–67. Strangely enough, this kind of demand for a renewed kind of Sabbath experience has surfaced recently in Christian circles as well, as noted above in note 35.

[126] In halakhic literature, the punishments for those who break the Sabbath laws on the level of *d'oraita* (*avot m'lakhah* or *toladot*) are principally as follow: death by stoning for all who offend intentionally; excision at the hands of Heaven for those who cannot be tried in court due to a lack of witnesses; and the obligation to atone via a sin offering for those who offend unintentionally. See Maimonides,

M.T. Hilkhot Shabbat 1:1–2.

[127] For a survey of halakhic sources related to my first example, see Yehoshua Yeshaya Neuwirth, *Sh'mirat Shabbat K'hilkhatah*, 3rd ed. (Jerusalem: Feldheim, 5770 [2009/2010]), vol. 1, pp. 61–62, §24. For a survey of sources relating to my second example, see Neuwirth, p. 31, §63. (According to the strictest sources, it is forbidden to pour hot water into a teacup on Shabbat even if the vessel from which it is being poured is not the vessel in which it was originally boiled.)

[128] See the material above referenced in note 48.

[129] Without suggesting that we have exhausted all there is to say on this complex topic, I wish to focus now on two kinds of evaluative thought regarding Shabbat in its theological guise that have developed in rabbinic *halakhah* with respect to Shabbat observance. I will present two opinions to demonstrate that both are plausible ways to understand the issues involved.

A positive evaluative effort regarding this development (i.e., as I presented it here: the adoption of the theological rationale for Shabbat observance as the basis for the elaboration of the Sabbath laws) can be found in the writing of Moshe Greenberg (1928–2010), who sees something positive in the dimension of holiness that inheres in this approach—something he feels would be lacking if Shabbat observance had developed throughout the generations solely in light of the societal/humanitarian rationale simply as a day of rest from weekday work. In his *Al Ha-mikra V'al Ha-yahadut* (Tel Aviv: Am Oved, 1984), Greenberg opens his discussion of this matter by citing the observation of someone who said to him: "My problem [is that] Shabbat [as observed according to the *halakhah*] is overflowing with ceremonies…yet does not serve as an actual day of rest or as a [kind of] true vacation [from weekly toil]" (p. 168). Greenberg responds to this question by presenting his own observation, opening with a quote from Abraham Joshua Heschel, who claimed that a family's weekly effort to prepare for Shabbat may be seen as akin to preparing to receive a guest of the greatest importance, whose arrival in their modest home as the sun sets on Friday they all anticipate with the greatest eagerness. Greenberg observes that the whole point of such frenzied efforts to prepare for Shabbat is rooted in the fact that they must be completed before the guest arrives. He then goes on to describe the sense of intense pleasure that he personally feels as he prepares for the advent of Shabbat—pleasure that he understands to flow from the fact that the much-anticipated guest is finally about to arrive, and that the guest's arrival is going "to change my life entirely and in every way. And so I abandon my [daily] chores, including all those secular tasks that burden me daily [in the course of the week], and I focus all my efforts on the guest. And I do this even to the extent of altering my schedule of daily activities to accommodate the new arrival" (ibid., p. 169). Greenberg explains that the "guest" who arrives with Shabbat in the home of a Jewish family *is* the unique atmosphere of a traditional Shabbat, "an atmosphere beloved above all others that has the capacity to make joyous the soul more than can any other kind of ambience, that embraces individual Shabbat observers and envelops them and their community, and that fixes in place what may [and may not] be done on Shabbat, leaving its imprint on all deeds undertaken on that specific day. In this kind of atmosphere, no deed that could be construed as a profanation of the Sabbath may ever be undertaken legitimately" (ibid., p. 170). And cf. also Michael Wyschogrod, "On the Christian Critique of the Jewish Sabbath," pp. 51–52, who writes about traditional Shabbat observance in a similar vein.

From a different vantage point, however, Mordechai M. Kaplan (in his *Judaism as a Civilization: Toward A Reconstruction of American Jewish Life* [1934; rpt. Skokie, Illinois, Varda Books 2001) writes that he finds in the laws that govern traditional Shabbat observance as they are understood today as merely multiplying endless difficulties that mostly just make those who observe Shabbat suffer: "We cannot receive any guidance from the list of works forbidden by traditional Judaism. A consistent attempt to live up to it would be attended with unnecessary hardship and deprivation" (p. 443). Kaplan does write respectfully about those who do find satisfaction in the kind of extremist behavior with respect to Shabbat observance that he himself decries. But he concludes: "We cannot expect such Sabbath observance from the majority of Jews" (ibid., p. 444). For the larger part of the Jewish community, Kaplan prefers the version of Shabbat observance suggested by Rabbi Joseph Morris of London (1848–1903), who writes (in his *Judaism as Creed and Life* [London: George Routledge and Sons and New York: Macmillan, 1910], p. 158, cited by Kaplan, op. cit., pp. 444–445) as follows: "It is difficult, almost impossible, to lay down a definite rule on this point, to say 'this sort of amusement is allowable, that sort improper on the Sabbath.' The matter must be left to the individual conscience, to each person's sense of what is seemly. What we have to do is to keep in mind the general principle already set forth, that the Sabbath is above everything a holy day, a 'Sabbath unto the Lord,' and honestly strive to make our observance conform to it...there are people who see no harm in spending part of the Sabbath day in struggling with a crowd at some exhibition, or in rushing to and fro from a concert or a theatre. Surely these amusements cannot fairly be called recreation. They are certainly not a 'sanctification' of the Sabbath.'" On this discussion in the modern time see also Elliott Horowitz, "Day of Gladness or Day of Madness: Modern Discussions of the Ancient Sabbath," in *The Jewish Contribution to Civilization: Reassessing an Idea*, eds. Jeremy Cohen and Richard I. Cohen (Oxford: Littman Library, 2008), pp. 57–79.

A Sign Between Me and the People Israel

Elliot N. Dorff

And the Eternal spoke to Moses, saying: Speak to the people Israel and say: Nevertheless, you must keep My Sabbaths, for this is a sign between Me and you throughout the generations, that you may know that I, the Eternal, have consecrated you. You shall keep the Sabbath, for it is holy for you. Anyone who profanes it shall be put to death: whoever does work on it, that person shall be cut off from among their kin. Six days may work be done, but on the seventh day there shall be a Sabbath of complete rest, holy to the Eternal; whoever does work on the Sabbath day shall be put to death. The people Israel shall keep the Sabbath, observing the Sabbath through the generations as a covenant for all time; it shall be a sign for all time between Me and the people Israel. For in six days the Eternal One made heaven and earth, and on the seventh say He ceased from work and was refreshed.
                                                                    —Exodus 31:12–17

A Sign Between Me and You

One could interpret this passage as saying that the Sabbath is a sign for all time only between God and the people Israel, but it is stated specifically that way in the Torah because the Torah is addressed to the people Israel. In reality, the Sabbath could be a link between God and the other nations of the world as well, for they too are the beneficiaries of the fact that God created the world. If interpreted this way, the Sabbath could have universal authority and meaning.

The earliest rabbinic commentary on this verse, however, interprets these verses narrowly rather than broadly:

> "For this is a sign between Me and you" (Exodus 31:13)—and not between Me and the other nations of the world. "Between Me and the people Israel" (Exodus 31:17)—and not between Me and the other nations of the world.[1]

This limiting of the Sabbath to Jews is reflected also in the Sabbath morning liturgy. The last two verses cited above, beginning with "The people Israel shall keep the Sabbath…" (Exodus 31:16–17), are included in the middle section of the Sabbath morning Amidah, and they are followed immediately by this paragraph:

> You have not granted this day, Adonai our God, to other peoples of the world, nor have You granted it, our Sovereign, as a heritage to idolaters, nor do those outside the covenant (literally, "the uncircumcised ones") know its rest that You have lovingly given to the people Israel, the descendants of Jacob whom You have chosen, the people who sanctify the seventh day. May they all find satisfaction and delight in Your goodness, in the seventh day that You have wanted and sanctified, declaring it the most precious, a day recalling the work of creation.

Reasons for Restricting the Sabbath to Jews

Why did the rabbis see the Sabbath as exclusively applying to the people Israel?

One reason is textual. After all, these verses begin with God telling

Moses to speak "to the people Israel" when announcing the imperative to observe the Sabbath. Furthermore, the commandment to observe the Sabbath in the Decalogue ("the Ten Commandments") is given to the Israelites when they alone stood at Mount Sinai (Exodus 20:8–11), and it is repeated when Moses speaks to the Israelites before he dies (Deuteronomy 5:12–15). In all of these cases, the text indicates that God is commanding observance of the Sabbath specifically to the Israelites, and not to other nations. Conversely, there is no source in the Torah that suggests that other nations are obliged to observe the Sabbath. So the biblical contexts in which the commandment to observe the Sabbath is announced may be the most direct reason why the rabbis of ancient times interpreted these verses to say that Sabbath observance applies only to the Jews.

Another reason that the rabbis limit Sabbath observance to Jews, however, may be historical. None of the other nations at the time of Moses—or, for that matter, at the time of the rabbis—observed the Sabbath. Christians observe Sunday as "the Lord's Day" because they believe that Jesus rose from the dead on that day. Catholics do not derive the command to observe a day of rest from the Torah. Some Protestants, however, reflecting the Protestant emphasis on the Bible for authority in place of the Catholic institutional hierarchy, describe Sunday using the biblical term "Sabbath." They do not define what is entailed in such a day in the ways that the Jewish tradition did, but historically some (for example, the Puritans) created strict bans against work on that day (which are the source of "blue laws" in some states, requiring businesses to be closed for all or part of Sundays), together with the demand that Christians attend worship services that, in some denominations in the past, lasted most of the day. The nations of the Middle East during the time of Moses, and the other nations among whom Jews lived in First Temple and Second Temple times, did not observe such a day at all. In fact, it was a commonplace among Greeks and Romans that Jews were lazy, for they took one day off from work each week.[2] So the rabbis' restriction of the Sabbath to the Jewish people may simply have been a recognition of the reality that only Jews observed it.

A third reason the rabbis may have limited the Sabbath to Jews is theological. As the Torah says in the passage cited above, the Sabbath is sign of the covenant between God and the Jewish people. The rabbis maintained that God created another covenant, the Noaḥide Covenant, with all descendants of Noah—that is, with all nations of the world. The Noaḥide Covenant has seven stipulations: prohibitions against murder, idolatry, adultery/incest, taking a limb from a living animal, blasphemy, and theft, and the positive commandment that each nation establish a system of justice.[3] Jews, however, are obligated to observe not only these seven commandments, but all the commandments of the Torah, numbering 613 by traditional count.[4] So the rabbis limited Sabbath observance to Jews because they believed that God demands of non-Jews only the seven commandments of the Noaḥide Covenant, and observing the Sabbath is not one of them.

Another theological tenet may have motivated the rabbis here as well, however. In the first rendition of the Decalogue in Exodus 20 and also in Exodus 31, the reason given for observing the Sabbath is in recognition that God created the world in six days and rested on the seventh. We thus observe the Sabbath to imitate God and/or to respect the world as God's property that we are allowed to use for our purposes only six days out of seven. These lines of reasoning could apply to non-Jews as well as to Jews. In the second rendition of the Decalogue in Deuteronomy 5, however, the reason given for observing the Sabbath is that God liberated us from slavery in Egypt, and so the Sabbath symbolizes the fact that we are not slaves and makes that status real by freeing us from work one day in seven. The liberation from slavery in Egypt, however, happened only to the Israelites. Thus, the fact that one of the Torah's rationales for observing the Sabbath applies *only* to the Jewish experience of liberation from Egyptian bondage is undoubtedly another theological reason for limiting the Sabbath to Jews.

Yet another theological reason that the rabbis limited the Sabbath to Jews is based on the verses in Exodus 31, the verses that we are considering here. The Torah here specifically defines the Sabbath as "a sign between Me and the people Israel" (Exodus 31:13, 17). That they are eternally bound in a covenantal relationship is unique to these two parties, God and Israel, whom God has "consecrated." The Sabbath is "holy *for you*," which seems to imply: not for others. So the rabbis are asserting the exclusive obligation of the people Israel to observe the Sabbath as an assertion of the special relationship that God and the people Israel have. This is part of being the Chosen People—that is, a people chosen to have additional obligations beyond those of other nations, including ritual obligations like the Sabbath and moral duties beyond those listed in the Noaḥide Covenant but contained in the Sinai Covenant and its rabbinic interpretations and applications. Some modern Jewish thinkers (such as Mordecai Kaplan and Richard Rubenstein[5]) have argued against maintaining the concept of the Chosen People, for fear that it will be misinterpreted now (as it has been in the past) by Jews and non-Jews alike as an assertion that Jews think that they are better than everyone else and more beloved by God. Kaplan has therefore preferred to speak of each nation's "vocation."[6] The original concept, however, meant that Jews are chosen by God for special responsibilities so that they might become a model nation, and God therefore holds them up to a higher standard.[7] In any case, given that non-Jews were not obligated to observe the Sabbath, it can be—and is, according to the Exodus 31 passage we are considering—specifically "a sign between

Me and the people Israel," excluding other nations.

Finally, the rabbis' restriction of the Sabbath to Jews was also motivated by legal concerns. After all, as this passage announces, the penalties for violating the Sabbath are death and excommunication from one's kin. Those are very harsh penalties, and if you have any love for your fellow human beings, you want to keep the number of people potentially subject to those penalties as small as possible. Indeed, the rabbis have a pattern of limiting the death penalty as much as possible,[8] and one way they did that was by making the domain of those potentially subject to it as small as possible.[9] In this case, that means limiting the number of people who are obliged to observe the Sabbath to Jews, who are specifically commanded to observe it, and leaving out all others—despite the fact that they too benefit from God's creation, one of the rationales for the Sabbath.

The Legal Implications of Limiting the Sabbath to Jews

Even if it is clear that non-Jews are not obliged to observe the Sabbath when they are living their own private lives or interacting with other non-Jews, what does this mean for the interactions of non-Jews with Jews? May Jews arrange for non-Jews to do things for them that Jews are not allowed to do personally on the Sabbath (such as lighting fires, carrying on a business, and building structures)? Or is the exemption of non-Jews from the Sabbath laws restricted to what they do for themselves or for other non-Jews, so that Jews may not employ non-Jews to do anything for Jews that Jews could not do for themselves on the Sabbath?

The rabbis sought to avoid both of those extremes by defining a middle ground on this issue. They first sought to distinguish what non-Jews do primarily for themselves and for other non-Jews, on the one hand, from those acts that non-Jews do specifically for Jews, on the other. Jews may benefit from such actions in the former case, but not in the latter, as the Mishnah makes clear:

> If a gentile lights a lamp, an Israelite may make use of its light; but if [the gentile does it] for the sake of the Israelite, it is forbidden [for the Israelite to use it]. If he [a gentile] draws water to give his animal to drink [and there is water left over], an Israelite may give water to his [own animals from what the gentile drew after the gentile completes watering his own animals]; but if he [the gentile] draws water for the Israelite's sake, it is forbidden [to use it]. If a gentile makes a stairway to descend by it, an Israelite may descend after him; but if [the gentile made the stairway] on the Israelite's account, it is forbidden [for the Jew to use it]. It once happened that Rabban Gamaliel and the elders were traveling in a ship, when a gentile made a stairway for getting down [to the shore], and Rabban Gamaliel and the elders descended by means of it.[10]

What is clear, then, is that if gentiles do something for themselves, such as laying a plank from a boat to the pier so that people on the boat can disembark on the Sabbath, Jews may use what the gentiles have done for themselves. If, on the other hand, the gentile is doing something on the Sabbath specifically for the Jew, it is forbidden for the Jew to benefit from it.[11]

This distinction, however, rooted as it is in the fact that Jews are obliged to observe the Sabbath but non-Jews are not, is easier to understand in principle than in specific situations. For example:

1. May a Jew ask a gentile on Shabbat to do something for the Jew or for other Jews if that act is forbidden for Jews to do on Shabbat but permitted in Jewish law for non-Jews to do?

2. What if the act that the Jew asks the gentile to do on Shabbat

will benefit them both?

3. May a Jew arrange with a gentile on a weekday for the gentile to do something for the Jew on Shabbat that is not permissible for Jews to do on Shabbat (e.g., light a fire?)

4. If a Jew hires a gentile to, say, build a building, may the gentile work on the Sabbath in order to complete it on time?

These are certainly not the only legal questions that arise in the interactions between Jews and non-Jews with regard to the Sabbath, but they will suffice to give readers a sense of the complexity of this issue of determining what a gentile may or may not do for a Jew on the Sabbath and some of the principles and precedents that Jewish law has developed over time in order to deal with it.

The answer to the first question and even to the second question, where the gentile will benefit also, is "no." By a ruling of the classical rabbis, a Jew may not ask a gentile on the Sabbath to do something for the Jew that the Jew may not do on that day (*amirah l'nokhri sh'vut*),[12] even though speaking to anyone is not otherwise prohibited on the Sabbath. The reason for this is that the rabbis were worried that asking a gentile on Shabbat to do something for you that you as a Jew are not allowed to do will all too quickly become doing it yourself if the gentile refuses, or does not understand the request, or does it incorrectly. Rabbi Moses Isserles asserts that a minority of rabbis, for example Rabbenu Nissim (1320–1376), would allow asking a gentile on the Sabbath to do something prohibited to Jews by the laws of the Sabbath when that is necessary for Jews to fulfill a commandment— for example, lighting a candle so that the Jew(s) can eat a meal in honor of the Sabbath or a wedding feast (on a Friday night after a Friday wedding) or a feast accompanying the circumcision of an eight-day-old boy on a Saturday, since all such meals are rabbinically commanded in order to celebrate the occasion. Isserles maintains that the majority of rabbis who have written about this, however, do not allow violating this rabbinic prohibition of asking a gentile to do something prohibited to Jews on Shabbat, even to enable Jews to fulfill another rabbinic commandment.[13]

The exception to this general rule is if a serious illness or a medical emergency is involved, for then Jews are required to violate the Sabbath to attend to the medical need.[14] When the disease is not life-threatening, Jews may violate rabbinic (but not biblical) prohibitions on the Sabbath,[15] including asking gentiles to do what is biblically prohibited to assist such ill Jews.[16]

Although the prohibition of asking a gentile to do for you, a Jew, what you are not allowed to do for yourself on the Sabbath is well established, Jews historically have developed ways of indirectly asking Jews to do what they need done on the Sabbath, such as lighting a fire or turning on a light. They say to the gentile, for example, "It is cold in here" or "It is dark in here"—and if the gentile knows the ways of the Jews well enough or simply wants to help others in need, he or she will get the hint and light the fire or turn on the light. This use of the "Shabbes Goy," the gentile who helps Jews observe the Sabbath, while widespread,[17] is still frowned upon by official rabbinic opinion as "repugnant…and in most cases it has become unnecessary because of modern automatic devices"[18] that can be programmed before Shabbat to do whatever is desired on Shabbat.

May a Jew on a day *other than the Sabbath* arrange with a gentile for the latter to perform work on the Sabbath that is forbidden to the Jew on the Sabbath? Rabbinic opinion and law permit this hiring a gentile when the work is part of a contract that includes other days of the week as well (for example, a guard or custodian), for then the gentile voluntarily agrees to take on work that is not for the Sabbath alone. He is doing it because that is part of the way he earns a living.

What, though, if the gentile's tasks include making coffee in the morning for the Jews of the household or, in an institutional setting, for campers and staff at breakfast at a summer camp or for worshipers at a synagogue to accompany the food at Kiddush following services? If it is part of the gentile's contract, one would presume that that would be permissible, for there too the gentile decides to do it as part of his work duties.

The classical codes, though, require that the work that the gentile does for Jews be done in private (*b'tzinah*).[19] The medieval rabbis were worried that if the gentile's activities were public, Jews seeing the gentile working for a Jew would think that the Jew or Jewish institution did not observe the Shabbat rules at all or had violated the rabbinic ruling that prohibits asking the gentile on the Sabbath to do the work prohibited to Jews on that day. So if, say, a synagogue arranges on a weekday for non-Jews to do custodial work on the Sabbath and to turn on lights before services and turn them off after the Jews have left, they should do their work as much as possible before the Jews arrive for services or after they leave, and that is the practice in most synagogues. Similarly, if the non-Jew is putting up coffee on Saturday morning for breakfast at a Jewish summer camp or for a Kiddush following Saturday morning or afternoon services at a synagogue, it should be a clear part of the gentile's work agreement and done in private. Even if non-Jews do some of their work while the Jews are in attendance (such as guards standing at the synagogue entrance), that is permissible if the work is such that most Jews attending services will understand that this is part of the gentiles' contracted work. This will clearly be the case if they also work at the synagogue during the week. Even those who visit the synagogue only rarely, though, will probably understand that the synagogue hires people for these tasks as part of a long-term contract, rather than hiring them on the Sabbath for work on that day. Still, Jews have to be careful not to tell the gentile workers directly that the air conditioning or heat needs to be turned on; they must rather engage in the kind of indirect discourse mentioned above: "It is too hot (or cold) in the sanctuary"—leaving it to the gentile to decide what he or she should do as a result of that statement of fact.

The fourth question above has to do with a Jew who hires a gentile to do a task (such as making a dress or suit, or building a building) with a deadline for when it needs to be completed but no stipulation that the gentile must work on the Jewish Sabbath to accomplish the task; is it permissible for the gentile to do such work on Shabbat and for Jews to benefit from it, because it is the non-Jew who decides when he or she wants to work to fulfill the contract?[20] This arrangement is called *kablanut*, "contracted work," but in this case it is not for work by the hour but for a specific product. Here again, though, the codes permit this only if it is not obvious that the gentile is doing this work on the Sabbath for a Jew, for the rabbis worried that Jews walking by the place where the gentile is working for a Jew will not know that the Jew hired the gentile to complete a task, leaving it to the gentile to determine the timing—but will instead think that the Jew is violating the Sabbath by paying the gentile to work on the Sabbath.[21] There are some medieval and modern rabbis, however, who maintain that even if it is clear that the gentiles in a particular case are working for a Jew or Jews (such as building a synagogue or a Jewish school or camp), they may work on the Sabbath if they think that they cannot finish the job unless they use Saturdays to advance their work, or even if they simply choose to work on the project then.[22]

As one might expect, rabbis disagree about the extent to which Jews who intend to observe the Sabbath rules may employ gentiles to do work on the Sabbath that Jews are not allowed to do themselves then, as well as the conditions under which gentiles may be employed for such work. This issue would never even arise, though, if gentiles were equally obligated to observe the Sabbath as Jews are. So the

Mekhilta's interpretation of our passage in Exodus 31 that restricts the requirements of Shabbat observance to Jews exempts gentiles from Sabbath observance but raises the question of what non-Jews may do for Jews on the Sabbath, and under what conditions. We have explored some aspects of that question above.

The Gift of the Sabbath

As the paragraph of the Shabbat morning liturgy quoted above asserts, Jews experience the Sabbath as a gift, one given to Jews and not to others. Along these lines, an ancient midrash says:

> The Roman Emperor [Hadrian] asked Rabbi Joshua ben Ḥananiah: "Why is it that Sabbath dishes have such a fragrant scent?"
> Rabbi Joshua answered: "We put in a certain spice called Sabbath."
> The Emperor said: "Please give me some of that spice."
> Rabbi Joshua answered: "It is effective only for those who keep the Sabbath."[23]

The medieval Jewish thinker Judah Halevi (1075–1141) points out the special character of Shabbat even more starkly. In his book *The Kuzari: An Argument for the Faith of Israel,* the rabbi is having an imagined conversation with the king of the Khazars, and Halevi puts into the latter's mouth a list of the ways the Sabbath differs from other vacation days, even for kings:

> The Rabbi: No people can equal us at all. Look at the others who appointed a day of rest in the place of the Jewish Sabbath. Could they contrive anything that resembles it more than statues resemble living human bodies?

The King of the Khazars: I have often reflected about you, and I have come to the conclusion that God has some secret design in preserving you, and that He appointed the Sabbath and [other] holy days [to be] among the strongest means of preserving your strength and luster. The nations broke you up and made you their servants….They would even have made you their warriors were it not for those festive seasons observed by you with so much conscientiousness….Had these not been, not one of you would put on a clean garment; you would hold no gathering to remember the Torah, on account of your everlasting affliction and degradation. Had these not been, you would not enjoy a single day in your lives. Now, however, you are allowed to spend a seventh part of your life in rest of body and soul. Even kings are unable to do likewise, as their souls have no respite on their days of rest [i.e., vacations]. If the smallest business calls them on that day to work and stir, they must move and stir, complete rest being denied to them. Had these laws not been, your toil would benefit others, because it would become their prey. Whatever you spend on these days is your profit for this life and the next, because it is spent for the glory of God.[24]

Or, as another midrash puts it: "What was created on the Sabbath day after God rested? Peace of mind, rest, contentment, and quiet."[25] As such, it is, as yet another midrash puts it, "a foretaste of the world to come."[26]

The Sabbath also serves to identify and reinforce the Jewish community. It can function in this way precisely because it is a distinctly Jewish institution, not shared by others. The special day each week for each of Judaism's daughter religions, Christianity and Islam, does not have either the same rules or the same meanings as the Jewish Sabbath. Aḥad Ha-Am (1856–1927), a cultural Zionist, articulates this communal meaning of the Sabbath well:

A Jew who feels a real connection with the life of his people throughout all the generations will find it utterly impossible—even if he does not accept the doctrines of the world to come or a state of the Jews—to imagine the existence of the people Israel without "Queen Sabbath." One can say without exaggeration that more than Israel has kept the Sabbath, the Sabbath has kept Israel. Had the Sabbath not restored the Jews' "soul" and weekly renewed their spirit, their weekday afflictions would have pulled them further and further downward until they sank to the lowest depths of materialism and moral and intellectual lowliness. Therefore it is not necessary to be a Zionist to feel all the sacred grandeur that historically hovers over this "good gift" and to rise up with all one's strength against anyone who harms it.[27]

These may sound like nice virtues of the Sabbath, but ultimately unnecessary and maybe even unrealistic qualities to hope for in one's life. In modern times, though, when families and communities are scattered during the week and when people feel tethered to their electronic devices all day every day, the fact that the Sabbath provides these qualities for one's life is nothing less than life-saving, as Aḥad Ha-Am says. As I have heard Rabbi Edward Feinstein say a number of times, "The Sabbath is the antidote to American civilization." Hence Reboot, the movement to turn off all electronic devices at sunset on Friday and to leave them off until after sunset on Saturday, has become popular among Jews who are otherwise not religious.

Reboot is just one example of how the Sabbath, in its unique Jewish form, can not only separate us from others, giving us a sense of our unique identity as a Jewish community, but also separate us from our working and technological lives one day each week and thus redeem us from being enslaved to our work. In both these ways the Sabbath is experienced as the great gift that it is.

NOTES

[1] Mekhilta D'rabbi Yishmael, *Parashat Ki Tissa*, s.v. *ki ot hi beini u-veineikhem*.

[2] For example, cf. the insulting reference to Jewish Sabbath observance in the fourteenth satire of the Roman poet Juvenal (c. 67–c.145), verses 105–106.

[3] T. Avodah Zarah 8:4; B. Sanhedrin 56a–56b; Bereishit Rabbah 16:6; Shir Hashirim Rabbah 1:16; Peskita D'rav Kahana, *Ba-ḥodesh* §§202–203.

[4] B. Makkot 23b; Bereishit Rabbah 24:5; Shemot Rabbah 33:7; Bemidbar Rabbah 13:15–16; and many other sources.

[5] Mordecai M. Kaplan, *Questions Jews Ask: Reconstructionist Answers* (New York: Reconstructionist Press, 1956), pp. 204–211, 429–432, 451–452, 500–502; Richard Rubenstein, *After Auschwitz: Essays in Contemporary Judaism* (Indianapolis: Bobbs-Merrill, 1966), chap. 2.

[6] Kaplan, *Questions Jews Ask*, especially pp. 500–502.

[7] See, for example, Exodus 19:6; Deuteronomy 7:1–11; Amos 3:2.

[8] Thus the Mishnah (at Makkot 1:10) says that a court that decrees a death penalty once in seven years is "a bloody court," and another opinion says once in seventy years. Rabbis Akiva and Tarfon say that if they had been on the court, they would have found a way to avoid a death penalty in every case where it is possible to interpret the law to warrant one—thus abrogating it in practice, even if not in theory.

[9] Probably the starkest example of that is "the stubborn and rebellious son" of Deuteronomy 21:18–21 who is, according to the Torah, to be stoned to death, but by the time the rabbis have narrowed the category of who qualifies as "a stubborn and rebellious son" for purposes of this law, they themselves admit that "a stubborn and rebellious son" that would be put to death under this law "never was and never will be" (B. Sanhedrin 71a).

[10] M. Shabbat 16:8.

[11] The codes codify the Mishnah's distinction: M.T. Hilkhot Shabbat 6:2, 3; S.A. Oraḥ Ḥayyim 276:1 and 325:11 and 12.

[12] B. Shabbat 150a; B. Eruvin 67b–68a; B. Bava Metzia 90a; Beit Yosef, Yoreh Dei·ah 297:6; S.A. Oraḥ Ḥayyim 586:21.

[13] Rabbeinu Nissim, Shabbat 55b–56a (end of chap. 19); see S.A. Oraḥ Ḥayyim 276:2, gloss.

[14] B. Shabbat 151b; B. Yoma 85b; M.T. Hilkhot Yesodei Hatorah 5:1–2; M.T. Hilkhot Shabbat 2:1–3.

[15] B. Shabbat 129a.

[16] M.T. Hilkhot Shabbat 2:10, 6:9.

[17] See Jacob Katz, *The Shabbes Goy: A Study in Halakhic Flexibility*, trans. Yoel Lerner (Philadelphia: Jewish Publication Society, 1989).

[18] Isaac Klein, *A Guide to Jewish Religious Practice* (New York: Jewish Theological

Seminary of America, 1979), p. 90.

[19] S.A. Oraḥ Ḥayyim 244:1, 252:3, 325:14.

[20] S.A. Oraḥ Ḥayyim 244:5, 252:2.

[21] S.A. Oraḥ Ḥayyim 244:1, 252:3.

[22] Cf. the gloss of Rabbi Moses Isserles (1520–1572, called the Rema) to S.A. Oraḥ Ḥayyim 244:3.

[23] B. Shabbat 119a.

[24] Judah Halevi, *The Kuzari: An Argument for the Faith of Israel*, trans. Hartwig Hirschfeld (New York: Schocken Books, 1964), part three, sections 9 and 10, pp. 142–143.

[25] Bereshit Rabbah, chap. 10, end.

[26] Bereshit Rabbah 17:5 (17:7 in some editions); Mekhilta D'rabbi Ishmael to Exodus 31:3.

[27] Aḥad Ha-Am, "*Shabbat V'tziyyonut*," first published in *Ha-shilo·aḥ* 3:6 (Sivan 1898) and available online at http://benyehuda.org/ginzburg/Gnz051.html.

Nothing Is Something Worth Doing[1]

Alon C. Ferency

You only do two days in the joint,
The day you get locked up and the day you go home.[2]

During my work with convicts, I am often surprised by the many ways in which they see themselves as free persons.[3] Obviously, their meals are at set times, their movements are restricted, and they live in confined spaces. Still, they speak of freedom within those circumscribed circumstances—mental freedom, if you will. Theirs is the choice of what to do in cramped quarters: the choice of what to eat among limited options; the moral freedom to become a convict in mind or only in body. What sort of training or mental fortitude could lead someone to experience freedom instead of privation while incarcerated? How do people survive stress, distress, even the inhumane? Are there lessons therein for lives of relative ease?

In a modern, peaceful, liberal society, the stresses we experience are often mild in comparison to the kinds of stress experienced by incarcerated convicts, though the physiological responses triggered are often similar: dilated pupils, constricted blood vessels, increased heart rate, activated adrenal glands, and enhanced metabolism. Such fight-or-flight responses had value to our hunter-gatherer ancestors but prove paralyzing in an office cubicle. In general, autonomic responses that serve us well through periods of acute stress are deleterious in dealing with the ongoing stressors that are features of our daily lives: inter-office politics, the daily commute, children's persistent school trouble. In any case, the long-term effects of chronic stress are near-catastrophic: heart disease, diabetes, auto-immune or inflammatory disease.

It's unlikely that our pre-modern ancestors of biblical and talmudic times were naïve about stress.[4] Indeed, Shabbat observance seems clearly designed to alleviate the stresses of our everyday world. What is the effect of Sabbath-keeping on the practitioner?[5] Why was Jewish Shabbat practice so demanding and why did its attendant *halakhah*, its practices, become so exacting? What does Shabbat observance portend, and intend to teach us?

In a word: *mindfulness*.

Shabbat creates the ability to focus and to charge the mind, thereby drawing the mind to what truly matters. Shabbat teaches us to *be*, rather than to *do*. There is a rhythmic structure to Shabbat: we prepare for the experience; we experience Shabbat; and then we carry the experience of Shabbat through the week. Since rest is both necessary and undervalued, how might one cultivate rest through a deeper commitment to Shabbat? And, what are the prerequisites to such cultivation?

It is crucial to realize that rest takes effort. Nothing is something worth doing. And rest transforms our focus.

Mindful Readiness

Let's begin from a premise that work and rest are two sides of the same coin. Shabbat and labor are both commandments. An early midrash on the Decalogue says that working on non-Shabbat days is itself a commandment: just as Israel is commanded to observe Shabbat, "so too [is it commanded to engage in] daily labor."[6] Rest is hard work: doing it right is actually a practice that requires forethought. Rest is not simple. Just as working has requirements—a tie, an alarm clock, an email address, a pencil sharpener—so, too, does rest.

Let us consider our sages' understanding of Exodus 31:16–17, a core text so familiar in Jewish liturgy that it is generally known simply by its first word, v'shamru. In the biblical text, the word v'shamru is followed by the infinitive la·asot ("to make" or "to do"), and Rabbi Baḥya ben Asher ibn Halawa (1255–1340) offers an explanation of that word, used in the passage somewhat cryptically to qualify Shabbat observance. How *does* one "make" or "do" Shabbat? It's paradoxical that one would need to "do" something in order to observe Shabbat, which is usually recognized by refraining from action. Baḥya infers that la·asot thus means "to observe the Shabbat actively." But what exactly is meant by "active rest," and how might one observe the Shabbat actively? He suggests: "The plain meaning of this [Scripture] line is [to require the Israelites] to provide themselves with the necessities required on the Shabbat…to encourage people to prepare for the Shabbat in time so that they can enjoy the day when it occurs. Our sages understand the exhortation to mean that one is to plan from one Shabbat for the next."[7] Like planning a meal or even a vacation, Shabbat rest demands time—what you put into it correlates to what you get out of it. Furthermore, both Abraham ibn Ezra (1089–1167) and Rashi (1040–1105), medieval sages with very different backgrounds and outlooks, come to a similar conclusion about what Shabbat observance entails. To the former, it requires that "one set one's needs and ways on Friday";[8] to the latter, "When Shabbat comes, it is in your eyes as though all your work were done, and there should not be rumination of working."[9]

By way of analogy, I consider the motto of Shabbat similar to the motto of camping: "Take only memories; leave only footprints." Let things be things. That is, on a Saturday as in, for example, Glacier National Park, our effort is to effect as little change as possible. Whether observing Shabbat or backpacking in nature, we try not to disturb the natural order—by not consuming, cutting, burning, or modifying the environment any more than is necessary. Just as you have to prepare for a camping trip because there are no supermarkets in Glacier, so too must you be industrious before Shabbat because you can't work on it.

On this analogy: if Shabbat were a camping trip, how would we pack?

First and foremost, we ought to get excited for the journey. During my last year of college, a friend and I prepared for a cross-country bicycle trip. We could imagine the saddle-sores, the fear of climbing the Continental Divide, the inclement weather, and the irate motorists, but our trepidation was tempered by excitement as we ordered maps from a cycling society, studied a road atlas, purchased tools, conferred with family and friends about where we might stay and with whom, and formulated a packing list. This process got us ready logistically, and it also spiritually enthused us about the upcoming voyage—for the road we'd mapped and the vistas and friends we'd see. Such experience is common to event planning, whether a concert, a weekend congregational retreat, or a dinner date: half the fun is in the anticipation.

Just as cresting a mountain pass requires hours of furious pedaling, so too does liberation from anxiety require a period of preparation. The thirteenth-century French exegete Hezekiah ben Manoaḥ (1250–1310, called Ḥizkuni) read our biblical passage similarly, asking what v'shamru could mean in this passage and what it would take to fulfill that commandment of Scripture. What does v'shamru—to guard or keep—mean, in regard to Shabbat? How might one "guard" or "keep" a day in its sanctity? Ḥizkuni's answer to this question is that "they [i.e., the Israelites] shall have in mind the next Shabbat during the six working days, looking forward to it, and preparing for it in order not to need to desecrate it when it comes."[10]

Any good spiritual practice requires forethought, preparation, and fussing the details. There are lovely images, homilies, and folktales about how one might do so, in order to make Shabbat an *oneg*, a source of pleasure (Isaiah 58:13). We reserve our best and our finest for Shabbat: clothing, food, and dinnerware. Such setting aside allows our spiritual energy to be directed to the moments of rest. Again, this takes detail-oriented work. For example, the Talmud relates: "All his life Shammai the Elder ate in honor of the Shabbat. If he found a well-favored animal he said, 'Let this be for the Shabbat.' [If afterwards] he found one better favored he put aside the second [for the Shabbat] and had the first [prepared for a weekday meal] instead…The School of Shammai say: 'From the first day of the week [prepare] for the Shabbat'"[11]

Get ready; get excited; think ahead. If you prepare for rest, it can serve you well. Then, you can find ways to carry the experience forward. Perhaps a message of Shabbat is that mindfulness is an occasional state that enhances other states. We prepare for "presence" with anticipation, and we reflect on it with euphoric recall. Restless anticipation is the storm before the calm.

Mindful Rest

Wherefore all this maddening preparation? It may be as simple as cultivating quietude. A quote widely attributed to Blaise Pascal teaches us that "all of humanity's problems stem from man's inability to sit quietly in a room alone."[12]

I've been returning to mindfulness meditation of late—with the surfeit of apps available, it's much easier than ever. Meditation ought not be viewed as something weird, strange, difficult, or abstruse. It really doesn't have to be that hard; from some remove, the process is astoundingly simple: you're just taking advantage of the fact that the brain can only think one thought at a time. That is, if you're thinking about the rhythm of your breath then you aren't thinking about the deadline for the annual report. As I tell students, it's simply a re-orientation of our mind and self from the cognitive to the sensory. By attending to music, breath, forest breeze, lavender oil, a mantra, or any of a number of other sensory reminders, we can move into a place where our thoughts can't hurt us. We become aware of meta-cognition: mind as an emergent property of the brain. We know ourselves to be thinking our thoughts, and with such awareness we can create a little space between thinker (us) and thought (external anxiety). By this rubric, I realized that I've been meditating, broadly construed, for most of my life. Whether following guided visualization, counting my breath, listening to John Coltrane in the dark, or walking in the woods, I am often doing it.

Shabbat is another mindful meditation. Among the most alluring and famed images of Shabbat is that of the second soul. The Talmud relates: "On Shabbat eve, the blessed Holy One gives the human a *n'shamah y'teirah* and at the close of the Shabbat God withdraws it, for [Scripture] says: 'God ceased from work and rested' (Genesis 2:3)—once it [the Shabbat] has ceased, woe that the spirit is lost!"[13] Commonly, the phrase *n'shamah y'teirah* has been understood to connote an "additional" soul that supports and sustains one through the joy of Shabbat—a metaphysical escort, if you will.[14] Yet, in some way it's always suggested a dissociative personality disorder to me, or a clumsy calculus of body+soul+soul. (Personally, I do not accept the dualism of body-and-soul, and "souls" sounds to me quite busy and cacophonous.)

Then, I stumbled across the interesting translation of this phrase in the Soncino edition of the Talmud, which renders *y'teirah* as "enlarged" rather than as "additional."[15] Since *n'shamah* comes from the Hebrew root meaning "breath," "spirit," or "inspiration," what if we were to understand *n'shamah y'teirah* not as an "additional soul" but rather as "expanded breath"? What if breathing easy is the simple lesson of Shabbat? Shabbat rest is just reserving twenty-five hours to breathe adequately, with "expansive breath." It's not that we abandon our worldly enterprises; it's simply that we put them on hold. We move from work to rest, from anxiety to anticipation, from the cognitive to the sensory—food, song, intimacy—and lastly from the physical to the metaphysical. By circumscribing time, we consecrate a day.

As the Italian sage Ovadia ben Jacob Seforno (1475–1550) offers, in his commentary to the V'shamru passage: "This additional soul assists us in concentrating on the spiritual dimension of the day."[16] This over-soul, embodied in expansive breath, nourishes us and brings about what Michael Fishbane calls the "prepared and resolute heart (*lev nakhon*)."[17] Is it all just respiration? In some respects, yes. Excitement and anxiety are comparable emotions: they both increase heart rate, constrict blood vessels, and induce perspiration. The difference, I'm told, is that with eagerness we breathe deeply, and in anxiety we breathe shallowly. Is it all so simple then? Just take a moment to breathe deeply.

Rest transforms focus. At the very least, twenty-five hours of planned rest (or even a few hours for those with professional commitments on Saturday) fortifies us for the week to come, with its attendant trials, stresses, or excesses. There will be more than enough time to be breathless, so let's conserve our spirit today. At a minimum, the salutary effect of Shabbat is something to carry forward, invigorated before the moments to come. As Rashi notes,

"One regains one's soul and one's breath when one rests from the toil of work."[18]

Returning to the epigraph of this essay, "two days in the joint": there's imprisonment and there's liberation, and every other year incarcerated is a mental state brought on as a consequence of the first and last day. Rabbi Levi Yitzhak of Berditchev (1740–1809) expands on the dual-ensoulment paradox further in his work *K'dushat Levi.* Referring to a talmudic dictum that "if the Jewish people only observed two Shabbats, the Messiah would come," he considers the two Shabbatot as representative of the first Shabbat of creation and every other Shabbat that the Jewish people have observed since then.[19] Is Rabbi Levi suggesting that all of time can be encapsulated in two days? Is the workweek merely a corollary to the order of creation? Between the Platonic ideal of the mystical Shabbat of creation, and the natural order of Shabbat observance that comprises one-seventh of our human lives, what other day is there? There is the first Shabbat and this Shabbat: God's Shabbat and last Shabbat—"the rest is commentary."[20]

Mindful Restoration

By serendipitous etymology, the K'dushat Levi notes the relation of the word Shabbat (from the root shin-bet-tav) to the word meaning settling, returning, and repenting (having the root *shin-vav-bet*).[21] Shabbat is a sitting in mindful rest; it is a return to our essential nature; it is a repenting from our wayward acquisitiveness. By slowing down, Shabbat effects repentance by causing us to reflect on our best self and godly potential. We see where we fall short and resolve to reach higher in the coming week. Rabbi Levi writes: "This repentance involves recognition that the objectives pursued during the six working days were in the main the pursuit of transient values, as opposed to the enduring values that the Shabbat is to help us pursue."[22]

Mindful rest, like any other mindfulness practice, brings us into awareness of life's values that are not transient. Perhaps it does this by the paradox of reminding us that a day comes when we can no longer work. Life is short. Eventually we must all rest, as "all ignorance toboggans into know."[23] Would you rather live hurriedly? Levi Yitzhak draws a contrast between Shabbat observance and how Israel left Egypt, *b'hippazon*, "in haste."[24] Only by consciously decelerating into rest may we accurately recall what matters. The potency of this is far-reaching: the counterpoint of Shabbat repentance is growing in faith. This is precisely what the *Sefer Ha-hinnukh* (an anonymous work about the commandments apparently composed in Spain in the thirteenth century) describes: an outcome of Shabbat compliance is that "everyone will be strengthened in the true faith."[25]

Yet, it's hard to give up time now for productivity later. Telescoping from theology to pedagogy, and from the sublime to the absurd, we ask: What is a great struggle many college students face? To go to bed. One must train oneself to believe that it is worth going to sleep rather than waiting for the fun to show up, so that one can enjoy tomorrow's experiences better. There is always a great Fear of Missing Out: "It's always ten minutes after you leave," comedian Dave Attell says, "when all the fun shows up."[26] This is a false premise. Instead, take time off from work rather than answering the last email, so that when you return you're more productive. Or go for a walk rather than preparing a brief, so that you feel refreshed when you return to the library.

As suggested by Rashi, the reverberations after planned rest are not simply a re-invigoration for future toil.[27] We did not spend a week shopping, cooking, and cleaning simply to rest and then abruptly return to the manic industrial world. Shabbat is a reprieve, yes, and it is an expansion of breath. It is also an expansion of the possibility of breath and the reach of the spirit. Rabbi Levi Yitzḥak reminds us: "When a Jew observes the Shabbat properly, the spiritual uplift derived from that experience will leave its mark during the six weekdays following."[28]

Recall that mindfulness cannot be effected by fiat. It must be grasped through challenge, attention, and preparation. Rest must be earned—that's why the midrash (quoted above) says it's a *mitzvah*, just like work! Rest acquired through work leaves its mark, making itself immensely more precious by dint of effort. Since we took time to prepare for Shabbat, and mindfulness to savor its expansive breath, we are more inclined to cherish it beyond Saturday night. We may rush out to a movie, but Shabbat lingers within, even as we sit in the theater.

Mindful preparation and execution enhance life beyond the practice. They correctly shift our focus to values that are enduring rather than transient. By celebrating Shabbat—looking forward to it and hearkening back to it—we expand the possibility of life. We grow the ambit of our concern beyond the material and toward the eternal: the life-giving and the breath-expanding. In debating how one might save a life if it interferes with Shabbat observance, the sages of Talmud said that we must "'Live by them' (Leviticus 18:5), and not die by them."[29] Shabbat is ultimately life-affirming and life-giving. Mindful rest allows us to affirm the greatest, most transcendent part of our humanity: the place wherein we meet the Divine.

Shabbat is a foretaste of the world to come,[30] a time of true rest and bliss. Barring inherited wealth, we all must work to sustain ourselves. Planning moments of respite, dwelling therein, and taking that spiritual sustenance forward allows us to put work in its place. We are here to live, not only to toil. Seforno notes that guarding and keeping Shabbat (*v'shamru*) is this-worldly, whereas doing Shabbat (*la·asot*) is other-worldly. It is a taste of the afterlife, "a day that is totally Shabbat."[31] Or, as Paul Éluard said, "There is surely another world, but it is in this one."[32]

There is a reality more pressing than the paycheck. Work is not only the ends; it is often just the means. We are more than our heart rate or our wallet. We can transcend the biology of evolution by natural selection and the economics of free-market capitalism. To quote Lawrence Kushner, "Shabbos is more real than Wednesday. Jerusalem is more real than Chicago. The *sukkah* is more real than a garage. *Tzedakah* is more real than income tax."[33]

Ready. Rest. Restore.

Repeat.

NOTES

[1] Simon Posford and Raja Ram, "Nothing Is Something Worth Doing" on *Ineffable Mysteries from Shpongleland*, the fourth studio album released by Shpongle in 2009.

[2] Lyrics from Clifford Harris, Jr. and Christopher Gholson, T.I., "You Ain't Missin' Nothing," *Paper Trail*, 2008; similarly, "You only do two days…the day you go in and the day you come out," by David Simon and Ed Burns, *The Wire*, season 3, episode 12.

[3] I work with incarcerated individuals and in drug and alcohol rehabilitation centers, as a prison chaplain and as a community rabbi.

[4] Sarah Biskowitz's blog post for the Jewish Women's Archives, "Rabbi Hillel on Stress Relief," January 30, 2017, https://jwa.org/blog/risingvoices/rabbi-hillel-on-stress-relief.

[5] Christian colleagues talk about taking a Shabbat, or Shabbat-keeping, but as yet their practice appears relatively simplified compared to traditional Jewish observance.

[6] Mekhilta D'rabbi Shimon bar Yoḥai to Exodus 20:9, ed. J.N.L. Epstein and E. Z. Melamed (Jerusalem: Hillel Press, 1952), p. 149.

[7] Baḥya to Genesis 31:16.

[8] Ibn Ezra to Exodus 31:16, s.v. *v'shamru*.

[9] Rashi to Exodus 20:9, s.v. *v'asita kol m'lakhtekha*.

[10] Ḥizkuni to Exodus 31:16, s.v. *v'shamru v'nei yisrael*.

[11] B. Beitzah 16a.

[12] I have not been able to located the actual source of the quote.

[13] B. Beitzah 16a and Taanit 27b.

[14] With regard to the "additional" Shabbat soul, see the essays by Jacob Adler, Martin S. Cohen, Elyse Goldstein, Michelle Levine, and Orna Triguboff in *Havdalah*, eds. David Birnbaum and Martin S. Cohen (New York: New Paradigm Matrix, 2017).

[15] This is the translation in the Soncino Press translation of Tractate Beitzah, but not in that same edition's translation of Tractate Taanit. Both translations are by Isadore Epstein.

[16] Seforno to Exodus 31:17, s.v. *va-yinnafash*.

[17] Michael Fishbane, *Sacred Attunement: A Jewish Theology* (Chicago: The University of Chicago Press, 2008), p. 171.

[18] Rashi to Exodus 31:17, s.v. *va-yinnafash*.

[19] *K'dushat Levi* to Exodus, *Ki Tisa* §12; B. Shabbat 118b.

[20] B. Shabbat 31a.

[21] *K'dushat Levi* to Exodus, *Bo* §14.

[22] Ibid.

[23] In e. e. cummings, *Selected Poems*, ed. Richard S. Kennedy (1994; rpt. New York: Norton, 2007), p. 99.

[24] *K'dushat Levi* to Exodus, *Bo* §14.

[25] *Sefer Ha-ḥinnukh*, positive commandment no. 33, ed. Ḥayyim Dov Chavel (Jerusalem: Mossad Harav Kook, 5720 [1959/1960]), p. 90.

[26] Dave Attell, "Fun Happens Late," *Skanks for the Memories* (Comedy Central Records, 2003).

[27] See note 18 above.

[28] *K'dushat Levi* to Exodus, *Ki Tissa* §12, referencing Exodus 31:16.

[29] B. Yoma 85b.

[30] B. Berakhot 57b.

[31] Seforno to Exodus 31:16, s.v. *v'shamru v'nei yisrael*.

[32] In Paul Éluard, *Oeuvres Completes* (Paris: Gallimard, 1968), vol. 1, p. 986.

[33] Lawrence Kushner, *Honey from the Rock: An Introduction to Jewish Mysticism*, 2nd ed. (2000; rpt. Woodstock, VT: Jewish Lights, 2015), §80, p. 126.

A Belly, Not an Anchor

David Maayan

In the passage about Shabbat from which this collection of essays takes its title, V'shamru (Exodus 31:15–17), the verses emphasize the work of the six days as well as the cessation from work on Shabbat. Both divine and human activity, and divine and human rest, are specified. Of course, this is the parallel which underlies one of the meanings of Shabbat: a remembrance of the "works of creation" and the Creator. However, although the liturgy reminds us of Shabbat and of remembrance itself, what of the six days of activity themselves? What is the relationship between the six "ordinary" days of work and Shabbat as a remembrance of the works of creation? When the sixteenth-century kabbalistic author Elijah de Vidas (1518–1587) wanted to depict the relation of Shabbat to the six days of the week, he presented his readers with an illustration of a wheel with six spokes emanating from a central circle. He explained: "All of the days draw vitality from the day of Shabbat, for the day of Shabbat is the central point around which the circle of the six days of the week revolves….Shabbat is the root of all six weekdays."[1]

What led medieval Jewish thinkers to develop this model of Shabbat as the vital center of the week (and thus of time and of all creation), departing from the consistent biblical presentation of Shabbat as the end of the week, "the seventh day?"[2] As elsewhere in Jewish mystical reflections, a new model suggests that a new perspective—both theological and experiential—is coming to expression. Reflecting on this inner dimension can lead us to turn again to the Torah and to rabbinic teachings, which we may find surprising in some ways. Whether what we see is the development of wholly new views or, at least in part, the recovery of long-forgotten insights is a subtle judgment left to each reader.

I wish to present here a view of the significance of Shabbat which draws on kabbalistic and hasidic writings. As Shabbat is also called the day of the soul[3] and a day for the Eternal One (Exodus 16:25), to reflect on Shabbat is also to contemplate the nature of the soul and its relation to the body, as well as the relationship of the Divine and the world. Bringing in the God–world relation is, of course, true to the Torah's own introduction of Shabbat not in the context of human ritual observance, but rather at the heart of the narrative of God's creation of the world.

The view that I will present sees Shabbat as primarily about immanence rather than transcendence. Shabbat is not a turning aside from the week at its end, but a turning toward it from its true center, from within. Rather than calling us to absent ourselves to some separate "spiritual world," we can hear Shabbat as a "day of the soul" inviting us to become more present with the spirit that is already embodied and at home with the world. The great mystic virtue of longing and yearning—so emphasized in the Zohar and hasidic literature—should be understood, against certain impulses in those same mystical texts, principally as a longing to become more present. In this way we include transcendence, but understood as a component of the paradoxical richness of human experience and the phenomenological mysteries of presence. As opposed to some proponents of the simplicity of "just being," the view I explore (primarily drawing upon the powerful formulations of Rabbi Naḥman of Bratslav) suggests that presence requires a sensed absence, that there is a type of longing to be which brings forth more being. Furthermore, to be most deeply present is to be in relationship, in covenant. As proclaimed in the traditional Shabbat table song "D'ror Yikra" ("Freedom Be Proclaimed"), Shabbat is freedom in the sense of covenantal freedom, in the sense of freedom from coercion—but in the sense also of freedom from isolation and alienation. These reflections will ultimately lead us back to our starting-point, with Shabbat as the center of a rotating wheel and representing the difference between a living, breathing center and the external anchors that we often look to for stability at the cost of our own vitality.

Shabbat and the Tabernacle

The first verse of Psalm 104 reads *bar'khi nafshi et Adonai* ("Let my soul bless the Eternal One"). The Talmud records a teaching which suggests that it is appropriate for the soul to bless God, as the soul and God possess five parallel qualities.[4] It is the soul's likeness to God that makes it so fitting for it to bless the Divine. This text seems to imply that it is the soul, not the body, which is "in the image and likeness of God." However, it is the soul with the body which is being paralleled, as the first quality makes clear: "Just as the blessed Holy One sustains (*zan*) the whole world, so too the soul sustains the entire body." We may say that it is the embodied soul that is being called upon to bless the enworlded God. Indeed, Psalm 104 is a rapturous praise of God's glory as reflected in the power, beauty, and harmony of creation. God has "clothed" and "wrapped" Godself in a robe of light through the act of creation.

To reflect on the interrelationship of the soul and the body leads us to reflect upon the interrelationship of God and the world as well as its microcosm, the Divine Presence—called the Shekhinah in classical texts—in the Temple. The well-known midrash which teaches that Betzalel knew the secrets through which God created the world, and drew upon this wisdom in constructing the Tabernacle, points to this parallel between the sanctuary and the world.[5] A number of scholars, drawing on their own insights but also on many classical midrashic texts, have shown convincingly the vast number of textual parallels in the Torah's description of creation and its detailed account of the building of the Tabernacle.[6]

Where does the central role of Shabbat—as the culmination of the process of creation—find its parallel in the construction of the Tabernacle? Of course, there is a quite literal dimension here: it is true that the rabbis taught that, just as God ceased from the work of creation on Shabbat, so too we must cease from the work of building the Tabernacle (or, later, the Temple) on Shabbat. In fact, as is well known, the rabbis state that the very definition of the forbidden "labors" of Shabbat is derived from the list of the labors that were required to construct the Tabernacle. Should this fact lead us to conceive of Shabbat as a kind of "anti-Tabernacle," a turning aside from it to, perhaps, higher things? I think we have ample reasons, and indeed plenty of textual evidence, to resist such a reading.

I suggest instead that the parallel to Shabbat in the construction of the Tabernacle (and the Temple) is precisely the moment when the labor is completed—and the Shekhinah enters the sanctuary.[7] Just as the Shabbat of creation allowed God to bless, sanctify, and rest within creation, so the completion of the sanctuary allows God to settle into its center. This is a moment of immanence and presence, rather than transcendence.[8] It parallels the moment when, at the completion of creation, repeatedly "seen" and declared good by God, God rests on Shabbat. God is not turning aside from this freshly made creation teeming with life and possibility, let alone transcending it entirely. God is not returning home from work to escape the week. Rather, as the Tabernacle model suggests, God is settling in to enjoy the home that the week's work has built.

Shabbat and the Tabernacle are juxtaposed by the Torah, placed in the same passage (Exodus 35:1–20) and once even in the same verse (Leviticus 19:30). Commenting on this, Rashi draws upon a midrash which suggests that perhaps the building of the Tabernacle should override the prohibition of working of Shabbat. But no, concludes the midrash, we should cease from working on Shabbat, even from the work of building the Tabernacle.[9] At first glance, this midrash may seem to present a conflict between two different commandments and values. Shabbat observance "beats" the *mitzvah* of building the Tabernacle. Thinking in these terms, we may begin to conceive of Shabbat as a "sanctuary in time" that is competing with a "sanctuary in space."[10] I would suggest, rather, that the midrash is teaching that the Tabernacle itself will not be complete without Shabbat, for Shabbat is the being, the presence, that dwells within the space carved out by our—and God's—work during the week.

As many have noted, the fact that the Torah connects the sanctity of Shabbat with the cessation of labor should not be taken as a negative judgment on labor. Indeed, the model of "work" as constructing the Tabernacle teaches us that this is the primary meaning of work. Our work should aim to create a home for God in the world, and to create a space where we may devote ourselves to God. Our work can open the way to celebrating with God, sensing God's presence in the world *and* in the work of our own hands, hearts, and minds. This work is so holy, in fact, that the thought arises that it may be permitted to continue this important work on Shabbat itself. Here, the midrash cited by Rashi teaches us an essential lesson: all of our holy actions will come to little if we never learn how to *be*, and how to let God *be* with us. The moment of revelation of God's presence calls for a cessation of activity—not because there is anything inherently wrong with activity (indeed, our activity in building the Tabernacle is what leads to the divine revelation in the first place), but because activity is incomplete without being and presence. When Solomon's Temple was completed, the Tanakh tells us that the priests were not able to "perform the service" because "the Presence of the Eternal filled the House of the Eternal" (1 Kings 8:11). All of our *doing*, no matter how holy, needs to be completed by the practice of *holy being*, of bearing witness to the presence of God, and our presence to God. The goal is ultimately to join being and doing into a seamless whole. However, this stilled moment in which the priests become rapt witnesses to the revealed Presence reminds us that at times we too need to pause our activities to remember, and re-experience, presence.

This notion of Shabbat as completion and filling, rather than as transcendence of the world, was alluded to earlier in Elijah de Vidas's notion of Shabbat as the source of vitality at the center of all the six days, their "root."

Shabbat as the Soul of the World

Perhaps no teaching more thoroughly fleshes out this perspective than the remarkable words of Rabbi Ḥayyim ibn Attar (popularly called the Or Ha-ḥayyim Ha-kadosh, after his most famous work), in his commentary on Genesis 2:2. The verse reads: "And God completed (*va-y'khal Elohim*) on the seventh day the work that He had done, and He rested on the seventh day from all the work that He had done." Ibn Attar opens his remarks with a classic question: Why does the Torah imply here that God did work, and thus completed creation, on the seventh day rather than the sixth?[11] After citing the classical midrashic answers drawn upon by Rashi, he then proceeds to present his own reading.[12]

According to Ibn Attar, the work of the world was only truly completed on Shabbat: "The world was trembling and shaking until Shabbat came, and the world was upheld and established."[13] However, he emphasizes, this is not because "the world was lacking some thing (*haseir davar*)." Rather, all of the things in the world lacked that which could establish and sustain them—they lacked *soul*. Thus the Torah hints *u-va-yom ha-shevi·i shavat va-yinnafash*" (Exodus 31:17), that on Shabbat, God made the soul (*nefesh*) of the world, providing a soul for all of God's creations.[14] Indeed, the author seems to imply that Shabbat itself *is* this soul of the world. The Or Ha-ḥayyim thus presents us with a hyper-literal understanding of Shabbat as *yoma d'nishmata*, "the day of the soul": it is not a day *about* or *for* the soul, but the day itself, in its true essence, *is* the soul. However, we should note too his emphasis on Shabbat as the embodied, life-giving soul that enters into and establishes the world and all life in it.

The Zoharic source most often cited as the origin of the term *yoma d'nishmata* sees this reflected in the fact that the prayer of ecstatic praise, Nishmat Kol Ḥai ("The Soul of All Life"), is added to the liturgy on Shabbat morning. The passage in the Zohar emphasizes that "praise comes only from the aspect of the soul and spirit," thus this day is of the soul "and not the body."[15] We may note the irony that the text of Nishmat is one of the most explicit enumerations of the role of the parts of the body in praise and worship in all of Jewish liturgy—not only the spirit and soul, but so too "the organs that You set within us....the tongue that You placed in our mouth—all of them shall thank and bless, praise and glorify, sing about, exult and revere..." The text goes on to mention "every tongue," "every eye," "every knee," "every spine," "all the hearts," "all innards and kidneys," and all "bones" as each having their roles to play in praising God through embodied expressions and somatic feelings.

I thus appreciate the Or Ha-ḥayyim's notion here of Shabbat

as the soul that "upholds and establishes" the physical and somatic world. Further, the Or Ha-ḥayyim writes that the inner content of this Shabbat soul is hinted at in the words *va-y'khal Elohim*, which he interprets as a hint to the longing and desire that the Divine feels toward creation.[16] He writes: "This is the language of longing and desire (*t'shukah v'heishek*)," for God "desired and chose His world. And by means of the seventh day which sustained the world, as I have explained, the Eternal One desired and wanted his creatures."[17] Thus the soul-day of Shabbat is, in its essence, the active force of God's own desire, described not just as will but as longing and wanting for the world and its creatures. The very root of Shabbat—and what makes it a life-giving force—is that it is the sustaining flow of God's continual love toward and choice for creation. Rather than a turning away from the world, Shabbat as a "day of the soul" means a reaffirmation of the world as the home prepared and chosen by God for the soul, and indeed for God's own dwelling place.

This latter notion would be most dramatically represented by the construction of the microcosm of the Tabernacle and the Temple. Yet it is here that we touch as well on a subtler dimension to the longing we have just described. For the Tabernacle is a kind of miniature world which we must build and inhabit, which we must create for God. It thus also represents that, although there is deep truth in the thought that the world is God's home, there is also deep truth in the notion that God longs for a home to be made for God in this world; God is in exile from creation, and David swore not to give sleep to his eyes until he found a place for God (Psalm 132:1–5). We, too, cannot simply settle in to being at home in the world, for the world that the soul is fully at home with is God's world, and the gap between us and that longed-for world is all too clearly manifest in the broken realities all about us. Thus Shabbat is about longing too, but not longing for another world; it is longing for *this* world and within it all its potential, longing for what it (and we) could become. This *longing to be* (and create) is different from a *longing to escape*. We shall explore this inner terrain further with the help of Rabbi Naḥman of Bratslav.

Longing To Be Present

Presence paradoxically requires absence, longing. A fascinating description of the centrality of longing is conveyed by Rabbi Naḥman of Bratslav. The well-known motif of a *n'shamah y'teirah* or "extra soul" received by each Jew on Shabbat can be traced back to Resh Lakish's declaration, recorded in the Talmud, that *va-yinnafash* is shorthand for "Woe! The soul has been lost!" (*vai, av'dah nefesh*).[18] Many have wondered about this derivation, which sees the hint about the extra soul of Shabbat conveyed by marking the moment that a person laments its sensed absence and disappearance after Shabbat. Why not emphasize the moment of the joy of the soul's reception on Shabbat evening, of its coming into being, rather than its loss?

For Rabbi Naḥman, unlocking this puzzle reveals a deep truth about the very nature of spiritual being, of the soul. He taught:

> The essential coming-into-being of the soul (*hit·havvut ha-nefesh*) is by means of the longing and yearning of a person of Israel for the blessed God. For each individual, it is according to that individual's level of longing, yearning, and pining to reaching a yet higher level….Through these yearnings, the soul comes into being. This is as the verse states, "It yearns and pines—my soul!" (Psalm 84:3). That is, the pining and yearning that I have for God, from this itself my soul is created. And this is what our rabbis taught: *va-yinnafash*— as soon as He ceased working, *vai av'dah nefesh* ("Woe! The

soul has departed"). In other words, at the very *beginning* of Shabbat, when we need to receive additional soul, we recall the departure of the soul during the week, saying *va-yinnafash—Woe! The soul has departed*, and we start to long for it. And it is from this itself, that we *long* after the soul, from *this itself* the extra soul comes into being.[19]

There exists a type of longing, a pained response to a sensed loss or absence, which can be destructive and lead to a loss of vitality, joy, and hope. Much of the wisdom of Jewish mourning customs has to do with the ability to acknowledge and make space for these feelings, while also guiding the mourners gently back toward life. Yet Rabbi Nahman here teaches that there is another kind of longing too, itself a creative force and a secret of human vitality. We not only long for the soul, says Rabbi Nahman: the soul *is* this longing made manifest. And the extra soul of Shabbat, with its capacity for joy, rest, and a sense of wholeness, is inseparable from our yearning and longing for God, for Shabbat, and for our own soul.

This Shabbat longing is not a longing for escape, but a longing to be present. Although Shabbat is called a taste of *olam ha-ba*[20]—usually translated as "the world to come"—Zohar scholar and translator Daniel Matt emphasizes that this phrase (and its Zoharic Aramaic equivalent *al'ma d'ati*) is most literally translated as "the world that is coming." For the Zohar, this term often refers to the *s'firah* of Binah, and thus the awareness that all of reality is continually flowing forth from its source. The Zohar thus refers to "the world that is coming, constantly coming, never ceasing..."[21] This consciousness of the continual pulse of being, which is thus also always becoming, is the place where the longing of absence and the joyous resting of presence are seen to be inseparable, to give birth to one another. This is the joy of Shabbat as a celebration, and participation, in God's creation.

Staying with Rabbi Nahman's insights on longing for a moment, I wish to return to the image of Shabbat as a completion of the work of the building of the Tabernacle. I referred earlier to the midrashic teaching that Betzalel knew the secrets of the letters of creation and used this wisdom to construct the Tabernacle. Thus, letters are the inner code of the entire structure. And yet, although letters build a structure, they still need something to be complete. "The vowels," teaches Rabbi Naḥman, "are the love and the yearning, as in 'points of silver' (*n'kudot ha-kasef*, Song of Songs 1:11). And the yearning is the soul…"[22] In a quintessentially hasidic reading, Rabbi Naḥman renders *n'kudot ha-kasef* here as "vowel points of yearning"[23]—that which is necessary to complete the letters and give them life, activity, voice, and expression; otherwise they are just dead letters. Shabbat is not the cessation of the work of the Tabernacle, but its *activation*. The yearning, love, and inner life that we bring to the structures we dwell within—from the literal letters of Torah we study to our families, communities, and beyond—is what determines the nature of what truly is born of those structures.

Thus, Shabbat is the ability to cease building letters and structures, for one day, and focus on yearning to invest those structures with new life, richer presence, and more authentic being. It is the pausing that Rabbi Naḥman refers to as "preparing to come into being," opening ourselves up to the greater possibilities within ourselves and the world.[24] This longing to be is closely associated with another dimension of the Shabbat experience, which is about freedom of the particular kind that I term here "covenantal freedom."

Covenantal Freedom

The association of Shabbat with freedom is reflected in the Torah's declaration of Shabbat as a remembrance of the exodus from Egypt

(Deuteronomy 5:12–15). Of course, for those of us with oppressive jobs or responsibilities during the week (whether physically demanding, unfulfilling, or even morally compromised ones), the sense of Shabbat as freedom from work and the week can be a deeply sensed reality apart from any textual reference. This negative view of "work"—the opposite of the model of work as building the Tabernacle for God—is reflected vividly in the opinion cited in Tosafot that Shabbat is a remembrance of the exodus because the Israelites were forced to perform the thirty-nine categories of work during their enslavement in Egypt.[25] From this perspective, Shabbat is about escape, and its freedom is essentially what is called negative freedom—that is, freedom *from*.

I worry about the implications of this model. I have reservations when Heschel, in his immensely influential *The Sabbath*, speaks of Shabbat as offering freedom from the "world of things" and an entryway into the "world of spirit."[26] When Heschel defines this "freedom" as "detachment," "independence of external obligations," and proclaims that to be free is to have things "and to be able to do without them,"[27] I cannot follow. Are we able to do without our bodies, without the world? Is this not reminiscent of the Zohar's reference to Nishmat Kol Ḥai as the praise of the soul alone, disparaging and forgetting the praises of the body which are so lovingly recounted there? This may seem unfair; Heschel surely refers only to consumer luxuries and so on, and not to our bodies! Heschel himself writes that, for "Jewish piety, the ultimate human dichotomy is not that of mind and matter but that of the sacred and the profane." Yet when he writes in the next paragraph "With our bodies we belong to space; our spirit, our souls, soar to eternity, aspire to the holy," it is difficult not to see Heschel here lining up the body and space with matter, and defining the holy as the spiritual, the soul, the limitless.[28]

And yet, Heschel's prose is such that, elsewhere in the same work, he provides a succinct formulation of the alternate view that I would rather advocate: "The faith of the Jew is not a way out of this world, but a way of being *within* and *above* this world; not to reject but to surpass civilization."[29] Here, the theological conviction (so emphasized in kabbalistic sources) of the two great truths of God's immanence and transcendence is affirmed and seen as reflected in the dual movement of a Jew who enters deeply within, even while rising above, the world and civilization.

The tremendous influence of the medieval philosophical emphasis of the transcendence of God has all too often led Jews to lose sight of the biblical vision of God's immanence. The Torah emphasizes God's choice to not remain detached and independent but to create, and to invest Godself in creation, in relationship, in covenant. Shabbat itself is declared an "eternal covenant" between God and Israel. How can Shabbat as freedom be reconciled with its own status as an eternal, binding obligation?

We may recall here the famous reading of the rabbis that what was "inscribed (*ḥarut*) upon the tablets" (Exodus 32:16) was "freedom (*ḥeirut*)."[30] In modernity, the question is often asked how the Torah's commandments and obligations can be described as "freedom." Yet I wonder if perhaps this question needs to be reframed. Although the tablets do contain obligations, we should not be reductionist in our understanding here. The reality conveyed by the tablets cannot be summed up as commandments and obligations, just as the larger Torah can hardly be described as a long list of laws. The tablets are most fundamentally the verbal expression of an encounter and a relationship between human beings and God. Like creation, this encounter is something ongoing and alive rather than only existing in the past. Obligations grow organically out of a committed relationship; they express, preserve, and honor it. But they must not be allowed to entirely define it, else a rigid structure of obligations may come to replace the living relationship.

When human beings are oppressed and severely limited by circumstances, freedom *from* is a powerful call, as it should be. Yet for many of us with relatively greater external freedom, we yearn (sometimes without fully recognizing it) for a different freedom— the freedom to enter fully into a deeply committed relationship. This is the freedom of love which is not about "detachment" and "being able to do without," but precisely the freedom to be fully present, to care. I have in mind the joy and freedom realized in the ability to be attached and even vulnerable without being controlled or coerced.

A Breathing Center

Shabbat itself is referred to as a "sign" (*ot*) and an "eternal covenant" (*b'rit olam*) between the Eternal One and the people of Israel (Exodus 31:16). The verses explicitly tell us that it is a sign that the Eternal created the world, and that "on the seventh day, *shavat va-yinnafash*." As we have seen, according to the Rabbi Ḥayyim ibn Attar, this phrase teaches much more than the idea that God created the world. In his eyes, we are called by Shabbat to reflect seriously on the image of God desiring, loving, and treasuring the world. On Shabbat, God nestled into the newly created world, taking a deep breath. (*Nefesh* has as one root meaning "to breathe," just as the English word "spirit" does. The word "inspiration" literally means "breathing in.") Many of us have learned, through body-centered practices that usually go under the name "mindfulness" nowadays, how breathing can be part of becoming more present to ourselves and our environment—and to their interpenetration, their shared being-together.

Just as there are meditations that claim to be able to take us "elsewhere," there is a type of longing that is an attempt to escape, to leave the world and all of its phenomena in search of a supposedly higher *essence*. But there is also a kind of longing that *brings into being*, drawing us deeper into the world, into relationship. This is the type of longing that God expressed by breathing a soul into Adam—in this meditative breathing out from deep within, it was not a meditation to escape but rather to bring into being. From deep within the wellsprings of longing for relationship, God breathed into being a being capable of reciprocating with a longing and presence of its own. The structure of Adam as a body was complete, but life only came with this soul-breath. As Rabbi Naḥman taught, we need to add *n'kudot ha-kesef*, vowels of longing, to the letters of structure. This longing plants seeds for manifestation, expansion, ongoing creation. To be true to the biblical and rabbinic sources, Shabbat cannot be seen as a separate spiritual world-unto-itself. Shabbat must be understood as being about creation, about the world, about the Temple, about the body, about community. And yet, to be fully present we have to long, to yearn, for that which is not yet present. This is a yearning for freedom, but not a freedom to escape. Rather, it is the yearning for the freedom to manifest, to become part of a meaningful tapestry of being and relationship; it is the freedom to commit oneself totally.

Thus, when we speak of presence and being, we need to make sure that these concepts do not themselves become frozen idols, but remain living processes, ongoing breaths of yearning. True presence is alive and has its own inner rhythm. In Judaism, we can sense this in the rhythm of Shabbat and the week itself, taking their endless partnership in time to represent a kind of deep breathing-in and -out each week in search of presence, integration, wholeness, together with absence, distinctions, autonomy, and all held together by the longing for more and more authentic being. This is Elijah de Vidas's vision, transmitted to us through his sixteenth-century text, of Shabbat as the vitalizing center of a rotating wheel. On Shabbat, we take a deep breath and allow the Divine to breathe new life and soul into us, as into Adam. Sometimes we are able to awaken from the artificial stability of inflexible structures that are so prevalent in the modern world to discover the stability-in-flux of being a living, breathing organism. This is to discover a new root metaphor for Shabbat as breathing center: a belly rather than an anchor.

NOTES

[1] Elijah de Vidas, *Reishit Ḥokhmah* (Gate of Holiness) 2:25–26, ed. Ḥayyim Yosef Waldman (Jerusalem: Torah Mi-tziyyon, 5760 [1999/2000]), vol. 2, pp. 23–24.

[2] The emergence of this and other models and motifs of Shabbat is discussed in Elliot K. Ginsburg, *The Sabbath in Classical Kabbalah* (Albany: State University of New York Press, 1989), pp. 74–101; see esp. pp. 85–92, figs. 4 and 5, and p. 156, n. 115. On the kabbalists' usage of diagrams as aids to thought, see the recent study by J. H. Chajes, "Kabbalistic Diagram as Epistemic Image" (Hebrew), *Pe'amim* 150–152 (2018), pp. 235–288.

[3] The expression *yoma d'nishmata* is used widely to describe Shabbat in hasidic literature; see, e.g., Tsvi Elimelekh of Dinov, *B'nei Yissaschar*, vol. 1 (Jerusalem, 5757 [1996/1997]), *ma·amarei ha-shabbatot* 1:21, p. 4a; and Yehudah Leib Alter of Ger, *S'fat Emet* (Jerusalem: Mir, 5757 [1996/1997]), vol. 5 (*D'varim*), *Shabbat T'shuvah* 5662 [1901], p. 169. These authors are drawing upon Zohar II 205b: "This day is the day of souls (*yoma d'nishmatin*)," a passage discussed below.

[4] B. Berakhot 10a.

[5] B. Berakhot 55a: "Rav Yehudah said in the name of Rav: Betzalel knew how to combine the letters with which the heaven and the earth were created…"

[6] See Arthur Green, "Sabbath as Temple: Some Thoughts on Space and Time in Judaism," in *Go and Study: Essays and Studies in Honor of Alfred Jospe*, eds. Raphael Jospe and Samuel Z. Fishman (Washington D.C.: Bnai Brith Hillel Foundations, 1980), pp. 287–305. See also Jon D. Levenson, *Creation and the Persistence of Evil: The Jewish Drama of Divine Omnipotence* (San Francisco: Harper & Row, 1988), chap. 7.

[7] The association of Shabbat and the "Sabbath Queen" with the Shekhinah (also identified with the lowest *s'firah* of Malkhut) in medieval Kabbalah is well known and reflected in the liturgy of Kabbalat Shabbat, particularly in Shlomo HaLevi Alkabetz's "L'kha Dodi." See also Reuven Kimmelman's *L'khah Dodi V'kabbalat Shabbat: Ha-mashma·ut Ha-mistit* (Jerusalem: Magnes Press, 2003).

[8] I do not mean that God is thus grasped as "being" immanent rather than transcendent. Similarly, I would resist the language that it is God's "immanent aspect" or "part" which dwells in the Tabernacle—such formulations sacrifice Divine Oneness in order to avoid paradox. Rather, the thrust of the biblical view is precisely that God, though utterly transcendent, nonetheless somehow becomes radically available to us in the immanent realities of the Temple, the Torah, Shabbat, and so on. Note how Solomon emphasizes God's transcendence in his prayer at the dedication of the newly built Temple in 1 Kings 8:27. This same tension or paradox finds an important parallel in the interconnection between human *being* and the *longing to become* which I explore, through the

lens of Rabbi Naḥman of Bratslav's teachings, further in this essay.
⁹ See Rashi to Leviticus 19:30, presumably drawing from Sifra, *K'doshim* 7:6; see also the parallel *b'raita* cited in B. Yevamot 6a. These sources refer to building the Temple (*beit ha-mikdash*), though here this may include the Tabernacle. On the Tabernacle explicitly, see Rashi to Exodus 35:2, s.v. *sheishet yamim*. For an extended discussion of these multiple derivations and their possible interrelationships within Rashi's commentary, see Gur Aryeh to Exodus 35:2, s.v. *hikdim lahem*.
¹⁰ I of course have in mind Abraham Joshua Heschels's *The Sabbath* (New York: Farrar, Straus and Young, 1951), which famously refers to Shabbat as "a *palace in time* which we build" (p. 15). Discussing this work, Edward K. Kaplan notes that Heschel's "tendency to draw antitheses polarized critics" and he cites Ira Eisenstein's critique that despite Heschel's repeated declarations "that one should not disparage space—things; nevertheless, one gets the impression that he is always doing just that" (in his *Spiritual Radical: Abraham Joshua Heschel in America* [New Haven and London: Yale University Press, 2007], pp. 125–129). This assessment is echoed as well in Arthur Green's "Sabbath as Temple" (p. 292), where he writes that *The Sabbath* "inevitably wound up in deprecation of space, despite Heschel's claims to the contrary."
¹¹ According to the Talmud's description of the legend of the composition of the Septuagint (the ancient Greek translation of the Hebrew Scriptures), this question led the translators to deliberately mistranslate the phrase "completed on the *sixth* day" (see B. Megillah 9a). This change (unlike most listed in the Talmud there) actually is reflected in the Septuagint text, although the Vulgate (Jerome's fourth-century Latin translation of the Bible) followed the Hebrew here.
¹² The midrashic answers presented in Rashi on this verse are drawn from Bereshit Rabbah 10:9.
¹³ Ibn Attar, *Or Ha-vayyim* to Genesis 2:2. Although the author presents this quote as from rabbinic literature, I was unable to locate an earlier source. Moshe Teitelbaum, in his *Yismaḥ Moshe* to Exodus (Brooklyn: Gross Bros., 5722 [1961/1962)], pp. 168d–169a, quotes this line and gives credit to the *Or Ha-ḥayyim*.
¹⁴ It is of course true that Genesis 1:20 (and other verses in the chapter) refers to the creation of certain animals as the making of *nefesh ḥayyah* (NJPS: "living creatures"). See Ibn Attar's remarks on Genesis 1:20–25. Perhaps the "vitalizing soul" referred to there is something within the animal's structure essential to its biology, along the lines of the Torah's declaration (in relation to animal blood) that "the blood is the soul (*nefesh*)" in Leviticus 17:11 and Deuteronomy 12:23. However, for Ibn Attar, what fully "established" the world and the creatures in it is the soul force provided by God's love and desire for the world, as discussed

further in this section.

¹⁵ Zohar II 205b.

¹⁶ This is based on creatively reading *va-y'khal* in light of the expression "my soul yearns" (*kal'tah nafshi*) in Psalm 84:3.

¹⁷ Ḥayyim ibn Attar, *Or Ha-ḥayyim*, commentary to Genesis 2:2.

¹⁸ B. Beitzah 16a.

¹⁹ Naḥman of Bratslav, *Likkutei Moharan*, ed. Natan Sternhartz (Jerusalem: Meshekh Ha-naḥal, 5759 [1998/1999]), vol. 1, lesson 31:9, p. 44b.

²⁰ B. Berakhot 57b.

²¹ This is Daniel Matt's translation of Zohar III 290b, published in *The Zohar: Pritzker Edition, Volume One*, trans. and ed. Daniel C. Matt (Stanford: Stanford University Press, 2004), p. 4 n. 19.

²² Naḥman of Bratslav, *Likkutei Moharan*, lesson 31:6, p. 44a.

²³ Relating *kesef* to the term *kissufin*, "yearning," which is so ubiquitous in Zoharic and much hasidic literature.

²⁴ See Naḥman of Bratslav, *Likkutei Moharan*, vol. 1, lesson 6:2, p. 6b. Note his explicit comment on "to be": "that is, that one should have being in the world."

²⁵ Tosafot to B. Pesaḥim 117b, s.v. *l'ma·an tizkor*. This alternative, negative archetype of work as the slavery in Egypt rather than building the Tabernacle is further elaborated in some hasidic works by associating the thirty-nine categories of labor with the corporeal punishment of thirty-nine lashes.

²⁶ Heschel, *The Sabbath*, p. 76.

²⁷ Ibid., p. 28.

²⁸ Ibid., p. 75. The tension pointed to here between a kind of monistic affirmation of the dignity of matter on the one hand, and hierarchical neo-platonic leanings toward the transcendence of the spirit on the other, is often found in hasidic literature. The interpretation of this tension was the central question of the famous Buber–Scholem debate in the early 1960s. See Gershom Scholem, "Martin Buber's Interpretation of Hasidism," in *The Messianic Idea in Judaism* (New York: Schocken Books, 1971), pp. 228–250; and Martin Buber, "Interpreting Hasidism," *Commentary* 36 (September 1963), pp. 218–225. See also Seth Brody, "'Open to Me the Gates of Righteousness': The Pursuit of Holiness and Non-Duality in Early Hasidic Teaching," *Jewish Quarterly Review* 89:1–2 (July–October 1998), pp. 3–44. On Heschel's sources of inspiration, including hasidic and kabbalistic writings, see Michael Marmur, *Abraham Joshua Heschel and the Sources of Wonder* (Toronto: University of Toronto Press, 2016); on the scholarly debate about hasidic influences on *The Sabbath*, see pp. 122–123. The fundamental interpretive question is whether matter is granted intrinsic value or whether its dignity ultimately depends on its potential to be "converted" to spirit. In this light, note Heschel's comment that "to the spiritual eye space is frozen time," in *The Sabbath*, p. 97, and cf. Catholic existentialist

theologian Karl Rahner's oft-quoted definition of matter as "frozen spirit" on the final page of "The Unity of Spirit and Matter in the Christian Understanding of Faith," in his *Theological Investigations Volume VI* (New York: The Seabury Press, 1974), pp. 153–177.

[29] Heschel, *The Sabbath*, p. 27.

[30] Pirkei Avot 6:2. See as well the multiple explications of this "freedom" in Shemot Rabbah 41:7.

Why Is Moses So Happy? Intimacy with God and Shabbat

Elie Kaunfer

The title of this volume—*V'shamru*—is the popular name of a biblical passage (Exodus 31:16–17) well known to worshipers on Shabbat, when these two verses are recited on three separate liturgical occasions: (1) preceding the Amidah on Friday night, (2) as part of Kiddush for Shabbat morning (in some customs), and (3) as part of the fourth blessing of the Shabbat morning Amidah. The inclusion of the verses in the Shabbat morning Amidah is probably the oldest of the three occurrences, but their placement here is in fact quite strange. This is because the introduction to these verses earlier in the blessing, known as Yismaḥ Moshe, has very little to do with the verses in Exodus 31:16–17. This fact has been noted by modern scholars and medieval commentators alike; Rashi, for example, objected to saying the Yismaḥ Moshe introduction because he saw it as irrelevant to the biblical verses.[1] This essay will explore the literary sources of this introduction, in order to uncover an interpretation of the words that may give a new framing to the experience of Shabbat itself.[2]

First let's examine the text of the introduction itself:

1. Moses rejoiced[3] in the gift of his portion	1. *Yismaḥ moshe b'mat'nat ḥelko*
2. that You called him a faithful servant.[4]	2. *ki eved ne·eman karata lo.*
3. A crown of glory You placed on his head[5]	3. *K'lil tiferet b'rosho nattata*
4. when he stood before You on Mount Sinai.	4. *b'omdo l'fanekha al har Sinai.*

5. And two tablets of stone he brought down in his hand,[6]	5. *U-sh'nei luḥot avanim horid b'yado*
6. and observing the Shabbat was written on them.	6. *v'khatuv bahem sh'mirat Shabbat.*
7. So it is written in your Torah:	7. *V'khen katuv b'toratekha:*
8. "The people Israel shall keep the Shabbat, observing the Shabbat throughout the ages as a covenant forever. It shall be a sign between Me and people Israel forever. For in six days the Eternal made the heaven and the earth, and on the seventh day He ceased (*shavat*) and was refreshed." (Exodus 31:16–17)	8. *V'shamru v'nei yisrael et ha-shabbat, la·asot et ha-shabbat l'dorotam b'rit olam. Beini u–vein b'nei yisrael ot hi l'olam, ki sheishet yamim asah YHVH et ha-shamayim v'et ha-aretz, u–va–yom ha-sh'vi·i shavat va-yinnafash.*

Contextual and Textual Oddities of the Prayer

It is clear that the introduction to the biblical verses is odd on a number of fronts. First, at least through line 5, the prayer could be read as an ode to the Ten Commandments, not to Shabbat in particular. When the text finally gets to the Decalogue's reference to Shabbat in line 6, we would expect a quote about Shabbat from the Ten Commandments to follow. But instead of Exodus 20:7–10 or Deuteronomy 5:11–14 (the two mentions of Shabbat in the Torah's two Ten Commandments passages), we find the V'shamru passage (Exodus 31:16–17). Why the seeming non sequitur?

Another strange feature of this introduction is its first line, *yismaḥ moshe*. Since this is the beginning of the fourth blessing of the Amidah, we would expect it to start with the word "You," addressing God directly. Beginning a blessing with the word "You," after all, is hardly unusual—almost every version of the Amidah features blessings (always the second and third, and almost always the fourth blessing) begin that way. In other versions of the Amidah for Shabbat, recited at Arvit and Minḥah, the fourth blessing begins with the word *attah*, "You" (*attah kiddashta* and *attah eḥad*).[7] So why start here with the word *yismaḥ*?

This oddity was noticed already by Menaḥem Zulay, and expanded by Aharon Mirsky.[8] Their proposed solution is that this introductory liturgical selection is actually part of a longer poetic structure that runs through an alphabetical acrostic; it is an ingenious suggestion. And this becomes clear in examining versions of this introduction from fragments in the Cairo Genizah: the word *u-sh'nei* ("and two") is missing, and line 5 begins with the word: *luḥot* ("tablets").[9] This reads better with the meter of the selection (otherwise, line 5 seems to have an extra beat)[10], and also reveals a partial alphabetical acrostic, with lines 1, 3, and 5 using the letters *yod, kaf,* and *lamed*. These letters—the tenth, eleventh, and twelfth of the Hebrew alphabet—may point to an original longer poem in which triads of consecutive letters of the alphabet were associated with each of the Amidah's seven blessings (with four letters being used for the final blessing, to complete the acrostic using all twenty-two letters of the alphabet). But all that remains is the middle *yod-kaf-lamed* triad, used in the middle blessing. The theory goes that this longer poem celebrated each of the Ten Commandments, and the fourth commandment—Shabbat—appeared in the fourth blessing.[11]

But if this theory is correct, it only strengthens our question: Why is the prooftext of line 7 followed by V'shamru, instead of the selection about Shabbat from the Ten Commandments? Apparently, it is because this introduction was used as a substitute for an older text that introduced the fourth blessing (which does indeed begin with "You."):

Rashi would not say Yismaḥ Moshe, but would say

[instead] "You chose us" (*attah v'ḥartanu*). He would say: "Adonai our God gave us Sabbaths for rest," because he didn't know what the connection was between Shabbat and Yismaḥ Moshe![12]

Apparently Rashi would say a different liturgical text altogether to begin the fourth blessing of the Amidah, which began with the words "You chose us." Naphtali Wieder theorizes that the following text, found mainly in manuscript form, preserves the standard form that was used before the popularization of Yismaḥ Moshe and was possibly the text that Rashi would recite:

The one whose custom is to say "You have chosen us" says this: "You gave us, Adonai our God, with love, Shabbatot for rest—this day of rest on which to cease and to rest and to keep like the commandment of Your will, as it is written in Your Torah: "The people Israel kept [the Shabbat]…"[13]

In sum: it seems that V'shamru was a biblical selection used in an old version of the fourth blessing of the Amidah, predating the Yismaḥ Moshe passage. V'shamru was introduced by a liturgical selection recited by Rashi, among others, which conforms to the expectation of the fourth blessing: it begins with "You."[14] When the new—or borrowed—introduction, Yismaḥ Moshe, came to be included in the Amidah, it did not displace the old biblical text, V'shamru; rather, it came to co-exist alongside it, even if a bit awkwardly.

Medieval Connections

Wieder, who published the seminal scholarship on this prayer, collects various medieval commentaries that try to justify and bridge the connection between the Yismaḥ Moshe introduction—specifically, the element of Moses' joy (line 1)—and Shabbat. He points to three basic approaches in the traditional literature, which I will summarize below. Each approach struggles with the first line of the prayer, attempting to identify the joy that Moses experienced and to understand how it is related to his "portion." While much of this introduction reworks texts from the Bible, the actual phrase "the gift of his portion" is not found in the Bible.[15]

The first proposal is offered by Rabbi Nathan son of Rabbi Makhir of Mainz, a contemporary of Rashi:

> Rabbi Nathan son of Rabbi Makhir said: Therefore, the sages established Yismaḥ Moshe in the morning, because the Torah was given in the morning. And it is fitting to tell the praise of Moses in the Amidah.[16]

Rabbi Nathan son of Rabbi Makhir is drawing on the talmudic tradition that the Torah was given on the morning of Shabbat.[17] Therefore, the morning Amidah of Shabbat is an appropriate time to offer praise of Moses.[18] But this doesn't really explain what the "gift of his portion" refers to.

Rabbeinu Tam takes the explanation one step further, in a report outlining his disagreement with his grandfather Rashi about whether to say this prayer:

> But Rabbeinu Tam restored the matter to its original glory and said: There is a great reason to mention Yismaḥ Moshe, as we say in the first chapter of Shabbat: What is the explanation of "For I am the Eternal who sanctifies you" (Exodus 31:13)? God said to Moses: "I have a good gift in My storehouse and Shabbat is its name. I want to give it to Israel. Go and inform them…" That is why they established Yismaḥ Moshe, referring to that good gift of God.[19]

Here, the reason to recite the prayer is not just about timing, with Shabbat morning as the time of receiving the Torah. Rather, it is about a more specific connection to Shabbat: Moses' "portion" was to be able to inform the Israelites about the gift of Shabbat, which had previously been reserved in God's storehouse.

A third approach is offered by Rabbi David Abudarham (fourteenth century, Seville), citing a midrash:

> At the time when Moses went out to his brethren, and saw their suffering and that they didn't have any rest, this was very difficult for him. He went to Pharaoh and said: "My lord king, the way of the world is such that a master wants to sustain his slaves. But you want to kill them!"
> Pharaoh said: "How so?"
> [Moses] said: "Because you are enslaving them constantly, and they have no rest, they will die. Rather, give them one day during the week in which they will rest, and they will become stronger and be able to manage the enslavement."
> [Pharaoh] said: "Choose for them one day a week for them to rest."
> [Moses] said: "Give them the Sabbath day, because any work that they do on that day has no blessing, since Shabtai [Saturn] rules [that day]."
> They rested from their sufferings on it every week.
>
> When they left Egypt, the Sabbath was given to them. When Moses saw that his thoughts matched those of his Creator, he rejoiced greatly.
> And that is why they set [the prayer] Yismaḥ Moshe.[20]

In this explanation, Moses' gift is that he was able to anticipate God's intention to grant the people a weekly day of rest far in advance of the giving of the Ten Commandments. Moses saw it as an opportunity to relieve his people from suffering, at least one day a week, while in slavery. Only when Shabbat was given from God to the Jewish people did Moses realize his thoughts had "matched those of his Creator," and he therefore rejoiced greatly.[21]

A New Approach

I would like to offer a different approach to the connection between the prayer Yismaḥ Moshe and the experience of Shabbat, which takes into account the literary intertexts in the prayer. Indeed, prayers are best understood when recognized as part of a larger intertextual field, employing what I have called elsewhere "the literary-intertext method."[22] In Reuven Kimelman's words: "The meaning of the liturgy exists not so much in the liturgical text per se as in the interaction between the liturgical text and the biblical intertext. Meaning, in the mind of the reader, takes place between texts rather than within them."[23] In other words, a prayer text cannot fully be understood until one first recognizes which biblical text is being quoted in the prayer, and then examines the prayer in light of the biblical text referred to.

First, it seems to me that the gift that Moses is rejoicing in is not Shabbat per se, but rather the poem's claim that Moses was called God's faithful servant (line 2).[24] This line alludes to the biblical scene in Numbers 12:6–8, where God distinguishes Moses' relationship with the Divine from that of Miriam and Aaron:

> Hear My words: When a prophet of the Eternal arises among you, I make Myself known to him in a vision, and I speak to him in a dream. Not so with My servant Moses; he is faithful throughout My house. Mouth to mouth I speak to him, plainly and not in riddles, and he beholds the likeness of the Eternal. Why, then, did you not fear to speak against My servant Moses?[25]

In Yismaḥ Moshe, Moses is rejoicing in the relationship he has with God. The liturgical text emphasizes the close and deep communication that Moses and God enjoy, unique among all humans. Numbers 12:7 ("Not so with My **servant** Moses; he is **faithful** throughout My house") is clearly referenced by line 2 of the prayer: "You called him **faithful servant**."

The Yismaḥ Moshe prayer, I suggest, further develops this relationship of unique communication in lines 3–4 by describing the "crown of glory You placed on his head when he stood before You on Mount Sinai." What is this "crown of glory"? Although this phrase is not found directly in the Bible,[26] I believe the biblical narrative of Exodus 34:27–34 helps to elucidate the phrase:

> And the Eternal said to Moses: "Write down these commandments, for in accordance with these commandments I make a covenant with you and with Israel." And he was there with the Eternal forty days and forty nights; he ate no bread and drank no water; and he wrote down on the tablets the terms of the covenant, the Ten Commandments.
> So Moses came down from Mount Sinai. And as Moses came down from the mountain bearing the two Tablets of the Pact, Moses was not aware that the skin of his face was radiant, since he had spoken with Him. Aaron and all the Israelites saw that the skin of Moses' face was radiant; and they shrank from coming near him. But Moses called to them, and Aaron and all the chieftains in the assembly returned to him, and Moses spoke to them. Afterward all the Israelites came near, and he instructed them concerning all that the Eternal had imparted to him on Mount Sinai.
> And when Moses had finished speaking with them, he put a veil over his face. Whenever Moses went in before the Eternal to speak with Him, he would leave the veil off until he came out; and when he came out and told the Israelites what he had been commanded, the Israelites would see how radiant

the skin of Moses' face was. Moses would then put the veil back over his face until he went in to speak with Him.

This passage describes the impact of Moses' direct communication with God, as he came down with the tablets in his hand: his face shone with a radiant light (Exodus 34:29)—reflected in the poetic image of "a crown of glory."[27] In fact, Moses' interaction with God is so powerful that people cannot even stand to look directly into his face following the communication. He has to cover himself with a veil to shield them from this power.

In this reading, Moses' gift (line 1) was the gift of unique communication with God (line 2), illustrated by the crown of glory (line 3) that he is granted when he comes down the mountain with the two tablets (line 4). This radiant countenance is even considered by one talmudic source to be a gift: "Rabbi Ḥama son of Rabbi Ḥanina said: One who gives a gift to his friend doesn't need to inform him, as it says: 'But Moses didn't know that the skin of his face shone' (Exodus 34:29)."[28] Moses's shining face is the gift, which is the sign of his selection as a faithful servant—that is, one who can speak to God face to face.[29]

Divine Encounter and Shabbat

Up until now, this reading of the poem seems to sideline any connection to Shabbat. It seems simply to describe an interaction between Moses and God in which Moses emerges with the gift of intense divine encounter, the physical residue of which was still visible to the Israelites when Moses came down from the mountain with the Ten Commandments in his hand.

However, Shabbat also remains central in this reading, as is clear from the verses immediately following the scene of the veil (quoted above). The very first commandment that Moses gives Israel upon coming down the mountain—the direct continuation of the passage above—is none other than the Shabbat (Exodus 35:1–3):

> Moses then convoked the whole Israelite community and said to them: These are the things that the Eternal has commanded you to do: On six days work may be done, but on the seventh day you shall have a sabbath of complete rest, holy to the Eternal; whoever does any work on it shall be put to death. You shall kindle no fire throughout your settlements on the sabbath day.

When offered the chance to reintroduce the Ten Commandments after the people's sin of the golden calf, Moses headlines Shabbat. The flow of our prayer from line 5 (general Ten Commandments) to line 6 (specific focus on Shabbat) comes into clearer focus with this understanding.

What is the connection between Moses' deep encounter with God and the law of Shabbat? I want to suggest that while only Moses can have this kind of encounter with God (as is made clear by God in Numbers 12), the Jewish people have an opportunity for an analogous experience each week in their celebration of Shabbat. Shabbat is a day of encounter in which all who keep it have the opportunity to emerge with a version of the powerful glow that Moses experienced after having lived on the mountain of God for forty days and nights.[30]

This prayer, then, is not just an ode to the special connection between God and Moses (although that is certainly outlined in lines 1–5); it is also a nod to the ways in which all Israelites can connect intensely with God's presence—through the day of Shabbat.[31] In this reading, the poem becomes a powerful argument that Shabbat morning be considered as an opportunity, as a time when the experience of prayer is not used to put forward requests or to acknowledge moral or spiritual shortcomings, but rather to commune with God in some latter-day version of the intimacy Israel's greatest prophet once knew with the God of Israel.

NOTES

[1] See Naphtali Wieder, "*Yismaḥ Moshe: Hitnagdut V'senegoreha*," in *Hitgabshut Nusaḥ Ha-t'fillah Ba-mizraḥ U-va-maʿarav* (Jerusalem: Ben Zvi Institute, 1998), vol.1, pp. 295–322. As noted, Rashi himself was opposed to saying this prayer, and it did not gain widespread acceptance even through the time of Rabbi Isaac of Vienna. See Wieder, pp. 298 and 303, and Daniel Sperber, *On Changes in Jewish Liturgy* (Jerusalem and New York: Urim, 2010), pp. 176–178.

[2] For a recent analysis of this prayer and its linguistic features, see Moshe Bar-Asher, *L'shoneinu Rinnah* (Jerusalem: Reuven Mass, 2016), pp. 84–96.

[3] I translate *yismaḥ* in the past tense, even though it is in the imperfect, because the context clearly indicates a past event. As we will see, the use of the imperfect is probably more determined by the opportunity to start the prayer with the letter *yod* than any specific syntactic specificity. Note a similar dynamic with Exodus 15:1, where an imperfect form of the verb likewise seems to indicate past time (*az yashir moshe*)—although Rabbi Meir, at least, read it as the future tense (see B. Sanhedrin 91b).

[4] See Numbers 12:7, discussed further below.

[5] Perhaps alluding to Exodus 34:27–34; see discussion below.

[6] Apparently referencing Exodus 32:15 or 34:29.

[7] Even in the Shabbat Musaf Amidah, the fourth blessing begins with a second-person address to God (if not with specific word *attah*): *tikkanta*, which has the second-person masculine singular suffix *-ta*.

[8] Aharon Mirsky, *Ha-piyyut* (Jerusalem: Magnes Press, 1991), p. 88. Mirsky writes (p. 88, n. 9) that Zulay made a note of this possibility in the list of manuscripts in the Institute for the Research of Hebrew Poetry, although he did not publish the idea himself.

[9] Wieder points to four Genizah manuscripts with this wording (*Yismaḥ Moshe*, p. 299, n. 18); Ezra Fleischer brings an additional three manuscripts (in his *T'fillah U-minhagei T'fillah Eretz-Yisraeliyim Bi-t'kufat Ha-g'nizah* [Jerusalem: Magnes Press, 1988], p. 52, n. 86).

[10] For the style of this meter, common to other compositions for the fourth blessing of the Amidah, see Shulamit Elitzur, "*P'tiḥatah Ha-k'dumah shel Birkat K'dushat Ha-yom B'shabbatot*," *Netuʿim* 21, p. 2, n. 9.

[11] Mirsky, *Ha-piyyut*, p. 91.

[12] Recorded in Abraham ibn Yarḥi's work, *Sefer Ha-Manhig*, ed. Yitzḥak Raphael (Jerusalem: Mossad Harav Kook, 1978), vol. 1, p. 150.

[13] Wieder, *Yismaḥ Moshe*, pp. 300–301.

[14] For a discussion on how old this text might be, and other variations for this blessing, see Elitzur, "*P'tiḥatah Ha-k'dumah*," pp. 5–18. For the question of how old the other texts for the fourth blessing of the Amidah on Shabbat

are, see Fleischer, *T'fillah U-minhagei T'fillah*, pp. 19ff. There he discusses the possibility that there was originally only one introduction to the fourth blessing on Shabbat, which did not vary (as it does today) from service to service. Fleischer later suggested that the original text for this blessing was a different blessing, beginning with the words *hannah lanu*. See Ezra Fleischer, "*L'nusah Ha-kadum shel Birkat Ha-yom Ba-amidat Ha-shabbat*," *T'fillot Ha-keva B'yisrael B'hithavutan U-v'hitgabshutan* (Jerusalem: Magnes Press, 2012), vol. 1, pp. 267–276. Elitzur (p. 2, n. 8) dismisses this text also as being a later development.

[15] Bar-Asher, *L'shoneinu Rinnah*, pp. 87–88.

[16] Wieder, *Yismaḥ Moshe*, p. 301. The text refers to the morning as *yotzeir*, the first blessing of the morning blessings surrounding the Shema.

[17] B. Shabbat 86b.

[18] It should be noted that Moses rarely appears in the Amidah directly; see the aside by Meir Bar Ilan, "*M'korah shel T'fillat Aleinu L'shabbei·aḥ*," *Da·at* 43 (1999), pp. 5–24, particularly p. 10, n. 27.

In addition to Yismaḥ Moshe, Moses appears in two instances of the Amidah generally, but these are not core to the original text, and it is doubtful that they were known to worshipers in the talmudic era:

  (1) The prelude to the priests' blessing (Birkat Kohanim), recited as part of the public recitation of the morning Amidah, includes a reference to Moses as the scribe who recorded the priestly blessing in the Torah: "Our God and God of our ancestors, bless us with the threefold blessing in the Torah, written by **Moses** Your servant, said in the mouth of Aaron and his sons, priests, Your holy nation, as it says…" The blessing that this selection introduces, taken from Numbers 6:24–26, is in fact quite old (see M. Tamid 5:1 and M. Sotah 7:2, and, for its presence in the Amidah, M. Berakhot 5:4), as is the requirement for the *ḥazzan* to call the *kohanim*, which requirement is found in Sifrei Bemidbar §39 (ed. Menahem Kahane [Jerusalem: Magnes Press, 2011], vol. 1, p. 107, and cf. the discussion in vol. 2, p. 313). But the introduction, which mentions Moses, was already recognized by some early medieval authorities as a later addition. For example, Rabbi Meir HaKohen wrote in the thirteenth century: "But 'Our God and God of our ancestors…' was written in the later generations, and it is not known when they established to say it… (*Hagahot Maimoniyot* on Rambam's *Seder T'fillot Kol Ha-shanah*, §7 [ed. Shabbtai Frankel; Jerusalem: Shabbtai Frankel Press, 2007], p. 327, with corrections of Yitzḥak Kahane *Maharam Mi-rotenberg, T'shuvot P'sakim U-Minhagim* [Jerusalem: Mossad Harav Kook, 1957], vol. 1, p. 60).

  (2) Moses also appears in a variant of the middle blessing for the Shabbat Musaf Amidah, which first appeared (according to Fleischer, p. 23) in the Rambam's siddur: "To Moses on Mount Sinai You commanded

Shabbat, 'Remember' and 'Keep'" (Daniel Goldschmidt, *Meḥhḳ'rei T'fillah U-d'fiyyut* [Jerusalem: Magnes Press, 1980], p. 206, line 9). Fleischer (in his *T'fillah U-Minhagei T'fillah*, pp. 22–23) notes this is the oldest version of the text. But this is also likely a later poetic addition to the standard text of Musaf, with no precedent in rabbinic references to the Amidah. See Bar-Asher, *L'shoneinu Rinnah*, pp. 112–113, for a suggestion about why Moses was added here.

[19] *Sefer Manhig, Hilkhot Shabbat* §20, ed. Yitzḥak Raphael (Jerusalem: Mossad Harav Kook, 5754 [1993/1994]), p. 150; citing B. Shabbat 10b. See Wieder, p. 298.

[20] *Sefer Abudraham Ha-Shalem*, ed. Shlomo A. Wertheimer (Jerusalem: Usha, 1963), p. 170; ed. Eliyahu Grinzeig (Jerusalem: Re'em, 2017), vol. 2, p. 78; *Torah Sh'leimah* (New York: American Biblical Encyclopedia Society, 1944), vol. 8, p. 76. Abudarham is citing a midrash found in Shemot Rabbah 1:28. But cf. Shemot Rabbah 1:32.

[21] Wieder (*Yismaḥ Moshe*, p. 311) brings another version of this midrash that removes Pharaoh as a character in the origin of Shabbat, and has God play that role instead. For additional versions of this midrash and its connection to the prayer, see Wieder, pp. 309–310.

[22] Elie Kaunfer, *Interpreting Jewish Liturgy: The Literary-Intertext Method* (doctoral dissertation; New York: Jewish Theological Seminary, 2014; available online at http://www.hadar.org/torah-resource/interpreting-jewish-liturgy, p. 16. "Intertextuality" refers to the approach to reading in which "…a text cannot be studied in isolation. It belongs to a web of texts which are (partially) present whenever it is read or studied." See also Steven Moyise, "Intertextuality and the Study of the Old Testament in the New Testament," in *The Old Testament in the New Testament: Essays in Honour of J. L. North*, ed. Steven Moyise (Sheffield, England: Sheffield Academic Press, 2000), pp. 14–41; here, pp. 15–16.

[23] Reuven Kimelman, "The Shema Liturgy: From Covenant Ceremony to Coronation," in *Kenishta: Studies of the Synagogue World 1* (2001), pp. 9–105; quote appears on p. 28.

[24] Rabbi Yehudah ben Yakar, *Peirush Ha-t'fillot V'ha-b'rakhot*, ed. Shmuel Yerushalmi (Jerusalem: Me'orei Yisrael, 1979), vol. 1, p. 104.

[25] All extended biblical quotations in this essay are adapted from the NJPS translation.

[26] Although it appears in Ben Sira 45:8 (*Sefer Ben Sira Ha-Shaleim*, ed. Moshe Segal [Jerusalem: Bialik Institute, 1958], pp. 310, 313, where it refers to the priestly crown.

[27] Bar-Asher, *L'shoneinu Rinnah*, p. 90, claims this is why the word is "in" his face as opposed to "on his head" (using the preposition *b'* rather than *al*). Note also that the word *yismaḥ* has the connotation of shining light in Proverbs 13:9. See Jones C. Greenfield, "Lexicographical Notes II," *Hebrew Union College*

Annual 30 (1959), p. 147. I thank Shlomo Tanner bringing this connection to my attention. And see the *Otzar Ha-t'fillot* (Vilna: Romm, 1914), p. 686.

[28] B. Beitzah 16a. The talmudic passage goes on to describe the gift of the Shabbat, as noted by Rabbeinu Tam above.

[29] See, also in this vein, Bar-Asher, *L'shoneinu Rinnah*, pp. 89–90; Yosef Yahalom, *Piyyut U-M'tziut B'sheilhei Ha-z'man Ha-attik* (Jerusalem: Hakibbutz Hameuchad, 1999), p. 177.

[30] In this way, the verses of V'Shamru, which represent a relational connection between God and the Jewish people (*beini u-vein b'nei yisrael*), are well-suited to follow this introduction. See further Elitzur, *P'tihatah Ha-k'dumah*, p. 13.

[31] See, also in this vein, Gordon Tucker, "From Amidah to Amidah: The Flow of Shabbat Time," in his *Torah for Its Intended Purposes: Selected Writings 1988–2013* (Brooklyn, NY: KTAV, 2014), pp. 91–95.

V'shamru: The Bible's "Poetic Story" About Shabbat

Dan Ornstein

If you love it, do not photograph
the woods as it now is, the leaves
in sunlight and shadow hardly stirring
in the air of the hot afternoon.
Do not try to remember it, stopping
the flutters of leaves and wings,
the dead leaf slowly spinning
on an invisible thread. Do not ask
the trees to linger even to be named.
You must live in the day as it passes,
willing to let it go. You must set it
free. You must forget this poem.
Then, into its own time forever
gone, it is forever here.[1]

Wendell Berry (b. 1934, United States) is a Kentucky farmer and social activist whose poems about the cycles and mysteries of nature have established him as an outstanding American writer. The poem above, from his extensive collection of Sabbath poems, challenges us to take a more "in the moment" walk through the woods than we might be used to taking. Can we embrace the majestic beauty of leaves and trees just as they are, as they inevitably pass through time—changing from second to second, onward toward decay— without trying to freeze them in time? Berry discourages us from committing nature to human or photographic memory, so that we can give up our illusory quest to control it. Paradoxically, it is only through our fleeting experiences of the woods, not our attempts to imprint them in our minds, that we truly make them "forever here." Giving ourselves totally to these experiences in wonder, we can return to them repeatedly. Similarly, we only appreciate the preciousness of time—"each day's passing"—when we humbly accept that, once it has passed, time is forever gone; our task is to just live in it, letting it be. Trying to capture the world forever on our iPhones weakens our ability to let the world captivate us. Even focusing our "in-the-moment" experience of the forest through the poem's words is *itself* a way of weakening the immediacy of that experience. We must therefore even forget the poet's words, immediately after having taken them to heart.

I am struck by how Berry's tribute to being fully present with nature and time is punctuated by terms that are legal in tone. Three times the poet prohibits us, "Do not"; three times he commands us, "You must." To free the reader from turning her encounter with nature into a huge, crass selfie, he plays the role of a contemplative nature guide who is also a law-giver. We are not used to this mixing of law and literature, prohibitions and poetry. Certainly, a command or prohibition here and there in the mouth of a fictional character intensifies dialogue and develops narrative tension, but these are exceptions in Western literature. For the most part, we expect that dry law will remain in the law books; we look to fiction and poetry to entertain and inspire us without constraints on the characters' behavior, on our imaginations, or on the writer's self-expression. Remarkably, John Berry crosses the artificial line between law and literature by combining both in this poem, howbeit with gentle, tender, non-punitive indirection. His poem brings us into those woods: we are not merely watching those dead and living leaves, that sunlight and shadow, those trees, that glorious, passing day. We are living with and in them, as notes and beats in their magnificent song of transient beauty. As he is doing this, directing us away from losing our immediate connection with nature, Berry lays down "the law" by weaving expertly "no, do not do that" and "you must do this" into the artistry of the poem.

The interweaving of law and literature, often by infusing legal material into stories and by using elements of poetry, is a unique feature of the Bible, a book that seeks to integrate all aspects of human life and to infuse them with God's presence. It shuns what Chaya Halberstam calls "the compartmentalization of [literary] genres."[2] Jason Gaines has made the intriguing suggestion that many laws found in the Torah—the Five Books of Moses—can be read poetically in ways that deepen, clarify, and even modify their historically accepted meanings.[3] Assnat Bartor argues that the narrative reading of biblical laws—a method developed by the Law and Literature School of Bible scholarship—allows the reader to discern the human element found in law as an instrument for pursuing justice: "Narrative reading...treats legal material in a manner that also confers value and meaning upon it. It underscores the human and subjective aspects of the law and illustrates how law is an instrument for responding to the human condition and is not only an instrument for subordination and control."[4] Similarly, Chaya Halberstam writes: "I would suggest that in the Hebrew Bible, narrative may have overtly legal aims, while law may utilize the devices of narrative...Both narrative and law may offer us models of vision and praxis intertwined."[5]

In this essay, I suggest that Exodus 31:16–17, what Jewish liturgy refers to as V'shamru, can be read as a "mini-story" that uses poetic techniques to convey the religious and moral meaning underlying the laws of Shabbat. It is significant that V'shamru follows Exodus 31:12–15, which is a harsh, punitive *legal* expression of the Torah's prohibition against *m'lakhah*, creative work, on Shabbat. Though at first glance it appears to be a mere repetition of the previous passage's themes, V'shamru can, in fact, be reasonably read as a poetic and narrative response to this statement about Shabbat law. By re-telling the story of Shabbat, V'shamru inspires us to remember that Shabbat encompasses, yet ultimately transcends, its myriad laws and restrictions.

Biblical Poetry: What Is It? How Is It?

Before we examine V'shamru as a poetic "mini-story," we need to understand a little about biblical poetry.[6] The British poet Samuel Taylor Coleridge (1772–1834) once wrote: "I wish our clever young poets would remember my homely definitions of prose and poetry; that is, prose—words in their best order; poetry—the best words in their best order."[7] Certainly, such a brief summation of something as complex as poetry is too tidy, but Coleridge nonetheless made an excellent point: a great poem contains words carefully and succinctly chosen for their beauty and impact, which have been arranged in profoundly creative, meaningful ways. This is certainly true of biblical poetry, which is distinguished (although not exclusively) by its use of a literary technique called parallelism: expressing an idea or image within a poetic line in two parallel ways. Below is an excellent example of parallelism from Psalm 23, the renowned poem of consolation that is held in highest esteem by Jews and Christians alike:

God makes me lie down in green pastures;
God leads me beside still waters.[8]

If the poet had wanted to express this idea in simple prose, he could have written, "God leads and guides me to safety." However, this is a poem, as is made clear by its simple, yet vibrant first line: "The Lord is my shepherd, I shall not want." Rather than merely state that God protects him, the poet almost shocks us with the provocative yet soothing identification of God with the shepherd—the implication being, of course, that the poet is a sheep. None of this imagery needs to be taken literally: humans and God, after all, are not actually sheep and Shepherd. However, the psalm provokes us to take the imagery quite seriously. What better metaphor could the faithful poet use to describe concretely his sense of utter dependence upon God to protect him from harm?

Notice how both lines expand and lend color to this image of God: God is not a shepherd in name only, but a shepherd who lives up to the title through action. Consider how the two parallel lines relate to each other. A casual reading reveals what appears to be needless repetition: we know that God is a great shepherd who brings us to rest in green pastures, so why repeat this idea with the image of God leading us beside still waters—which seems to add nothing to the image already drawn? Conversely, we might casually assume that the parallel images, in fact, have no similarity and are therefore meaningless. Yet these casual readings miss an important dimension of parallelism: the poet presents an idea twice, often (though not always) in a different way, so as to intensify the idea from one line to the next. This develops the idea in ways that a single mention alone would not achieve. God the shepherd is great at the job! We can find God faithfully resting with the flock in those green pastures. Yet this passive image of God resting then gives way to a far more active one: God also successfully leading the flock, among it our "poet-sheep," to still waters where the flock can drink and live, all the while sheltering it from implied predators along the way to the water. We are thus confronted with a magnificent development: rest leads to activity, while passive oversight leads to active protection. Thus, we could read our two parallel lines in this way:

> God makes me lie down in green pastures;
> [And even more so] God leads me beside still waters.

Many other examples of biblical parallelism exist, placing the best words in a variety of best orders. For example, returning to the theme of trees, we find the following verse in Psalm 92, formally designated in its opening line as the psalm for Shabbat:

> The righteous man shall bloom like the palm tree;
> Like the Lebanon cedar [the righteous man] shall grow mightily. (92:13)

The righteous man is compared to the palm tree (most likely the date palm, which is common to the Middle East) and to the cedar tree, two very tall, slow-growing trees that take a long time to bear fruit after initial planting.[9] These parallel images are an illustrative response of faith to what the psalmist writes earlier in the psalm about evil people:

> The wicked may spring up like grass;
> The evildoers might blossom forth,
> But they will be destroyed forever. (92:8)

Using simple images culled from nature (grass, blossoming shoots, tall trees), the psalmist makes a profound poetic statement of hope about the fortunes of good and evil people. Like grass and shoots that seem to grow and spread with ease, unimpeded, the wicked appear to pop up and proliferate unstoppably. But soon, like quick-growing but lowly grass scorched by the sun, evildoers will die out. Good people may appear unable to grow and flourish, so powerful is the force of evil behavior. But a faithful person needs to be patient. Ultimately, like the Lebanon cedar and the date palm, good people will bloom, flourish, and overshadow the evildoers.

We should return for a moment to our verse comparing good people to trees to consider it more closely, this time labeling its different parts based upon their literal order in Hebrew:

A	*B*	*C*
The righteous man	like the palm tree	shall bloom

B'	*A'*	*C'*
Like the Lebanon cedar	[the righteous man]	shall grow mightily.

As we saw above in our discussion of Psalm 23, the image of the righteous man gradually growing mightily intensifies the image of the same man gradually blooming. Palm trees can reach a mature height of about seventy-five feet. Cedars can reach an even greater mature height of about 130 feet.[10] The image of the good person as a cedar intensifies the image of that same person as a palm tree. Rendered in prose, the psalmist's faith in the face of evil is essentially this: "If you think that good people do not have a chance to succeed, wait patiently. They will gradually bloom like palm trees—and with God's help, they will gradually get even bigger and stronger than palms, becoming like cedars."

Looking again at our verse, this time with its different parts labeled, we realize that we could draw an imaginary X between the two lines by connecting **A** with **A'**, and **B** with **B'**. The word-order of the palm and the cedar literally criss-crosses with references to the righteous man, as it were, surrounding the reader or worshipper with images of tall, mighty trees that protect him from evil. (Bible scholars call this kind of criss-crossing parallelism a chiastic structure, from *chi*, the Greek letter written as χ.) Further, while the righteous man is referred to explicitly (**A**) in line 1, in line 2 (**A'**) he seems to go missing, referred to elliptically by the verb "to grow mightily."[11] The poet seems almost to inject an element of doubt into his seemingly solid statement of faith: waiting patiently for justice to be served so gradually on the evildoer, might the righteous man be in danger of disappearing, out of despair? Recall that psalms are complex religious statements. Faith and hope interact dynamically with the anxiety of doubt, because that is the true nature of mature faith. Yet psalms are not just religious texts; they are poems, beautiful ones in fact. Their authors use these kinds of poetic techniques (such as parallelism and chiastic structure) to catch the careful reader's attention and deepen his or her engagement with the poem.

V'shamru, the Bible's Poetic "Shabbat "Story," from within

I could listen to Bruce Springsteen's songs, Bach's partitas, or Kreisler's Praeludium repeatedly, all day long. I know nothing about music theory, I cannot play an instrument, and I do not read music; but their music, nonetheless, moves me, literally, beyond words. Similarly, poetry is music in words, whose sounds and syllables can make you sing and dance even if you do not speak the language of the poet fluently, or even at all. Before we translate and examine its words as poetry, read—and listen to!—V'shamru in the original Hebrew, using my transliteration. Note the repeated sound that I have bolded:

> *V'**sh**amru v'nei yisrael et ha-**sh**abbat,*
> *la·asot et ha-**sh**abbat l'dorotam b'rit olam.*
> *Beini u–vein b'nei yisrael ot hi l'olam,*
> *ki **sh**eishet yamim asah Adonai et ha-**sh**amayim v'et ha-aretz,*

*u–va–yom ḥa-**sh**'vi·i **sh**avat va-yina**f**a**sh**.*

Even if you are not a Hebrew reader or speaker, if you are reading this essay you likely know the Hebrew word "Shabbat," meaning the Sabbath. The *sh* sound in Hebrew is produced by a consonant, the letter *shin*. The word "Shabbat" derives grammatically from the Hebrew verb root *shin-bet-tav*, meaning "to cease from work or movement." It seems to me no surprise that a word denoting a day for being at peaceful rest should begin with *shin*, whose sound is a near-universal onomatopoeia used to gently quiet someone down.[12] Yet also listen to the music of the *shin* letter as it dances through these two verses, Exodus 31:16–17: it occurs in this thirty-one-word passage eight times, three of these in the last half-verse alone. "Shhh…" these verses seem to be saying to the Israelites and to us: "Quiet down, stop working and building and producing. Be like John Berry's leaves in sunlight and shadow, hardly stirring in the air of the hot afternoon." The author of V'shamru has deployed a simple yet striking repetition of a mere consonant to convey poetically the rest and peace that define Shabbat at its best.

The poetry of this biblical passage is made even more manifest when we look at its structure. Below is my English translation of V'shamru (Exodus 31:16–17), retaining the word order and redundancies peculiar to the Biblical Hebrew:

(A) They shall observe—the children of Israel—Shabbat

(B) To make Shabbat throughout their generations, an eternal covenant.

(C) Between Me and between the children of Israel, a sign-is-She, eternally

(D) For in six days made Adonai the heaven and the earth

(E) And on the seventh day, (Adonai) ceased from creating and "re-souled."[13]

When we analyze this passage, what do we find? Once again, we will label the different parts of the first two lines, revealing interesting parallels:

A   *B*   *C*

They shall observe—the children of Israel—Shabbat.

A'   *C'*   *B'*

To make   Shabbat   throughout their generations, an eternal covenant.

Notice how A is intensified by A', its direct parallel. Observance of Shabbat (expressed using the Hebrew root *shin-mem-resh*, "to guard") refers to adherence to the legal restrictions of refraining from creative work; this is certainly an important aspect of Shabbat through which we imitate God, who ceased from creative work at the beginning of time. However, following those prohibitions—an essentially passive endeavor—is only one limited part of the Shabbat experience. The parallel Hebrew word *la-asot*, "to make" or "to create," challenges the faithful Shabbat observer to do something more active and more important: to imitate, weekly, God who made the world and who then created and observed the first Shabbat.[14] Moreover, Shabbat is not observed in isolation by hermits; it is a sacred celebration embraced with joy by an entire community, the children of Israel—and not only the children of Israel of biblical times, but by all Jews, throughout their generations, as an eternal covenant with God. Thus, the "criss-crossing" parallels of B and B', C and C': Shabbat, the eternal day, was given to the people of biblical times, and *even more so*, to all Jews of all times.

If V'shamru had given us only these poetic gifts, it would have been sufficient. Yet the passage offers us even more poetic artistry. Turning to the middle line, the center of the passage, we notice that it not only physically divides both line-pairs, but it also draws them together into a meaningful whole: "Between Me and between the children of Israel, a sign-is-She, eternally." As we saw above, the first line-pair focuses on us, the Jewish people, and our celebration of Shabbat in imitation of God. Below, we will see how the second line-pair focuses on God, who created the universe and celebrated the very first Shabbat. The third line literally (and literarily) brings us, God's people, together with God! Just as no one Jewish person should observe Shabbat alone, so too, the Jewish people's Shabbat celebration is not for us alone. It is for us to enjoy together with God, as an eternal sign of our abiding love for each other: "Between Me and between the children of Israel, a sign-is-She, eternally."

This now brings us to our second set of line pairs. Here too we discover a subtle yet evocative parallelism, howbeit one without chiastic structure:

A	*B*	*C*
For in six days	made Adonai	the heaven and the earth.

A'	*B'*	*C'*
And on the seventh day,	(Adonai) ceased from creating	and re-souled.

Six days of creative work lead up to the majestic seventh day of rest, of ceasing from creation. Over the course of these two brief statements, the Torah takes the entire history of the world's creation found in the first chapter of Genesis and boils it down to a gem of a miniature story. In doing so, it answers some nagging questions raised by the first part of V'shamru: What is Shabbat an eternal sign *of*, between us and God? Why should we human beings "make" Shabbat at all? The answer: because God created all of existence in six days, then ceased from creating (*shavat*[15]) on day seven. We are God's creatures, yet we are also God's co-creators, a direct reflection of God's presence in the world. God worked for six days to create a magnificent world? We do so as well. God ceased from that work on Shabbat to appreciate what

God had done? We do so as well, and we *must* do no less, for God is ultimately the Master in this co-creative relationship.[16]

Six days parallel day seven (*A* and *A'*): God creating the world parallels God resting and ceasing (*B* and *B'*). Each parallel presents us with a heightening tension, first between ordinary time and sacred time, then between creation and cessation. Yet, what meaningful parallel or tension can we draw between "heaven and earth" (*C*) and "re-souling"? (*C'*) More importantly, what is re-souling?[17] The standard translation of the Hebrew word *va-yinafash* is a figurative one: "God was refreshed." Yet such a rendering makes it difficult to understand what the Torah asserts God actually did. A number of the medieval Bible commentators wrote that God, who neither sleeps nor grows tired, would not *need* to refresh or re-soul; those are human needs based upon human physical and mental limitations. These commentators, many of whom were deeply influenced by the philosophical trends of their day, were quite uncomfortable with anthropomorphic descriptions of God, and would only explain them figuratively and symbolically.[18]

However, the Bible itself—at least in its earliest narratives—seems to possess no such discomfort. Drawing from the earlier account of the first Shabbat (Genesis 2:4), V'shamru seems to assert that even God, Creator of heaven and earth—that is, everything in existence—needed to rest, breathe, refresh, and re-soul after finishing the work of creation. If we follow this anthropomorphic vision of "God at rest" to its full conclusion, its parallel with "heaven and earth" reveals a fascinating spiritual insight. God, the ultimate Creator of all that is, ceased creative work on that first Shabbat. God did this not only as the Artist appreciating the masterwork, but also, as it were, as the first Laborer in need of genuine rest and refreshment. As a comment on our cyclical life of work and rest, six days and Shabbat, in imitation of God, V'shamru is giving us a "warning" on three different levels: (1)

like God, we must work, create, and build the world; (2) like God, we must desist weekly from creation, to leave it alone, especially to remind ourselves that we are not God, that our mastery of the earth is limited; (3) most provocatively, like God, we must desist weekly from creation because no human being can be fully human while constantly working, just as God cannot be fully God while constantly creating. We find, implicit in this last parallelism of V'shamru, the most significant intensification of language and ideas. If God, Creator of heaven and earth, ceased from work and needed to "re-soul" on Shabbat, *how much more so* do we, mere human creatures, need to cease and re-soul.[19]

Law and Literature: V'shamru in Context

As I suggested above, V'shamru is a poetic and narrative response to the Torah's very harsh legal expression of Shabbat prohibitions found in the preceding passage. Modern Bible scholars suggest that Exodus 31:12–15 and Exodus 31:16–17 represent two different schools of ancient Israelite teachers. Their disparate but overlapping approaches to Shabbat were placed together over the many centuries that the Torah was being edited into a final document: the latter passage, V'shamru, was possibly intended as a supplement to the former passage.[20] By contrast, the very popular traditional Torah commentary of Rabbi Ḥayyim ben Attar (1696–1743) offers a number of moralistic and sermonic reasons for V'shamru, on the assumption that the two passages were set down together by Moses at God's dictation.[21] Whichever approach one follows, I believe it is reasonable to assume that V'shamru is commenting on—or responding to—the passage before it, which reads as follows:

And the Eternal said to Moses: Speak to the Israelite people
and say:
Nevertheless, you must keep My sabbaths,
for this is a sign between Me and you throughout the ages,
that you may know that I the Eternal have consecrated you.
You shall keep the sabbath, for it is holy for you.
One who profanes it shall be put to death:
whoever does work on it, that person shall be cut off from
among his kin.
Six days may work be done,
but on the seventh day there shall be a sabbath of complete
rest, holy to the Eternal;
whoever does work on the sabbath day shall be put to death.[22]

We immediately detect three similarities between V'shamru and
this preceding passage: (1) the commandment to keep Shabbat, (2)
Shabbat as the sign of God's covenant with Israel throughout the
generations, and (3) the distinction between the six days of the week
and the seventh day. However, in significant ways, the two passages
could not be more different. The earlier passage repeats three times
the prohibition, *on pain of death*, against profaning Shabbat by
performing *m'lakhah* during the holy day. V'shamru mentions the
prohibition in only the most implicit terms and without reference to
any kind of punishment for violating Shabbat.[23] The reason offered in
the first passage for observing Shabbat is to remind the Israelites that
God makes them holy, and that they therefore must observe Shabbat
as a holy day in imitation of God. Though the concept of holiness
might be implicit in V'shamru, the word is never mentioned explicitly.
By contrast, V'shamru gives us a basis for God's people to observe
Shabbat as a form of direct *creative* imitation: we reenact God's
creation of the world and God's first Shabbat, and we remember that
we are God's co-creators. Daily and weekly, in our relationship with
God, work and rest, we act out and echo the great drama of God's

relationship with the universe.

Through the use of poetic elements and narrating a mini-version of the creation story, V'shamru complements the first passage by conveying to us that Shabbat is about far more than its laws and the threat of punishment for their violation. Shabbat is a dramatic reenactment—a kind of spiritual theater—in which we, together with God, weekly re-live the world's creation and God's covenant of love with us. Similar to Berry's poem, V'shamru recognizes that Shabbat is a weekly miracle, a glorious walk in the woods without your camera—with eyes and heart flung wide open. Every Saturday is a day passing through the week, never to be again. Yet Shabbat is more than merely Saturday; it is a day that eternity utters, reflecting that eternal covenant between the eternal Creator and Israel, the eternal people.[24] Shabbat's holiness is expressed through law that helps us, like God, to rest and be refreshed in body and spirit. Without law to help us create a boundary between work and the holiness of rest, we cannot accomplish this quest for holiness. However, law alone is never enough, for law without love, prohibitions without poetry, behaviorism without meaning, can transform Shabbat from that joyous walk in the woods into a prison sentence. In the true spirit of Judaism, the poetic words of V'shamru stand in balanced tension with the prior expression of the Bible's most inclusive Shabbat prohibition: *m'lakhah*, or creative work.[25] Together, law and love, prohibition and poetry, behavior and purpose, set you and me free from merely existing, by showing us how to truly live, in letter *and* in spirit.

V'shamru is also responding to Exodus 31:12–15 in another significant way. The first passage makes clear that Shabbat is of, by, and for the Jewish people as a holy people, in exclusive relationship with God. It is a particularistic institution. Creation, humanity, the world at large, and our vital role in creation are not given a voice here, at least not an explicit one. V'shamru does not abandon this particularistic theology: after all, Shabbat *is* an eternal sign between us and God; it is God's gift specifically to us, the Jewish people, one that we celebrate and nurture. But V'shamru also lends a distinctive, universalistic meaning to Shabbat as well. We observe Shabbat not only to treasure our holiness as God's chosen people, but also to reaffirm our task as God's choosing partners: together with God, we must strengthen the ongoing creation, maintenance, and protection of heaven and earth and all living things in between. One day a week, our celebration of Shabbat sets us *apart from the world*; during that time, God and God's Torah ask us to remember our responsibilities to all of humanity and creation, as *a part of the world*.

The Mark of Cain and the Sign of Shabbat

Imagine this scene from the biblical story of Cain and Abel. Cain stands over the corpse of his brother, whose life he has taken in a fit of brutality and jealous rage. The glorious creation song of God's first Shabbat has long since been muffled by the sins of Adam and Eve and their subsequent expulsion from paradise, and now this bloody end to one quarter of humanity, what Elie Wiesel has called the world's first genocide.[26] Stunned by this human being's propensity for violence and death, the Creator confronts Cain, the son and sibling turned murderer, an arrogant pretender to mastery over life and death (Genesis 4:9–10):

God said to Cain, "Where is your brother Abel?"
And he said, "I do not know. Am I my brother's keeper?"
Then God said, "What have you done? Hark, your brother's blood cries out to Me from the ground!

We imagine the last echoes of song of that first Shabbat being drowned out completely by Abel's blood screaming from the earth, demanding justice. This was not what God had planned for humanity. How has everything gone so terribly wrong?

God decrees that Cain's punishment will not be execution: after all, why would God, heavenly Parent of both these boys and the whole first human family, respond to murder by initiating more killing? No, Cain will wander ceaselessly in exile, subject to intimidation by human and animal predators alike. Aware of Cain's distress that whoever finds him might kill him, God performs a mysterious act of compassion: "The Eternal put a mark on Cain, lest anyone who met him should kill him" (Genesis 4:15).

What was the mark that God gave Cain? Long ago in an unnamed place in the Land of Israel, a group of rabbinic sages argued fiercely about this. Some of them said it was a fearsome horn on his forehead. Others suggested that it was fearsomeness itself. And still others taught that it was a dog to keep him company and protect him. Then a rabbi who had been listening spoke up:

"I disagree with all of you. The protective mark that God gave to Cain was Shabbat. It was as if Shabbat shut the door tight in God's face when God came to take Cain's life for his crime against his brother."

"Shabbat? That is absurd!"

"No it is not. The Torah tells us that God gave Cain a protective mark, in Hebrew *ot*. The Torah also calls Shabbat an *ot*, a sign of God's eternal covenant with us.[27] The use of this same word in both passages is hinting something important to us: God gave Cain, the world's first murderer, Shabbat, the world's first and greatest day of peace and love, as His sign of protection. So too, God gives it to us, Cain's descendants.[28]

V'shamru, like all poems, presents the best words in their best order. It calls to us: "When you celebrate Shabbat, it will remind you that humanity, descendants of Cain's legacy of brutality, is never beyond redemption." No matter how cruel humanity becomes, V'shamru calls to us, the Jewish people, but by extension all people: "Let Shabbat be your release from despair, let it be your blessing of respite, 'forever here,' that holds you through the violence, the hatred in the world, all week long. You, God's living poem, God's partners in creation, must be that living sign to all people, reminding them that death and destruction are not the only answers. People can—they must—choose life."

NOTES

[1] Wendell Berry, "If You Love It," in *This Day: Collected & New Sabbath Poems* (Berkeley, CA: Counterpoint Publishing, 2013), p. 352.

[2] Chaya Halberstam, "The Art of Biblical Law," *Prooftexts* 27:2 (2007), p. 346. Chaya Halberstam is an associate professor of Religious Studies at Kings University College at Western University in Canada.

[3] Jason M. H. Gaines, "Poetic Laws," published online at https://thetorah.com/poetic-laws/. Jason Gaines is an instructor in Religious and Judaic Studies at Smith College.

[4] Assnat Bartor, "Reading Biblical Law As Narrative," *Prooftexts* 32:3 (Fall 2012), pp. 292–311. Assnat Bartor is Professor of Jewish Studies at Tel Aviv University.

[5] Chaya Halberstam, "The Art of Biblical Law," pp. 345–364.

[6] One of the best books on biblical poetry is by Robert Alter, *The Art of Biblical Poetry* (New York, Basic Books, 2011), especially chap. 1.

[7] *Specimens of the Table Talk of Samuel Taylor Coleridge*, ed. Henry Nelson Coleridge (London: J. Grant, 1905), p. 48.

[8] Psalm 23:2. Translated literally from the Hebrew, the verse reads: "In green pastures God makes me lie down / By still waters God leads me."

[9] The date palm only begins to bear fruit four to eight years after being planted. See https://en.wikipedia.org/wiki/Date_palm.

[10] See the following Wikipedia articles: "Cedrus Libani," at https://en.wikipedia.org/wiki/Cedrus_libani; see also the article, "Date Palm," at https://en.wikipedia.org/wiki/Date_palm.

[11] These two techniques are known respectively as chiastic parallelism (as noted, from the Greek letter χ) and elliptical parallelism.

[12] See the Wikipedia article on cross-linguistic onomatopoeia: https://en.wikipedia.org/wiki/Cross-linguistic_onomatopoeias#Hushing.

[13] Regarding my translation of the Hebrew words *ot hi l'olam* as "a sign-is-She eternally" on line C, as opposed to the standard translation (as, e.g., in the JPS New Jewish Version: "It shall be a sign for all time"), my translation is an attempt to poeticize how the words are rendered in English. This is in keeping with my contention that the V'Shamru passage should be read as biblical poetry. Though Shabbat is neither male nor female, the biblical Hebrew pronoun, *hi*, is feminine, thus my reference to Shabbat as "She." Further, because rabbinic sources refer metaphorically to Shabbat as both a bride and a queen, capitalizing the word She is a reasonable poetic flourish. On line D, I have attempted to preserve the Hebrew word order in "made Adonai the heavens and the earth," whereas the more normal English word order would be "Adonai made the heavens and the earth."

[14] In fact, this word, *la-asot*, echoes its earlier use in the passage about that first Shabbat found in Genesis 2:3.

[15] The noun "Shabbat" is spelled in Hebrew with the same letters as the verb *shavat*. The Hebrew letter *bet* is at times vocalized with a *dagesh*, a diacritical mark that gives it a "b" sound in pronunciation. When, for grammatical purposes, the mark is absent, the *bet* letter is pronounced like a "v."

[16] This dynamic relationship between us and God is reinforced throughout our passage by the repetition of the Hebrew *asah*, to do or to make: we "make" Shabbat (*la·asot*) to echo when God made the universe (*asah*). Both uses of the verb, as well as the verb *shavat* ("ceased from work"), directly echo Genesis 2:3: "And God blessed the seventh day and declared it holy, because on it God ceased from all the work of creation that God had done."

[17] I suggest my neologism, "re-souling," based upon the verb root of *va-yinafash*, which is *nun-pei-shin*, "to be alive" or, more accurately, "to breathe." "To be refreshed" is certainly an adequate figurative rendering of the word, but it fails, in my opinion, to capture the full poetic texture and beauty of the Hebrew.

[18] For instance, see the comments of Rashi and of Abraham Ibn Ezra to this verse.

[19] I also suggest that this "how much more so" inference is hinted at in yet another way in our passage: through ellipsis, leaving out explicit mention of God in the second line, thus creating an intriguing ambiguity. Without explicit reference to God there, the line could also be read as: "And on the seventh day, he (=the human being) ceased from work and re-souled." This is, admittedly, a creative reading engendered by the line's elliptical quality, not the simplest or most logical contextual reading.

[20] Saul Olyan, "The Sabbath According to H or The Sabbath According to P And H?" *Journal of Biblical Literature* 124:2 (Summer 2005), pp. 201–209.

[21] Ḥayyim ibn Attar, *Or Ha-ḥayyim* (ed. Venice, 1742) to Exodus 31:16–17. For a translation, see *Or Hachayim: Commentary on The Torah By Rabbi Chayim ben Attar*, trans. Eliyahu Munk (Jerusalem: Lambda Publishers, 1999), vol. 2, pp. 839–846.

[22] The translation is from the Jewish Publication Society Torah, changing "Lord" to "Eternal" in keeping with the conventions of this series.

[23] As I wrote above, the Hebrew verb root *shamar* can be translated as "to observe a law or prohibition."

[24] "Day that eternity utters": after Abraham Joshua Heschel, *The Sabbath* (New York: Farrar Strauss & Giroux, 1951), chap. 7.

[25] *M'lakhah* is not primarily "work" as defined by physicists: the amount of energy expended when force is applied to an object to move it over a certain amount of distance. Rather, it is the act of creating or destroying something, particularly by changing its material state. According to Genesis 2:1–3, when

God reached the seventh day of creation—Shabbat—God ceased from all of God's *m'lakhah*, through which God created the universe. To create the *mishkan*, the desert sanctuary which was a sacred space, the Israelites imitated God's performance of *m'lakhah*, as is recorded in Exodus, chaps. 25–38. The talmudic sages possessed an ancient legal tradition that Exodus 31:12–17 interrupts this building narrative (human *m'lakhah*) to once more warn the Israelites that, like God, they are to perform creative work six days a week in order to build the sanctuary; yet on the seventh day, also like God, they are to refrain from this construction of sacred space in order to honor sacred time, Shabbat. The sages derived the list of the thirty-nine archetypal forms of *m'lakhah* forbidden on Shabbat, based upon this juxtaposition of the biblical passages. Whatever forms of creative work were forbidden in the building of the *mishkan* are similarly forbidden during Shabbat. See M. Shabbat 7:2 for a detailed list of *m'lakhah* labors.

[26] Elie Wiesel. *Messengers of God: Biblical Portraits and Legends* (New York: Touchstone-Simon and Schuster, 1976), pp. 37–64.

[27] Another standard translation of the Hebrew word, *ot*, used above to refer to "mark," is "sign." *Ot*, as we have read, is the word used in our V'shamru passage.

[28] Midrash Tanḥuma, *Parashat B'reishit* §10.

When Does the Shabbat That We Observe Begin and End?

Martin I. Lockshin

The Torah presupposes that the faithful know many things that it fails to spell out. Consider, for example, Exodus 31:16: What is meant by God's injunction that Israelites "keep" the Shabbat, *v'shamru v'nei yisrael et ha-shabbat* (using the same verb found in the version of the Ten Commandments presented at Deuteronomy 5:12)? There are many pieces to that puzzle, but one of the most basic concerns the boundaries of the Sabbath day, when it begins and when it ends. For anyone with even a modest Jewish education, that sounds like an extremely simple question. But, as with most things, the more deeply we look into it, the more complex it becomes.

The standard understanding is that Jews who observe Shabbat define a "day" differently from the rest of our culture. When Jews want to explain the timing of Shabbat, we have to mention the name of two days of the (secular) week, explaining that Shabbat begins just before sundown on *Friday* afternoon and lasts until three stars appear on *Saturday* night. Jewish law thus teaches us that all Jewish days, including Shabbat, conform neither to our calendars nor to our customary consciousness of a day.

But why *do* Shabbat and every other Jewish day begin in the evening? The traditional answer is based on the interpretation of a phrase repeated six times in Genesis 1: *va-y'hi erev va-y'hi boker*. Consider Genesis 1:3–5:

God said, "Let there be light"; and there was light. God saw that the light was good, and God separated the light from the darkness. God called the light Day, and the darkness He called Night. And there was evening and there was morning (*va-y'hi erev va-y'hi boker*), a first day.[1]

The Talmud explains that the biblical phrase means that in each "day" in the story of creation, daylight follows night.[2] This explanation was, and is, a standard part of a good Jewish education. And until the twelfth century, when Rabbi Samuel ben Meir (called Rashbam, c. 1080–c. 1160) wrote his controversial commentary on the Torah, this explanation was unquestioned.

Commentaries of Rashi and Rashbam on the Torah

Rashbam's grandfather and teacher, Rashi (1040–1105), was the most famous Ashkenazic rabbi of the Middle Ages. Both grandfather and grandson were pious Jews who spent most of their intellectual energy on the study of Talmud and *halakhah* (Jewish law). But each also wrote a commentary on the Torah, as a kind of hobby, it seems.

Rashi's Torah commentary captivated the Jewish world as soon as it was written. For traditional Jews, it is still the most authoritative commentary. Dozens (or perhaps hundreds) of super-commentaries on Rashi's Torah commentary have been written, and are still being written today. Thousands of printed editions of Rashi's commentary exist, since for the last few centuries, traditional Jews who write a new Torah commentary almost invariably publish it with Rashi's Torah commentary on the same page, perhaps in order to avoid creating the impression that they are attempting to supplant Rashi's work. In fact, Rashi's Torah commentary may have been the first Hebrew book printed, even before the first edition of the Hebrew Bible in the

1470s. So many manuscripts of Rashi's Torah commentary exist, and with so many differences among them, in fact, that no one has ever produced a universally accepted scholarly critical edition.[3]

His grandson Rashbam's Torah commentary had a totally different fate. In its own time, it apparently had very limited distribution. When the two leading Bible commentators of the generations immediately after Rashbam, Rabbi David Kimḥi (1160–1235) and Rabbi Moses ben Naḥman (Ramban or Naḥmanides, 1194–1270), wrote their works, they responded to Rashi's commentary frequently but never to Rashbam's. Later commentators such as Rabbi Levi ben Gerson (called Ralbag or Gersonides, 1288–1344), Don Isaac Abarbanel (1437–1508), and Rabbi Ovadiah Seforno (1475–1550) also do not seem to have seen Rashbam's commentary on the Torah. Authors of vast erudition, they would have tried to read whatever previous commentaries they could find. They would have been especially interested in a commentary written by a famous talmudist like Rashbam—and Rashi's own grandson, at that. But his commentary seems to have been unavailable. Indeed, even after the invention of the printing press when Jewish books, including many Torah commentaries, started to be printed, Rashbam's Torah commentary remained unpublished. If not for a wealthy German bibliophile, Rabbi David Oppenheim (1664–1736), the Torah commentary might have been entirely lost. Oppenheim found a manuscript of Rashbam's Torah commentary in an attic and purchased it.

This manuscript only began with Genesis chapter 18. The last chapters of Deuteronomy were also missing. According to Oppenheim, the manuscript showed evidence of having been eaten away at both ends by rodents. All printed editions of Rashbam's Torah commentary that we have today, including the first printed edition funded by Oppenheim in the early eighteenth century, are based on that manuscript. Sadly, the manuscript itself was lost during the Shoah. Like Rashi's Torah commentary, no scientific critical edition of Rashbam's Torah commentary exists, but for a very different reason: we have no manuscripts on which we could base such an edition.

In the nineteenth century, Rabbi Abraham Geiger (1810–1864) found a medieval manuscript in Munich containing almost all of Rashbam's commentary on Genesis chapter 1. This text abruptly ends in mid-sentence in the middle of a comment on the last verse of the chapter. Some traditionalists refused to believe that Rashbam was the author, mostly because of the surprising comment there on *va-y'hi erev va-y'hi voker* ("there was evening and there was morning"). But scholars agree that the manuscript contains Rashbam's authentic commentary on Genesis 1, and this chapter appears in almost all contemporary editions of the commentary.[4]

Rashbam's Comment on *Va-y'hi Erev Va-y'hi Voker*

Rashbam's comment on Genesis 1:5 is as follows (with the biblical verses presented in bold):

> **[God calls the light Day] and the darkness Night**: The text always writes about the light first and then the darkness. **There was evening and there was morning** (*va-y'hi erev va-y'hi voker*): The text does not say, "There was *night* and there was *day*." Rather it says, "There was evening"—i.e., the light of the first day subsided and the darkness fell—"and there was morning"—that morning [that came at the end] of the night when dawn broke. At that point, **one day** of those six described in the Decalogue (Exodus 20:11) was completed. Then the second day began when "God said, 'Let there be an expanse'" (Genesis 1:6). The text has no interest in stating that an evening and a morning regularly constitute one day.

The text is interested only in describing how those six days were constituted—that when the night finished and the dawn broke, one day was completed and the second day began. **God said, "Let there be an expanse."** When this first day finished, at dawn, God said this.

Rashbam points out the significant difference between what the Torah did not write, "There was night and there was day, one day," and what it did write, "There was evening and there was morning, one day." Accordingly, he says that we should not understand our verse as saying that "one day" consists of nighttime followed by daylight. As he puts it, "The text has no interest in stating that an evening and a morning regularly constitute one day." The text is describing how God created the world. On each day of creation, God "worked," and then, at the end of the work day, evening fell and then morning followed. At that point, when dawn broke, the previous day of creation finished and a new day of creation began. After that happened, God began the creation activities of the next day.

What Did Rashbam Mean to Say in His Comment
on *Va-y'hi Erev Va-y'hi Voker?*

While Rashbam was a radical advocate of *p'shat*, the plain or contextual meaning of the Bible, he firmly accepted midrash as a legitimate method of reading the Torah, aware as he was that much of Jewish law was derived through midrashic interpretation. In fact, he wrote that midrash was the most important method of reading the Torah, and certainly we know that he himself felt obligated to observe the laws derived through midrashic interpretation.[5] But he understood that the text of the Torah is multivalent. He argued that the *p'shat* should not be ignored, and so he dedicated his Torah commentary to *p'shat*. In part, his commentary was a veiled polemic against the commentary of his grandfather, who also declared allegiance to *p'shat*[6] but who, in Rashbam's assessment, often fell short of explaining the plain contextual meaning.[7]

Here in Genesis, Rashbam was offering a new *p'shat* interpretation of a verse but he was not advocating any change in Jewish law. We see this unmistakably in his commentary to Genesis 1:14, where the Torah says that the sun, moon, and stars serve "as signs for the set times—the days and years." Rashbam explains that the stars serve as signs for us, since "from one appearance of the stars until the next appearance constitutes one day." In other words, Jewish days, including the Sabbath day, were meant from the beginning to be reckoned from dusk to dusk, as they are reckoned in halakhic Judaism today. Rashbam insists, though, that this is not the contextual, plain-sense meaning of the words *va-y'hi erev va-y'hi voker* and that this is not the pattern that God followed when creating the world in six days. God's six days of creation were from dawn to dawn.

This is just one of many comments where Rashbam knowingly offers an interpretation that does not conform to the standard traditional understanding.[8] In fact, this passage is, in theory, less radical than many other comments of his, since Genesis chapter 1 is narrative and not law. It could be argued that Rashbam's non-traditional explanations of legal passages in the Torah are far more controversial, since they could potentially influence questions of Jewish practice.[9] Rashbam often does not explain how he reconciles what *halakhah* teaches with the *p'shat* meaning of the Torah.[10]

Reactions to Rashbam's Comment on *Va-y'hi Erev Va-y'hi Voker*

As mentioned above, when Rashbam's commentary on Genesis 1 was first published, some doubted its authenticity because of what they saw as the radical nature of his explanation of *va-y'hi erev va-y'hi voker*. Even today, some editions of the Torah text accompanied by traditional commentaries that are intended for the ultra-conservative market include all of Rashbam's Torah commentary except for the commentary on the first chapter of Genesis. ArtScroll Publications recently demonstrated an inconsistent approach by printing a Bible with all of Rashbam's commentary on Genesis chapter 1, except for the comment on *va-y'hi erev va-y'hi voker*. As Marc Shapiro has pointed out, either the one manuscript that underlies the commentary on Genesis 1 is legitimate or it is not.[11]

Iggeret Ha-shabbat

The most famous criticism of Rashbam's explanation of *va-y'hi erev va-y'hi voker* comes not from modern times, but from Rashbam's younger contemporary Rabbi Abraham ibn Ezra (1089–1167) in a polemical work entitled *Iggeret Ha-shabbat* ("The Epistle of the Sabbath"), written in England in 1159.[12] Ibn Ezra, like Rashbam, was a radical advocate of *p'shat* exegesis. On a few occasions, he hinted that his close reading of the text led to the conclusion that Moses was not the author of every verse of the Torah.[13] On other issues he was more conservative.[14] While Rashbam was untroubled by the idea of a text having more than one meaning, Ibn Ezra wrote: "There is only one correct explanation for the words of any author, whether the author was a scholar or a prophet."[15] If the rabbis teach that a day is from dusk to dusk, Ibn Ezra is not willing to tolerate the idea that the first chapter of the Torah says something different.

In Ibn Ezra's introduction to *Iggeret Ha-shabbat*, an entertaining piece of medieval Jewish literature, he writes that he was in a deep sleep in his bed one Friday night when, in a dream, he saw a messenger standing before him holding a letter. The messenger explained that he was sent by the Sabbath herself to deliver it. Ibn Ezra describes his excitement that the Sabbath had taken the trouble to write him a personal letter.[16]

The letter from the Sabbath is, not so coincidentally, written in standard Sephardic poetic style, the style of Ibn Ezra's own poetry. Ibn Ezra describes his pleasure as he reads the first part of the message where the Sabbath praises Ibn Ezra's past allegiance to her. However, his mood changes when he reaches the end and the Sabbath accuses him of disloyalty: "In your youth you observed me [= the Sabbath] faithfully, but now in your old age you have sinned inadvertently, for your students brought books into your house that encourage desecration of the eve of the Sabbath."

Ibn Ezra asks the Sabbath's messenger to explain. The messenger answers that the problem was in a Torah commentary that Ibn Ezra's students had recently brought into his home. He relates that in his vexation he hurriedly took the newly-arrived Torah commentary out into the moonlight (presumably because no lights were available in his house at night on the Sabbath) and saw that, in the interpretation of the phrase *va-y'hi erev va-y'hi voker*, the unnamed sinful commentator wrote that "when the morning of the second day began, that was the completion of one full day" of creation.[17]

Ibn Ezra describes his consternation (real or exaggerated for dramatic effect; it's hard to tell) that such a dangerous book was in his home. He claims that he even considered burning it then and there, invoking the talmudic principle that one may desecrate one Sabbath if it will ultimately lead to the observance of many Sabbaths.[18] But he restrains himself, vowing to write an excursus immediately after the Sabbath explaining why a biblical day must be seen as beginning at dusk. Thus was born *Iggeret Ha-shabbat*.

Ibn Ezra explains:

- The purpose of presenting the story of creation at the beginning of the Bible is to encourage Jews to observe the Sabbath. It makes no sense that a day in the creation story would have a different structure than the day that the Jews are supposed to observe.

- If this interpretation were to circulate, Jews would become a laughingstock for Christians. Ibn Ezra does not explain why, but a reasonable explanation is since the Jews had always claimed that the Bible advocates a dusk-to-dusk day, and since the Christians observed their Sabbath beginning at dawn, a Jewish Bible commentary that found support in Genesis 1 for the Christian understanding of a day was to be shunned.

- Even the Karaites teach that a day begins at dusk. The Karaites were a Jewish sect that did not accept the authority of the Talmud. Ibn Ezra had expended considerable energy during his lifetime polemicizing against them. But on this issue Karaites and mainstream Jews who accept talmudic authority (Rabbanites) agreed, so the existence of this new divisive commentary was especially irksome to him.

Ibn Ezra did not identify the author of the offending Bible commentary, leaving scholars to debate the question. One theory, first proposed by Samuel Poznanski,[19] is that Ibn Ezra had heard about an obscure dissident Jewish group living in Cyprus called the Meshawites, who observed Shabbat from Saturday morning to Sunday morning, and he wrote his *Iggeret Ha-shabbat* to counter their claims.[20] But there is no evidence that Ibn Ezra had ever heard of the Meshawites, and indeed it seems certain that at the end of his life he was acquainted with Rashbam's works.[21] Furthermore, the offending quotation that Ibn Ezra cited in *Iggeret Ha-shabbat*, "when the morning of the second day began, that was the completion of one full day," seems to be taken almost verbatim from Rashbam. Finally, Ibn Ezra reports that the messenger told him, in the name of the Sabbath herself, *v'lo tissa p'nei ish*—that is, that Ibn Ezra was not to show deference to the offending exegete. It would not have crossed Ibn Ezra's mind to show deference to the tiny group of Meshawites, thousands of miles away, who were considered heretics by the very few Jews, Rabbanite or Karaite, who knew anything about them. But he might have considered showing deference to Rashbam, the respected talmudist, who was a scion of perhaps the most illustrious family of French rabbinic scholars.

Modern Bible Commentators on *Va-y'hi Erev Va-y'hi Voker*

In modern times, a few Jewish Bible commentators have come to the defense of the traditional understanding of *va-y'hi erev va-y'hi voker*.[22] But most acknowledge the logic of Rashbam's position. The respected Bible scholar Moshe David Cassuto (Italy and Israel, 1883–1951) writes:

> This method [i.e., the one used in Genesis 1] of reckoning the day from sunrise appears to be at variance with the accepted Israelite practice of connecting the day-time with the preceding night—that is, the custom of regarding sunset as the starting-point of the day. In order to remove this inconsistency, Jewish exegetes, both medieval and modern… sought to place forced and improbable interpretations on the words, *and there was evening and there was morning*. Only a few, like Rashbam, gave the correct explanation of the verse, which Ibn Ezra, nevertheless, attempted to refute by composing his *Sabbath Letter*.[23]

Cassuto, like Rashbam, was a rabbi who was loyal to Jewish tradition;

still he takes Rashbam's insight a step further. He says that both the Bible and later Judaism teach that ritual observances of Judaism are observed from dusk to dusk. Consider the verse about observing Passover (Exodus 12:18): "In the first month, from the fourteenth day of the month at evening, you shall eat unleavened bread until the twenty-first day of the month at evening."[24] This verse unambiguously stipulates that the holiday is celebrated from dusk to dusk. However, Cassuto writes, the biblical conception of a day, not just in Genesis 1 but in many places throughout the Bible, is of a unit of time that lasts from dawn to dawn. For one example, after Lot's older daughter sleeps with her father at night, the verse says that "the next day" (*mi-maḥorat*) she and her sister planned what would happen on the following night (Genesis 19:33–34). This verse proves that the morning following the night is considered a different day. In fact, even Exodus 12:18, which is cited above to prove that Passover begins in the evening and ends in the evening, can also be used to prove that the definition of a biblical day follows the pattern that Rashbam suggested, as follows: The verse says to begin eating *matzah* on "the fourteenth day of the month at evening." But the standard understanding of Jewish law is that when we begin to eat *matzah* at the seder, the date is the fifteenth of the month since the sun has already set. Yet the Torah still refers to that time as "the fourteenth day of the month at evening," which must mean that the underlying biblical conception of a day is from dawn to dawn.

Conclusion

Cassuto, like Rashbam, is able to tolerate contradictions in the tradition. With his insight into the differing conceptions of "day," Cassuto circles back to the Bible, showing that the contradiction that Rashbam pointed out many centuries ago was actually part and parcel of a contradiction contained within the Bible itself. Perhaps both Cassuto and his medieval predecessor felt that if the Bible could contain such contradictions, there was room for them to experiment with new textual interpretations while still holding fast to the traditions of their people.

NOTES

[1] Translations of biblical texts throughout this essay are taken from the NJPS.

[2] See, for example, B. Ḥullin 83a and Rashi's comment there, s.v. *ma'aseh b'reishit*.

[3] Currently, the best text of Rashi's Torah commentary is generally felt to be the one that appears in *Mikraot G'dolot Ha-keter*, ed. Menachem Cohen, 7 volumes (Ramat Gan: Bar Ilan University Press, 1997–2013).

[4] I have published an annotated Hebrew edition of Rashbam's Torah commentary, *Peirush Ha-rashbam al Ha-torah*, in two volumes (Jerusalem: Ḥorev, 2009 and reprinted with corrections in 2013). The text in this edition is based on the Oppenheim and the Geiger manuscripts.

[5] See, e.g., his commentary to Genesis 1:1 and 37:2.

[6] See, e.g., Rashi's comment to Genesis 3:8.

[7] See my *Rabbi Samuel ben Meir's Commentary on Genesis: An Annotated Translation* (Lewiston: Edwin Mellen, 1989), pp. 17–23.

[8] For lists of such passages, divided into categories, see my *Peirush Ha-rashbam al Ha-torah*, pp. 532–534.

[9] For one example, see his explanation that the scapegoat of Leviticus 16 is not killed but is set free to graze with other goats (commentary to Leviticus 16:10). The traditional explanation is that the goat is killed by pushing it off a cliff.

[10] Hillel Novetsky, a contemporary scholar, feels that he is able to reconstruct many of Rashbam's lost comments on the Torah and he presents his evidence in his website *alhatorah.org*. One of his reconstructions involves completing the text of Rashbam's commentary on the last verse of Genesis 1. In his notes, Novetsky explains that in this comment Rashbam offers a way to harmonize the *halakhah* with the *p'shat* concerning the issue of the definition of a day. The explanation is too complicated for the purposes of this essay but may be found at http://alhatorah.org/Commentators:Rashbam's_Torah_Commentary/1#ShabbatControversyandCensoringofRashbam.

[11] See point 7 in Shapiro's post: http://seforim.blogspot.co.il/2014/12/self-censorship-in-arukh-ha-shulhan.html.

[12] At least since the eighteenth century, some have doubted the attribution of *Iggeret Ha-shabbat* to Ibn Ezra. See Naftali Ben-Menaḥem, *Inyanei Ibn Ezra* (Jerusalem: Mossad Harav Kook, 1978), pp. 305–306, quoting the eighteenth-century rabbi Refael Ashkenzi. (Ben-Menaḥem does not agree with Ashkenazi.) Leading contemporary Ibn Ezra scholar Uriel Simon is convinced that the attribution is correct and so am I. See Simon's *Ozen Milin Tivḥan: Meḥkarim B'darko Ha-parshanit Shel Rabbi Avraham Ibn Ezra* (Ramat Gan: Bar Ilan University Press, 2013), especially pp. 101–133. Some have also expressed doubt about whether it was specifically Rashbam's position that Ibn Ezra was attacking; for more on this point, see below.

[13] See, for example, Ibn Ezra's commentary to Genesis 12:6 and to Deuteronomy 1:2.

[14] On differences between the two approaches see my "Tradition or Context: Two Exegetes Struggle with Peshat," in *From Ancient Judaism to Modern Israel*, eds. Jacob Neusner and Ernest Frierichs (Atlanta: Scholars Press, 1989), vol. 2, pp. 173–186.

[15] Ibn Ezra, *Sefer Y'sod Dikduk Hu S'fat Yeter*, ed. Neḥemiah Aloni (Jerusalem: Mossad Harav Kook, 1984), p. 86. See also Ibn Ezra's comment in his introduction to his *shittah aḥeret* Torah commentary where he says that when we find a contradiction between what tradition teaches and what the verse appears to say, "we search out which one of them is actually true, and we correct [our understanding of] the one that opposes it" (*n'vakkeish eizeh mei-hem hu ha-emet l'vado u-n'takkein et ha-sheini ha-omeid k'negdo*). The comment is found in the *Mikraot G'dolot Ha-keter*, ed. Menachem Cohen (Ramat Gan: Bar Ilan University, 1997), vol. 1, p. 29.

[16] Many editions of *Iggeret Ha-shabbat* are available. The one used here was edited by Samuel David Luzzatto (called Shadal, 1800–1865) and published originally in the journal Kerem Ḥemed 4 (1839). It is available at http://www.daat.ac.il/daat/shabat/luach/igeret-2.htm.

[17] The Hebrew reads *v'hinneih sham katuv peirush va-y'hi erev va-y'hi voker v'hu omeir ki ka·asher hayah voker sheini az alah yom eḥad shaleim*.

[18] B. Yoma 85b.

[19] Samuel Poznanski, "Meshwi al-Okbari, chef secte juive," *Révue des Etudes Juives* 34 (1897), pp. 161–191.

[20] On the Meshawites, see Zvi Ankori, *Karaites in Byzantium* (New York: Columbia University Press, 1968), pp. 372–415; and Golda Akhiezer, "Byzantine Karaism in the Eleventh to Fifteenth Centuries," in *Jews in Byzantium: Dialectics of Minority and Majority Cultures*, ed. R. Bonfil (Leiden: Brill, 2012), pp. 745–748.

[21] Ibn Ezra had lived in France, around where Rashbam lived, before moving to England. Ibn Ezra is known to have had contact with Rashbam's younger brother, Rabbenu (Jacob) Tam. So it is reasonable to assume that he had opportunities to encounter Rashbam's Torah commentary. See the discussion in Simon, *Ozen Milin Tivḥan*, pp. 100–133, especially p. 126.

[22] See, e.g., *Sefer B'reishit M'forash Biydei Ha-rav David Tzvi Hoffmann*, the Genesis commentary of Rabbi David Zvi Hoffmann (Germany, 1823–1921) to Genesis 1:5, translated from the German to Hebrew by Asher Waserteil (Bnei Brak: Nezaḥ, 1969), pp. 26–28.

[23] *A Commentary on the Book of Genesis*, trans. Israel Abrahams (Jerusalem: Magnes, 1961), part 1, pp. 28–30.

[24] See similarly Leviticus 23:32 about observing Yom Kippur from dusk to dusk.

Creating Shabbat

Zvi Grumet

There is one key passage in the Book of Exodus describing the command for Israel to observe, *lishmor*, Shabbat:

> The Israelites shall observe (*v'shamru*) the Shabbat, to make the Shabbat, for all generations, an eternal sign. It will be an eternal sign between Me and the Israelites, because in six days God created the *shamayim* and the *eretz* but on the seventh day He desisted, and inspired. (Exodus 31:16–17)

As this passage invokes creation of *shamayim* and *eretz*, it is appropriate to begin our exploration of the *v'shamru* passage there:

> The *shamayim* and the *eretz*, with everything that fills them, were completed. On the seventh day Elohim completed the creative work He had done; on the seventh day Elohim desisted from any of the creative work He had done. Elohim blessed the seventh day and distinguished it, for on it He desisted from creating any of the creative work which Elohim had created to do. (Genesis 2:1–3)[1]

The creation epic described in the first chapter of Genesis is marked by its organization and structure. Each of the six days of creation (with a few exceptions[2]) follows a formula, which includes the following elements:

- Elohim said…
- Let there be… (or some other verb of creation)
- There was… (or: It was so)
- Elohim sees that the creation was tov ("good")
- Elohim names the creation
- It was *erev* and it was *boker*,[3] *yom*___ ("day #____").

Every one of these elements is absent from the description of the seventh day, on which there is no divine speech, no act or verb of creation, no "it was *tov*," no naming, and no *erev* or *boker*. It is therefore not surprising that Stephen Langton (1150–1228), the Archbishop of Canterbury credited with the chapter divisions of the Bible, saw fit to end the creation epic with the close of the sixth day.[4] The seventh day is so dramatically different structurally that it does not seem to belong with the accounts of the other six days; Langton ended chapter 1 of Genesis with the sixth day, and the description of the seventh day opens the second chapter (2:1–3).

However, the difficulty with ending chapter 1 after the sixth day and beginning a new chapter with the description of the first Shabbat is multifold. Since the description of the seventh day opens by referring to the completion of the *shamayim* and the *eretz*, the very items mentioned in the opening of Genesis 1, the passage describing the seventh day seems to be a literary coda to the creation epic begun in the previous chapter. Furthermore, although there is no formulaic closure of *yom* ___ ("day ___"), as we find with the previous six days, the text repeats three times in three verses that this is the "seventh day." A seventh day makes no sense without the context of the first six, and so the description of the seventh day presumes the previous six. Finally, the name used to identify God throughout the creation epic is Elohim, whereas the name used in Genesis 2–3 (beginning after the description of the seventh day) is consistently Adonai Elohim.[5]

This analysis points to the conclusion that the narrative description of the seventh day *is* an integral part of the opening creation epic, yet is dramatically different from the description of the previous six days in both substance and form. This essay will explore the nature of the seventh day in light of the biblical text in its own literary context, as well as its intertextuality with the above-cited text in Exodus.

Context[6]

The sense of structure in the creation narrative extends beyond the formula repeated for each day of creation. A careful reading reveals that the six days of creation comprise two parallel cycles of three days each. Note the correspondences between days 1 and 4, days 2 and 5, and days 3 and 6 (highlighted by reading the columns in this table vertically):

Day 1 *Or* ("light" or "time"[7])	**Day 2** Separation between "upper" and "lower" waters	**Day 3** Emergence of land and vegetation
Day 4 *Me'orot* ("luminaries" or "timekeepers"[8])	**Day 5** Animals that inhabit the "upper" and "lower" waters (flying creatures and fish, respectively)	**Day 6** Animals that inhabit the land and consume the vegetation

These two cycles reflect an orderly and carefully designed creation process. The first cycle of three days is filled with potential, but is static. The second cycle of three takes the potential inherent in each of the first three days and animates it, both literally and figuratively. The luminaries/timekeepers appear to move through the sky,[9] and the animals of the fifth day are described primarily by their mode of locomotion.

Beyond the structural view, the entire creation story describes a movement from an initial state of chaos to a clearly organized and differentiated world. The *tohu va-vohu* of Genesis 1:2, the unformed and undistinguished mass brimming with the potential for everything, is methodically organized via a series of separations—light from dark, day from night, upper waters from lower, land from water. The plants and animals are created "each according to its species," and both are designed to reproduce only according to their species.[10] And closing of each day of creation with the words *erev* and *boker*, usually translated as "evening" and "morning" respectively, likely refer to the movement from confusion to clarity. The root of *erev* means "to mix," while the root of *boker* means "to clarify."[11]

The entire creation saga thus describes a carefully organized and planned process involving a series of creative acts, each effected by divine speech, after which God announces that a meaningful stage of creation has been completed. It is *tov*. Each day of creation marks a significant phase in the movement from chaos/*erev* to clarity/*boker*. When the physical universe and its inhabitants are finally completed, God announces that not only are the individual components complete but that the whole—clearly greater than the sum of the parts—is very good, *tov me'od* (Genesis 1:31).

The daily formula for the creation narrative reflects all of these processes. The seventh day, however, is different. On the one hand, it is part of the creation story; on the other hand, it lacks all of the formulaic elements found in the description of the previous six days—precisely because they describe the creative process, of which the seventh day is *not* a part. There is no divine speech of creation, no creative verbs, *no ki tov*, no *erev* and no *boker*—because there is no physical creation on this day. Nonetheless, the Bible insists that we consider the seventh day as an integral, albeit radically different, part of creation.

Text

The nature of the seventh day becomes clearer when we look more carefully at the biblical text. This short text consists of only three verses. The first verse introduces the seventh day as the day *after* all of the processes of creation in the physical domain have been completed: "The *shamayim* and the *eretz*, with everything that fills them, were completed" (Genesis 2:1). The *shamayim* and *eretz* are an explicit reference back to the opening of the creation story, in which Elohim creates *shamayim* and *eretz* (Genesis 1:1). The Hebrew *kol tz'va·am*, which I translated as "everything which fills them," refer to everything else that was created in the rest of the opening six days.

The next verse presents us with a paradox: "On the seventh day Elohim completed the creative work He had done; on the seventh day Elohim desisted from any of the creative work He had done" (Genesis 2:2). While the first half of the verse states that God completed the creation on the seventh day, the second half explicitly avers that God desisted from creative actions on that day. According to one opinion found in an ancient midrash,[12] the paradox was so troubling that the elders who translated the Torah into Greek changed the text to avoid the contradiction. According to others, the created world was missing Shabbat and so the act of "creating" Shabbat completes the creation.[13] This second opinion is actually grounded in a careful reading of the text itself. The Hebrew *ba-yom ha-sh'vi·i* is usually translated as "on the seventh day," yet an equally plausible translation would render it as "through the seventh day"—that is, through the very creation of the seventh day, the greater creation is completed.

This begs the question of why a seventh day was necessary. Certainly God does not need to rest, and could have simply stopped creating at the end of day six when everything was complete. During the first six days a process unfolded in which everything in the physical universe was completed, but the seventh day describes the creation of an idea, a day on which there is no physical creation. The implication of this is quite startling, as it begins to suggest a purpose for the seventh day. Put simply: the seventh day is a day on which to continue the creative process beyond just the physical realm.

The final verse in the biblical description of the seventh day provides further clarification, but also presents new challenges: "Elohim blessed the seventh day and distinguished (or: sanctified) it, for on it He desisted from any of the creative work which Elohim had created to do" (Genesis 2:3). Two distinct ideas emerge in this verse. The notion that Elohim distinguished (or sanctified) the seventh day, found in the end of the verse, is clear: the seventh day is unique in that its creative nature is expressed in the non-physical world. Indeed, some would call that sanctification. But what does it mean to say that Elohim "blessed" the seventh day? What is a blessing, and what does it mean for a period of time to be blessed?

To explore this idea more fully, we need to first understand what a blessing is. This is not the first blessing in Genesis, nor will it be the last. On the fifth day of creation, Elohim blesses the fish and birds, that they be fruitful and multiply, and on the sixth day Elohim likewise blesses the humans.[14] Divine blessing in this context does not mean that the result is *inevitable*, but rather that it is *possible*. A blessing from Elohim means that Elohim has endowed the recipient with a potential, or perhaps has shared some of the divine creative power with the recipient. Thus, blessing people or animals (such as fish and flying animals) is an act empowering them to be fruitful and to dominate their respective domains.

This definition of blessing, however, is more difficult when it comes to understanding the blessing of the seventh day. What could it mean for a time period to be blessed? Perhaps the answer is that in planning creation, Elohim designed it so that there were six days devoted to creative activity in the physical world, and one day devoted to creative activity in the non-physical realm. That special time period, the seventh cycle of time, is endowed with a special capacity for fostering non-physical creativity and bringing it to fruition.

Intertextuality

The idea of the seventh day as time set aside for, and endowed with, special capabilities for non-physical creativity both sheds light upon and is illuminated by the presentation of Shabbat to the Israelites in the Exodus version of the Decalogue:[15]

Exodus 20:8–11	Genesis 2:1–3
Remember the Day of Desisting (or: the Sabbath Day), to distinguish it. For six days you shall work and do all of your creative work, but the seventh day—it is a day of desisting, for the Eternal, your God. You shall do none of your creative work—you, your son and your daughter, your male and female servants, your animals, and the foreigner in your gates. Because for six days the Eternal made the *shamayim* and the *eretz*, the seas and all that is in them, and He rested on the seventh; it is for this purpose that the Eternal blessed the Day of Desisting and distinguished it.	The *shamayim* and the *eretz*, with everything that fills them, were completed. On the seventh day Elohim completed the creative work He had done; on the seventh day Elohim desisted from any of the creative work He had done. Elohim blessed the seventh day and distinguished it, for on it He desisted from creating any of the creative work which Elohim had created to do.

Some elements of the Genesis text are easily recognizable in the language of the Decalogue: the creation of the *shamayim* and *eretz* and all that is in them parallels the opening verse of the Genesis text, and the six days of creative work followed by a day of desisting (which is finally named) is another clear parallel element. It is clear that the Decalogue text is built on the foundation of the creation text.[16]

There is another subtle yet powerful link between the two texts. The verbal roots *bet-resh-kaf* (meaning "bless") and *kof-dalet-shin* (meaning "sanctify" or "distinguish") appear in both texts. In fact, these are the only two passages in the entire Bible in which both roots appear as twin verbs predicated on the same subject,[17] and it is these two roots which identify the seventh day and set it apart from all others.

While the Decalogue text is unquestionably building upon the creation passage, it also explicates it. The final line of the Decalogue text reads: "It is for this purpose that the Eternal blessed the Day of Desisting (or: Sabbath Day) and distinguished it." This phrase is somewhat obtuse; what "purpose" is the Torah talking about?

If we parse the entire Decalogue passage carefully we discover that there is an initial instruction, followed by filling some historical background, and concluding with some kind of clarification. If we remove, for the sake of clarity, the background section, we are left with the following: "Remember the Day of Desisting (or: the Sabbath Day), to distinguish it.…It is for this purpose that the Eternal blessed the Day of Desisting (Sabbath Day) and distinguished it."

God's purpose in blessing and distinguishing the seventh day was so that Israel would do the same. While many traditional interpretations understand that we rest on the seventh day because God did,[18] a careful reading of the text suggests that it is precisely the reverse: God desisted from creative work on the seventh day so that we would do so as well. Building on our earlier understanding, God endowed this seventh day with a potential for creativity in the non-physical world so that people would develop that potential and bring it to fruition.

A fascinating midrash captures this idea exquisitely: "'Each day of week has a partner,' complained Shabbat, 'but I am all by myself.' God responded: 'Israel will be your partner.'"[19] Indeed, as we saw in the beginning of this essay, the potential of Day 1 of creation is fulfilled on its corresponding Day 4, Day 2 has Day 5 to complete it, and Day 3 has Day 6 to bring out its potential.[20] Shabbat is unfulfilled until there are human beings to bring out its potential. Fulfilling that potential required considerable waiting until God was ready to give the Torah and charge Israel with its fulfillment. Let us return to our opening passage:

> The Israelites shall observe (*v'shamru*) the Shabbat, to make the Shabbat, for all generations, an eternal sign. It will be an eternal sign between Me and the Israelites, because for six days God created the *shamayim* and the *eretz* but on the seventh day He desisted, and inspired. (Exodus 31:16–17)

As Israel observes *v'shamru*, it actualizes Shabbat's potential, which has been waiting since creation. When we fulfill that mission, essentially completing the creation itself on a weekly basis, we transform it from the Day of Desisting into Shabbat—and in the process it becomes a symbol of Israel's partnership with God as co-creators.

NOTES

[1] All the translations in this article are my own. In this passage, I have chosen to retain the Hebrew *shamayim* and *eretz* because the usual translations, "heavens" and "earth," are problematic. For more on these words see my *Genesis: From Creation to Covenant* (Jerusalem and New Milford, CT: Maggid, 2017), pp. 3–16.

[2] The first day opens with what appears to be two introductory verses prior to "Elohim said." The number of the day on the first day is a cardinal number whereas all the others are ordinal numbers, and on the sixth day the number is highlighted by the addition of the definite article: "*the* sixth day." There is no "it was good" on the second day but that phrase appears twice on the third day. Naming happens only on days one, two, and three. For more on the structure of the creation story, see Grumet, *From Creation to Covenant*, pp. 3–16.

[3] These words are usually translated as "evening" and "morning" respectively. See discussion below regarding an alternate translation, which more closely reflects the context.

[4] While most scholars agree that he played a significant role, there is debate regarding who else was involved and how much of a role he played.

[5] The Hebrew text has *YHVH Elohim.* "Adonai" is the traditional pronunciation of the Tetragrammaton.

[6] The ideas in this section are developed further in my *Genesis*, pp. 3–26.

[7] This is an unconventional translation, but is borne out by a close reading of the text. For an explanation see Grumet, pp. 3–16.

[8] See the previous note.

[9] Although it is actually the earth that rotates, we experience the heavenly bodies as "moving" through the sky. Even professional astronomers refer to "sunrise" and "sunset," although of course the sun does not actually move.

[10] The word *min* ("species") is repeated in a variety of forms three times regarding the plants and seven times regarding the animals.

[11] See Leviticus 13:36 and 27:33. According to M. Berakhot 1:2, morning is defined by the ability to visually distinguish between colors or identify people.

[12] Bereshit Rabbah 10:9. According to the midrash, the translation they offered was, "On the sixth day Elohim completed the creative work He had done; on the seventh day Elohim desisted from any of the creative work."

[13] Bereshit Rabbah 10:9. It is cited as a second opinion in Rashi's comment to Genesis 2:2.

[14] It is interesting that the land animals do not receive a blessing, even though they do reproduce. Perhaps because the standard blessing of reproduction (as used with the fish, the flying animals, and humans) includes the idea that they are to dominate their respective domains (see Genesis 1:22, 28), a blessing to

the land animals would clash with that of humanity. This concern later finds a different expression in Exodus 23:30 and in the plague of the wild beasts in Egypt.

[15] The distinction between the seventh day of the week and its six predecessors is actually introduced earlier in Exodus (16:22–30). The manna, which fell daily, did not fall on Shabbat, and the Israelites were instructed not to go out to collect it on Shabbat. In Bereshit Rabbah 11:2, Rabbi Yishmael links the Shabbat of the manna to the blessing and distinction of the seventh day in the creation narrative. The Torah text first makes the connection in the Decalogue.

[16] This is dramatically different in the second account of the Decalogue, in Deuteronomy 5:12–15. In that account there is no reference at all of the creation narrative.

[17] They do appear elsewhere as nouns, or as a verb and a noun, but nowhere else as a pair of verbs.

[18] See, for example, Bekhor Shor's comment to Exodus 20:11.

[19] Bereshit Rabbah 11:8.

[20] In the midrash, Day 1 is paired with Day 2, Day 3 with Day 4, and Day 5 with Day 6.

Am I My Brother's Guardian or Are You?
Cain's *J'Accuse* in the Midrash

Noam Zion

The Biblical Human Calling: To Be A Guardian/*Shomeir*

The innovative Jewish educator Joel Lurie Grishaver once commented that the biblical calling of the human being is to be a guardian/ *shomeir* in three distinct senses. One form of guardianship is Israel's calling to guard or keep the covenant, as in *v'shamru v'nei yisrael et ha-shabbat...b'rit olam*, "Israel shall keep the Shabbat...as an eternal covenant" (Exodus 31:16). More generally, Israel is to keep (*shomeir*) the *mitzvot* of God. The covenantal laws in the Book of Exodus bind not all humanity but Israel alone (Genesis 17:9–10). These laws are to be guarded for one's own good and then God will guard our life (Joshua 23:11).

Second, all humans in the Garden of Eden are expected to guard God's garden of pleasures—God's paradise, the archetypal land— and also to cultivate it, *l'ovdah u-l'shomrah* (Genesis 2:15). Here the human task is not to rule and to conquer, to tyrannize the earth and its creatures (as in Genesis 1:28), but rather to care for and to serve the ecological niche that God has designated and generously planted for Adam's habitat. In Genesis 2, the human is designed as a creature— not unlike the animals of the earth—to live in a mutually beneficial symbiosis with nature. Therefore, neither the animals nor the land belongs to humanity by the right of divine assignment to rule all (Genesis 1:26) or by conquest (Genesis 1:28). Instead humans (*adam*) emerge from and belong to the earth (*adamah*), from which they are taken and to which they will return in death (Genesis 3:19). Adam is not a slave, but a guardian of God's world: responsible for the earth as a trust, just as a guardian of property is culpable for malfeasance for failure to protect the trust (Exodus 22:6–14). Thus, when human beings fail to follow the rules and steal from God's garden, they are expelled for violating various tasks of guardianship: most explicitly, they did not guard the garden according to its Owner's rules.

The third biblical usage of the term "guardian" (*shomeir*) refers not to keeping God's land in good order, but rather to keeping one's brother from harm. God never explicitly instructs brothers to care for one another in Genesis, but brotherly solidarity is so thoroughly ingrained in the biblical ethos that Cain knows he has violated that moral axiom in killing his brother—and so he explicitly denies that responsibility when God asks him "Where is Abel, your brother?" (Genesis 4:9). As Philo explains, the guilty criminal knows he is culpable, so he denies his responsibility:

> Why does God who knows everything ask of the fratricide [Cain], "Where is Abel, your brother?" God wishes that the human himself shall confess of his own free will…for he who killed through necessity would confess…But he who sins of his own free will denies it.[1]

Throughout Genesis, the fratricidal conflicts can be healed not simply by each sibling worrying about himself and avoiding the harm of others, as does a good citizen of a liberal state, but by taking responsibility to serve as collateral, as a substitute to redeem his brother from responsibility. Judah wins his father's consent to take Benjamin to Egypt and he earns Joseph's forgiveness when

Judah takes upon himself Benjamin's punishment for purportedly stealing Joseph's cup (Genesis 43:9; 44:32–33). As codified in the Torah, brothers are expected to be the financial redeemer (*go·eil*) of their nearest kin by buying them out of slavery and buying back their debt-confiscated land even before the Jubilee year (Leviticus 25:25, 25). One must never exploit and abuse a brother as an abject slave (Leviticus 25:46). The full irony and scandal of Cain's denial of responsibility for the whereabouts and the material support of his brother is highlighted for latter-day readers by comparing his story with the passages that actually require an Israelite to be his brother's blood redeemer: "The redeemer (*go·eil*) of blood shall put the murderer to death" (Numbers 35:19, 27). Instead of acting in this way, Cain himself was the murderer—spilling his brother's blood, which is also related to the prohibition on desecrating the divine image in which every human being is born (Genesis 5:1–3). When God makes a covenant with Noah after the flood caused by human violence (*ḥamas*, Genesis 6:11), God demands accounting for all bloodshed:

> Surely I will require your lifeblood; from every beast I will require it. And from every man, from every man's brother I will require the life of man. Whoever sheds man's blood, by man his blood shall be shed, for in the image of God He made man. (Genesis 9:4–6)

While only made explicit in Genesis 9, the Bible assumes that Cain is aware of this judicial principle and now God must become the blood avenger for Abel's blood that cries out to God (Genesis 4:10; see also Isaiah 41:14). In Genesis, Cain's crime violates not the image of God, but the solidarity of brothers implicit in their biological bond. This bond is expressed philologically in the midrashic wordplay on *dam/adam/adamah* (whose Hebrew letters echo one another, and which is reiterated by the repetition of this root eight times in the same passage). *Dam/adam/adamah* in Hebrew are roughly parallel to hemoglobin/human/humus in English.

Midrashim on "My Brother's Keeper"

In this essay, I will focus on the interpretation of Cain's denial of guardianship for his younger brother in midrashic literature. These rabbinic-style narratives are more than objective, analytic commentaries. Rather, they rewrite the story by imaginatively identifying and filling its lacunae. To understand responsibility is to see how its violation generates guilt. Feeling guilty, Cain preemptively denies that God has the right to expect him to be answerable for Abel's absence. Cain insists that he has no liability for his failure to be his brother's guardian. The novelist John Steinbeck, in *East of Eden*, his great novel about Adam, Cain, and his brother, writes:

> No story has power, nor will it last, unless we feel in ourselves that it is true and true of us.….I think this is the best known story in the world because it is everybody's story. I think [the tale of Cain and Abel] is the symbol story of the human soul…The greatest terror a child can have is that he is not loved and rejection is the hell he fears.….And with rejection comes anger, and with anger some kind of crime in revenge, and with the crime guilt. And there is the story of mankind.… The human is the only guilty animal…Therefore I think this old and terrible story is important because it is a chart of the soul—the secret, rejected, guilty soul.….What a great burden of guilt men have![2]

Cain is not really angry at Abel, but at God who rejected his gift ("For Cain and his gift God had no regard; Cain became exceedingly upset and his face fell," Genesis 4:5). Cain refuses to listen to God's warning about ruling over his impulses ("God said to Cain: Why are you so upset? Why has your face fallen? Is it not thus: If you intend good, bear-it-aloft.³ But if you do not intend good, at the entrance is sin, a crouching demon—toward you is his lust, but you can rule over him," Genesis 4:6–7). Then Cain takes out his anger and shame at having lost in the competition for gifts and at having failed to win divine favor. He strikes back at his brother who upstaged him: "And as for Abel, he too brought—from the firstborn of his flock, from their fat-parts. God had regard for Abel and his gift" (Genesis 4:4).

It is God's favor, not Abel's, that Cain seeks. Ignored by God, he will now get attention by acting out. In disregard for God's warning and in order to be contrary, Cain kills his brother because Abel was favored by God (Genesis 4:4). His failure as a guardian is the outcome not of his failure to understand that he is responsible and not out of indifference to his brother, but precisely because his brother threatens to usurp his place as the firstborn, both in the family and in the eyes of God. It is not clear whether Cain considers his violent act as a means to advance his own standing by removing his only competitor or as vengeance on his upstart brother, or as a protest against the discriminatory God who had effaced his dignity.

The narrative could reasonably have ended with Abel's death, followed immediately by divine punishment, but instead God enters a conversation with the murderer. The formulation of the questions shows that God obviously was already aware of the murder, as well as the whereabouts of the victim and the identity of the perpetrator whom God had just warned about controlling his anger. Nevertheless, God interrogates Cain in an extended exchange that opens with God asking naively, "Where is your brother Abel?" Next Cain plays dumb by lying: "I don't know!" Then God asks rhetorically, "What have you done?" and punishes Cain. Cain responds, then, with what might be construed as a confession, or at least with a plea for clemency: "My sin/punishment is too great to be borne!" God responds by swearing to protect Cain, the fugitive wanderer, by assigning him the mark of Cain (though the form that mark takes, whether physical or symbolic, is unspecified in the Torah).

So much divine and human speech is devoted in this chapter to a criminal—first in cautioning him about his reaction to the rejection of his sacrifice and later, after his greater crime of fratricide, in God's conversing with Cain to evoke remorse and confession. The Bible wants us to understand the criminal mind, and it seeks to deliver a pedagogic message so that the arch-criminal and all his descendants can learn about human responsibility for sins—even when the criminal thinks he was provoked and mistreated. The Torah's educational task is difficult because the guilty one denies his culpability in multiple ways and in fact considers himself to be the victim of great injustice.

In the *midrashim* on God's dialogue with Cain, the rabbis imaginatively explore Cain's point of view. There are so many excuses Cain can use as rationalizations: "I couldn't help myself" (lack of impulse control)—despite God's claim that Cain can rule over his *yeitzer*/impulses (Genesis 4:7); "You made me the way I am"; "You treated me unjustly by rejecting my gift and favoring my brother"; and "Who said I am supposed to be my brother's keeper in the first place?" In truth, the Torah does not make God's moral expectations— do not murder; guard your brother— explicit before this first murder. Rather, the positive obligation of guardianship is first formulated when it is denied by the criminal.

Several *midrashim* rewrite the dialogue between God and Cain, thereby articulating Cain's response to the divine presumption that he is supposed to be his brother's guardian. These retellings derive somehow from an oral tradition one of whose earliest written manifestations is Josephus' retelling of biblical history:

> Thereupon Cain, incensed at God's preference for Abel, slew his brother and hid his corpse, thinking to escape detection. But God, aware of the deed, came to Cain, and asked him whither his brother had gone, since for many days God had not seen him, whom God had constantly before beheld in Cain's company. Cain, in embarrassment, having nothing to reply to God, at first declared that he too was perplexed at not seeing his brother, and then, enraged at the insistent pressure and strict inquiries of God, said that he was not his brother's guardian to keep watch over his person and his actions. Upon that word God now accused Cain of being his brother's murderer.... [4]

Josephus suggests that Cain denies responsibility in response to God's meddling questions. Pushed into a corner with no reasonable excuse, Cain blurts out an axiomatic denial of his task as guardian. Of course, the problem is not that Cain failed to protect his brother, but that he killed him. His problem is not dereliction of duty (i.e., criminal negligence), but murder! He was not apathetic to his brother's fate; he was in fact malignantly hostile to his welfare.

Perhaps later *midrashim* realize the incongruity of denying you are a "babysitter" (*shmartaf*) when accused of fratricide. Who, then, failed to defend and guard Abel from his brother Cain?[5] The midrash places in Cain's mouth the accusation that God, not Cain himself, is malfeasant in guarding his brother. As in God's interrogation of Adam and then Eve after the theft of the fruit of the Tree of Knowledge, the one accused shifts the blame. Eve blamed the snake, while Adam blamed both God and Eve: "The woman You gave me, she gave me from the tree, so I ate" (Genesis 3:11–13). Adam portrays himself as a bundle of instinctually obedient responses to whatever is proffered him without an independent mechanism of discretion and self-control. That same recidivism is attributed by a midrash to Cain—like father, like son:

When God asked; "Where is your brother, Abel?" Cain replied: "I don't know, am I my brother's keeper? After all, You are the guardian of all creatures, so why seek him from me?"

It is like the parable of the thief who stole some items one night without being caught, but he was arrested by the gatekeeper the next morning. The gatekeeper challenged him: "Why did you steal the items?" The thief responded, "I am a thief who does not neglect his profession, but your professional duty is to guard. Why did you abandon *your* duty? Now, how can you blame *me*?"

Similarly, Cain admitted, "I killed him, but You created the evil impulse in me. You are the keeper of all, yet You let me kill him!? You really killed him, as it says: "I am (*anokhi*) my brother's keeper." If You had accepted my sacrifice just as You did his, then I would never have been jealous of him!"[6]

The midrash reads Cain's response, "Am I my brother's keeper," not as a rhetorical question but as a statement: You—the one called *anokhi* (the One who self-identifies as the divine "I" in the Ten Commandments)—are my brother's keeper, not me! The term *anokhi* was invoked at Mount Sinai when God self-identified in the first commandment as "I am Adonai your God, who took you out of Egypt" (Exodus 20:2). Cain transmutes the phrase from "my brother's keeper," a concrete familial relationship, to the guardian of creatures of all sorts. So God should have been protecting Abel, just as the night watchman ought to prevent thefts.

Further, for the midrash at least, God is the guardian not only of innocent victims, but even of criminals who cannot be expected to have effective self-control or moral conscience. God fell down on the job of policing Cain and hence of protecting Abel. Cain suggests that people are socially constructed to break rules; they are always trying to evade responsibility. Like students stealing answers left unintentionally by the teacher on his or her desk, Cain is *supposed* to be a thief, not a guardian of his own impulses—let alone the defender of his brother's well-being. In a competitive world such as the one God has created by preferentially treating some sacrifices and some of those bringing the sacrifices over others, and by legislating privileges of the firstborn over second-born sons, people are effectively being encouraged to compete by any means possible, since loss of face and failure cause unbearable humiliation.

Further, the midrashic Cain mouths off to God like an impudent teenager, claiming that whatever bad impulses he has were inherited from his parents. Adam and Eve stole, so Cain steals. His impulses are simply part of human nature; God created him with a *yeitzer ha-ra*, powerful negative impulses. Cain describes himself as a bundle of uncontrollable impulses—such as jealousy and anger which lead to violence—and God knows that, observing: "At the entrance is sin, a crouching demon. Toward you its lust—but you can rule over it" (Genesis 4:7). Cain's denial of responsibility begins by rejecting God's premise that "you can rule over it," and that leaves Cain wholly vulnerable to instinctual responses such as jealousy and revenge.

Given his natural lack of self-control, Cain contends that the divine rejection of his gift inevitably led to killing his brother. God is at fault for not taking the proper precautions and for exacerbating Cain's desire to murder. God has disregarded the rabbinic understanding of the commandment "Do not place a stumbling block before a blind person" (Leviticus 19:14). As Rashi explains, this means that one should "not place a stumbling block before one who is blind to a particular matter."[7] Similarly, the Talmud relates: "The Rabbis taught: 'You shall not put a stumbling block before the blind' refers to one who beats his grown-up son [in order to discipline him]." Rashi explains: Since the son is grown-up, he might resent this treatment and then he will deal his father a blow [which is a capital crime]—thus the father is effectively prompting his son to commit a crime."[8] When God provoked Cain, whom God knew to be jealous and surly, by showing indiscriminate preference for Abel's gift, the midrashic Cain can say *J'accuse*:[9] "If You had accepted my sacrifice just as You did his, then I would never have been jealous of him!"[10]

The midrash makes an excellent case for Cain's absolution, but its point is not to justify murder. Rather it wishes to make explicit the apparently reasonable excuses people invoke to mitigate or erase culpability for lack of self-control. Educationally speaking, the midrash says that God has heard all those justifications before, but you are still expected to be your own guardian who must exercise self-control, and therefore you *are* your brother's guardian. God is not expected to protect one brother from the jealousy of the other. We may live in a world without absolute justice, but injustice, favoritism and inequality are not valid justifications for murder.

In the next midrash the debate between Cain and Abel and between God and Cain turn into a Jobian argument over theodicy:

According to [one] opinion, the [missing] conversation [between Cain and Abel[11]] was as follows: Cain suggested that they take a stroll in the fields, and when they were alone, he said, "It seems that God shows favoritism. That's why your offering was accepted and mine wasn't."
"Heaven forbid," answered Abel. "That's not true at all. I am better than you, and my offering was of higher quality. That's why it was accepted."
"There is no judgment! There is no world to come! Good people don't receive any reward, and the wicked receive no punishment," exclaimed Cain.
Abel replied, "You don't know what you're talking about! Of course God will give good reward in the world to come. He

will also punish the wicked for their misdeeds."
Thus began a debate. But before long, tempers flared…[12]

In this midrash, long before God accuses Cain of killing his brother and before Cain accuses God of failing to be Abel's guardian, the brothers were debating the Jobian question: Can we learn from our own fate—for good or for bad—either that God's world is a meritocracy or that God's tyranny is arbitrary? Abel maintains that he deserved divine preference, and that divine favor justly reflects human worthiness. On the other hand, Cain is sure that his gift was rejected on no rational grounds, that the system is rigged against him. As the Israeli artist and sculptor Yigal Tumarkin once said:

> The real hero is Cain. The loser. In a world of five (God, Adam, Eve, Cain. and Abel), four did not like him. I have no time for Rashi's explanations or Cassuto's. Cain was born screwed. The farmer as opposed to the shepherd. But God always loved shepherds. God knows how strong the emotion of jealousy is, and how destructive. It is the first feeling He put in nature. So what's the big deal here? God drove Cain crazy. And never gave him a chance since he was born. I understand him [Cain]. Jealousy, strong, barren, the most destructive of emotions.
> What did the poet Natan Alterman say? "If you ever laugh without me, at a party of your friends, My silent jealousy will burn your house down upon you."
> I'm Cain. And how! So are you.[13]

In short, the midrash presented above assumes that God is at fault and humans are exempt from all responsibility—but not because people cannot control their emotions, and not because divine competition tantalizes the *yeitzer*/impulse. Rather the problem is systemic: the world lacks justice due to divine arbitrariness. When the leader and the system are amoral, then there is no claim on the individual citizen to act morally. Sin is justified not by human irrationality and lack of impulse control, but by human rationality. It is only reasonable to conclude that, in an irrational world, it is irrational to observe the law. So in a world without a judge or judgment, no one should be law-abiding. When God fails to guard the innocent and reward the virtuous, God is teaching criminals that to react in kind is the most equitable thing to do.

What biblical textual clue gives rise to the midrash? Cain's emotional and moral crisis results directly from the two gifts brought to God—one accepted and one ignored. The detailed adjectives describing the sacrifices reveals that Cain's sacrifice was inferior: Cain's offering comes simply "from the fruit of the earth," in comparison to Abel's gift "from the firstborn of the flock, from the fat ones" (Genesis 4:3–4).[14] Cain does not see what is wrong with his gift, but only what is wrong with the Judge evaluating the gift, who has rejected him: "God paid no heed to Cain and his gift" (Genesis 4:5). Cain could have produced a better quality gift that would have been accepted by God, but Cain sees nothing wrong with his gift. He sees no reason to blame himself, and hence no way to earn honor through greater effort and excellence. God is prejudiced against him and favorably disposed toward his brother.

In another midrash, Abel himself joins Cain in accusing God of failing to be a true guardian, by not intervening in a violent situation whose outcome God could foresee:

> Rabbi Shimon bar Yoḥai said: It is difficult to say this thing, and the mouth cannot utter it plainly. Think of two athletes wrestling before the king; had the king wished, he could have separated them. But he did not so desire, and one overcame the other and killed him. He [the victim] cries out before he

died, "Let my cause be pleaded before the king!" As it says: "The voice of your brother's blood cries out *against* Me!"[15]

In these self-consciously impudent *midrashim* which a pious Jew can barely utter, Abel's blood cries out not *to* God to take vengeance on the murderer, but rather *against* God for creating this competition between brothers for divine favor, just as a Roman emperor takes pleasure in allowing enslaved gladiators to fight to the death. The competition may be judged by fair criteria: one competitor performs better than the other. But fair or unfair, one will be a winner and the other, a humiliated loser. One will kill and one will be killed. Neither brother is culpable, because neither had a choice about entering this competition in the first place.

On different levels, the parable may refer either to Cain and Abel or to Rome and Jerusalem. God decreed that the two kingdoms should fight to the death. The rabbinic expositor of this midrash is Rabbi Shimon bar Yoḥai, who supposedly saw his own teacher Rabbi Akiva tortured to death by the Romans for the transgression of publically teaching Torah. The God of history is the God of injustice. Therefore God generated impossible moral conflicts and hence necessary victims of the struggle: both gladiators, the winner *and* the loser, complain to the emperor that neither wished to participate, whether they are the murderer *or* the victim.

On yet another level, the parable may apply psychologically to Cain who is undergoing an inner struggle between the good and the wicked impulses. God grants free will and takes pleasure in human striving for self-control, as God said to Cain: "You can rule over it!" By creating a moral struggle in a world of free will, God knows that often the evil will out-battle the good impulse—as in the case of Cain.

It is not easy to countermand Cain's midrashic arguments with rational argumentation, even though we feel intuitively that Cain ought to feel guilty for the inexcusable crime of killing his brother. As social scientific and psychological thinking has evolved in the last hundred years, Western legal systems have become more and more forgiving of premeditated murderers. Indeed, when Cain was "retried" thirty years ago by experts in human responsibility, he was acquitted. In 1988 *The Jerusalem Post* reported in a news item:[16]

> Cain was not guilty! It took a few thousand years to get it straight, but humanity's first (alleged) capital crime— Cain murdering his brother Abel—was finally retried. The acquittal came in a simulated trial held in Venice recently by lawyers, moral theologians, historians, and anthropologists. The trial saw the defense successfully extricate the accused from the moral dictum in the Bible "Thou shalt not kill," with arguments about the psychological and sociological circumstances in which Cain slew Abel, of whom he was jealous.
>
> Cain's defenders conceded that he did kill his brother but that it was unpremeditated and in the context of an economic power struggle between pastoralists and the first agriculturalists, Abel representing the former and Cain the latter. From this point of view, Cain's crime should be seen as "rightful" in terms of the "law" of the time, his lawyers maintained. Defense and prosecution each called rabbis as witnesses. After an hour's deliberation, the jury pronounced Cain "not guilty" by a majority of five votes to four.

The *midrashim* succeed in making us aware of the logic of Cain, but I think it is a mistake to confuse understanding his point of view and forgiving his crime. In her controversial book *Eichmann in Jerusalem*, Hannah Arendt invented the theory of the banality of evil to explain Adolf Eichmann's behavior.[17] He was not a monster but a good bureaucrat, she explained. Then she was attacked viciously for exonerating the mass murderer of her people. She responded with passion: "I wrote no defense of Eichmann, but I did try to reconcile the shocking mediocrity of the man with his staggering deeds. Trying to understand him is not the same thing as forgiveness. And furthermore, I see it as my responsibility to understand. It is the responsibility of anyone who dares to put pen to paper on this subject."[18] So too, our *midrashim* seek to understand the first fratricide, not to condone it.

Now I think we do need new *midrashim* to help law-abiding members of society, educators and parents who still believe in free will, self-control, and moral conscience to effectively argue back against Cain. In the perennial disputation begun by Cain, speaking for all criminals who have a serious beef against injustice, the rationalizations, psychological motives, and environmental social causes have gained greater cogency and nuance with every passing generation. The lyrics of Stephen Sondheim's "Gee, Officer Krupke" run the gamut on scientific grounds for exonerating criminals.[19]

Rabbinic midrash itself ironizes Cain's hypocritical pleas for mercy, cautioning against Abel's soft-hearted liberal guilt in feeling compassion for his violent brother:

> "And Cain rose up against his brother Abel" (Genesis 4:8):
> Rabbi Yoḥanan said: Abel was stronger than Cain, for the expression "rose up" can only imply that he [Cain] lay beneath [Abel]. He [Cain] said to [Abel]: "Only the two of us are in the world: What will you go and tell our father [if you kill me]?"
> At this [Abel] was filled with pity for him; immediately [Cain] rose against [Abel] and slew him. Out of that incident was born the proverb, "Do not do good to an evil man, then evil will not befall you."[20]

The midrash intentionally misreads "Cain rose up" (*va-yakom*), usually understood as figurative language for incipient action, taking it instead literally: he stood up from a reclining posture. In the midrashic narrative Cain assaulted his brother but Abel, who was stronger, wrestled Cain to the ground and pinned him down. Once Abel had prevailed over his assailant, Cain pleaded for mercy—in a way reminiscent of the Yiddish joke defining chutzpah as "that quality enshrined in a man who, having killed his mother and father, throws himself on the mercy of the court because he is an orphan."[21] Cain appeals to his brother's potential guilt feelings toward his parents, should he kill Cain even in self-defense. Abel falls for that plea for pity and releases Cain from his clutches. Then Cain, feeling none of the moral compunctions of Abel and no gratitude for Abel's leniency, assaults Abel again—this time, murdering him. Apparently, the cynical Cain is unconcerned about he himself telling his parents what he has done and taking responsibility for the pain he has inflicted on them and on his brother.

In general, the rabbis believed that one's *yeitzer ha-tov*, one's moral conscience, is too weak to overpower its counterpart, the *yeitzer ha-ra*, and this is why Cain was unable to master his impulses.[21] More important, Cain is unable to justify to himself why he should even try to restrain his vengeful thoughts. Our moral thinking is often incapable of coping with the rational weapons in the arsenal of self-exoneration that we have honed. Judges have become too lenient, and angry people who feel victimized have abandoned moral compunctions about taking vengeance. We must be our own guardians, taking responsibility for our own actions—and not projecting our task on God as the guardian of humanity. Only then can we also become guardians of our brothers and sisters.

NOTES

[1] Philo, *Questions in Genesis* 1:68, from the Loeb Classical Library edition of Philo's *Questions and Answers on Genesis*, trans. Ralph Marcus (1953; rpt. Cambridge, MA: Harvard University Press and London: William Heinemann, 1961), p. 41; as cited in James Kugel, *The Bible As It Was* (Cambridge, MA: Harvard University Press, 1997), p. 93, with some changes.

[2] John Steinbeck, *East of Eden* (1952, rpt. New York, London, and Toronto: Penguin Books 2002), p. 269.

[3] Alternative translation: "If you do better, then there is uplift [of Cain's fallen face by winning divine favor; or divine forgiveness for his sin in bringing an inferior gift to God]."

[4] Josephus, *Jewish Antiquities* 1:55–56, trans. H. St. J. Thackery in the Loeb Classical Library edition of Josephus (1930; rpt. Cambridge, MA: Harvard University Press and London: William Heinemann, 1967), p. 27; as cited in Kugel, *The Bible As It Was*, p. 93.

[5] Ironically, Cain's sin is that he did not guard his brother against his own drives—from which he should have guarded himself.

[6] Midrash Tanḥuma, chap. 9, commenting on Genesis 4:3. Note that the verb "to be" is not expressed in the present tense in Hebrew, so the word *anokhi* in the verse quoted means both "I" and "I am."

[7] Rashi to Leviticus 19:14, s.v. *li-f'nei ivveir.*

[8] B. Mo·eid Katan 17a and Rashi ad locum, s.v. *d'ka avar mi-shul v'li-f'nei ivveir lo tittein mikh·shol.* Regarding this idea, cf., Maimonides, M.T. Hilkhot Rotzei·aḥ 12: 14: "It is forbidden to sell a pagan weapons of war, and we neither sharpen their spears, nor sell them knives, manacles, iron chains, bears, lions, and anything that is a public danger; but we may sell them shields that are only for defense purposes. Whatever is forbidden to sell to a heathen is likewise forbidden to sell to a Jew who is a robber, since in doing so we make ourselves an accessory to criminals and tempt them to unlawful acts. Whoever misleads an innocent party [literally: the blind in a matter] and gives them dishonest advice, or strengthens the hand of a transgressor who is blind since the desires of his heart blind him from seeing the true path, violates a negative precept, as it is stated: 'You shall not put a stumbling block before the blind.' Whoever comes to consult you, give him advice in good faith." And cf. the similar comment attributed to Rabbi Natan at B. Pesaḥim 22b and cited below in note 10.

[9] "*J'accuse…!*" (= "I accuse…!") was an open letter published on 13 January 1898 in the newspaper *L'Aurore* by the influential writer Emile Zola. In the letter, Zola addressed President of France Félix Faure and accused the government of anti-Semitism and the unlawful jailing of Captain Alfred Dreyfus.

[10] Rabbi Nathan said: "Whence do we know that a person should not serve wine

to a Nazirite?….From the verse, 'You shall not put a stumbling block before the blind'" (B. Pesaḥim 22b).

[11] There seems to be a lacuna in the biblical text at Genesis 4:8: "Cain said to his brother Abel…But then it was, when they were out in the field that Cain rose up against Abel his brother and killed him"—no direct speech is reported.

[12] Cited in the Spanish anthology *Mei·am Lo·eiz*, an eighteenth-century Ladino reworking of the midrash that first appears in the Aramaic translation called the Targum Yerushalmi composed sometime before the eighth century in the Land of Israel.

[13] As published in the *Yediot Aḥaronot* newspaper on October 14, 1987.

[14] Numbers 18:12–13 presents a law requiring that agricultural gifts to God must be from the "fat" (i.e., the best) of the crop of new oil, wine, and grain and further directs that the first fruits must be donated to God. Apparently, that was the standard that Abel upheld but that Cain failed to meet, bringing "from the fruit of the earth" harvested "at the end of the season "(*mi-keitz yamim*, Genesis 4:3). I do not think this is an anachronistic reading of the story, but the law shows what the original readers would have known. The use of the identical adjectives in Numbers 18:12–13 and Genesis 4:4 cue the reader to that high sacrificial standard.

[15] Bereishit Rabbah 22:0, citing Genesis 4:10. In a later version of that midrash, God is blamed for failing to guard Abel, even though he did not create the competition as does the Emperor. God and all humanity are implicated for being apathetic bystanders:

> *Crying out to Me*: Don't read "to Me" but "about Me." A parable will explain. Two persons quarreled and one killed the other. A third person was standing between them and did not intercede to separate them. Who will everyone be buzzing about? Certainly about the third person. (*Midrash Ha-gadol* on Genesis 4:10; Yemen, thirteenth century).

[16] Jewish Telegraphic Association reports that Dec 20, 1988, a mock trial was sponsored by the Venice municipality and the Venetian Bar Association before a judge and jury with expert witnesses testifying (historians, rabbis, criminologists, etc); see https://www.jta.org/1988/12/21/archive/cain-cleared-of-abels-murder.

[17] Hannah Arendt. *Eichmann in Jerusalem: A Report on the Banality of Evil* (New York: Viking Press, 1964).

[18] Cited in the script of Margarethe von Trotta's film *Hannah Arendt* (2012), from her final speech at the end of the movie, and available online at https://www.springfieldspringfield.co.uk/movie_script.php?movie=hannah-arendt.

[19] In *West Side Story* (1959; rpt. London: William Heinemann, 1972), p. 106f. In the course of the song, Sondheim offers as excuses for juvenile delinquency the delinquent's parents' drug abuse and alcoholism, the delinquent's own neuroses

and mental illness, the delinquent's lack of a healthy home environment while growing up, the delinquent's inability to find employment, and the delinquent's basic laziness. But even the experts can't quite agree: toward the end of the song, various professionals (including a judge and a social worker) argue for mental illness, alcoholism, inbred laziness, poor personal hygiene, and immaturity as the reasons for juvenile delinquency. Nor can they agree on remediation. More to the point, no one will take responsibility to help the delinquent, preferring to generate endless reasons for excusing the delinquent from making mature moral choices.

[19] Bereishit Rabbah 22:7.

[20] Leo Roston, *The New Joy of Yiddish* (New York: Three Rivers Press, 2001), p. 81.

[21] Rabbi Reuven son of Astrubilos says: "How can a person distance himself from the evil impulse which in is in his intestines?...The evil impulse is thirteen years older than the good impulse [which is born only at puberty]...The evil impulse has become habitual and it triumphs." (*Midrash Ha-gadol* on Genesis 4:70. *Midrash Ha-gadol* is an anonymous fourteenth-century compilation of aggadic *midrashim* on the Torah collected from the two Talmuds, earlier *midrashim* of Yemenite provenance, the Targums, and Maimonides.)

V'Shamru: Guarding the Vulnerable in an Uncertain World

Shmuly Yanklowitz

We live in precarious times. Years of recession and the rise of a new class of political and economic demagogues have cleaved our nation into haves and have-nots. Welfare—so demonized for the struggling family, the working single mother, the recovering addict, the refugee—flows plentifully, not to those who need it the most, but into the pockets of undeserving people who have sought to swindle and bankrupt our society. For too long, policies injurious to the vulnerable have proliferated and tragically become normal, leaving a significant void in the capacity for developing empathy in the next generation. This generation's normative purpose—indeed, the goal every generation—is to rectify this gap, and fill its chasm with love toward all of creation. We must hear the voiceless and see the invisible.

In the Book of Genesis, why does God choose Abraham, of all people in creation and the son of an idol-maker, to be the progenitor of many nations, including the righteous nation of Israel? The way the Torah justifies this choice is fascinating: "For I have loved him, because he commands his children and his household after him that they keep (*v'shamru*) the way of God, doing charity and justice, in order that God might then bring upon Abraham that which God had spoken to him" (Genesis 18:19). What is happening here? Just keeping your brood in check hardly merits an everlasting covenant.

Yet, that is precisely what Scripture says is the case. Abraham chose to commit to following God's compassionate and just ways, rather than remaining imprisoned by the iniquities of idol worship; because of this choice, he was chosen to be the father of the Jewish people and all monotheists.

To be a *shomer* ("guardian") of the ways of God is to live a life devoted to walking in God's ways, which is itself a scriptural commandment: "God shall make you into a holy nation…if you keep God's commandments and you [commit to] walking in God's ways" (Deuteronomy 28:9). This concept is also known as *imitatio Dei*. God is merciful, patient, and kind. And human beings, when on their best and most moral behavior, should strive to emulate those attributes (and countless others). The challenge is that many virtues are often in tension. Should we be gentle and quiet in this moment, or bold and courageous? Should we prioritize kindness or strength? Should we be led or be in retreat? The scriptural commandments read almost simply. But to say how *exactly* to walk in God's ways—to emulate the manifold dimensions of divine behavior in the world—is simply not a straightforward matter. Rather, this emulation requires substantial learning and reflection.

Throughout their voluminous commentaries on the Bible, the rabbis urge us to emulate the attribute of compassion. They devised a simple formula for encouraging our highest potential in this world: we are, most of all, to emulate God's compassionate ways. We are to think locally and globally, simply and broadly. But with supporting Israel, helping the Jewish poor, funding Jewish day schools, and countless other Jewish concerns and needs, how can one justify giving time to broader universalistic social justice issues? Rabbi Avraham Yitzḥak Hakohen Kook (1865–1935), the first Ashkenazic Chief Rabbi of British Mandatory Palestine (what was to become the State of Israel), wrote:

> There are some righteous individuals who are very great and powerful, who cannot limit themselves to *k'nesset yisrael* [the Jewish community] alone, and they are always concerned for the good of the entire world…These *tzaddikim* [righteous people] cannot be nationalists in the external sense of the term because they cannot stand any hatred, or iniquity, or limitation of good and mercy, and they are good to all, as the attributes of the holy Blessed One for "He is good to all and His compassion is over all of His works" (Psalm 145:9).[1]

Sadly, I have met too many Jewish social justice leaders who feel marginalized and think of themselves as "bad Jews." In fact, the opposite is true: those who dedicate themselves to supporting the poor, sick, abused, and alienated are indeed model Jews. Abraham was "chosen" precisely because he was committed to being a *shomer* for *tzedakah u-mishpat* (pursuing justice). Indeed, Lurianic Kabbalah (based on the mystical teachings of sixteenth-century Rabbi Isaac Luria) taught that our role in this world is to access hidden sparks, liberate them from their evil shells (*k'lippot*), and elevate ourselves. Social justice activists who go out to support the most vulnerable are doing precisely this. One can be a decent person and only engage with one's own family and one's fellow Jewish neighbor, but this is only part of the job, part of the *tzedakah u-mishpat* mandate. Rav Kook, a pluralist attuned to the diversity and complexity of souls, taught that there are others who cannot remain parochial but need to go out beyond the Jewish community: these are, he taught, righteous individuals.

Everywhere, there are invisible people with inaudible, hidden cries. They are victims of deep injustices and violent oppression. They are the boys who wash our dishes at restaurants and the men who wash our cars. They are the girls who make our hotel beds and the women who serve in our homes. They are the slaves confined by our penal codes and the bodies objectified by raw sexual appetites. They are the homeless, spending their days in the shadow of our contempt and their nights in our parks of denial. Our task is to hear the hidden cries in our generation. Theirs are the loud cries of the streets and the subterranean cries of those yearning for support and comfort, and the open cries reverberating within our souls. The late Rabbi Yehuda Amital, Rosh Yeshiva of Yeshivat Har Etzion and a member of the Knesset, once said in an interview: "Every generation has its own cry, sometimes open, sometimes hidden; sometimes the baby himself doesn't know that he's crying, and hence we have to try to be attentive to the hidden cries as well."[2]

Isn't it true that a person who lacks even the most basic of needs often wishes not to be seen, for any pretense of dependence on greater society is seen as capitulation? There is a deep shame that is felt when a person is at his or her lowest, without the means to improve one's station in life. This engenders anger, which morphs into shame. And this shame limits people's ability to reach out for help, to be visible to others who want to help them. After Nelson Mandela rose to become the first democratically elected president of South Africa, a country marred by a history of injustice the likes of which modern societies had so rarely experienced, he shared the following thought: "Those who conduct themselves with morality, integrity and consistency need not fear the forces of inhumanity and cruelty."[3] It is our duty to take his admonition to heart. We need the courage to see and make seen the victims of injustice among us.

But these words are from another generation. Surely, haven't we learned much since then?

***

The Maggid of Mezritch, one of the most influential of the hasidic masters, thought deeply about the notion of *yeish mei-ayin*, "creation out of nothing." This concept, while not an innovation from by

Maggid per se (the idea had been discussed as early as the medieval scholar Saadiah Gaon), was re-contextualized by the Maggid for a new Jewish audience. In his mystical way, the Maggid believed that helping those who lurk in the shadows is akin to something that had not previously existed coming into existence and providing light to something that had previously been unseen—for this is compared to the creation of the universe itself.[4]

Without question, Jewish law demands not only that we *see* but that we *be seen* in Jerusalem on the festivals.[5] Such a law is not a relic. Rather, it is moral training for our eyes and our hearts; we are to be open to the multifaceted ways to see God. In this way, we are not only *seeing* God but we are also *being seen* by God, thus helping us to learn that in our post-Temple world, the way to see God is to see the unseen in our midst. Connecting and supporting the unseen is not a distraction from tradition, but rather its actualization. Greater than lending money or giving *tzedakah* to a poor individual, the rabbis tell us, is providing partnership to them.[6] Seeing all people as equal goes far toward treating them with respect and dignity. And we cannot discount those who are different from us, even in the slightest of ways.

Fortunately, we have been granted the ability to help make visible those who society would deem invisible. We accomplish this by letting the vulnerable seek out the succor they desperately need. We offer unconditional love, with no judgment of status—only hope. Indeed, only hope and love can bring consolation. Every time we encounter the people who dwell in the shadows, who are ignored and considered as the dregs of society, we must transcend our own pride, our own ego, and bend down proudly to lend an outstretched hand. Some of the most terrifying times in my own life have been when I didn't really feel like I existed; in these moments, I didn't feel acknowledged by the world, let alone appreciated or loved. I often reflect on these times before beginning a mission to help those who are still left to wander the world without guidance and love.

These ideas I've set forth here may seem self-evident, but I've found that they are also truly embedded in traditional rabbinic lessons about the world. Consider, for example, the following midrashic passage: "That which is said about Aaron is greater than that which is said about Moses. Regarding Moses, it is said that only men wept for him, whereas for Aaron both the men and the women wept—because he pursued peace and loved peace, and placed peace between a man and his wife and between a woman and her friend."[7] What are we to make of this perplexing passage? If Moses is *the* paradigmatic leader for the Israelites—and, by extension, for humankind—then why did only half the nation, only the men, weep for him? The deaths of Moses and Aaron are representative of human potential for compromise. If the former showed love by being strict in his demeanor toward his flock, then the latter was a transformative leader who did not lead from a distance but rather walked among the people, building and healing fractured relationships. These models provide us with the paradigmatic tussles between love and justice, where love and compassion becomes the victors over justice.

This dialectic leads, accordingly, to compromise. The art of compromise is demanding and arduous; all of us can learn and grow much by learning how to compromise. So much more work needs to happen on global, national, and interpersonal fronts. But first we must consider our own egos, not letting our latent tribal tendencies take hold of our better nature. We must be willing to retract on our absolutes for the sake peace on earth. One might think that absolutism is a sign of strength. If one has "moral clarity" then one shouldn't budge on one's well-heeled position. Judaism proposes a novel, almost counterintuitive, approach, arguing that compromise is the approach of the wise:

> Rabbi Joshua son of Korḥa says: It is a *mitzvah* to seek compromise, as it is written, "Truth and peaceful judgment should you judge in your gates" (Zechariah 8:16). It would seem that where there is judgment there is no peace, and where there is peace there is no judgment. What is the judgment that incorporates peace? Compromise.[8]

The rabbis valued religious compromise. In the Talmud, Rabbi Yoḥanan is quoted as saying that Jerusalem was destroyed in the time of the Romans only because the people judged according to the Torah. In astonishment, the other rabbis reply: "What kind of judgment should they have applied—that of the sorcerers?" The reply: "What Rabbi Yoḥanan meant was that litigants insisted on strict enforcement of the law and were unwilling to compromise." And Maimonides affirmed this value of religious compromise.[10]

One's character should never be solely measured by one's ideals, but also by how one is willing to compromise for the sake of preserving human dignity. There are, of course, values that should not be compromised. But for the sake of peace, often we must compromise our upper hand even when we feel certain of the truth. Rashi taught that doing "the right and the good" specifically "refers to a compromise, within the letter of the law."[11]

Part of our guardianship of this world must be focused on building more compassion, healing, and peace rather than insisting on harsh, uncaring justice, law, and punishment. Where can we take the higher road in our own lives today? And looking beyond on the personal, how can we take these spiritual notions of compromise into the realms of government and business? God knows, they need it as well. It is our duty to work toward compromise no matter the circumstance, so that the world can become more just, more equitable, and more peaceful. It may be difficult, but it's a sacred imperative.

The Talmud teaches that God prays to God's self:

> May it be My will that My mercy may suppress My anger, and that My mercy may prevail over My [other] attributes, so that I may deal with My children in the attribute of mercy and, on their behalf, stop short of the limit of strict justice.[12]

If God, as it were, needs to pray for God's own kindness to prevail over justice, then all the more so should our own prayers be filled with such intentions. Jewish law tells us that it is unjust to be biased and swayed by poverty, favoring the case of the poor over the rich in a dispute. Within the realm of a formal court's judgment this is crucial (see Exodus 23:3, 6). Does this notion still apply today, however, where the disparity of wealth between the poor and the rich has become so large that the poor often can no longer properly advocate for themselves?

This notion of equality before the law is mostly a delusion today in America, since the poor have such a serious disadvantage in the courtroom. In a *New York Times* article, Michelle Alexander, visiting Professor at Union Theological Seminary and author of *The New Jim Crow: Mass Incarceration in the Age of Colorblindness*, commented that more than 90 percent of criminal cases are never tried before a jury; most people charged with crimes just plead guilty, forfeiting their protected constitutional (I'd argue God-given) rights.[13] The prosecution usually promises to give a deal to those who plead guilty and go all-out against anyone who tries to go to trial. It is simply cheaper to plead guilty than to try to pay for legal counsel (or, for that matter, to rely on underpaid, understaffed public defenders).

If we are truly committed to truth and justice, every individual should have the same fair opportunity before the law. But this is not the reality today. Even if it were true, Judaism teaches that we must go over and above the law (*li-f'nim mi-shurat ha-din*)[14] to support those individuals who are more vulnerable.[15] Furthermore, we are taught that God created and destroyed many worlds that had been built upon the foundation of *din* (judgment), before finally creating this world built upon *rahamim* (divine mercy).[16] Our world can't exist on pure judgment; rather, as fallible beings, we rely upon the grace, empathy, and kindness of God and people.

We must act toward those who are suffering with mercy and compassion, and this must affect how we build society. Former President Barack H. Obama explained the importance of empathy in jurisprudence when he chose the type of individual whom he wanted to be his Supreme Court justices: "I will seek someone who understands that justice isn't about some abstract legal theory or footnote in a casebook; it is also about how our laws affect the daily realities of people's lives. I view the quality of empathy, of understanding and identifying with people's hopes and struggles, as an essential ingredient for arriving at just decisions and outcomes."[17] Law is not only about principle; it is also about life.

Numerous Jewish teachings remind us that our primary responsibility is to protect and prioritize the most vulnerable individuals and parties. Indeed, Kohelet says: "God takes the side of the aggrieved and the victim" (3:15). When there is conflict, God simply cannot withhold support for the one suffering. Rabbi Aaron Soloveichik wrote: "A Jew should always identify with the cause of defending the aggrieved, whosoever the aggrieved may be, just as the concept of *tzedek* is to be applied uniformly to all humans regardless of race or creed."[18] This is what it means to be Jewish: to prioritize the suffering in conflict. This point is made time and time again by the rabbis of classical times. The Talmud, based on the verse "Justice, justice, you shall pursue" (Deuteronomy 16:20), teaches that everything else being equal, the disadvantaged should be given preference[19]; Maimonides teaches that even if the disadvantaged arrive later than other people, they should be given precedence.[20]

In a court of law, all parties are ideally treated equally, as we are guided by the Jewish value of *din* (judgment). Today, however, justice often does not prevail. Further, in the pursuit of social justice activism we must favor the vulnerable, since we are guided by the Jewish value of *ḥesed* (lovingkindness). In life, we must learn to balance all of our values, including love, justice, and mercy. But in the pursuit of justice for all, we cannot choose a simple guiding principle: as Isaiah Berlin taught, moral life consists of embracing a plurality of values.[21]

To be guardians of the vulnerable, we have to ensure the system is fair and just for all parties. Yet as changemakers, we also have a special and holy role: to give voice to the voiceless and to support the unsupported in society. This is the role of Jewish activism. The ancient rabbis taught: "Even if a righteous person attacks a wicked person, God still sides with the victim."[22] All people deserve our love and care but we must follow the path of God and make our allegiances clear: with the destitute, oppressed, alienated, and suffering.

While "underclass" invisibility is caused initially by systems of oppression, the propensity to accept shame invariably leads these vulnerable individuals to perpetuate this depressed psychological and social state. "Shame involves the realization that one is weak and inadequate in some ways in which one expects oneself to be adequate. Its reflex is to hide from the eyes of those who will see one's deficiency, to cover it up," explains legal scholar Martha Nussbaum.[23] One who basic needs are not being met may often wish not to be seen out of shame. This can be made worse by our discomfort at seeing those who are afflicted by penury, economic exploitation, or circumstance and not taking action, which contributes to the further clouding of visibility for these populations.

Yet, we have been granted the power to help make visible the invisible. We can accomplish this by letting the vulnerable hiding in the shadows know, every time we encounter them, that they are recognized members of society, members in good standing even. We can do this especially by letting the public know they exist by advocating for their rights and welfare. As we already saw, Jewish law demands not only that we see but that we be seen in Jerusalem on the festivals.[24] This is training for the rest of the year that our eyes, and hearts, be open to see those who are unseen. Connecting and supporting the unseen is not a distraction from the tradition but its actualization.

To be sure, one of the primary goals of Jewish spiritual life is to see beyond the physical, to sanctify the unseen, and to transform the mundane into a holier purpose. This is the meaning of the quote by Rav Amital brought earlier in this essay: our task is to hear the unique cries of people who are often torn asunder from normal society, from normal time, from normal life; we need to uncover the hidden cries that call to us. In many ways, the cultivation of this ability to listen and respond is the central goal of religious living.

Each morning when I prepare for my morning prayer by putting on my *t'fillin*—phylacteries, the boxes that contain the words of the holy Torah close to my mind and heart—I feel so privileged. Indeed, during my morning prayer, when I notice the right strap hanging down from the *shel rosh* on my head (which is made to be longer than the left strap), I am reminded that this is the kabbalistic sign of the ethic of *ḥesed* (love and kindness). This in turn reminds me that the traits of love and kindness should prevail against the traits of *g'vurah* and *din* (strength and judgment). But as I remove the *t'fillin* from head and arm at the conclusion of my morning prayers, the following question often passes through my head: How exactly shall I prioritize my potential to make the world more kind and more loving over my potential to bring absolute truth and strict justice to the world? I have been fortunate to have the support of an engaged community to help me answer my own question during those introspective moments each morning. I would venture to say I am not alone in having had these feelings, and neither am I alone in recognizing the crucial role played by friends and family members to remind me of my visibility and humanity.

I turn back to the Torah's reflective principle of *v'shamru*, which calls on the faithful to guard that which is truly holy in this world. And so, I conclude by co-opting this holy word as I call out to my readers in the name of the downtrodden: Let us be those friends, *v'shamru*! Let us be those family members, *v'shamru*! Let us be those advocates for those who have none, *v'shamru*! May we be blessed with the good sight to see the unseen, and the vision to increase their visibility in our daily lives.

NOTES

[1] Avraham Yitzḥak Hakohen Kook, *Orot Ha-kodesh* (Jerusalem: Mossad Harav Kook, 5723–5724 [1962–1964], vol. 3, §349; See Yitzchak Blau, "The Implications of a Jewish Virtue Ethic," in *The Torah U-Madda Journal* 9 (2000), p. 36.

[2] This quote can be found in a film honoring Rabbi Amital for his eightieth birthday. Excerpts of the film, titled "A Tribute to Rav Amital zt'l," can be found on YouTube at https://www.youtube.com/watch?v=JPxq_p8L-MM (with the quote beginning at 12:40).

[3] These words were part of Mandela's British Red Cross Humanity Lecture, delivered at the Queen Elizabeth Conference Center in London on July 10, 2003; the quote was later included in Nelson R. Mandela and The Nelson Mandela Foundation, *Nelson Mandela By Himself: The Authorised Book of Quotations* (New York: MacMillan, 2010), p. 206.

[4] Magid D'varav L'ya·akov (Brooklyn, NY: Kehot Publication Society, 1972), p. 11.

[5] B. Ḥagigah 2a.

[6] B. Shabbat 63a.

[7] Midrash Aggadah to Numbers, *Parashat Ḥukkat*, chap. 2.

[8] B. Sanhedrin 6b.

[9] B. Bava Metzia 30b.

[10] M.T. Hilkhot Sanhedrin 22:4.

[11] Rashi's commentary on Deuteronomy 6:18, s.v. *ha-yashar v'ha-tov*.

[12] B. Berakhot 7a.

[13] Michelle Alexander, "Go to Trial: Crash the Justice System, *The New York Times*, (March 10, 2012), http://www.nytimes.com/2012/03/11/opinion/sunday/go-to-trial-crash-the-justice-system.html?_r=2.

[14] Rabbi Abraham Yitzḥak Kook, *Ig'rot Ha-ra·ayah* (Jerusalem: Mossad Harav Kook, 1985), vol. 1, p. 97.

[15] B. Bava Metzia 83a.

[16] Rashi to Genesis 1:1, s.v. *bara Elohim*: "The world could not [thus] endure and therefore gave precedence to [divine] mercy."

[17] "The President's Remarks on Justice Souter", at https://obamawhitehouse.archives.gov/blog/2009/05/01/presidents-remarks-justice-souter.

[18] Ahron Soloveitchik, *Logic of the Heart, Logic of the Mind* (Brooklyn, NY: Genesis Jerusalem Press, 1991), p. 67.

[19] B. Sanhedrin 32b.

[20] M.T. Hilkhot Sanhedrin 21:6, cf. S.A. Ḥoshen Mishpat 15:2.

[21] See "The First and The Last" by Isaiah Berlin, *New York Review of Books*, Vol. XLV, Number 8 (1998).

22 Yalkut Shimoni, as cited by Aaron Soloveitchik in his *Logic of the Heat, Logic of the Mind*, p. 67.
23 Martha Nussbaum, *Hiding from Humanity: Disgust, Shame, and the Law* (Princeton, NJ: Princeton University Press, 2004), p. 183.
24 B. Ḥagigah 2a.

Preserving What? Reassessing Foundation Myths and Exploring (Actual) Jewish History

Barbara Thiede

Acknowledging Heaven, Earth, King, Parent, and Teacher, you are not far from the correct road of Reason and Virtue. Cultivating the virtues of Benevolence, Righteousness, Propriety, Wisdom, and Faith, you reach the source of sages and philosophers.
    –Inscription from synagogue in Kaifeng, China

The life of Judaism is preserved by its people. The title of this book, *V'shamru*, is rooted precisely in that expectation. But the question remains: What are we guarding in the first place? What can we surely equate with "Judaism"? Answering this question has been left largely to a clergy steeped in Western ideas and Western traditions—despite the multifaceted geography and history of the Jewish people.

Shamor: to guard, to keep, to preserve. So many rabbis assume that to do these things is to do what many Jews won't: understand and embrace the *halakhah*, Jewish law, as a way of life. Even the most liberal of rabbis bemoan the halakhic apathy of their congregants, their apparently boundless ignorance, their indifference. For clergy, the task can seem obvious. Find a way to educate the flock in *halakhah* and halakhic thinking. Practice and observance will enrich congregants' lives and inspire them to commit to living Jewishly. And so Judaism will be preserved, guarded, and made safe for the future.

This entire discussion is based, however, on flawed assumptions.

Rabbinic Judaism is not Judaism per se. The *halakhah* we think of as both essential and traditional to Jewish identity and to Jewish life is nothing of the sort. Present-day rabbis are operating on a set of myths that are manifestly failing to accomplish their goals. Preserving Rabbinic Judaism is not working for most Jews and it will certainly not work to preserve Judaism as such.

Judaism is based on a set of complex factors including tribal identity, a corpus of inherited narratives and stories, rituals and custom, philosophy, borrowed ideas from surrounding cultures, and more. The rabbis have played an important part in Jewish history, but they are hardly the whole of it. Jews can certainly benefit from intensive engagement with rabbinic texts and traditions. But if we want to preserve Judaism, we must go beyond the territory defined and regulated by the rabbis. Moreover, clergy and teachers should acknowledge that the account so often employed to support the equation of Judaism and rabbinic tradition—the Yavneh narrative—is not historical, but polemical in nature.

Rabbis have constructed their own biography—one that licensed their authority over Jewish communal life in Europe, the Middle East, North Africa and, later, in the Americas. Even today, they depict the destruction of the Second Temple as a cataclysmic event that left the Jewish people lost and leaderless. The narrative continues: the rabbis stepped into the gap and reconstructed Judaism.

According to the popular story, Rabbi Yoḥanan ben Zakkai was smuggled out of Jerusalem and succeeded, as the city fell, in winning Roman permission to establish a yeshiva at Yavneh. Jewish practice, Jewish tradition, and Jewish identity were thus rescued from wholesale obliteration.[1] A grand coalition of rabbinic sages, the narrative tells us, preserved and saved Judaism.[2]

Every aspect of this narrative is, however, without historical support. "Yavneh itself…is a legend," Daniel Boyarin writes, "or rather, a series of changing legends of foundation."[3] The destruction was not a cataclysmic event for the vast majority of Jews at the time and the rabbis were, for centuries afterwards, largely irrelevant to Jewish life.[4]

By the time the Second Temple was destroyed, Jews had been living far from their ancestral homeland for many centuries. They had created communities and built synagogues everywhere they went—in Egypt, in Rome, on the North African coast, in Cyprus, Greece, the Aegean Islands, and in Asia Minor. Historical evidence does not suggest that synagogues of Second Temple times and the first centuries of the Common Era were centered around prayer services—far from it.[5] Instead, they served a multitude of functions: from fundraising to adjudicating the emancipation of slaves to offering meeting space for burial societies. The Temple was not paramount to Jewish communities.[6] Those who held positions of influence and power both in and outside of Palestine were called *archontes* (chiefs), *ethnarch* (governor), and a host of other similar titles, depending on community and local social and political structures of governance.[7] The *rosh* of a synagogue, the data demonstrate, could even be a woman.[8] Or a non-Jew.[9] Rabbis neither invented synagogues nor appear in the record as synagogue leaders. In short: thriving Jewish communities existed across the Roman Empire. They did not depend on rabbis.

Most diaspora literature leaves the Temple wholly unmentioned; Jewish writers prefer featuring biblical characters in their narratives.[10] Even the second-century BCE *Letter of Aristeas*, with its flowery description of the Temple cult, presents a romanticized travelogue of sorts, rather like videos one could find on today's Internet soliciting tourists for a trip to the "Holy Land."[11] Second Temple Jews paid their half-shekel to the Temple; that was an important obligation worth fulfilling and defending. But the Temple cult was not essential to living a satisfying Jewish life abroad. As Eric Gruen has written, there is no "diaspora narrative" to be found in Second Temple times because diaspora Jews didn't need one. Life outside of Palestine was evidently not marked by longing or loss for a Temple priesthood and sacrificial cult.[12]

The destruction of the Temple did not produce Jewish literature describing a lost and distraught people. That vision comes later—the product of a rabbinic agenda placing rabbis at the center of the narrative.[13] But for diaspora Jews, not much changed. As before the destruction, they were largely given the right not to take part in official cults in deference to their beliefs. In Rome, the Jewish community agitated for—and won—permission not to have to receive official allotments of grain on the Sabbath. Jews functioned as tradesmen, craftsmen, tax collectors, farmers, bankers, and granary officials across Europe, North Africa, and Asia Minor. Their rituals and observances were attractive to gentiles: Juvenal and Seneca wrote—albeit with some concern—about the number of Romans taking up Jewish practices.[14]

Jews of the so-called "rabbinic period" of the post-Second Temple period were hardly influenced by the rabbis who, according to our mythology, "saved" Judaism. The second-century CE Babatha papyri, an archive of an ancient woman's personal documents found at the southern tip of the Dead Sea, do not demonstrate concern with Jewish law and do not indicate that rabbis were called upon for either officiating at life-cycle events or solving legal matters. Babatha kept marriage documents written in Greek; no *ketubot* (Jewish marriage contracts) are found among the extant texts.[15] In fact, the Babatha collection shows that legal issues of all kinds, large and small, were brought to the Roman governor or his lieutenants.[16] Jews gave their children Greek names and wrote their legal documents in Greek. Synagogues were not always built so that worshippers would be facing Jerusalem as they recited prayers, and they featured imagery based on pagan motifs and alluding to pagan deities.[17] Jews were living Jewish lives, all right, but those lives were neither rabbinically defined nor halakhically determined.

Most telling of all is this fact: there is no objective evidence that Yavneh, as later talmudic texts constructed it, ever actually existed. Present-day rabbis congratulate themselves for representing a tradition that encourages dissent and argument, but this is based on overstated claims. Early talmudic texts reveal that halakhic controversy was certainly not always amicably tolerated. Rather, it could sometimes result in the wholesale excommunication of rabbis who did not fit the majority mold.[18]

Despite the myths that seminaries continue to teach as matters of historical record, the rabbis neither saved nor "democratized" Judaism. Indeed, the term "democratization" is an untenable retrojection of modern ideas into an ancient context. Moreover, Rabbinic Judaism was the work of a specific male constituency. However rich and compelling the outcome, there is hardly anything democratic about a process in which an elite first self-selects and then canonizes its authority.

Yet, though the rabbinic narrative is Eurocentric, androcentric, and even fictitious, today's rabbis—male and female—espouse it. It is hardly surprising that they would; they have positions and institutions to protect. And the fact that European and American Jewry have inherited a Judaism that is reliant on rabbinic authority cannot be disputed. But the idea that this is the only kind of Judaism that can inspire today's Jews to identify as such certainly can be.

The history of the Second Temple period and Late Antiquity, which features a self-confident Diaspora Judaism, is evidence that Jews have lived vibrant communal lives without rabbinic systems in place to guard or define their practice. Diaspora communities engaged with the cultures surrounding them without giving up their Jewish identity. Gravesites adorned with figures from Greek mythology (including Leda and the swan), incantations that included plentiful mention of a variety of angels, reading in Greek and the practice of giving children Greek names—these were all part and parcel of Jewish practice.[19] Such practices did not stop Second Temple Jews from abstaining from pork, circumcising their sons, and observing Shabbat. Coinage of Jewish cities in Palestine could depict both pagan deities and Jewish symbols; incantation bowls could invoke the demoness Lilith; synagogue inscriptions could honor local and even pagan royal families and benefactors—none of this stopped Jews from identifying themselves as Jews.[20]

Jewish identity was then, as it is today across North America, flexibly expressed. Inscriptions and epigraphs in Greek and Latin demonstrate that one might be called Jewish by ethnicity, Jewish by religion or belief, or Jewish by geographic origin. Such inscriptions used varying terms: *Ioudaia, Ioudaios, Iudaeus,* and *Iudea.* Some of those named as *Ioudaia* may well have been Jews according to present-day rabbinic definitions. There were also other possibilities, however. Some could have been proselytes, while others may have been men and women who happened to be born in Judea, and still others the God-fearers of ancient texts who attended synagogue and lived Jewishly without fully converting.[21] We cannot find the deep and lasting fear of assimilation so often expressed by the rabbis of the modern era. Rather, Jewish life demonstrates a wholehearted embrace of creative Jewish experience in the light of what was—at that time—global culture. In this regard, aspects of contemporary Jewish life share some elements with that lived 2,000 years ago in Rome, in Alexandria, in Sephorris, and elsewhere.

Jewish communities of the Second Temple period or Late Antiquity are hardly the only examples demonstrating how Jews have lived without rabbinic texts, authorities, or foundations for their practice. The Karaites, who certainly claim to do just that, are examples of this lifestyle, and there are many other examples of Jewish communities who could not even have known that the Talmud existed. They tell us that Judaism can adapt and flourish even when it is not dependent on rabbinic authority of any kind.

Imagine a Jewish community completely isolated from all others. Its library does not include Talmud or rabbinic texts; its literary resources consist only of Torah scrolls. For perhaps as much as 800 years, this community survives—and even thrives—essentially on its own. It possesses, in addition to its scrolls, a synagogue. For centuries, despite its tiny size, this community circumcises its sons, abstains from eating pork, and observes both Shabbat and major festivals. It leaves behind inscriptions describing the community's practice; in one, Yom Kippur is described as a day when "Emotions were forgotten. / Knowledge put aside. / Focused the mind and nourished the nature / to cultivate the return to good. / All people were silent. / At the end of the day / Desires were eliminated and principles expanded."[22] Words that Rabbinic Judaism considers essential to the observance of the Day of Atonement—words like "awe," "fear," or "judgment"—are entirely missing from the text.

These Jews, the Jews of Kaifeng, probably arrived in China from Persia via the Silk Road sometime in the tenth or eleventh century. They received permission to build their first synagogue in 1163 and they became, apparently, part of the city's merchant class. China observed a patrilineal system of descent, so Jewish men married Chinese women; the children were considered Jews. A 1512 inscription describes the success of the community's members; Jews are described as civil and military officials, farmers, artisans, traders, and shopkeepers. Some Jews appear to have attained high posts in China's political and military realms; others became doctors and academicians.[23] The community reached its greatest size of about 4,000 individuals before a devastating flood in 1642. While it regained some lost ground, it never fully recovered. Scholars debate how and why the community all but disappeared in the nineteenth century. Possible causes include the city's own decline, repeated floods, uprisings, and even China's waning power as a whole.[24]

But it is nevertheless an impressive fact that the Kaifeng Jewish community managed to survive and even thrive for many hundreds of years without Rabbinic Judaism to sustain it. Like Jews of the Roman Empire, Kaifeng Jews did acknowledge the power of their emperor, but the inscription they placed above an Imperial tablet housed in the synagogue praised God as supreme, making clear that God's power trumped that of any earthly ruler.[25] Like Jews elsewhere in the world—and unlike their Chinese neighbors—they organized their community as a congregation: a form of religious organization rare in Eastern societies.[26]

Scholars debate whether the evidence of Confucian thought in stone inscriptions demonstrates that Kaifeng Jews adapted to their surroundings or adapted their surroundings to their Jewish practice, but one thing is clear: the lives these Jews lived for at least three-quarters of a millennium were not rabbinically determined. They were, nevertheless, Jewish. We should marvel at their resilience and their commitment; despite various vicissitudes of history, the Kaifeng Jews sustained their community's existence for well over 700 years.

Other Jewish communities have been partly or mostly isolated from Rabbinic Judaism as most Europeans and Americans know it. The Kaifeng Jews are not at all alone. A number of African Jewish communities provide other examples of Jews living Jewishly in ways that are not dependent on rabbinic systems. Their canons are not equivalent to those of the modern European Jews and their descendants. They may not celebrate the same holidays. Where most

American Jews have never heard of the *Testament of Abraham*, the *Book of Enoch*, or the *Book of Jubilees*, Ethiopian Jews have read and embraced these texts, and regarded them as authoritative for their culture, beliefs, and practices.

A few salient examples are easily summarized: The Beta Israel of Ethiopia celebrate the Sigd (Amharic for "prostration"), a holiday largely unknown to other Jews. On the twenty-ninth day of the eighth month according to their calendar, exactly fifty days after Yom Kippur, they will gather, climb a nearby mountain, fast, read from Torah, and pray. Christians and Muslims frequently appear to have attended this holiday to observe the goings-on. The Beta Israel continued a practice of animal sacrifice long after the Second Temple was destroyed. In short: their community, like the Kaifeng community, lived Jewishly—but not because they had the Talmud to instruct them on how to do so.[27]

When today's rabbis argue for preserving and keeping rabbinic law as way to assure the survival of Judaism, they are doing so from a perspective that ignores historical realities: Jews have lived without *halakhah*; many Jews live now without *halakhah*. They are nevertheless Jews and identify as such. Should we insist that all Jews play the game according to rabbinic rules—rules that constitute only one segment of Jewish history and that were produced by a self-selected group of male elites?

Jews of today's America are often described as ignorant of tradition and texts. In each Pew report of every decade, we discover—and lament—the disconnected Jews all around us. They no longer support their Federations, they don't bother with affiliating congregationally, and they intermarry in numbers that portend the certain death of Judaism. After the latest such report in 2013, doom and gloom permeated the media: "It's a very grim portrait of the health of the American Jewish population in terms of their Jewish identification," warned Jack Wertheimer, professor of American Jewish history at New York's Jewish Theological Seminary.[28] When, in the fall of 2017, *The Forward* asked seventeen rabbis across denominational settings what most threatens the Jewish people, a good number insisted that it was the ignorance and apathy of their people.[29]

And so rabbis lobby for ways to bring apathetic and ignorant Jews "home" to shul. They long to succeed in engaging them in halakhic practice, and they work hard to achieve just that.

But what if today's Jews won't embrace what most rabbis deem essential to Jewish life? How might we react to Jews whose idea of a healthy eating practice might be outraged by a system ruled by a male elite, a system that can grant halakhic approval to a product with food dyes but that will take no note of issues of sustainability and ecology? For such Jews, buying groceries may well be a moral and ethical practice that originates from a competing understanding of what it means to be a good Jew. They may not feel at home with rabbis who cannot acknowledge their environmental concerns when hiring kosher caterers for this year's Ḥanukkah celebration or deciding which homes can be declared kosher enough to contribute snacks for communal get-togethers.

Berel Lang notes that Jews of our own time are "hyphenated creatures," well aware of global economies of cultural identity.[30] Yes, they are often intermarried. Yes, they may come in various ethnic iterations. Many Jews today are non-Jews who came to Judaism as adults, resulting in bona fide Jews who nonetheless don't "look" Jewish according to the descendants of European Jewry who dominate most American synagogues.[31] The diversity of Judaism can and should not be contained or qualified: it is enhancing and expanding us, and it is often doing so without reference to *halakhah*.

Rabbis may prefer to anguish over the ignorance of today's Jews, about what their leaders identify as Judaism. But such a definition of Judaism captures a mere piece of Jewish history, not the whole. That piece, however rich, cannot possibly reflect the full diversity, the richness, and the power of multiple ways of creating and living Jewish lives. Neither the rabbis nor their *halakhah* is our sole means for keeping, guarding, and protecting what is ours.

Or at least, they shouldn't be.

Rabbinic *halakhah* is part of our history; it is rich, fascinating, and worth our study. It is just not *the* definition of Judaism. To learn our history is to see just how variegated, resilient, and creative Judaism is, in how many ways it can be read, and how many are its forms of nourishment. The multiple ways we have created thriving Jewish communities offer us insight about the many forms Jewish identity can take.

Judaism is a mother lode of meaning. Our traditions, our rituals, our multifaceted texts, and our variegated history will teach us skepticism and humor. We can find ourselves charmed by the inventiveness of our forefathers and surprised by that of our foremothers who were neither silent nor powerless in the making of Jewish prayer, tradition, ritual, and text. Judaisms of all kinds can inform how we live, how we eat, how we advocate, and what we advocate for. Being Jews can be part of our explanation for why we fight for the downtrodden or attempt to live lives of service. There is no question that rabbinic texts have much to say about all these questions.

Judaism deserves to be guarded and preserved. The name of this volume suggests we do just that. But to guard who we are, we should know much more about who we have been, where we have lived, and how we have created and recreated what we call Judaism. It is a grand discovery.

NOTES

[1] B. Gittin 55b–56b. Popular versions of this narrative may be found by conducting a simple Google search on the word "Yavneh." See, for example, Chabad's retelling at http://www.chabad.org/library/article_cdo/aid/2713638/jewish/Spiritual-Leadership-in-Yavneh.htm.

[2] The keynote speech at the Ohalah Association of Rabbis for Jewish Renewal Conference of 2017, given by Rabbi Benay Lappe, played on just such themes. Lappe described the destruction of the Second Temple as a "crash" and the rabbis as cutting-edge saviors, of a sort, of Judaism. See a video from this session at the conference at http://2017conferenceohalah.weebly.com/videos.html.

[3] Daniel Boyarin, "A Tale of Two Synods: Nicaea, Yavneh, and Rabbinic Ecclesiology," *Exemplaria* 12:1 (2000), p. 28.

[4] In the early 1980s, Shaye Cohen's survey of "epigraphical rabbis" showed that there was no evidence that rabbis enjoyed any particularly special role in either Palestine or the Diaspora. See Shaye J.D. Cohen, "Epigraphical Rabbis," *The Jewish Quarterly Review* 72:1 (1981), pp. 1–17. Scholarship has, over the past decades, proven that Cohen was clearly on the right track. See, for example, "Rabbis and Patriarchs on the Margins," in Seth Schwartz's seminal work *Imperialism and Jewish Society, 200 B.C.E. to 640 C.E.* (Princeton: Princeton University Press, 2001), pp. 103–128. Contrary to the mythology of early academies and *yeshivot*, Jeffrey Rubenstein has, through a close examination of different strata of the Babylonian Talmud, concluded that rabbinic academies did not emerge until the years when the Bavli was redacted, between 450 and 600 CE. See Jeffrey L. Rubenstein, "The Rise of the Babylonian Rabbinic Academy: A Reexamination of the Talmudic Evidence," *Jewish Studies Internet Journal* 1 (2002), pp. 55–68, available online at http://jewish-faculty.biu.ac.il/files/jewish-faculty/shared/JSIJ1/rubenstein.pdf.

[5] Esther Chazzan points out that "the venue for regular public prayer during the Second Temple period remains difficult to determine. As is well known, the burgeoning data for the early synagogue attest a variety of communal activities, including public Torah reading but not regular prayer services" ("Liturgy Before and After the Temple's Destruction: Change or Continuity?" in *Was 70 C.E. a Watershed in Jewish History? On Jews and Judaism Before and After the Destruction of the Second Temple*, eds. Daniel R. Schwartz and Zeev Weiss [Leiden: Brill, 2012], p. 376, n. 19).

[6] As Schwartz and many others have pointed out, prayer in synagogues is "uncertain"—it appears that much activity centered around fund-raising and common meals (Schwartz, *Imperialism and Jewish Society*, p. 221). For a rich description of Jewish life in various diaspora settings, see also Erich Gruen, *Diaspora: Jews amidst Greeks and Romans* (Cambridge: Harvard University Press,

2002). For a survey of the self-confident, humorous, and revealing literature produced by Jews in the Diaspora, see Erich Gruen, *Heritage and Hellenism: The Reinvention of Jewish Tradition* (Berkeley: University of California Press, 1998). For an edited volume of recent scholarship addressing the vibrant life of Jews in the Diaspora, see also *Was 70 C.E. a Watershed in Jewish History?*, eds. Schwartz Weiss (cited in the previous note).

[7] In 47 BCE, Caesar gave John Hyrcanus and his descendants the title of "ethnarch" of the Jews (Gruen, *Diaspora*, p. 88). As Gruen points out, such titles were not consistently applied across every Jewish community of the Roman Empire. The term *politeuma*, a semi-autonomous civic unit with both administrative and judicial authority over its members, is a term used about the Jews of Alexandria and, as Gruen writes, "new papyrological texts disclose the existence of a Jewish *politeuma* in Herakleopolis, with a 'politarch' and other 'archons' in the officialdom, who, among other things, adjudicated disputes between Jews in the city, occasionally even between a Jew and a Gentile" (ibid, p. 74).

[8] Ross Kraemer, "Jewish Women in the Diaspora World of Late Antiquity," in *Jewish Women in Historical Perspective*, ed. Judith R. Baskin (Detroit: Wayne State University Press, 1998), pp. 46–72. Kraemer describes an inscription from second-century Smyrna referring to one "Rufina *Ioudaia*, president of the synagogue."

[9] T. Rajak and D. Noy, "*Archisynagogoi*: Office, Title, and Social Status in the Greco-Jewish Synagogue," *The Journal of Roman Studies* 83 (1993), pp. 75–93. For the role of non-Jews in ancient synagogues, see also R. S. Kraemer, "On the Meaning of the Term 'Jew' in Greco-Roman Inscriptions," *The Harvard Theological Review* 82 (1989), pp. 35–53; Louis H. Feldman, "Proselytes and 'Sympathizers' in the Light of the New Inscription from Aphrodisias," *Revue des Études Juives* 148 (1989), pp. 265–305; Dietrich Alex Koch, "The God-fearers between Facts and Fiction," *Studia Theologica* 60 (2006), pp. 71–75; W. van der Horst, *Ancient Jewish Epitaphs* (Kampen, Netherlands: Kok Pharos, 1991), pp. 71–72 and 135–137; and Shaye J. D. Cohen, "Crossing the Boundary and Becoming a Jew," *The Harvard Theological Review* 82:1 (January 1989), pp. 13–33.

[10] Michael Tuval, "Doing without the Temple: Paradigms in Judaic Literature of the Diaspora," in *Was 70 C.E. a Watershed in Jewish History?*, pp. 181–239.

[11] The *Letter* was based on a romantic legend created to sanctify the Septuagint, the Greek translation of biblical texts. According to the legend, seventy-two elders were imported to Alexandria to generate the translation. They managed, despite being separated from one another, to choose exactly the same words for every part of the Hebrew texts, thus "proving" that the Septuagint was divinely authorized. See "Aristeas, Letter of," in *Encyclopaedia Judaica*, eds. Michael

Berenbaum and Fred Skolnik (2nd ed.; Detroit: Macmillan Reference USA, 2007), vol. 2, pp. 456–457.

[12] Gruen, *Diaspora*, p. 6.

[13] Boyarin, "A Tale of Two Synods," *passim*.

[14] Juvenal (first to second century CE) wrote: "Some who have had a father who reveres the Sabbath, worship nothing but the clouds and the divinity of the heavens, and see no difference between eating swine's flesh, from which their father abstained, and that of man; and in time they take to circumcision. Having been wont to flout the laws of Rome, they learn and practice and revere the Jewish law, and all that Moses handed down in his secret tome, forbidding to point out the way to any not worshipping the same rites, and conducting none but the circumcised to the desired fountain. For all which the father was to blame, who gave up every seventh day to idleness, keeping it apart from all the concerns of life" (cited in Menahem Stern, *Greek and Latin Authors on Jews and Judaism* [Jerusalem: The Israel Academy of Sciences and Humanities, 1980], vol. 2, pp. 102–103). Seneca, in turn, insisted that Jewish customs had gained such strength "that they have been now received in all lands." He added: "The conquered have given laws to their victors" (ibid., vol. 1, p. 431).

[15] Schwartz, *Imperialism and Jewish Society*, p. 70.

[16] Ibid., p. 112.

[17] Ibid., p. 247. The fifth-century synagogue of Sepphoris features an abstract representation of Helios, the Greek sun god.

[18] See the story of the excommunication of Rabbi Eliezer, for example, in B. Bava Metzia 59a–b. Boyarin concludes that this particular talmudic narrative, among others, demonstrates that "Rabbinic Judaism is…the end-product of an extended history of struggle for hegemony by a particular version of religious authority" (p. 39). We should also remember that the rabbis limited the roles of women and non-Jews in synagogal life; the God-fearers are a feature of the synagogues of Late Antiquity, not of the medieval period.

[19] Schwartz, *Imperialism and Jewish Society*, pp. 133–136, 156–158.

[20] There is a wealth of scholarship dealing with all these many facets of Jewish life in this time period. See Schwartz, *Imperialism and Jewish Society, passim*; and Gruen, *Diaspora, passim*. For the role Jewish women might have played in composing the inscriptions of incantation bowls, see Rebecca Lesses, "Exe(o)r-cising Power: Women as Sorceresses, Exorcists, and Demonesses in Babylonian Jewish Society of Late Antiquity," *Journal of the Academy of Religion* 69:2 (June 2001), pp. 343–375.

[21] This is a phenomenon that could be compared to the many spouses or relatives of Jews who live Jewishly in today's communities, without converting. See Kraemer, "On the Meaning of the Term 'Jew' in Greco-Roman Inscriptions," *passim*.

[22] Tiberiu Weisz, *The Kaifeng Stone Inscriptions* (New York: iUniverse, Inc., 2006), p. 39.

[23] Stephen Sharot, "The Kaifeng Jews: A Reconsideration of Acculturation and Assimilation in a Comparative Perspective," in *Jewish Social Studies* 13:2 (Winter 2007), p. 181.

[24] Ibid, p. 194.

[25] Ibid, p. 183.

[26] Ibid, p. 197.

[27] Hagar Salamon, "The Religious Interplay on an African Stage: Ethiopian Jews in Christian Ethiopia," in *Cultures of the Jews: A New History*, ed. David Biale (New York: Schocken Books, 2002), pp. 977–1008.

[28] http://www.nytimes.com/2013/10/01/us/poll-shows-major-shift-in-identity-of-us-jews.html.

[29] https://forward.com/opinion/385223/rabbi-roundtable-biggest-threat-jewish-people/.

[30] Berel Lang, "Hyphenated Jews and the Anxiety of Identity," *Jewish Social Studies* 12:1 (New Series, Fall 2005), pp. 1–15.

[31] I have spoken to several Asian Jews about this issue, particularly. One wonders how Kaifeng Jews would have responded.

Observing the Commandments: Thoughts of
a Non-Halakhic Religious Jew

Dalia Marx

For this mitzvah that I am commanding to you today
is not too wondrous for you and neither is it far beyond you.
It is not in heaven, which would make it reasonable to ask
"Who shall ascend to heaven on our behalf and retrieve it for us,
and communicate to us so that we may fulfil it?"
And neither is it beyond the sea,
which would make it reasonable to ask,
"Who will cross the sea to retrieve it for us,
and communicate it to us so that we may fulfil it?"
Indeed, very near is the matter to you;
it is in your own mouth and your own heart to fulfill it.
                                    —Deuteronomy 30:11–14

Standing in a circle, holding hands, and singing together at the top of our voices "*v'shamru v'nei yisrael et ha-shabbat*" in an upbeat melody composed be Moshe Rothblum was part of my Israeli Reform youth movement Shabbat experience. These words from Exodus 31, which are recited as part of the Shabbat morning service and also in the Kiddush (the sanctification prayer recited over wine), speak for themselves. However, I have often paused to think about what they actually mean for us liberal Jews: what they should mean, and what it does mean for us to keep or to observe the Shabbat. This question, about Shabbat in particular but about religious commandments more generally, is still an important one for me—one that informs my religious choices and through which I measure my Jewish conduct. This essay presents a preliminary and tentative attempt to deal with the one aspect of the vast matter of *sh'mirat mitzvot*, the question of what the concept could or should mean for non-halakhic Jews such as myself.

The phrase *sh'mirat mitzvot* can be translated as "guarding," "observing," or "keeping" the commandments. All these translations have their proponents in the world of progressive Judaism with which I am affiliated. This is not simply an arcane matter of translation: each translation sheds a slightly different light on the concept of religious duty. In any event, they all stress the same central concept: that Judaism is an enacted religion far more about what one *does* than what one *believes*. The concept of "doing" has traditionally been understood in terms of allegiance to certain patterns of behavior rather than as mere obligation to a philosophical system. And that brings me to the question at the heart of this essay: Can the concept of *sh'mirat mitzvot* be of value to contemporary Jews who do not see themselves compelled by the classical *halakhah* to behave in this or that specific way?

What Is a *Mitzvah*?

The term *mitzvah* is generally used in one of two ways. It sometimes denotes a specific and formal religious duty, namely one of the 613 commandments recorded in the Torah according to the traditional count. At other times, it refers to a good and worthy deed that an individual undertakes out of a sense of personal obligation, such that the concept of commandedness comes from within rather than from without.

The first understanding assumes that the commandments are of divine origin, as is traditionally set forth in authoritative Jewish legal sources. The second understanding corresponds to the inner sense of duty that individuals often feel to do good in the world, a sense of obligation that can also be understood as obedience to one's conscience or to one's inner ethical imperative regardless of one's personal religious faith that may well involve adherence to Jewish beliefs and practices. To denigrate this latter approach as unrelated to religion is to take an extremely narrow stance regarding the question of what religion is.

The two understandings of *mitzvah* are not mutually incompatible: both definitions suggest actions rooted in a relationship between a commanded individual and a commander (even if both turn out to be the same entity), and both share the sense that the *mitzvah* is a worthy and well-intended act. But not all worthy or well-intended deeds can be labelled as *mitzvot*. A *mitzvah* is, at its core, a deliberate deed undertaken out of a sense of responsibility related to the action at hand, one rooted in the doer's faith that he or she is acting out of a sense of responsibility, of being commanded; such an action is thus a function of the doer's chosen lifestyle and set of personal beliefs.

Commander, Commanded, Commandment

It seems reasonable to assert that there are three aspects at play when dealing with the concept of *mitzvah*, each serving as the others' partner: the *m'tzavveh* (commander), the *m'tzuvveh* or *m'tzuvvah* (commanded individual), and the *mitzvah*, the commandment itself.[1]

In traditional terms, the *m'tzavveh*, the commander, is the God who speaks to us through the commandments and who, by creating humankind in the divine image, has granted us the task of ongoing partnership in the ever-continuing creation of the world. The *m'tzuvveh* or *m'tzuvvah*, the commanded individual, traditionally is characterized by his or her responsiveness to the perceived reality of God's commanding voice. Judaism teaches us that we are not mere nomads wandering about in the world and that each of us has a task (or set of tasks) to perform. The pleasure we derive from our actions can never be sufficient grounds to justify their performance, but we must also predicate our actions on responsivity to what we perceive to be the voice of God. In recent decades, it has become common to refer to this understanding as a commitment to *tikkun olam*, work undertaken by mending, changing, even transforming the world—beginning with ourselves and working our way to effect change in ever-expanding circles. This approach, however, requires from us even more than mere obedience: in fact, it calls us to be partners with God (albeit junior ones) in creating the world and governing it.

And the *mitzvah* (commandment) itself is the agent that brings the Commander and the commanded party into partnership. The ineffable speaks to us through the commandments, such that when we perform a *mitzvah* we are responding to a divine call—and not in a theoretical or cognitive or symbolic manner, but in a supremely practical way. Even a very practical deed, when undertaken as a response to a sense of commandedness, can acquire meaning that extends far beyond the deed itself—and so becomes a *mitzvah*. The *mitzvah* thus serves as a bridge to mediate our communication with the ineffable, at the same time making possible a dialogic, enduring relationship between ourselves and God.

All of this works well for people who consider God as the *m'tzavveh*, as their personal Commander. But what about those who feel *m'tzuvvim* (commanded) from within, and whose actions in the world are specifically *not* informed by a sense of an external transcendent force commanding them to behave as they do? For people who feel commanded, compelled, and obligated from *within* to follow a moral code and to do good, the *mitzvot* of life are not necessarily the 613 commandments recorded in the Torah (see below). Such people may undertake an ongoing process of consideration and reconsideration in order to decide which mode of behavior is the right and worthy one for themselves.

In many corners of the Jewish world, this approach—of being commanded from within and making personal decisions about appropriate behavior—is denigrated as unserious (or worse). But that evaluative judgment misses two important points. First, it may ultimately take much more serious efforts to frame one's own set of values and then to identify the actions they require than to obey a set of formal rules; following prescribed rules may be challenging, but it is also more straightforward (and, to many, more reassuring) than charting one's own idiosyncratic course in life. Second, choosing a personal path forward does not necessarily mean invariably taking an easier route: indeed, people may choose to take upon themselves actions that are not part of the traditional system of *mitzvot* at all. The formal laws concerning *kashrut*, for example, are complex and demanding, yet also quite straightforward. Indeed, one who chooses to keep *kashrut* in a more profound sense—by asking, say, if one's food was produced, handled, marketed, and served in an ethically appropriate manner (which is, after all, the original sense of the Hebrew word *kasher*)—may be faced with a challenge far beyond simply looking for a kosher stamp on the food's packaging. There are many food items and products that are kosher according the traditional *halakhah*, but may not be considered ethically or socially kosher—that is, just or appropriate to consume—when other criteria are brought into play.[2]

This presentation of two types of *mitzvah*, each with its own relation to the concepts of "commandment" and "commandedness," may strike some as too rigid—and it surely the case that, at least for many people, the external and the inner "commander" are indistinguishable. This may explain why so many Jews are active in social justice endeavors, such as working for women's rights, LGBTQ rights, minorities' rights, refugees' rights, environmental issues, and many more such struggles. This intense involvement of Jews in such endeavors may attest to the fact that there is something essential that drives us to do the right thing, to strive for *tikkun olam*. It may not necessarily be about Jewish law per se, but there is definitely something about Jewish lore and experience that compels that kind of behavior and commitment.

In the end, living our lives with a strong sense of being commanded—whether we identify the origin of that sentiment as a "commander" from within, or one (or: One) from without—places us in a constant and ongoing conversation with the transcendent, with the ineffable. The concept of living a life of *mitzvot*, thus understood, is not exclusively a Jewish endeavor, but it is certainly very Jewish.

The Merits of the Commandments

Rabbi Judah the Patriarch, the redactor of the Mishnah, taught that one must observe all the commandments carefully because "it is impossible to know the reward attached to any specific *mitzvah*" (M. Avot 2:1). So far, I have been discussing primarily *mitzvot* that lead to doing good in the world and to those who dwell in it, what medieval scholars called *mitzvot sikhliyyot* ("rational commandments"). But we also need to address the more challenging task of identifying the rationale behind the *mitzvot shimiyyot*, those commandments of which we have "heard" but may find it hard to rationalize or to explain.

(For a classical approach to the difference between *mitzvot sikliyyot* and *mitzvot shimiyyot,* see Sandia Gaon's *Sefer Emunot V'dei·ot* 3:2–3.) Can we identify the religious, social, or educational purpose of commandments such as those related to such arcane matters as ritual purity and impurity?

This question is discussed extensively by Jewish thinkers. Some commentators go so far as to explain the reason behind each and every *mitzvah*. Others point to the spiritual or material reward one may reap from the performance of each *mitzvah*. Still others believe that there is no explanation or merit to the *mitzvot* other than the opportunity they afford us to obey the Commander who gave them to us and to educate ourselves. In fact, the very wording of the blessing recited before performing religious commandments ("Blessed are You, Eternal, Sovereign of the universe, who has sanctified us through the commandments…") clearly indicates that we are *not* innately sanctified (i.e., simply because we are Jews), but that we attain sanctity through our observance of the *mitzvot*—that is, through choosing to lead worthy and attentive lives.

Rabbi Abba bar Aibo, the third-century CE sage almost always referenced in classical literature simply as "Rav," maintained that "the *mitzvot* were only given to the people of Israel in order to refine them (*litzrof otam*)."[3] The purpose of the commandments, then, is to refine and purify—and thus improve—those who perform them, just as a goldsmith purifies and cleanses gold of any dross before working with it. Interestingly, some manuscripts of this text preserve a slightly different reading of Rav's statement: "The *mitzvot* were only given to the people of Israel to bring them together (*l'tzareif otam*)."[4] According to this version of Rav's statement, the function of the commandments is to bring people together, with the underlying idea that the way to create a community is to share a meaningful set of values that lead to a meaningful set of actions. People who observe together, stay together.

We will never know whether Rav actually said *litzrof* or *l'tzareif*, but what a rich field of meaning these two very similar, yet so very different readings, open for us! The understanding that the commandments came *litzrof* people is all about self-improvement, reflecting the notion that people become better and more refined through observance. The understanding that the commandments are meant *l'tzareif* people, on the other hand, makes them primarily about community building.

These two approaches are complementary, suggesting that neither can exist meaningfully without the other: individuals must always consider themselves as part of a *k'lal*, a collective, yet the collective cannot be considered as anything other than the sum of unique individuals. Even though Rav obviously didn't utter both versions of his remark, we can embrace them both as profound truths and assert that the purpose of the *mitzvot* is both to improve and refine the individual and, at the same time, also to set in place the guidelines that characterize the community and guarantee that it will be made up of decent and worthy individuals.

What is this collective to which we are being called to relate? Obviously, there are many concentric circles of collectivity to which we all belong: first our families and friends, then our immediate communities, then our people and our country, and finally humankind—and perhaps every living thing and the world itself, considered independently of those who dwell in it. We must lament that some Jews are passionately committed only to their innermost circles, while neglecting responsibility to the larger ones. But just as the two different accounts of Rav's statement teach that we must begin from within, refining (*litzrof*) ourselves, it also suggests that we must look beyond ourselves and develop a strong sense of social responsibility (*l'tzareif*) so that our commitments do not end with our immediate family, circle of friends or our neighborhood or our synagogue or our town. The tension between the individual and the communal is vital to a sense of engaged Jewishness, and so is the tension between the communal and the universal. In my opinion, this deeply rooted tension is something to be celebrated, not regretted or endured.

Commandedness may feel like a heavy burden to some, and indeed it is. However, the sense of being commanded can also lead to a very optimistic worldview, one that suggests that we are not mere passengers in the world but real players in it. Living with such a sense entails believing that we human beings can effect change—both in our own lives and in the world in which we live. And it teaches us that life matters, but that our mode of living also does.

Mitzvot in the Non-Orthodox Jewish World

The Talmud says: "Rabbi Simlai taught that 613 commandments were given to Moses at Sinai."[5] However, since the Talmud does not specify what these *mitzvot* are, rabbis of later generations offered their own lists.[6] Because 613 is not a round number and does not carry any obvious typological connotations, Rabbi Simlai's number appears to be his actual sense of how many commandments are found in the Torah.[7]

The talmudic passage continues by citing various biblical personalities who found some specific number of commandments to be the truly essential ones. King David, for example, is said to have considered the eleven basic commandments presented in Psalm 15 as constituting the foundation stones upon which the rest of the Torah's laws rest.[8] Similarly, the prophet Isaiah suggests as truly foundational the six injunctions embodied by one who "walks righteously and speaks uprightly, despises the gain of oppression, and refuses to take a bribe, to ignore an individual's acts of violence, and even to look upon evil" (Isaiah 33:15). And Micah narrows the list further, highlighting only three commandments as constituting the basis of all Torah law, all of which enjoin the faithful Israelite to embody just interpersonal conduct by doing only "what is good and what the Eternal requires of you: to act justly, to love mercy, and to walk humbly with… God" (Micah 6:8). The talmudic discussion concludes by citing the prophet Habakkuk, who is said to have imagined the entire system of commandments as a kind of midrashic development of one single injunction, embodied in the verse "The righteous shall live according to their faith" (Habakkuk 2:4).

How should we understand this passage? I believe that it does not mean to deny that the Torah is comprised of many, many *mitzvot*. Rather, it suggests that they are all elaborations or expansion of certain basic principles, which are far fewer in number than the total number of commandments that embody them. Positing that all 613 *mitzvot* are derived from a very few core principles suggests that religious observance that does *not* revolve around these values risks turning into mere ritual, hollow and empty. This seems to be what the text has in mind by declaring that Habakkuk taught that *all* the commandments concretize a single principle—namely, that that the core of divine service rests on the individual's choice to be a faithful person. Thus, any deed can be sacred if it grows from an individual's choice to be a faithful person, acting in constructive and helpful ways in the world and searching for the sacred. While the prophet's point (as understood by the Talmud) is certainly not to denigrate the importance of the other commandments, his lesson underscores that the essence of the entire system of *mitzvot* is to promote a specific path in life—the one that derives from the search for holiness and that embodies that search through action.

Moreover, this talmudic passage suggests that observing the commandments does not mean "collecting" *mitzvot* (or, as it is sometimes referred to, "climbing the ladder of the *mitzvot*"). Rather, it should mean leading a holistic life based on fairness and justice. The *mitzvot* are thus acts that bring a person—both as an individual and within the framework of the larger community—to reflect about the core values that guide one's life and to yearn to experience holiness.

Liberal Judaism has always stressed the importance of social justice, honesty in all matters, and the importance of uncompromising commitment in all areas of moral conduct. But what about the practical *mitzvot*, those that appear, at least at first glance, not to have a moral aspect at all? This question seems especially apropos regarding the so-called ritual commandments, the *mitzvot shimiyyot*. Classical Reform Judaism, as it thrived in the United States in the nineteenth and the beginning of the twentieth centuries, clearly distinguished between ethical and ritual commandments. Many classical Reformers were thus prepared to abandon any of the *mitzvot* that they felt had lost their power and importance over time. On the other hand, the ethical commandments—like those mentioned in the talmudic discussion above—were deemed to be eternal and in force permanently.[9] Today, however, many leaders and rabbis of the Reform Movement understand that, apart from the vital moral imperatives, practical and ritual *mitzvot* are essential too, both *l'tzareif* and *litzrof*, to "refine" the individual and "to bring together" the community.[10]

Many Jews today do not see themselves either compelled or confined by the traditional *halakhah*, but do appreciate the essential importance of the concept that Judaism is something you *do*, not merely something that you *are* or something in which you believe. *Sh'mirat ha-mitzvot*, keeping or observing the commandments, means keeping in tune with our past and with *k'lal yisrael*, the entirety of Israel, as well as guarding and cultivating a life of attentiveness and thoughtful choosing.

While moral and ethical commandments are essentially non-negotiable (one cannot say "I don't feel that 'do not steal' fits me today"), it is our right—perhaps even our duty—to examine the ritual *mitzvot*…and to do so over and over again. We should want to be at home with the entirety of the Jewish concepts, ideas and practices, even those which seem strange to us, and even those which we strongly oppose (for example, those that promote gender inequality). They all are ours, even if we choose not to keep them! Judaism stresses the importance of choice, but we need to be fully educated and informed in order to make informed choices.

In some cases, we may feel a need overtly to reject certain aspects of the specific way the *halakhah* is understood today (for example, the strong emphasis that is placed on technical and commercial aspects that characterizes the way the laws of *kashrut* are widely understood in today's world, while the moral and social aspects of those laws are often ignored).[11] In other cases, we need to think more broadly about the *mitzvot*. For example, should unhealthy food or food items produced by child labor be considered kosher at all, even if the package it comes in has all the right rabbinic "stamps"? *Sh'mirat mitzvot*, the keeping and/or observing of the commandments, after all, has to with our duty to sustain and keep the world and all that dwell in it safe. That was our initial task, or commandment, on earth, as encapsulated in the biblical mandate *l'ovdah u-l'shomrah* ("to cultivate it [the world] and to preserve it," Genesis 2:15). This is what should underline and motivate all our deeds.

Obviously, many people—and not only Jews—strive for *tikkun olam* and attempt to do good in the world. But Jews do it Jewishly. We, Jews of all denominations and streams, do it in tune with our heritage, our sacred texts, and the people in our past and our present, thus allowing our deeds to infuse our lives with holiness. Indeed, as the Torah says, "The matter is very near to us. In fact, it is in our own mouth and our own heart to fulfill it" (Deuteronomy 30:14).

NOTES

[1] *M'tzuvveh* and *m'tzuvvah* are the masculine and feminine versions of the same word, derived from the same root (*tzadi-vav-hei*) that generates the word *mitzvah*.

[2] For example, I created for myself a few years ago the following list of values, which I take upon myself to examine in addition to traditional rules of *kashrut*, when I decide whether a particular product is "kosher":

1. **Social justice, concern for those who lack:** "[Are you not] to share your bread with the hungry?" (Isaiah 58:7).
2. **Preservation of nature and avoidance of waste:** "You shall not destroy" (based upon Deuteronomy 20:19).
3. **Sensitivity to animals:** "You shall not cook a kid in its mother's milk" (Exodus 23:19).
4. **Fair employment practices:** "You shall not oppress your fellow and you shall not steal" (Leviticus 19:13).
5. **Health and preservation of the body:** "For your own sake, therefore, be most careful" (Deuteronomy 4:15).
6. **A sense of gratitude:** "Let all that breathes praise the Eternal, Hallelujah" (Psalms 150:6).
7. **Family and community:** "How good and how pleasant it is that brothers dwell together" (Psalms 133:1).
8. **Attentiveness and consciousness:** "And the living shall lay it to the heart" (Kohelet 7:2).
9. **Taste and pleasure:** "Honey and milk are beneath your tongue" (Song of Songs 4:11).
10. **Moderation:** "If you find honey, eat only what you need, lest, surfeiting yourself, you throw it up" (Proverbs 25:16).

[3] Vayikra Rabbah 13:3. The text was probably redacted in the fifth or sixth century CE.

[4] The two words in question, *litzrof* and *l'tzareif*, have identical consonants and differ only with regard to their vowels, and would thus appear identically in an unvocalized text.

[5] B. Makkot 23a.

[6] The most well-known accounts of the 613 commandments is *Sefer Ha-ḥinnukh* ("The Book of Education"), which deals systematically with each of the commandments. The book, published anonymously, has traditionally been considered the work of Aaron Halevi of Barcelona, a well-known thirteenth-century Spanish talmudist, but that attribution has been rejected by many scholars today in favor of one attributing the book to one or another of his contemporaries.

[7] The discussion in Tractate Makkot explains the number as the sum of 365 (understood to be both the number of negative commandments and the days of the solar year) and 248 (understood to be both the number of possitive commandments and the number of a man's body parts). The number 248 as the number of limbs in a man's body appears also a M. Ohalot 1:8. At B. Bekhorot 45a, women are said to have bodies composed of 252 parts.

[8] Psalm 15 is attributed to David in its first verse. The point is not that the rabbis imagined David to be denigrating the other commandments or recommending that they be ignored, just that he found these fifteen to be truly foundational.

[9] The first Reform Platform (Pittsburgh, 1885) says: "We recognize in the Mosaic legislation a system of training the Jewish people for its mission during its national life in Palestine, and today we accept as binding only its moral laws, and maintain only such ceremonies as elevate and sanctify our lives, but reject all such as are not adapted to the views and habits of modern civilization." The full text is available to the public on the CCAR website at www.ccarnet.org.

[10] The latest American Reform platform (1999), which too was agreed upon in Pittsburgh, reads: "We respond to God daily: through public and private prayer, through study and through the performance of other *mitzvot*, sacred obligations—*bein adam la-makom*, to God, and *bein adam l'haveiro*, to other human beings" (cited from the CCAR website at www.ccarnet.org).

[11] Cf. note 2 above.

The Jewish Paradigm for Problem-Solving: Why Not Applied to New Testament?

Michael J. Cook

The Torah does not present the commandments in any sort of clear hierarchy of importance or worth, yet some—presumably the more difficult or fragile or complicated ones—we are told not merely to obey but actually to "guard," presumably from non-compliance or laxity. Most of the essays in this volume address one or another of those scriptural commandments, or groups of commandments, which the Torah commands the Israelites not merely to obey but to guard and to protect.[1] But the Torah itself uses the noun *mishmeret*, a nominal form derived from the verb *shamar* used to reference that act of guarding and protecting *certain* specific commandments, to denote the *entire* covenantal set of obligations that bind Israel and God, thus suggesting that the pious Israelite will bring a measure of protective watchfulness to all the commandments and not *just* to those regarding the observance of which the Torah uses the verb *shamar* ("to protect" or "to guard"), either in the familiar form of *v'shamru* or in some other related form.[2] And it specifically uses a version of shamar to denote specifically what it is the Israelites are to do to with respect to the laws of the covenant called *mishmeret* in the text of the Torah.[3]

In this essay, I would like to take that notion of acting forcefully to safeguard the covenant just one step further and apply it not to a

Torah-based commandment at all, but rather to a rabbinic one and, at that, to the specific rabbinic command to which I have devoted my entire professional life: Rabbi Eleazar's famous dictum in Pirkei Avot, *da mah l'hashiv l'epikoros* (M. Avot 2:19), which enjoins us to know how to respond when we, or our faith or our Jewish practice, are attacked by others eager to demonstrate the superiority of their own religion through the denigration of ours, or to disparage Judaism as part of a larger effort to discredit the concept of religion itself.[4] This is not a simple matter Rabbi Eleazar is placing before us: to take his advice meaningfully does not mean responding to our attackers tetchily or dismissively, but actually acquiring the tools necessary to defend Judaism and Jewishness vigorously and convincingly. Nor is this concept in opposition somehow to the idea in its original scriptural setting: to my way of thinking, relating to the covenant as a *mishmeret* means specifically to learn how successfully to respond to its would-be disparagers.

Since the most famous scriptural passage that commands the Israelites to "guard" a specific ritual applies to the Sabbath—I am thinking, of course, of Exodus 31:16–17, one of the most liturgically prominent passages relating to Shabbat—I would like to illustrate my point with respect to the Sabbath specifically. In my experience, secular America mostly finds it irritating that Jewish people continue to observe the Sabbath on Saturday instead of Sunday, which they think of as the "real" (as opposed to, if they speak generously, the "Jewish") Sabbath. And indeed, all our American institutions, public and private—to the extent that they are committed to any Sabbath observance at all—take it for granted that Sunday is the Sabbath, the Seventh Day Adventists merely serving here as the exceptions that prove the rule. But when a Jew is confronted with this phenomenon and challenged to obey the Torah's commandment to "guard" or "protect" the Sabbath in the most elemental way possible by insisting that it be observed on the correct day, what percentage of American Jews have even the vaguest sense of what to say? A few may be possessed of a vague sense that Christians somewhere along the line changed the Sabbath from Saturday to Sunday. But when that happened, almost none could say even inexactly. Asking how such an elemental change in the clear meaning of Scripture could be countenanced by people who claimed to be faithful, at the very least, to the Ten Commandments would also be met with blank stares by most. And how all of this can have been almost totally forgotten by Christians themselves, who (in my experience, at least) *also* only have a vague sense of why and when Christian worship became scheduled for the so-called Lord's Day instead of on the actual Sabbath, which was then allowed to fall away entirely from Christian worship as though Sunday had somehow been Shabbat all along—explaining that issue too would confound, if not totally flummox, most American Jews, including savvy, university-educated ones.

Sticking for a moment with the Sabbath, Aḥad Ha-am famously wrote that "even more than the Jews have kept [*shamru*] the Sabbath has the Sabbath kept the Jews."[5] That is surely true, but we can state the same truth more broadly by asserting that even more than we have preserved our Torah has our Torah preserved our people. And—to use the most embracing and encompassing paradigm of all—that even more than we Jews have amassed *learning* has our cultivation of *learning* safeguarded our people. How, then, can we explain the mandate promulgated by our rabbinic sages of old that Jews *should* keep themselves ignorant of the New Testament—when we see that such avoidance has jeopardized Jewish well-being in a Christian environment?[6] How were we to allow our learning to guard and keep us, if we were to make a virtue out of avoiding the specific areas in which ignorance threatened to do us the most damage? To know how to respond to those who disparage our faith is to obey the Torah's command to guard and protect the commandments. And, indeed, this has become my life's work as well.

Raised decades ago in Forest Hills, an almost entirely Jewish section of New York City's borough of Queens, I had felt reproved, even chastised, by Jewish family and friends alike—in religious school, in the synagogue, and especially at home—whenever I ventured the slightest question concerning Jesus or the Gospels. Only upon embarking on my undergraduate studies at Haverford College, just outside Philadelphia, did I experience a radical reversal. Now living in as non-Jewish an atmosphere as Forest Hills was Jewish, Harvard's Quaker scholar of the New Testament, Henry J. Cadbury, encouraged me to take classes with Haverford professor John Flight, in whose courses I was almost always the sole Jewish student. I grew convinced that, by studying the New Testament, Jews would no longer be induced to wallow in a sea of ignorance that left them flustered, and often severely embarrassed, within their Christian environment. Why could not that same overarching paradigm for Jewish problem-solving—*learning*, not *shirking*—be operative and helpful here as well? If we are devoted to fulfilling the Torah's mandate to "guard" the Sabbath, why should we not also guard ourselves—from charges of ignorance, of willful rejectionism, of falsifying the biblical record, and of denying the truth of Christianity?

What eventuated was my four-decades-long tenure as the sole rabbi in America to hold a full professorial chair in New Testament per se, and Cincinnati's Hebrew Union College becoming the sole Jewish seminary in history to make a basic knowledge of the New Testament a prerequisite to rabbinical ordination.[7] My long-range strategy? To establish a method of teaching I coined "Gospel dynamics," enabling hundreds of rabbinical candidates to assimilate the workings of these dynamics by the Jew in the pew—i.e., Jewish laypeople—and thereby generate programming about Jews and the Gospels within synagogue adult education courses and speaker programs.[8] The prime focus of "Gospel dynamics"? To lay out how and why certain traditions had arisen, or had editorially morphed, to frame and meet the needs of the developing Church, thereby becoming dramatically redirected to the severe detriment of Jews' well-being. By incorporating and applying this focus, modern Jews would better recognize, comprehend, and resolve their insecurities and establish and solidify their comfort level with Christian friends and acquaintances.

The Problem: Sample Anecdotes

Roused by the Pope (October, 1965)—3:00 a.m.! Pounding on a dormitory door awakens my friend, a Jewish co-ed at Miami University (in Oxford, Ohio). A casual acquaintance from across the hall: "TV just announced: the Pope has freed you from killing Jesus. Thought you'd want to know as soon as possible!"[9] Mumbling "thank you," the co-ed stumbles back to bed, annoyed primarily with herself for not having known how to have responded.

Shortening Bible at Both Ends (Hanukkah, 1969)—Putnam Valley, New York, my synagogue pulpit (before I entered academia). Jewish parents gloat to me how they have just coped with a Ḥanukkah gift that their son, Danny, received from Christian neighbors: an illustrated children's Bible—whose second half was a New Testament! To "protect" Danny from depictions of Jesus, Mary, John the Baptist, Paul, et al, the parents sliced away the last hundred pages with a razor! Of course, the volume's now-weakened binding renders it likely that Genesis, Exodus, and half of Leviticus will soon likewise slither to the floor. Who better than his parents to teach Danny about Jesus' edifying *Jewish* teachings?[10] Yet instead they trumpet their ostrich-like solution!

Infamous "Mary" Faux Pas (Fall, 1973)—Regarding the film version of *Jesus Christ Superstar*, New York City press courteously "alerts" the Interreligious Affairs Department of the Union of American Hebrew Congregations that a query is imminently coming their way: "Is this movie anti-Semitic?" The prepared Jewish response? "Hardly anti-Semitic, but we disapprove of the film's depicting Jesus as incestuously involved with Mary Magdalene." A public relations debacle, traceable again to Jewish ignorance! Magdalene was a different Mary from Jesus' mother (hence no incest)! Ironically, the Talmud itself appears to mis-identify Mary Magdalene with Jesus' mother, Mary—so at least the faux pas was consistent with (erroneous) Jewish "tradition"![11]

A Unique Crèche (Christmas, 2002)—A wintery side street: I am walking behind a Jewish mother and her little boy. We approach, on the right, a Methodist church's crèche and its nativity display. Mom averts her gaze to the left, across the street, as if to induce her son to follow suit. No such luck! As I gain on and pass them, I overhear the boy's animated query: "Say, Mama, who's that baby over there?" Without missing a beat: "Oh, that's baby Judah Maccabee!"

Boston High School Basketball (2016)—When squaring off against Cambridge Rindge & Latin in a Massachusetts boys' basketball semifinal, Catholic Memorial high school had banned much of its fan base: the fifty to seventy-five spectators who, after at the previous game, had chanted "You killed Jesus" toward Jewish fans of Newton North High School. "The chant alarmed Jewish fans in the crowd," causing a municipal crisis (featuring, as well as anti-Jewish chanting, Jews not clearly knowing what to say).[12]

Distraught Baby-Sitter (2016)—One of my former Jewish students (in New Testament), while babysitting two young children, urgently texts me: the Christian parents have instructed her to occupy the youngsters with Mel Gibson's *Passion of the Christ*. But now the little ones are petrified by the film's violence. Unable to reach the parents, the sitter instead has contacted me: "What should I do? They explicitly instructed me to show the movie." I suggest: "Switch the screen immediately to a more appropriate program! Later, tell the returning parents what happened. Get back to me if I can help further!"

Each of the foregoing anecdotes—easily multiplied by dozens of others—was here traceable to Jews' having failed to think of the covenant as a *mishmeret*, that is, as something to be protected and guarded, in this case by assimilating *in advance* the kind of confidence-building and solid knowledge that will enable them to respond forcefully to attacks from the outside, even if that knowledge is related to the New Testament itself rather than traditional Jewish sources.

A Workable Jesus Model?

Preliminary to rolling out such a program is the daunting disagreement, certainly true among gentile scholars themselves, as to who Jesus actually was: a pacifist or militant, a prophet, reformer, liberator, apocalyptist, Pharisee, Essene, magician, charismatic, healer/exorcist, cynic-philosopher, or savior.[13] For this essay, agreement in defining the historical Jesus will not be the issue but rather identifying those urgent problems that Gospel writers felt constrained to resolve for their Christian adherents: dilemmas and challenges arising especially from the second half of the first Christian century. As this initial juncture, however, we require some modest consensus as to a working model concerning Jesus' identity—that is, a proposed rudimentary formulation of a Jesus-image that a majority of scholars will find at least plausibly and tolerably correct.

Such a modest consensus might well include the details that Jesus was a Galilean Jewish teacher who died c. 30 CE and who, seeing himself as Heaven's last envoy before God's imminent intervention in history, worked to purify society of the evil resulting from human misbehavior and to achieve places of societal acceptance for the poor, outcast, and lowly. He may have anticipated a royal role in this coming "Kingdom of God," whose arrival he heralded not only through especially artful Jewish parables but by one exceptionally emblematic demonstration precipitating his arrest: overturning Temple furniture to symbolize overturning of the current Jewish societal order by the dawning ruling power of God.[14] Presumably, the Jewish personnel ruling this new kingdom would differ from those governing the old, so those feeling most acutely provoked by Jesus' portent would be the then-current Jewish leaders: some of the chief priestly elements under sway of Roman occupiers charged with maintaining law and order and payment of taxes. Jesus' varied and multi-faceted preaching of a coming of a new kingdom could not but spark intercession by authorities—Roman as well as some Jewish. It fell to the Jewish High Priest Caiaphas to deliver Jesus to the Roman prefect, Pontius Pilate, who in turn consigned Jesus to the cross for sedition, here defined as aspiring to be "king of the Jews," a status reserved for the Roman Emperor alone.

The Legacy of Jesus' "Passion"

Jewish ineptitude in coping with the Gospels is nowhere more manifest than respecting the "Passion narratives" that establish the Jews' alleged corporate and perpetual blame for Jesus' execution.[15] Episodes here comprise Jesus' Last Supper, his betrayal by Judas

Iscariot, his arrest by Jewish personnel, his subjection to a brutal Jewish Sanhedrin trial (a key focus of this essay), and a Jewish mob screaming for his crucifixion (despite less than a week earlier having en masse welcomed him as he entered Jerusalem riding humbly on a donkey). Over the sweep of almost two millennia, scurrilous accusations of Jewish villainy intensified exponentially, unrestrained by (what I coin) the "hybrid riddle": if Jesus' death was indispensable for humanity's salvation, why blame Jews as the determinative cog in bringing it to pass? (This is *the* most frequent question I have encountered from my rabbinical and adult students.)

During the Crusades, the "Christ-killer" taunt became a pretext for Christian armies, trekking from Europe to recapture Jerusalem from the Muslim "infidels," to ransack the communities of Jews (who, of course, were also "infidels" in their eyes) en route.[16] And that notion, that Christians had displaced Jews as God's chosen people, was in turn exploited by Hitler's ideologues to teach that the existence of the Jews in the twentieth century was nothing but an unfortunate quirk of history, little more than a fossil that ought reasonably to have disappeared far earlier. This ploy lessened potential resistance to Hitler's "Final Solution," the plan to exterminate the Jewish people. While it is far too much to say simply that the Gospels caused the Holocaust, it is not at all exaggerated to say that the Gospel literature provided many with a kind of before-the-fact justification of the kind of virulent anti-Semitism that led to the Shoah and its horrors.

A Litmus Test: The Jewish Inability to Counter Mel Gibson's "Passion" Film

The production process of this infamous film, lasting for two years before its actual release, profoundly disturbed elements of the U.S.

Conference of Catholic Bishops.[17] They feared that Gibson's (extremist conservative[18]) Catholicism might compromise the four decades of progress that followed the Second Vatican Council's monumental repudiation of the deicide accusation.[19] That happened in 1988, but later on another Catholic document went so far as to question the reliability of Gospel depictions of the Sanhedrin trial,[20] mandating instead "extreme caution and, perhaps, even abandoning the device" (e.g., in dramatic re-enactments of Passion trial-productions).[21]

In 2003, I was invited to be among four Roman Catholic and three Jewish scholars charged by the Secretariat to evaluate an advance script of Gibson's film and convey to him our (independently arrived at) results.[22] My personal critique enumerated forty-eight problematic motifs that I construed to bode ill for modern Jews' societal security (thirty-seven made it to the screen). Many of these were lacking all basis in the Gospels: for example, Jews throwing Jesus off a bridge, the bribing of Jerusalem Jews to vote for his crucifixion, and even Satan cueing Jews' actions.

Jewish Federation directors were urged by synagogue boards to pen concise statements that Jews could circulate, to interested gentiles and for press releases—to account for Jews' radioactive behavior.[23] But Federations were, generally speaking, discomfited that they simply had no reservoir of Gospel knowledge to draw upon in determining how best to respond to Gibson's film. As a rule, they had but the foggiest of notions as what to say. Upon their invitation, I myself (and I imagine many others) crafted for Federations a usable response. My response follows:

SOME JEWISH REACTIONS TO MEL GIBSON'S "THE PASSION OF THE CHRIST"

Jews…affirm Mel Gibson's right of artistic license. They also realize that many Christians will experience his controversial film differently from the way many Jews will view it. To foster

mutual understanding, the following explains why some
Jews...find the film objectionable:

[1] In significant departure from Gospel testimony, Mr.
Gibson draws heavily upon visions by a nineteenth-century
German nun, Anne Catherine Emmerich. The pervasive
tenor of his movie as well as aspects of his personal
theology—and...scenes where Jesus is tortured by Jews
and...other characters are assigned antisemitic actions or
expletives—...are...demonstrably inspired by this nun (who
had no expertise in first-century history).[24]

[2] While Mr. Gibson has...praised his production as the
most historically reliable...he knows little of, or ignores, a
century of recent *Christian*...scholarship concerning...Jesus'
death, and has instead restricted his consultants to those [of
his own mindset]...

[3] Mr. Gibson's powerful influence could...undercut...four
decades of advances in Christian-Jewish relations...in which
our community prides itself. (Already, the film has polarized
some who otherwise used to engage in friendly...discourse
with one another.)

[4] Mr. Gibson refuses to take seriously enough the...
relationship between European Passion plays and the
ensuing trauma, even death, they brought at least indirectly
to countless Jews. Hitler himself used the Oberammergau
Passion Play to indoctrinate Nazis as to why Jews as a *people*
had to be exterminated. The Holocaust alone (whose Jewish
dimensions Mr. Gibson has seemed reluctant fully to accept)
explains why Passion Plays are so "radioactive" for the Jewish
psyche.

[5] The movie radiates the potential of jeopardizing the
welfare of Jews abroad, where images...duplicative of some...
of Gibson's film have been...appropriated...as vehicles for
conveying antisemitism.

[6] DVDs in video chains, libraries...and Christian religious
school curricula could poison the minds of some Christians

(especially children) toward Jews of Jesus' time, if not also...
of today....

[7] Mr. Gibson's "over-the-top" fascination with torture...
reinforces..."unchristian" values and vile violence pervading
our secular culture—by which so many Christians claim to
feel assaulted today (which aversion...Jews...share).

[8] The rage and name-calling...generated by the film are
inconsistent with the dawning of the Jewish Kingdom of God
so ardently anticipated by Jesus through his own (Pharisaic)
parables.

Nonetheless, the Jewish community remains committed
to...pursuit of wholesome interfaith relations, and hopes...
heartfelt dialogues over this film may...engender...mutual
understanding...toward the Messianic Age conceptualized
and bequeathed to...the world by Jewish tradition.

*This statement is prepared by Michael J. Cook, Ph.D., Sol & Arlene
Bronstein Professor of Judaeo-Christian Studies, Hebrew Union
College, Cincinnati. It reflects his sense of the stance of most Jews
in communities he has addressed, but does not necessarily bear the
official approval of Jewish communities where it is distributed
(February 2, 2004).*[25]

What were the principal Federation reactions to this posting? They
were generally welcoming, but reticent—even paralyzed by the
question of how this piece was going to play out in the press and how
Federation directors were going not to sound ill-equipped to respond
to ensuing "letters to the editor." The majority decision? Better to take
no action at all! Yet I found that my personal internet circulation of
the statement elicited favorable response from Jewish *and* Christian
laypersons grateful for help in knowing how to respond.

By contrast, alas, as matters panned out, three self-professed
"talmudic" Jews[26] aided Gibson by calling his attention to the utterly
irrelevant talmudic passage in Sanhedrin 43a:

> On the eve of Passover they hanged Yeshu [the Nazarene].
> And a crier went forth before him forty days [saying],
> "[Yeshu the Nazarene] goes forth to be stoned because
> he has practiced magic and deceived and led astray Israel.
> Anyone who knows aught in his favor, let him come and
> declare concerning him." And they found naught in his favor.
> And they hanged him on the eve of Passover.

This fictional recounting stemmed from at the very least a century and a half after Jesus died, and in Babylonia no less—a land far removed from Jesus' locale. The passage was undoubtedly predicated on the Gospels, hardly confirming of them: thus "to drag this [talmudic] text into the picture [was] 'dangerous, utterly meaningless and irrelevant.'"[27] So what was its original purpose? To demonstrate that Jews, not in haste but with all due deliberation, *tried to save Jesus*—but that over as long as forty days there was not a soul in the entire Holy Land who came to his aide. Gibson, however, overjoyed, eagerly appropriated this bogus text—bogus because it was intended to exonerate Jews, not to incriminate them! Here Jewish ignorance of how to process the Gospels extended to not knowing how to avoid misprocessing the Talmud as well!

A Sample Analysis: Jesus' Alleged Sanhedrin Trial

The broad application of this essay is that the traditional Jewish premium on amassing knowledge and problem-solving should now, as a matter of course, likewise entail gaining familiarity with New Testament. Given the confines of our present discourse—and extending as well to our discussion of the Gibson ordeal—it becomes apt now to select and intensify our focus on a singularly injurious subject of Jewish history: Jesus' alleged Jewish Sanhedrin trial.

Mark 14:55–65 sets the trial on Thursday night, immediately after Jesus departs the Last Supper for the Garden of Gethsemane.[28] There he is arrested and delivered to the High Priest, who convenes a Sanhedrin comprising the "chief priests, elders, and scribes." Immediately summoned to defend himself, Jesus remains silent; summoned a second time, Jesus now abruptly affirms that he *is* "the Christ, the Son of the Blessed." The High Priest decries this as "blasphemy" (a Jewish, not Roman, concern), and the Sanhedrin en masse roundly condemns Jesus as deserving death.[29]

This episode has been so repeatedly damaging throughout almost two millennia of Jewish persecution by Christianity that even some modern Jews—desperately seeking to exculpate our people— predicate their defense on a litany of "discrepancies" (i.e., procedural inconsistencies) between how the Talmud allegedly conducted capital trials in general, compared to what Mark claimed for Jesus' interrogation in specific! (I have discussed this above in my analysis of the Gibson film.)

I myself am one of those scholars, predominantly gentile, who champion a radically different reconstruction. I am convinced of a "pre-Markan Passion Narrative" and feel certain that, underlying our earliest Passion account (the one bequeathed us by Mark in about 70 CE) was an earlier, pre-70 CE, rudimentary, oral, and only later-on written down version relating what befell Jesus during his last days. This hypothetical version was co-opted and editorially reworked (revised, expanded, etc.) over time, thereby enlarging the initially briefer storyline with themes and nuances (even a Sanhedrin trial!) so as to serve needs of the developing Christian community. Note that no recourse is needed here to any theory of procedural discrepancies or inconsistencies between any Sanhedrin protocols involving the

Talmud.[30]

Indeed, I contend we may still actually be able to discern two rudimentary sentences peering up through today's canonical Markan veneers, both about specific "deliveries." The first, Mark 14:53, spans the *delivery* of the arrested Jesus from the Garden of Gethsemane to the High Priests's whereabouts on Thursday night. The second pre-Markan verse, 15:1, then narrates the High Priest's *delivery* of Jesus to the Roman prefect, Pontius Pilate, on Friday morning.

Observe, whether by pure happenstance or not: these two proposed *early* skeletal verses "happen" to telescope in and of themselves a *complete* antecedent "mini" Passion account with *no Sanhedrin trial intervening at all.* Consider an alternate text, possibly something like:

> **14:53.** And they *led Jesus to the High Priest*; and all the chief priests and the elders and the scribes were assembled…**15:1.** And as soon as it was morning, the chief priests, with the elders and scribes, and the whole council held a consultation; and they bound Jesus and *led him* away and delivered him *to Pilate.*

If this juxtaposition even approximates an actual antecedent rendition, we would naturally then ask where the Sanhedrin scene fits in. And our answer is clear: it does not! In terms of the plot, we would not need this element because the "consultation," still present from 15:1, covers that need. The original account would have featured only Friday morning's "consultation" *into which* Mark, possibly decades later, editorially intruded (i.e., added) an entirely fictional Thursday-night Sanhedrin trial.

This would account for the oddity of a Sanhedrin convened to serve and finish Thursday night, with an eye-raising but not needed "consultation" Friday morning. Again, the most plausible explanation is that the Thursday-night "Sanhedrin" was Mark's literary invention, but that the author then somehow forgot to cut the Friday morning "consultation"—which now had not only had lost its raison d'être but actually was "in the way" of the passage reading smoothly and logically.

Consider, also, the oddities solved by our removing the "Sanhedrin" paragraph, which I contend that Mark intruded into what he inherited. Gone is the dubious irregularity of convening Sanhedrin delegates immediately after (or even perhaps during) Thursday's festive Passover meal on the first evening of the Feast of Unleavened Bread. Further, are we genuinely to believe that Jewish Sanhedrin delegates would return home after a nighttime trial only to reconvene almost immediately on Friday morning to re-discuss an outcome which had been verbalized with such finality just hours before?

Other problematics also abruptly dissipate upon this reconstruction—for example, in drumming up attendees for his Sanhedrin Thursday-night trial Mark errs in narrating "the chief priests, with the elders and scribes, ***and the whole council***," for "the chief priests with the elders and scribes" *themselves* constitute "the whole council." Again, the inexplicable excess and sequencing in grouping of attendees is but another by-product of insufficiently careful editing.[31] Finally, recall that Rome could consign suspected seditionists to the cross even without any *Jewish* Sanhedrin trial beforehand.

Inferring Motives for the Sanhedrin Paragraph?

The matter of Mark's motives, while of course speculative, demands reflection. Here we leave aside the two bookend verses and focus on what they now enclose:

Mark 14:32. And they led Jesus to the High Priest….[32]

[Now Mark's Inserted Constructed Trial (14:55–65)]
[55]Now the chief priests and the whole council [Sanhedrin] sought testimony against Jesus to put him to death; but they found none. [56]For many bore false witness against him, and their witness did not agree. [57]And some stood up and bore false witness against him, saying, [58]"We heard him say, 'I will destroy this temple that is made with hands, and in three days I will build another, not made with hands.'" [59]Yet not even so did their testimony agree. [60]And the High Priest stood up in the midst, and asked Jesus, "Have you no answer to make? What is it that these men testify against you?" [61]But he was silent and made no answer. Again the High Priest asked him, "Are you the Christ, the Son of the Blessed?" [62]And Jesus said, "I am; and you will see the "Son of Man" seated at the right hand of Power, and coming with the clouds of heaven." [63]And the High Priest tore his garments, and said, "Why do we still need witnesses? [64]You have heard his blasphemy. What is your decision?" And they all condemned him as deserving death. [65]And some began to spit on him, and to cover his face, and to strike him, saying to him, "Prophesy!" And the guards received him with blows....

15:1 And as soon as it was morning, the chief priests, with the elders and scribes…held a consultation; and they bound Jesus and led him away and delivered him to Pilate.

Confirming the artificiality of the purported trial (14:55–65) is its stilted construction: five loosely cohering layers piled on one another, labeled A through E (emphasis added):

A [55]Now the chief priests and the whole council [Sanhedrin] sought testimony against Jesus to put him to death; but they found none. [56]For many *bore false witness against him,* and *their witness did not agree.*

B   [57]And some stood up and *bore false witness against him,* saying, [58]"We heard him say, 'I will destroy this temple that is made with hands, and in three days I will build another, not made with hands.'" [59]*Yet not even so did their testimony agree.*

C   [60]And the High Priest [Caiaphas] stood up in the midst, and asked Jesus:

[Query #1] *"Have you no answer to make? What is it that these men testify against you?"* [61]But he was *silent* and made no answer.

[Query #2] Again the High Priest asked him, *"Are you the Christ, the Son of the Blessed?"* [62]And Jesus said, "I am; and you will see the "Son of Man" seated at the right hand of Power, and coming with the clouds of heaven."

D   [63]And the High Priest tore his garments, and said, "Why do we still need witnesses? [64]You have heard his *blasphemy.* What is your decision?" And they *all* condemned him as deserving death.

E   [65]And some began to spit on him, and to cover his face, and to strike him, saying to him, "Prophesy!" And the guards received him with blows.

Commentary:

Layer A (verses 55–56) shows the Sanhedrin as predisposed to condemn Jesus.

Layer B (verses 57–59) virtually repeats the previous verse (the italics showing the correspondences). Because verse 56 neglected to specify the *content* of the false witness, layer B now provides it (which may suggest a time-lapse between the formulations of A and B—a tell-tale sign of editing).[33]

Layer C (verses 60–62) seeks to supply words that were ascribed to more important persons, Jesus and the High Priest. Recourse here is to Jewish scripture—a standard Gospel editorial practice. Also, Jesus here manifests clashing demeanors because he is harnessed to clashing proof-texts! His initial silence toward the High Priest was determined by the silence of Isaiah's Suffering Servant (53:7, "he opened not his mouth"), and Jesus' stridency toward the High Priest's second question was mandated by importing the "Son of Man" text from Daniel 7:13 (along with Psalm 110:1).

Layer D (verses 63–64) conveys Mark's key message: that Jesus' strident response to the High Priest constitutes blasphemy (and not sedition, the latter which would have awakened Rome's concern and hence which posed danger to the church).

Layer E (verse 65) concludes the artificial culmination.

For good measure, we should also discover what appear to be even more subtle editorial fingerprints. First, the High Priest's two supposed questions of Jesus are not a genuine quote but a reworking and borrowing from Pilate's interview of Jesus (Mark 15:2 and 4); and Jesus' alleged responses (Mark 14:60–61) are simply "proof-texting" intended respectively to cohere with borrowings from Isaiah (53:7) and Daniel.(7:13).[34] Further, a close examination of the two questions Pilate asks Jesus to field (Mark 2:4) reveals that editor Mark likewise imported these into the Sanhedrin trial and assigned them to the High Priest instead (naturally adjusting the phraseology to adjust the new context). All these connections betray literary craftsmanship, not recall of authentic history.

Turning now from suspicious details to inferences of their likely specific application by the Markan editor, it would appear that Mark felt it woefully inadequate, if indeed not insulting, that the Jesus whom Christians deemed the Son of God would be disposed of by nothing more potent than a mere Friday morning "consultation" in the course of which Jesus says nothing and is not even mentioned as being present. Did Mark believe instead that only a full-fledged trial before the "supreme court" of the land could suggest a suitable level of deference for its details to indict the entire Jewish nation (but not Roman officialdom) of blasphemy (a concern to Jews, not Rome) even though sedition must surely have been the actual Roman charge? Did not Mark transform a Jew put to death by the Romans as a "Christian" put to death by "the Jews"—the latter thus depicted not solely as people pre-rejecting Christianity but also threatening, and repeatedly, rebellion against Rome?[35]

Summation

This essay has been fundamentally concerned with the detriment Jews have done themselves by tolerating, even on occasion promoting as virtuous, ignorance of Gospel studies. Jesus' Sanhedrin trial has been noted merely as a single, albeit most powerful, example justifying why, for their own well-being (and especially the well-being of a new generation of young people) to end the ghettoization of the Jewish mind when it comes to New Testament and to take seriously the Torah's reference to itself as a *mishmeret*, as something to be guarded and watched over, as something to be protected from assault by hostile or even well-meaning others.

NOTES

¹ In this regard, see especially the essay of Martin S. Cohen, "The Fragile Sabbath," elsewhere in this volume.

² The Torah uses the word *mishmeret* to reference the covenant at Genesis 26:5 and Deuteronomy 11:1, and cf. the passage at Joshua 24:3 that speaks specifically of "the *mishmeret* of divine commandments."

³ The verbs in use are *va-yishmor* at Genesis 26:5 and *v'shamarta* at Deuteronomy 11:1.

⁴ The Hebrew literally means "know what to respond to an Epicurean," which is an example from Rabbi Eleazar's day of a kind of non-Jewish opponent who routinely disparaged Judaism. Rabbi Eleazar himself is Eleazar ben Shamua, a teacher of the fourth generation of mishnaic teachers and one of the premier pupils of Rabbi Akiva.

⁵ Aḥad Ha-am (1856–1927), "*Shabbat V'tziyyonut*," available online at http://benyehuda.org/ginzberg/Gnz051.html. And cf. David Novak, *Zionism and Judaism: A New Theory* (New York: Cambridge University Press, 2015), p. 81.

⁶ E.g., T. Shabbat 13:5; cf. T. Yadayim 2:13.

⁷ In this position, I succeeded my mentor, Samuel Sandmel (1911–1979), Professor of Bible and Hellenistic Literature.

⁸ "Gospel dynamics" is a term I coined for those skillful techniques (evinced by the Gospel writers) by which early Christians molded traditions about Jesus to address *their* needs decades after he died.

⁹ The clear reference is to Vatican II's "Nostra Aetate" Declaration (paragraph 4), promulgated under Pope Paul VI in October of 1965.

¹⁰ E.g., the Shema (Deuteronomy 6:4–9), Golden Rule (Leviticus 19:18), Lord's Prayer (cf. Kaddish in Jewish liturgy), designations of God in royal terms (cf. "our Father, our King"), etc.

¹¹ See B. Shabbat 104b and 106a.

¹² Cf. https://www.washingtonpost.com/news/early-lead/wp/2016/03/15/you-killed-jesus-taunt-gets-boston-high-school-students-banned-from-playoff-game/.

¹³ The classic ground-breaking survey of more than fifty eighteenth- and nineteenth-century historical reconstructions of Jesus is Albert Schweitzer, *The Quest for the Historical Jesus*, trans. William Montgomery (1910; rpt. Mineola: Dover, 2005)—exposing the disconcerting tendency to see Jesus more as scholars themselves were rather than as he himself may have been.

¹⁴ Analogous are other prophets whose singular demonstrations were deemed instrumental in bringing God's will to fruition: Ahijah (1 Kings 11:29ff.), Jeremiah (32:1ff.), Ezekiel (4:4ff.), etc.

¹⁵ "Passion" (from the Latin for "suffering") signifies Jesus' last days of travail.

The New Testament sources are Mark 14–15, Matthew 26–27, Luke 22–23, and John 18–19.

[16] Although not themselves employing the exact term, presaging "Christ-killers" were Matthew 27:25, John 8:44, Acts 3:13–15, and 1 Thessalonians 2:14–16 (the last possibly mis-ascribed by Christian tradition to Paul).

[17] Cf. specifically its Secretariat for Ecumenical and Interreligious Affairs declaration, *Nostra Aetate* ("In Our Time"), Section 4 (1965), which aimed to lay to rest the deicide accusation.

[18] Gibson's sect, "Catholic traditionalism," recognizes neither papal authority nor the universality of Second Vatican Council teachings.

[19] The text there reads as follows: "What happened in His passion cannot be charged against all the Jews, without distinction, then alive, nor against the Jews of today...." Dismissed was the notion that Jews were corporately rejected by God for complicity in Jesus' death and for failing to recognize him as Messiah then and since. Also, Roman Catholic teaching materials were overhauled, including Catholic textbooks.

[20] *Sanhedrin* is a hebraisized form of the Greek *synedrion*, literally "sitting together" (hence "council"; "assembly").

[21] This was the *Criteria for the Evaluation of Dramatizations of the Passion*, National Conference of Catholic Bishops, 1988, #C.1.c.

[22] The four Roman Catholics were Mary Boys, Philip Cunningham, Lawrence Frizella, and John Pawlikowski. The three Jews were myself, Paula Fredriksen, and Amy-Jill Levine.

[23] "Federation" is a Jewish community's major organization providing charitable, recreational, and cultural services.

[24] *The Dolorous Passion of Our Lord Jesus Christ According to the Meditations of Anne Catherine Emmerich* (1923; rpt. Mineola, NY: Dover Books, 2004).

[25] Available online at http://huc.edu/news/2004/02/02/dr-michael-cook-some-jewish-reactions-mel-gibson-s-film-passion-christ#.

[26] The Jewish commentators were Rabbi Daniel Lapin, movie critic Michael Medved, and author and *Forward* columnist David Klinghoffer. Cf. Ami Eden's essay in the *Forward* in their regard, available online at https://forward.com/culture/6362/some-of-mel-gibson-s-best-friends-are-jewish/.

[27] Ellis Rivkin, quoted by Erich J. Greenberg in "The Talmud on the Death of Jesus," available online at https://theshalomcenter.org/content/talmud-death-jesus. Also, cf. Ronald Modras, *The Catholic Church and Antisemitism Poland, 1933–1939* (London: Routledge, 2004), p. 192, who writes: "The unhistorical nature [of this passage]...indicates that third-century Judaism had no independent information about Jesus...the reference...[an] obvious attempt... to counter Christian missionary efforts among Jews." And see further David Instone-Brewer, "Jesus of Nazareth's Trial in Sanhedrin 43a," online at http://

www.tyndale.cam.ac.uk/Tyndale/staff/Instone-Brewer/prepub/Sanhedrin%20 43a%20censored.pdf.

[28] Note that the verse numbering of Gospel texts was not present from the start, but added later on.

[29] The term "blasphemy" here is meant to denote speaking disparagingly of God and using God's name in the process.

[30] Canvas the scholarship in Gerd Theissen and Annette Merz, *The Historical Jesus: A Comprehensive Guide* (Minneapolis: Fortress, 1998), *passim*. Note that linguistic studies have not determined whether Mark retained pre-Markan wordings verbatim, preserved *all* of the suspected forerunner, or interwove additional sources with it.

[31] My contention that Mark copied their mention into 14:53 from that in 15:1.

[32] Note that the story of Peter's denial of Jesus (14:54 and 66–72) is a late-stage editorial addition separate from the subject of this essay. See Cook, *Modern*, pp. 137–138 and 184–186.

[33] Otherwise verse 56 might simply have been rewritten altogether.

[34] Along with Psalm 110:1.

[35] Mark inserts "blasphemy" (2:5b–10) into 2:1-5a,11–12; a Passover meal 14:12–16 between verses 14:11 and 17; a "Barabbas" unit (15:6–15a) between 5:5 and 15:15b; also the paragraph embarrassing Peter (Mark 14:54,66–72). All this is to say that Mark habitually leaves tell-tale fingerprints of his similar intrusions and insertions elsewhere.

Translation
Grant peace everywhere goodness and blessing,
Grace, lovingkindness and mercy to us and unto all Israel

Transliteration
Sim shalom tovah u-v'rakhah
ḥein va-ḥesed v'raḥamim aleinu ve-al kol Yisrael amekha

שִׂים שָׁלוֹם*

שִׂים שָׁלוֹם טוֹבָה וּבְרָכָה
חֵן וָחֶסֶד וְרַחֲמִים עָלֵינוּ וְעַל כָּל יִשְׂרָאֵל עַמֶּךְ

* **Sim Shalom** (Hebrew: שִׂים שָׁלוֹם; "Grant Peace") is a blessing that is recited near the end of formal Jewish prayer services. The precise form of the blessing varies depending on the service and the precise denomination along the Jewish spectrum.

www.BlechTapes.com

a focused YouTube channel

Benjamin Blech Exegesis

on 10-theme Mesorah Matrix

sequence of 12 twenty-minute tapes:

intro + 10 themes + outro

www.UnifyingScienceSpirituality.com

About the Contributors

Reuven P. Bulka, C.M., is Rabbi Emeritus of Congregation Machzikei Hadas in Ottawa, Ontario, Canada. He is President and CEO of Kind Canada Généreux and founding Chair of Kindness Week in Ottawa. Rabbi Bulka is the author or editor of close to forty volumes on a wide range of topics. His most recent book, Honeycombs (written with his granddaughter Rikki Ash), deals with a novel way to understand the Amidah. He and his wife Leah share many generations of children.

Martin S. Cohen is the rabbi of the Shelter Rock Jewish Center in Roslyn, New York, and one of the senior editors of the Mesorah Matrix series. He is the author of *Our Haven and Our Strength: The Book of Psalms* (Aviv Press, 2004), *The Boy on the Door on the Ox* (Aviv Press, 2008), four books of essays, and four novels. Rabbi Dr. Cohen served as senior editor of *The Observant Life* (2012) and *Pirkei Avot Lev Shalem* (2018), both published by the Rabbinical Assembly. His new translation and commentary on the Torah is forthcoming. The rest of his books, essays, and stories can be surveyed at www.martinscohen.net.

Michael J. Cook, Ph.D., is Bronstein Professor of Judeo-Christian Studies at Hebrew Union College, Cincinnati, and the only American rabbi with a full professorial chair in New Testament. He has served on the Executive Board of the Central Conference of American Rabbis and many advisory groups in Jewish-Christian relations. Aside from his widely-used *Modern Jews Engage the New Testament* (Jewish Lights, 2012), his publications treat Jewish views of Jesus, Paul, Jewish symbols in Christian art, anti-Semitism, and the Talmud in Gospel study.

Elliot N. Dorff is Rector and Distinguished Service Professor of Philosophy at the American Jewish University and Visiting Professor at UCLA School of Law. Rabbi Dorff chairs the Conservative Movement's Committee on Jewish Law and Standards, and he is a past president of the Society of Jewish Ethics, the Academy of Jewish Philosophy, the Jewish Law Association, the Academy of Judaic, Christian, and Islamic Studies, and Jewish Family Service of Los Angeles. Of the thirteen books and over two hundred articles he has written on Jewish thought, law, and ethics, his book most germane to the essay printed in this volume *is Knowing God: Jewish Journeys to the Unknowable* (Jason Aronson, 1992), especially the third chapter.

Alon C. Ferency is the rabbi of Heska Amuna Synagogue in Knoxville, Tennessee. He is a founding board member of the Community Coalition Against Human Trafficking, and was the rabbi-in-residence at Bonnaroo Music and Arts Festival and the religious consultant on *The Last Movie Star.* He was a contributor to the volumes on Birkat Kohanim and Modeh Ani in this series, as well as to *Conservative Judaism* quarterly and *Sh'ma*, and has forthcoming work on connections between physicality and spiritual care. His sermons are available on iTunes.

Baruch Frydman-Kohl is the Anne and Max Tanenbaum Senior Rabbi of Beth Tzedec Congregation in Toronto and a Rabbinic Fellow of the Shalom Hartman Institute. He received his doctorate in Philosophies of Judaism from the Jewish Theological Seminary and was trained in dispute resolution at the Osgoode Hall Law School of York University.

Zvi Grumet is Director of Education at The Lookstein Center for Jewish Education, a Bible teacher at Yeshivat Eretz Hatvi, and a mentor for the Pardes Educators Program. He is a popular speaker at many venues and has published two full-length studies on the Bible, Moses and the Path to Leadership (Urim, 2014) and Genesis: From Creation to Covenant (Maggid, 2017).

Elie Kaunfer is president and CEO of the Hadar Institute, an organization committed to furthering Torah, Avodah and Hesed through Jewish learning and community building. A Wexner Graduate Fellow and Dorot Fellow, he is the author of *Empowered Judaism: What Independent Minyanim Can Teach Us about Building Vibrant Jewish Communities* (Jewish Lights). Rabbi Kaunfer holds a doctorate in liturgy from the Jewish Theological Seminary, where he was also ordained. He has served as faculty for Wexner Heritage, Scholar-in-Residence at the Federation's General Assembly, and has lectured widely on prayer and building grassroots Jewish communities.

Admiel Kosman, a renowned poet, is Professor for Jewish Studies at Potsdam University as well as the academic director of Geiger College, a training school for liberal rabbis, in Berlin. He is the author of several books and many articles in the field of talmudic research and of collections of Hebrew verse, and he also writes a regular column for *Haaretz* in which he interprets current events in light of traditional sources. His latest academic book is *Gender and Dialogue in the Rabbinic Prism* (Walter de Gruyter, 2012) and his most recent collection of poetry is *Approaching You in English: Selected Poems* (Zephyr Press, 2011).

Berel Dov Lerner and his wife Batsheva are members of Kibbutz Shluḥot. He is an associate professor of philosophy at Israel's Western Galilee College and has published widely in Western and Jewish thought.

Michelle J. Levine is an associate professor of Bible at Stern College for Women, Yeshiva University. She has a Ph.D. in Jewish Studies from New York University, is the author of *Naḥmanides on Genesis: The Art of Biblical Portraiture* (Brown University Press, 2009), and has written academic articles on topics of the Bible and medieval biblical exegesis. She is also a noted lecturer on Bible topics to communities throughout the United States and Israel. In 2011, she was voted Stern senior class Jewish studies "Professor of the Year."

Martin I. Lockshin lives in Jerusalem. He is University Professor Emeritus at York University in Toronto, where he taught Jewish Studies for thirty-eight years. Rabbi Lockshin is the author of six books and many articles, mostly dealing with the history of Jewish Bible commentaries.

David Maayan is a student and teacher of Jewish texts, with a particular interest in the literature of Kabbalah and Hasidism. He is currently a doctoral student in Comparative Theology at Boston College, where he is researching the development of the modern self and models of embodiment in Jewish mystical theologies in a comparative context.

Dalia Marx, Ph.D., is Professor of Liturgy and Midrash at the Jerusalem campus of Hebrew Union College-Jewish Institute of Religion, and teaches in various academic institutions in Israel and Europe. Marx, a tenth-generation Jerusalemite, earned her doctorate at the Hebrew University and her rabbinic ordination at HUC-JIR in Jerusalem and Cincinnati. She is involved in various research projects and is active in promoting liberal Judaism in Israel. Marx writes for academic and popular journals and publications. Among her publications are *A Feminist Commentary of the Babylonian Talmud* (Mohr Siebeck, 2013) and the Hebrew-language book *About Time: Journeys in the Jewish-Israeli Calendar* (Yediot Sefarim, 2018).

Dan Ornstein is rabbi at Congregation Ohav Shalom and a writer living with his family in Albany, New York. He is the author of the book *Cain v. Abel: A Jewish Courtroom Drama* (Jewish Publication Society, 2020).

Barbara Shulamit Thiede is a faculty member of the Department of Religious Studies at the University of North Carolina at Charlotte. She teaches Hebrew Bible, Jewish history, the history of anti-Semitism, and the legacy of the Holocaust for both the undergraduate and graduate programs. In addition, she also offers a range of classes in Hebrew Bible and Jewish history for ordination programs at ALEPH, the Alliance for Jewish Renewal, and serves as a member of the ALEPH Academic Council. The spiritual leader for Temple Or Olam in Concord, North Carolina, Rabbi Dr. Thiede blogs at adrenalinedrash.com.

Shmuly Yanklowitz is President & Dean of Valley Beit Midrash, the founder and president of Uri L'Tzedek, the founder and CEO of The Shamayim V'Aretz Institute, the founder and president of YATOM: The Jewish Adoption and Foster Network, and the author of fourteen books on Jewish ethics, including *The Soul of Jewish Social Justice* (Urim Publications, 2014) and *Pirkei Avot: A Social Justice Commentary* (CCAR Press, 2018). Newsweek named Rav Shmuly one of the top fifty rabbis in America in 2012 and 2013, and *The Forward* named him one of the fifty most influential Jews in the nation in 2016 and 2017. Shmuly and his wife Shoshana live in Scottsdale, Arizona, with their four children.

Noam Zion, on the faculty of the Hartman Institute in Jerusalem since 1978, specializes in in-service learning for rabbis, educators, and theologians. His popular publications include books about the Jewish holidays: *A Different Night: Haggadah*; *A Different Light*: *Hanukkah; A Day Apart: Shabbat at Home*; and *A Night to Remember: A Haggadah of Contemporary Voices.* His academic books are a trilogy on *Jewish Giving in Comparative Perspectives* (Biblical, Greek, Rabbinic, Christian, and Muslim narratives of generosity) and nine volumes on *Talmudic Marital Dramas*, published by Zion Holiday Publications and available online at www.haggadahsrus.com.

LIGHTS OF CREATION & TRANSCENDENCE
David Birnbaum / Mesorah Matrix Series

MESORAH MATRIX
10-BOOK SERIES
150+ Essayists

dimensions of

Spirituality & Kedushah

THE SPARK OF THE INFINITE DIVINE

Mesorah Matrix
Series

David Birnbaum

Editor-in-Chief

MESORAH
MATRIX

Sanctification	TIKKUN OLAM	BIRKAT KOHANIM
2015	2015	2016
KADDISH	Modeh Ani	HAVDALAH
2016	2017	2017
SEARCH FOR MEANING	U-VACHARTA BA-CHAYIM	Ehyeh asher Ehyeh	U'shamru
2018	2018	2019	2019

200+ original essays

150+ global thought leaders

jewish thought & spirituality

a decade-long unified endeavor

LIGHTS OF CREATION & TRANSCENDENCE
David Birnbaum / Mesorah Matrix Series

MESORAH MATRIX

10-BOOK SERIES
150+ Essayists

Sanctification

Tikkun Olam

Birkat Kohanim

The Kaddish

Modeh Ani

Havdalah

Search for Meaning

U-VACHARTA BA-CHAYIM

Ehyeh asher Ehyeh

V'Shamru

THE SPARK OF THE INFINITE DIVINE

Mesorah Matrix Series

Sanctification *("Kedushah")*

Tikkun Olam *("Repair the World")*

Birkat Kohanim *(The Priestly Blessings: a contemporary take)*

The Kaddish *(specifically, The Mourner's Praise of God)*

Modeh Ani *(The solo daily morning prayer of Gratitude)*

Havdalah *(separating Holy from Secular: Sabbath > secular)*

Search for Meaning *(pegging-off of Viktor Frankl's classic)*

U-VACHARTA BA-CHAYIM *(The 613th precept-Choose Life)*

Ehyeh asher Ehyeh *("I Will Be That Which I Will Be" – at the Burning Bush)*

V'Shamru *(The Sabbath)*

21st CENTURY PUBLISHING

David.Birnbaum.NY@gmail.com

www.NewParadigmMatrix.com

VOLUME 1

David Birnbaum / Mesorah Matrix Series

LIGHTS OF CREATION & TRANSCENDENCE

Sanctification

Editors

David
Birnbaum & Blech
Benjamin

LEAD ESSAY: **Jonathan Sacks**

New Paradigm Matrix™

EXPLORING HIGHER DIMENSIONS

MESORAH MATRIX
VOLUME 2

TIKKUN OLAM
JUDAISM, HUMANISM & TRANSCENDENCE

David Birnbaum / Mesorah Matrix Series
LIGHTS OF CREATION & TRANSCENDENCE

Editors

David
Birnbaum & Martin S. **Cohen**

Associate Editor: **Saul J. Berman**

New Paradigm Matrix™

EXPLORING HIGHER DIMENSIONS

MESORAH
MATRIX
VOLUME 3

BIRKAT KOHANIM

David Birnbaum | Mesorah Matrix Series

LIGHTS OF CREATION & TRANSCENDENCE

EXPLORING HIGHER DIMENSIONS

Editors

David
Birnbaum & **Cohen**
Martin S.

Associate Editor: **Saul J. Berman**

New Paradigm Matrix®

MESORAH MATRIX
VOLUME 4

KADDISH

Editors

David
Birnbaum &

Martin S.
Cohen

Associate Editor: **Saul J. Berman**

New Paradigm Matrix

EXPLORING HIGHER DIMENSIONS

David Birnbaum / Mesorah Matrix Series

LIGHTS OF CREATION & TRANSCENDENCE

MESORAH MATRIX
VOLUME 5

David Birnbaum / Mesorah Matrix Series

LIGHTS OF CREATION & TRANSCENDENCE

Modeh Ani

THE TRANSCENDENT PRAYER OF GRATITUDE

Editors

David
Birnbaum & Martin S. **Cohen**

Associate Editor: **Saul J. Berman**

New Paradigm Matrix™

EXPLORING HIGHER DIMENSIONS

MESORAH MATRIX
VOLUME 6

LIGHTS OF CREATION & TRANSCENDENCE
David Birnbaum
Mesorah Matrix Series

HAVDALAH

Editors

David
Birnbaum & Martin S. **Cohen**

Associate Editor: **Saul J. Berman**

EXPLORING HIGHER DIMENSIONS

New Paradigm Matrix™

David Birnbaum / Mesorah Matrix Series

LIGHTS OF CREATION & TRANSCENDENCE

SEARCH FOR MEANING

Editors

David
Birnbaum
Martin S.
& Cohen

Associate Editor: **Saul J. Berman**

New Paradigm Matrix™

EXPLORING HIGHER DIMENSIONS

MESORAH
MATRIX
VOLUME 8

LIGHTS OF CREATION & TRANSCENDENCE

David Birnbaum / Mesorah Matrix Series

U-VACHARTA BA-CHAYIM

Editors

David
Birnbaum & Martin S.
Cohen

Associate Editor: **Saul J. Berman**

New Paradigm Matrix®

EXPLORING HIGHER DIMENSIONS

MESORAH MATRIX
VOLUME 9

David Birnbaum / Mesorah Matrix Series
LIGHTS OF CREATION & TRANSCENDENCE

Ehyeh asher Ehyeh

Editors

David
Birnbaum & Martin S.
Cohen

EXPLORING HIGHER DIMENSIONS

New Paradigm Matrix™

LIGHTS OF CREATION & TRANSCENDENCE / Mesorah Matrix Series

David Birnbaum

U'shamru

Editors

David
Birnbaum & Martin S.
Cohen

New Paradigm Matrix

EXPLORING HIGHER DIMENSIONS

ESSAYISTS

Avivah Zornberg
Author

London, UK

David Ellenson
HUC-JIR

New York, NY

Saul Berman
Y.U. / Stern

New York, NY

Jonathan Sacks
United Hebrew
Congregations
London, UK

James Kugel
Bar Ilan University

Ramat Gan, Israel

Shalom Carmy
Yeshiva University,
Tradition Magazine
New York, NY

Rachel Barenblat
Bayit

Williamstown, MA

Rachel Friedman
Lamdeinu

New York, NY

W. Zeev Harvey
The Hebrew University of Jerusalem
Jerusalem

Rachel Adelman
Hebrew College

Newton Centre, MA

Shlomo Riskin
Ohr Torah Stone Colleges
Efrat, Israel

Mark Goldfeder
Emory University

Atlanta, GA

Hillel Goldberg
Intermountain Jewish News
Denver, CO

Lawrence Schiffman
NYU
New York, NY

Alan Cooper
Jewish Theological Seminary
New York, NY

Yonatan Feintuch
Bar Ilan University

Tel Aviv, Israel

Jacob Schacter
Yeshiva University

New York, NY

Aryeh Cohen
American Jewish
University
Los Angeles, CA

Avram Reisner
Chevrei Tzedek
Congregation
Baltimore, MD

Elliot Dorff
American Jewish
University
Los Angeles, CA

Michael Graetz
Congregation Eshel
Avraham
Omer, Israel

Steven Kepnes
Colgate University

Hamilton, NY

Reuven Bulka
Congregation
Machzikei Hadas
Ottawa, Canada

Adena Berkowitz
Kol Ha-neshamah

New York, NY

Alan Mittleman
Jewish Theological
Seminary
New York, NY

Tzvi Sinensky
Rosh Beit Midrash

Lower Merion, PA

Bradley Artson
American Jewish
University
Los Angeles, CA

Jill Jacobs
T'ruah: The Rabbinic
Call for Human Rights
New York, NY

Michael Broyde
Emory University

Atlanta, GA

Noam Zion
Hartman Institute

Jerusalem

Sid Schwarz
CLAL

New York, NY

Raḥel Berkovits
Pardes Institute

Jerusalem

Howard Addison
Temple University

Philadelphia, PA

Robert Harris
Jewish Theological
Seminary
New York, NY

Samuel Lebens
Rutgers University

New Brunswick, NJ

Richard Hidary
Congregation
Shearith Israel
New York, NY

Jonathan Schorsch
Universität Potsdam
Potsdam
Germany

Eliezer Shore
Hebrew University
of Jerusalem
Jerusalem

Roberta Kwall
DePaul University
Law School
Chicago, IL

Alon Ferency
Heska Amuna
Synagogue
Knoxville, TN

Aubrey Glazer
Congregation Beth
Shalom
San Francisco, CA

Rebecca W. Sirbu
Rabbis Without
Borders, CLAL
New York, NY

Geoffrey Claussen
Elon University

Elon, NC

Jeremy Gordon
New London
Synagogue
London, U.K.

Shoshana Klein
Poupko
Ahavath Torah
Englewood, NJ

Michael
Wasserman
The New Shul
Scottsdale, AZ

Daniel Greyber
Beth El Synagogue

Durham, NC

Gail Labovitz
American Jewish
University
Los Angeles, CA

James Jacobson-Maisels
Or HaLev, Center for Jew-
ish Spirituality & Meditation
New York, NY

Yeshaya Dalsace
Dor Vador Com-
munaute Massorti
Paris, France

Kari Tuling
Congregation
Kol Haverim
Glastonbury, CT

Karyn Kedar
B'nai Jehoshua
Beth Elohim
Deerfield, IL

Nina Cardin
Rabbinical
Assembly
New York, NY

Aryeh Klapper
Center for Modern
Torah Leadership
Sharon, MA

Jonathan Wittenberg
New North London
Synagogue
London, UK

Michael Knopf
Temple Beth-El

Richmond, VA

Rivon Krygier
Congregation
Adath Shalom
Paris

Elie Spitz
Congregation
B'nai Israel
Tustin, CA

Ira Bedzow
Aspen Center for
Social Values
Aspen, CO

Yitzchak Blau
RCA

Jerusalem

Alfred Cohen
YU High School

New York, NY

Elliot Cosgrove
Park Avenue
Synagogue
New York, NY

Yehonatan
Chipman
Hitzei Yehonatan
Israel

David Flatto
Penn State Law

University Park, PA

Shohama H. Wiener
Temple Beth-El

City Island, NY

David Evan Markus
Temple Beth-El

City Island, NY

Nathaniel Helfgot
Yeshivat Chovevei
Torah
New York, NY

Cass Fisher
University of South
Florida
Tampa, FL

Admiel Kosman
Postdam University

Germany

Simcha Krauss
Eretz Hatzvi

Jerusalem

Melanie Landau
Monash University

Australia

Vernon Kurtz
North Suburban
Synagogue Beth-El
Highland Park, IL

Rolando Matalon
B'nai Jeshurun

New York, NY

Shmuly Yanklowitz
Valley Beit Midrash
President & Dean
Scottsdale, AZ

Peter Knobel
Beth Emet

Evanston, IL

Harvey Meirovich
Zacharias Frankel
College
Berlin, Germany

Aryeh Frimer
Bar-Ilan University

Ramat Gan

Martin Lockshin
York University

Ontario, Canada

Shai Cherry
Shaar Hamayim

Del Mar, CA

David Shatz
Yeshiva University

New York, NY

Jeremy Rosen
Persian Jewish
Center
New York, NY

David Greenstein
Congregation
Shomrei Emunah
Montclair, NJ

Avraham Walfish
Herzog College and
Michala Jerusalem
Tekoa, Israel

David Mescheloff
RCA

Israel

Barbara Thiede
UNC Charlotte

Concord, NC

Lawrence Troster
GreenFaith

Highland Park, NJ

Ruth Walfish
Herzog College and
Michala Jerusalem
Tekoa, Israel

Lenn Goodman
Vanderbilt
University
Nashville, TN

Dan Ornstein
Ohav Shalom

Albany, NY

Dena Freundlich
Ma'ayanot AMIT

Jerusalem

Elaine Goodfriend
California State
University
Northridge, CA

Berel Dov Lerner
Western Galilee
College, Herzl Inst
Northern Israel

Orna Triguboff
Neshama Life
Organisation
Sydney, Australia

Nehemia Polen
Hebrew College

Newton Centre, MA

Mark Greenspan
Oceanside Jewish
Center
Oceanside, NY

Richard Claman
Zeramim Journal

New York, NY

Avi Olitzky
Beth El Synagogue

St. Louis Park, MN

Michelle J. Levine
Stern College for Women
Yeshiva University
New York, NY

Yehuda Gellman
Ben-Gurion
University
Negev, Israel

Herbert Bronstein
Lake Forest
College,
Lake Forest, IL

Avraham Feder
Beit Knesset
Moreshet Yisrael
Jerusalem

Elyse Goldstein
City Shul

Ontario, Canada

Kerry M. Olitzky
Big Tent Judaism

New York, NY

Dalia Marx
Hebrew Union
College
Jerusalem

Jason Rubenstein
Mechon Hadar

New York, NY

Herbert Yoskowitz
Adat Shalom
Synagogue
Farmington Hills, MI

Mark Sameth
Pleasantville Com-
munity Synagogue
Westchester, NY

Catharine Clark
Congregation
Or Shalom
London, Ontario

Jacob Adler
Temple Shalom of
Northwest Arkansas
Fayetteville, AR

Jonathan Jacobs
John Jay College,
CUNY
New York, NY

David Kunin
Beth Shalom
Synagogue
Edmonton, AB

Michael Marmur
Hebrew Union
College
Jerusalem

Mordechai Luria
Institute for Jewish
Ideas & Ideals
New York, NY

Noah Farkas
Valley Beth Shalom

Encino, CA

Alex Maged
Yeshiva University

New York, NY

Hayyim Angel
Yeshiva University

New York, NY

Elie Kaunfer
Mechon Hadar

New York, NY

Alex Sztuden
The Herzl Institute

Jerusalem

David Golinkin
Schechter Institute
of Jewish Studies
Jerusalem

Mark Washofsky
Hebrew Union
College
Cincinnati, OH

Edwin C. Goldberg
Temple Sholom of
Chicago
Chicago, IL

Baruch Frydman-Kohl
Beth Tzedec
Congregation
Toronto, Canada

Ora Horn Prouser
Academy for
Jewish Religion
Yonkers, NY

Howard Wettstein
University of
California
Riverside, CA

Zvi Grumet
Yeshivat Eretz
Hatzvi
Jerusalem

Erica Brown
The Jewish
Federation
Rockville, MD

Meesh Hammer-Kossoy
Pardes Institute
of Jewish Studies
Jerusalem

Michael J. Cook
Hebrew Union
College
Cincinnati, OH

James Diamond
University of
Waterloo
Ontario, Canada

Shira Weiss
Ben Gurion
University
Beer Sheba, Israel

Gidon Rothstein

Bronx, NY

Ariel Mayse
Stanford University
Stanford,
California

Dr. Elyssa Wortzman
Mindful art-based
spiritual education
San Francisco

Ellen LeVee
Spertus Institute

Chicago, IL

Kim Treiger-Bar-Am
Tel Aviv

Israel

David Maayan
Boston College

Newton, MA

Senior Editors

Benjamin Blech
Yeshiva University

New York, NY

Martin S. Cohen
Shelter Rock,
Jewish Center

Roslyn, NY

21st CENTURY PUBLISHING

David.Birnbaum.NY@gmail.com

www.NewParadigmMatrix.com

Sanctification

'Sanctification'
from Essay by Chief Rabbi Lord Jonathan Sacks

... And there is the priestly task of kedushah, sanctifying life by honouring the sacred ontology, the deep moral structure of the universe, through the life of the 613 commands, a life of discipline and self-restraint, honesty and integrity, respect and love, the code set out in the chapter of the Torah that opens with the momentous words, "Be holy for I, the Lord your God, am holy." Other cultures and faiths drew inspiration from its wisdom and prophetic traditions, but kedushah remained a specific Jewish imperative that made us different. Even so, it contains a message for the world, which Jews bear witness to whenever and wherever they remain faithful to it.
Our vocation remains, to be mamlechet cohanim vegoi kadosh, "a kingdom of priests and a holy nation."
                                                    - The Ethic of Holiness, August 2012

to view series updated authors list,

see www.MesorahMatrix.com

Mesorah Matrix Series

Editors

David Birnbaum

Martin S. Cohen

Benjamin Blech
Editor

Benjamin Blech
Yeshiva University,
"Understanding
Judaism"

- born in Zurich in 1933, is an Orthodox rabbi who now lives in New York City.

Rabbi Blech has been a Professor of Talmud at Yeshiva University since 1966, and was the Rabbi of Young Israel of Oceanside for 37 years. In addition to his work in the rabbinate, Rabbi Blech has written many books on Judaism and the Jewish people and speaks on Jewish topics to communities around the world.

Education

Rabbi Blech received a Bachelor of Arts degree from Yeshiva University, a Master of Arts degree in psychology from Columbia University, and rabbinic ordination from the Rabbi Isaac Elchanan Theological Seminary.

Milestones

Rabbi Blech is the author of twelve highly acclaimed and best selling books, with combined sales of close to half a million copies, including three as part of the highly popular Idiot's Guide series. His book, *Understanding Judaism*: The Basics of Deed and Creed, was chosen by the Union of Orthodox Jewish Congregations as "the single best book on Judaism in our generation".

Wikipedia online, http://en.wikipedia.org/wiki/Benjamin_Blech (accessed November 8, 2012)

Martin S. Cohen

Martin S. Cohen

Martin S. Cohen has been a Senior Editor of the inter-denominational Mesorah Matrix series since 2012.

From 2000-2014, he served as Chairman of the Publications Committee of the quarterly journal *Conservative Judaism*, which was under the joint auspices of the JTS (Jewish Theological Seminary) and the RA (Rabbinical Assembly) during that span.

Rabbi Cohen also served as the senior editor of *The Observant Life*, a compendium of Jewish law, custom published by the Rabbinical Assembly in 2012.

Martin's weekly blog can be viewed at www.TheRuminativeRabbi. blogspot.com. He serves as rabbi of the Shelter Rock Jewish Center in Roslyn, New York.

Rabbi Cohen was educated at the City University of New York and at Jewish Theological Seminary of America, where he was ordained a rabbi and received his Ph.D. in Ancient Judaism. He is the recipient of fellowships at the Hebrew University (Jerusalem) in 1983 and Harvard University in 1993.

Martin Cohen has taught at Hunter College, the Jewish Theological Seminary of America, the Institute for Jewish Studies of the University of Heidelberg, as well as at the University of British Columbia and the Vancouver School of Theology.

His published works include *The Boy on the Door on the Ox* (2008) and *Our Haven and Our Strength: A Translation and Commentary on the Book of Psalms* (2004).

Rabbi Cohen is currently writing a translation and commentary on the Torah and the Five Megillot.

Saul Berman
Mesorah Editor

Saul J. Berman is one of the world's leading Jewish intellects.

He is an American Jewish scholar and Modern Orthodox rabbinic.

Rabbi Berman was ordained at Yeshiva University, from which he also received his B.A. and his M.H.L. He completed a degree in law, a J.D., at New York University, and an M.A. in Political Sciesnce at the University of California, Berkeley, where he studied with David Daube. He spent two years studying mishpat ivri in Israel at Hebrew University of Jerusalem and at Tel Aviv University. He did advanced studies in Jewish Law at Hebrew University and Tel Aviv University Law Schools. Since 1971 Rabbi Berman serves as Associate Professor of Jewish Studies at Stern College for Women of Yeshiva University. Rabbi Berman was Rabbi of Congregation Beth Israel of Berkeley CA (1963-1969), Young Israel of Brookline, MA (1969-1971) and of Lincoln Square Synagogue in Manhattan (1984-1990.) Since 1990 he has served as an Adjunct Professor at Columbia University School of Law, where he teaches a seminar in Jewish Law. Aside his academic appointments, from 1997 until 2006.

Rabbi Berman is a contributor to the *Encyclopedia Judaica* and is the author of numerous articles which have been published in journals such as *Tradition, Judaism, Journal of Jewish Studies, Dinei Yisrael*, and others.

Rabbi Berman was the founder and director of the Edah organization for the promotion of Modern Orthodoxy. Edah was ultimately absorbed into Yeshivat Chovevei Torah.

He is married to Shellee Berman; they have four children and seven grandchildren.

Saul Berman
Yeshiva University,
Stern College

Wikipedia online, http://en.wikipedia.org/wiki/Saul_Berman (accessed February 15, 2013) +
The Tikvah Center for Law & Jewish Civilization online, http://www.nyutikvah.org/fellows/saul_
berman.html (accessed February 15, 2013)

Shalom Carmy
Contributing Editor

Shalom Carmy is an Orthodox rabbi teaching Jewish Studies and philosophy atYeshiva University, where he is Chair of Bible and Jewish Philosophy at Yeshiva College. He is an affiliated scholar at Cardozo Law School of Yeshiva University. He is also Editor of Tradition, an Orthodox theological journal.

Shalom Carmy
Yeshiva University,
Tradition Magazine

A Brooklyn native, he is a prominent Modern Orthodox theologian, historian, and philosopher. He received his B.A. in 1969 and M.S. from Yeshiva University, and received his rabbinic ordination from its affiliated Rabbi Isaac Elchanan Theological Seminary, studying under Rabbis Aharon Lichtenstein and Joseph Soloveitchik. He has edited some of R. Soloveitchik's work for publication. Carmy has written many articles on Biblical theology, Jewish thought, Orthodoxy in the 20th century, and the role of liberal arts in Torah education. He edited "*Modern Scholarship in the Study of Torah*: Contributions and Limitations" (ISBN 1-56821-450-2), "*Jewish Perspectives on the Experience of Suffering*", as well as several other works. He writes a regular personal column in *Tradition*, and contributes regularly on Jewish and general subjects to *First Things* and other journals. In addition to his exegetical and analytic work, Carmy's theological contribution is distinguished by preoccupation with the way religious doctrine and practice express themselves in the life of the individual.

http://en.wikipedia.org/wiki/Shalom_Carmy (accessed May 7, 2014)

LIGHTS OF CREATION & TRANSCENDENCE

David Birnbaum

Mesorah Matrix Series

Sanctification	TIKKUN OLAM	BIRKAT KOHANIM	KADDISH	Modeh Ani	HAVDALAH	SEARCH FOR MEANING	U-VACHARTA BA-CHAYIM	Enyeh asher Enyeh	U'shamru
VOLUME 1	VOLUME 2	VOLUME 3	VOLUME 4	VOLUME 5	VOLUME 6	VOLUME 7	VOLUME 8	VOLUME 9	VOLUME 10
MESORAH MATRIX	MESORAH MATRIX	MESORAH MATRIX	MESORAH MATRIX	MESORAH MATRIX	MESORAH MATRIX	MESORAH MATRIX	MESORAH MATRIX	MESORAH MATRIX	MESORAH MATRIX
Birnbaum & Blech	Birnbaum & Cohen	Birnbaum & Cohen	Birnbaum & Cohen	Birnbaum & Cohen	Birnbaum & Cohen	Birnbaum & Cohen	Birnbaum & Cohen	Birnbaum & Cohen	Birnbaum & Cohen
New Paradigm Matrix	New Paradigm Matrix	New Paradigm Matrix	New Paradigm Matrix	New Paradigm Matrix	New Paradigm Matrix	New Paradigm Matrix	New Paradigm Matrix	New Paradigm Matrix	New Paradigm Matrix
2015	2015	2016	2016	2017	2017	2018	2018	2019	2019

March 2018

www.MesorahMatrix.com

Kaunfer

Lockshin

Maayan

Dorff

Cook

Marx

Cohen

Yanklowitz

Ferency

Ornstein

Bulka

Lerner

Thiede

Levine

Frydman-Kohl

Grumet

Zion

Kosman

For the mountains shall erode

and the hills indeed collapse,

but My grace towards you shall never waver.

- Isaiah 54:10

כִּי הֶהָרִים יָמוּשׁוּ

וְהַגְּבָעוֹת תְּמוּטֶינָה

וְחַסְדִּי מֵאִתֵּךְ לֹא יָמוּשׁ

– יְשַׁעְיָהוּ 54:10

21st CENTURY PUBLISHING

David Birnbaum
Editor-in-Chief

New Paradigm Matrix
att: David Birnbaum
Tower 49
12 E 49th St.
18th Floor
New York, NY 10017

David.Birnbaum.NY@gmail.com

$16.00 / book

V'shamru

ISBN 978-0-9843619-8-4